RF 'OLUTIONARY RUSSIA

The Russian Revolution of 1917 is one of the crucial events of the modern era and is central to understanding the modern world and its history. The repercussions of 1917 are still evident today. Although the importance of the event was recognized immediately, significant historical research on the subject did not begin until the late 1960s.

Rex Wade presents a collection of some of the most important articles, with particular focus on the very latest research, together with a thorough and explanatory introduction, maps, a glossary of terms, and a chronology. Students are provided with the essential materials to gain an understanding of the major debates surrounding the events of the Russian Revolution of 1917. The book also provides a clear guide to the events themselves.

The collection begins with examples of the "social history" of the 1980s. The author continues by illustrating the recent interest in the use of language and symbols in the revolution, the greater attention being paid to nationalities and the provinces, the new political history, and the very recent fundamental reinterpretation of the October Revolution and the Bolshevik seizure of power. *Revolutionary Russia* is indispensable reading for all students and teachers of Russian history.

Rex A. Wade is Professor of History at George Mason University in Fairfax, Virginia. He is the author of *The Russian Revolution, 1917* (2000).

REWRITING HISTORIES
Series editor: Jack R. Censer

REVOLUTIONARY RUSSIA

New Approaches

Edited by *Rex A. Wade*

Routledge
Taylor & Francis Group

NEW YORK AND LONDON

First published 2004
by Routledge
29 West 35th Street, New York, NY 10001

Simultaneously published in the UK
by Routledge
11 New Fetter Lane, London EC4P 4EE

Routledge is an imprint of the Taylor & Francis Group

Typeset in Palatino by
Florence Production Ltd, Stoodleigh, Devon
Printed and bound in Great Britain by
The Cromwell Press, Trowbridge, Wiltshire

Library of Congress Cataloging in Publication Data
A catalog record for this book has been requested

British Library Cataloguing in Publication Data
A catalogue record for this book is available from the British Library

ISBN 0–415–30747–3 (hbk)
ISBN 0–415–30748–1 (pbk)

CONTENTS

CONTENTS

MAPS

SERIES EDITOR'S PREFACE

Rewriting history, or revisionism, has always followed closely in the wake of history writing. In their efforts to re-evaluate the past, professional as well as amateur scholars have followed many approaches, most commonly as empiricists, uncovering new information to challenge earlier accounts. Historians have also revised previous versions by adopting new perspectives, usually fortified by new research, which overturn received views.

Even though rewriting is constantly taking place, historians' attitudes towards using new interpretations have been anything but settled. For most, the validity of revisionism lies in providing a stronger, more convincing account that better captures the objective truth of the matter. Although such historians might agree that we never finally arrive at the "truth," they believe it exists and over time may be better approximated. At the other extreme stand scholars who believe that each generation or even each cultural group or subgroup necessarily regards the past differently, each creating for itself a more usable history. Although these latter scholars do not reject the possibility of demonstrating empirically that some contentions are better than others, they focus upon generating new views based upon different life experiences. Different truths exist for different groups. Surely such an understanding, by emphasizing subjectivity, further encourages rewriting history. Between these two groups are those historians who wish to borrow from both sides. This third group, while accepting that every congeries of individuals sees matters differently, still wishes somewhat contradictorily to fashion a broader history that incorporates both of these particular visions. Revisionists who stress empiricism fall into the first of the three camps, while others spread out across the board.

Today the rewriting of history seems to have accelerated to a blinding speed as a consequence of the evolution of revisionism. A variety of approaches has emerged. A major factor in this process has been the enormous increase in the number of researchers. This explosion has reinforced and enabled the retesting of many assertions. Significant

ideological shifts have also played a major part in the growth of revisionism. First, the crisis of Marxism, culminating in the events of Eastern
Europe in 1989, has given rise to doubts about explicitly Marxist accounts.
Such doubts have spilled over into the entire field of social history which
has been a dominant subfield of the discipline for several decades.
Focusing on society and its class divisions implied that these are the
most important elements in historical analysis. Because Marxism was
built on the same claim, the whole basis of social history has been questioned, despite the very many studies that directly had little to do with
Marxism. Disillusionment with social history, simultaneously opened the
door to cultural and linguistic approaches largely developed in anthro-
pology and literature. Multi-culturalism and feminism further generated
revisionism. By claiming that scholars had, wittingly or not, operated
from a white European/American male point of view, newer researchers
argued that other approaches had been neglected or misunderstood. Not
surprisingly, these last historians are the most likely to envision each
subgroup rewriting its own usable history, while other scholars incline
towards revisionism as part of the search for some stable truth.

Rewriting Histories will make these new approaches available to
the student population. Often new scholarly debates take place in the
scattered issues of journals which are sometimes difficult to find.
Furthermore, in these first interactions, historians tend to address one
another, leaving out the evidence that would make their arguments more
accessible to the uninitiated. This series of books will collect in one place
a strong group of the major articles in selected fields, adding notes and
introductions conducive to improved understanding. Editors will select
articles containing substantial historical data, so that students – at least
those who approach the subject as an objective phenomenon – can
advance not only their comprehension of debated points but also their
grasp of substantive aspects of the subject.

This collection of works on the Russian Revolution comes at a particularly propitious moment from the point of view of revisionism. After
a generation or more of historians, influenced by social history and the
linguistic turn, a rather new understanding of the Russian Revolution
has emerged. Before this last wave of scholarship, Russia apparently
succumbed to revolution through the action of the Bolsheviks dominated
by Lenin who seized control by ignoring majority will. Replacing this
Lenin-centered and conspiratorial model is an interpretation that emphasizes the strength of the Bolsheviks and the weaknesses of other
revolutionary parties. Specifically, the Bolsheviks' popularity depended
upon their seeming ability to deter the Germans and satisfy peasant
demands for land. Furthermore, Lenin's own plans were modified and
undermined by his own comrades. Thus, in 1917, power came, rather
expectedly, to the Bolsheviks. It was, indeed, only in January of 1918, at

the dispersal of the Constituent Assembly, that the Bolsheviks expanded their authority by seizing direct control. This action, which helped to precipitate a civil war in which the Bolsheviks ultimately prevailed, produced the dictatorship for which the regime is so well known. Reading this volume reveals this new understanding of the Russian Revolution as well as important examples of innovative approaches.

CONTRIBUTORS

Orlando Figes is Professor of History at Birkbeck College, University of London. He is the author of *Peasant Russia, Civil War: The Volga Countryside in Revolution, 1917–1921* (1989), *Natasha's Dance: A Cultural History of Russia* (2002), and, with Boris Kolonitskii, *Interpreting the Russian Revolution: The Language and Symbols of 1917* (1999). His *A People's Tragedy: The Russian Revolution, 1891–1924* (1996) won the Wolfson History Prize, the NCR book award, the W.H. Smith literary award, the Longman/History Today book of the year award and the Los Angeles Times book prize.

Tsuyoshi Hasegawa is Professor of History at the University of California, Santa Barbara. His books include *The February Revolution: Petrograd 1917* (1981), *The Northern Territories Dispute and Russo-Japanese Relations*, vol. 1: *Between War and Peace, 1967–1985*, vol. 2: *Neither War nor Peace, 1985–1998* (1998), and as co-editor with Jonathan Haslam and Andrew Kuchins, *Russia and Japan: An Unresolved Dilemma between Distant Neighbors* (1993). He also has published articles and books in Japanese on Russian history.

Michael C. Hickey, Professor of History at Bloomsburg University, Pennsylvania, has engaged in detailed study of the city and region of Smolensk during the revolution. Articles published include "Local Government and State Authority in the Provinces: Smolensk, February–June 1917," *Slavic Review* 55, no. 1 (1996): 863–881; "Discourses of Public Identity and Liberalism in the February Revolution: Smolensk, Spring 1917," *The Russian Review* 55, no. 4 (1996): 615–637; "Revolution on the Jewish Street: Smolensk, 1917," *Journal of Social History* 31, no. 4 (Summer 1998): 823–850; and "Urban *Zemliachestva* and Rural Revolution: Petrograd and the Smolensk Countryside in 1917," *Soviet and Post-Soviet Review* 23, no. 2 (1996): 143–160, among others.

Diane P. Koenker is Professor of History at the University of Illinois and currently editor of the *Slavic Review*. She has published *Moscow*

Workers and the 1917 Revolution (1981), *Strikes and Revolution in Russia, 1917* (1989, with William G. Rosenberg), numerous articles focused especially on workers and Moscow during the revolution and civil war, and is co-editor of *Party, State, and Society in the Russian Civil War: Explorations in Social History* (1989) and *Notes of a Red Guard / Eduard M. Dune* (1993).

Boris Ivanovich Kolonitskii, senior researcher at the Institute of History of the Academy of Sciences in St. Petersburg, is the author (with Orlando Figes) of *Interpreting the Russian Revolution: The Language and Symbols of 1917* (1999). Articles in English include "Anti-Bourgeois Propaganda and Anti-Burzhui Consciousness in 1917," *Russian Review* 53, no.2 (1993): 183–196. He has published extensively in Russian, including *Simboly vlasti i bor'ba za vlast'* (Symbols of Power and the Struggle for Power: Toward the Study of the Political Culture of the Russian Revolution, 1917) (2001).

Michael S. Melancon, Professor of History at Auburn University, is the author of *The Socialist Revolutionaries and the Russian Anti-War Movement, 1914–1917* (1990); "The Syntax of Soviet Power: the Resolutions of Local Soviets and Other Institutions, March–October 1917," *Russian Review* 52, no. 4 (1993): 486–505; "Who Wrote What and When: The Proclamations of the February Revolution," *Soviet Studies* (July 1988): 479–500, and numerous other articles on the revolution and Russian history. He is co-editor (with Alice Pate) of *New Labor History: Worker Identity and Experience in Russia, 1840–1918* (2003).

Lev Grigor'evich Protasov, Doctor of Historical Sciences, is professor and department head at Tambov Pedagogical Institute, Russia. He has published extensively in Russian, on the Constituent Assembly in particular, including *Vserossiiskoe Uchreditel'noe sobranie: Istoriia rozhdeniia i gibeli* (The All-Russia Constitutent Assembly: the History of its Birth and Death) (Moscow, 1997).

William G. Rosenberg, Professor of History at the University of Michigan, has written extensively on the Russian Revolution and Russian history. Books include *Liberals in the Russian Revolution: The Constitutional Democratic Party, 1917–1921* (1974) and (with Diane Koenker) *Strikes and Revolution in Russia, 1917* (1989). He is editor of *Bolshevik Visions: First Phase of the Cultural Revolution in Soviet Russia* (1990), co-editor of *Critical Companion to the Russian Revolution 1914–1921* (1997) and *Party, State, and Society in the Russian Civil War: Explorations in Social History* (1989), and author of numerous articles.

Steve A. Smith is Professor of History at Essex University. He is the author of *Red Petrograd: Revolution in the Factories, 1917–18* (1983), *The Russian Revolution: A Very Short Introduction* (2000); *A Road is Made:*

Communism in Shanghai, 1920–1927 (2000), *Like Cattle and Horses: Nationalism and Labor in Shanghai, 1895–1927* (2002), co-editor of *Notes of a Red Guard/Eduard M. Dune* (1993), and author of many articles on Russian and Chinese history.

Ronald Grigor Suny is Professor, Department of Political Science, University of Chicago. His numerous publications include *The Baku Commune, 1917–1918: Class and Nationality in the Russian Revolution* (1972); *The Revenge of the Past: Nationalism, Revolution, and the Collapse of the Soviet Union* (1993); *Looking toward Ararat: The Armenians in Modern History* (1993); *The Making of the Georgian Nation* (1994); and *The Soviet Experiment: Russia, the USSR, and the Successor States* (1998). He also has edited or co-edited several books and published many articles.

Rex A. Wade is Professor of History at George Mason University. His books include *The Russian Search for Peace, February–October 1917* (1969); *Red Guards and Workers' Militias in the Russian Revolution* (1984); *The Russian Revolution, 1917* (2000); *The Bolshevik Revolution and Russian Civil War* (2001); and as editor, *Documents of Russian History*, Vols. 1–3 (1991–1995) and (with Scott Seregny), *Politics and Society in Provincial Russia: Saratov 1590–1917* (1989).

James D. White is Reader in the Institute of Russian and East European Studies, University of Glasgow. He is the author of *Lenin: The Practice and Theory of Revolution* (2001); *The Russian Revolution: A Short History* (1994); *Karl Marx and the Intellectual Origins of Dialectical Materialism* (1996); and numerous articles and essays.

ACKNOWLEDGMENTS

The permission of the following publishers to reprint articles or selections is gratefully acknowledged:

American Association for the Advancement of Slavic Studies (AAASS) for Boris Kolonitskii, "'Democracy' in the Political Consciousness of the February Revolution," *Slavic Review* 57, no. 1 (1988): 95–106.

Blackwell Publishers for Orlando Figes, "The Russian Revolution in 1917 and its Language in the Village," *Russian Review* 56, no. 3 (1997): 323–345.

Cambridge University Press for Steve A. Smith, "Petrograd in 1917: the View from Below," in Daniel H. Kaiser, ed., *The Workers' Revolution in Russia, 1917: The View from Below* (1987), pp. 59–79, and for the selection from Rex A. Wade, *The Russian Revolution, 1917* (2000): 206–244.

Charles Schlacks, Jr., Publisher, for Michael S. Melancon, "From Rhapsody to Threnody: Russia's Provisional Government in Socialist-Revolutionary Eyes, February–July 1917," *The Soviet and Post-Soviet Review* 24, nos. 1–2 (1997): 27–42.

Princeton University Press for the selection from Diane P. Koenker and William G. Rosenberg, *Strikes and Revolution in Russia, 1917* (1989), pp. 3–8, 14–18, 326–329.

M.E. Sharpe, Inc., for the English Language Translation Copyright of L. G. Protasov, "The All-Russian Constituent Assembly and the Democratic Alternative: Two Views of the Problem," *Russian Studies in History* 33, no. 3 (Winter 1994–95): 67–93.

Stanford University Press for Ronald Grigor Suny, "National Revolutions and Civil War in Russia," from Ronald Grigor Suny, *The*

ACKNOWLEDGMENTS

Revenge of the Past: Nationalism, Revolution and the Collapse of the Soviet Union (1993), pp. 20–23, 29–30, 43–51, 55–58, 76–83. Copyright 1993 by the Board of Trustees of the Leland Stanford Jr. University.

University of Pittsburgh Press for Michael C. Hickey, "The Rise and Fall of Smolensk's Moderate Socialists: The Politics of Class and the Rhetoric of Crisis in 1917," in Donald J. Raleigh, ed., *Provincial Landscapes: Local Dimensions of Soviet Power, 1917–1953* (2001), pp. 14–35.

University of Washington Press for Tsuyoshi Hasegawa, "Crime, Police, and Mob Justice in Petrograd during the Russian Revolutions of 1917," in Charles E. Timberlake, ed., *Religious and Secular Forces in Late Tsarist Russia. Essays in Honor of Donald W. Treadgold* (1992), pp. 241–271.

James D. White for James White, "Lenin, Trotskii and the Arts of Insurrection: The Congress of Soviets of the Northern Region, 11–13 October 1917," *The Slavonic and East European Review* 77, no. 1 (January, 1999): 117–139.

I also wish to acknowledge the help and encouragement of several people. George Enteen, Michael Hickey, and Michael Melancon read over some of the introductory materials and made helpful suggestions. Mollie Fletcher-Klocek ably prepared the maps. Jack Censer, the series editor and a friend, was helpful and encouraging throughout. Thanks are due to Deborah Gomez and Stuart McLauchlan for help with scanning the articles into word processing text. Vicky Peters of Routledge has made association with the press a pleasure, as have Jane Blackwell, Della Tsiftsopoulou and Nigel Hope.

GLOSSARY

Black Hundreds – General term for ultra-rightist, ultra-monarchist, often anti-Semitic, groups; popular revolutionary mythology saw them behind various disorders and as very dangerous.

CEC – Central Executive Committee (executive of the Congress of Soviets)

Cheka (Vcheka) – Common name for the All-Russia Extraordinary Commission for Combating Counter-Revolution and Sabotage, the secret, or political, police of the Soviet Union. Established by the Bolsheviks in December, 1917; forerunner of later secret police under different names (GPU, OGPU, NKVD, KGB) during the Soviet Union.

Commissar – Term used to designate revolutionary officials, especially agents of the soviets, in 1917. After the October Revolution it was incorporated into the official name for the main government ministers (i.e., People's Commissar for Foreign Affairs, etc.), the equivalent for "secretary" in the American government and "minister" in European governments (including Russia before 1917 and after 1946).

Constituent Assembly – The assembly to be elected by a universal, free, secret, and direct ballot after the overthrow of Nicholas II and which was to establish the future basic political structure and principles for Russia.

Constitutional Democrats (Kadets) – The main liberal party in Russia, based on a program of civil liberties and constitutional and parliamentary government.

Council of People's Commissars (Sovnarkom, CPC, SNK) – Formal name for the government formed by the Bolsheviks after the October Revolution, and used until 1946, when the name of the government was changed to Council of Ministers.

Delo naroda (People's cause) – Main Socialist Revolutionary Party newspaper.

Duma – Usually means, especially if capitalized, the State Duma, the lower house of the elected legislature established after the revolution of 1905, which lasted from 1906 to 1917. Also name of city councils before and during the revolution.

guberniia, guberniya – A province, the main administrative subdivision of the Russian state.

Izvestiia (News) – Usually refers to the official newspaper of the Petrograd Soviet; often name of newspapers of other soviets as well.

Kadets – See Constitutional Democrats.

Kornilovite – Pejorative term implying a counterrevolutionary person, threat, or tendencies; derived from General Kornilov's failed effort to seize power in August.

Kronstadt – Naval base in the harbor of Petrograd; became a synonym for radicalism.

Left SRs – Left wing of the Socialist Revolutionary Party, cooperated with the Bolsheviks in the radical left coalitions of the fall of 1917; became a separate party after the October Revolution and participated in the Soviet government from December 1917 to March 1918.

Mensheviks – The more moderate branch (in opposition to the Bolsheviks) of the Russian Social Democratic Labor Party, the main Marxist Russian revolutionary party; by 1917 effectively a separate party.

Menshevik-Internationalists – Left wing of the Mensheviks in 1917; opposed Revolutionary Defensism and often cooperated with the Bolsheviks and Left SRs in the radical left bloc in 1917, but opposed the October Revolution.

Mezhraiontsy (Interdistrict Group) – Association of Social Democratic intellectuals standing between the Mensheviks and Bolsheviks; most joined the Bolsheviks in July 1917.

Militia – Term introduced after the February Revolution for the police. Also used in the names of some volunteer armed bands in 1917, such as workers' militias.

MRC – Military Revolutionary Committee, formed by the Petrograd Soviet in October; played a key role in the October Revolution and in maintaining the new Soviet government for a few weeks thereafter. MRCs existed in some other cities also.

Narod – "The people," often with semi-romantic overtones.

Narodnik(s) – Populist(s). Often used to refer to agrarian socialists, including SRs.

oblast' – Large administrative territory.

obshchina – The traditional village commune, the village as a political and economic entity.

Octobrists – The Union of 17 October Party, the main moderate conservative party.

Okhrana – Tsarist secret police.

Pravda (Truth) – Main Bolshevik newspaper. After July Days named variously *Rabochii i soldat, Proletarii, Rabochii, Rabochii put'*.

Rabochaia gazeta (Workers' gazette). Main Menshevik newspaper.

xvii

Rada – Literally the Ukrainian equivalent of the Russian "soviet," a council. During the revolutionary period usually refers to the Ukrainian Central Rada in Kiev, which asserted leadership of the Ukrainian national movement.

Rech' (Speech) – Main newspaper of the Kadet Party.

Revolutionary Defensism – Political position, developed by Irakli Tsereteli and others, mostly Mensheviks and SRs, that dominated the Petrograd Soviet from March to September 1917 and, to a degree, the Provisional Government as well. It stressed the importance of a swift negotiated peace, but with defense of the country and revolution until that could be achieved, and cooperation with the liberals in "coalition" Provisional Government ministries.

RSDLP or RSDWP or RSDRP – Russian Social Democratic Labor (or Workers') Party, the main Russian Marxist revolutionary party; by 1917 it had long since split into Bolshevik and Menshevik wings, although both still claimed and used the formal party title. The Bolsheviks often used the acronym RSDLP(b).

SD, SDs – Social Democrats; see RSDLP.

Socialist Revolutionary Party – Peasant-oriented revolutionary party but with a strong appeal to workers and intelligentsia, it stressed the opposition of "toilers" to oppressors of all kinds. Largest political party in 1917 and in the Constituent Assembly. Tended toward internal divisions, and in 1917 had right, center, and left wings, which weakened its effectiveness. (See also Left SRs.)

soviet(s) – Literally "council," the term has come to be used historically to refer to the soviets (councils) of workers', soldiers', and peasants' deputies formed in 1917. Usually capitalized when referring to the Petrograd Soviet in 1917 and to the Soviet government formed after the October Revolution.

Sovnarkom – Common abbreviation for the Council of People's Commissars, the government formed by the October Revolution, based on the first syllable of each word in Russian.

SR, SRs – See Socialist Revolutionary Party.

Stavka – Front military headquarters of the Russian army in World War I.

uezd (*uyezd*) – a rural district, subdivision of a province (*guberniia*).

VTsIK, TsIK – see CEC.

volost' – a rural subdistrict, subdivision of a *uezd*.

Zemlia i volia (Land and Liberty) – Newspaper of the Petrograd SRs.

zemstvo – Elected local rural government institutions of late Imperial Russia with limited authority to deal with health, agriculture, education, and other issues. Abolished after the Bolshevik Revolution.

Zimmerwaldists – anti-war left wing of European (including Russian) socialism during World War I, named for conference held at Zimmerwald, Switzerland.

NOTE ON SPELLING
AND DATES

Writing about Russia introduces special issues of spelling and dating. Russian is written in the Cyrillic alphabet and thus all Russian names and words must be transliterated into the Latin alphabet. While modern transliteration is more consistent than in earlier times, there are minor variations according the preferences of the authors of the various articles in this collection. Probably the most common problem is whether to use "sky" or "skii" for name endings (Kerensky and Trotsky or Kerenskii and Trotskii). Another is whether or not to include the "soft sign" – Lvov or L'vov. Other common variations are the insertion of a "y" before the letter "e" (*uezd* and *uyezd*), and whether to transliterate one vowel as "ia" or "ya" (Ulianov or Ulyanov) and another as "iu" or "yu" (Miliukov or Milyukov). Some authors use the English version of first names with common equivalents, others use the Russian version: Nicholas/Nikolai, Alexander/Aleksandr, Paul/Pavel, etc. In some instances authors use the Russian convention of two initials instead of a first name. Similarly, cities and places are usually but not always given in the manner most familiar to contemporary readers and in their Russian variant rather than in the various nationality language forms (Kharkov rather than Kharkiv).

All dates are in the Russian calendar of the time. In 1917 and until February 1/14, 1918, the Russian (Julian) calendar was 13 days behind the Western (Gregorian) calendar. Thus the February Revolution and the October Revolution (Russian calendar in use in 1917) are called the "March Revolution" and the "November Revolution" (Western calendar) in some books, although not by any of the authors in this collection. To get the Western date, simply add 13 days. An early act of the new Soviet government was to bring the Russian calendar into line with the Western calendar by making February 1, 1918, into February 14, 1918 (i.e., jumping forward 13 days).

CHRONOLOGY

Note: All dates here and in the articles are according to the Russian calendar, which was 13 days behind the Western calendar until February 1/14, 1918.

1917

Feb. 9–22   Rising tide of strikes in Petrograd

Feb. 23–26   Women's demonstrations (23rd) expand to include most of population of Petrograd by 25th; troops reluctant to act against demonstrators; government barricades streets and orders troops to fire on demonstrators (26th).

Feb. 27   Garrison mutiny; Petrograd Soviet formed; Temporary Committee of the State Duma formed and announces assumption of authority.

Mar. 1   Order No. 1 of the Petrograd Soviet regarding troops of the garrison.

Mar. 2   Provisional Government formed; abdication of Nicholas II.

Mar. 3   Formation of Provisional Government and abdication of Nicholas announced.

Mar. 14   Soviet "Appeal to the People of the World" for a "peace without annexations or indemnities."

Mar. 20   Provisional Government abolishes all discriminations based on nationality or religion.

Mar. 20   Irakli Tsereteli arrives in Petrograd from Siberian exile.

Mar. 21–22   Tsereteli and Revolutionary Defensists establish leadership of Petrograd Soviet.

Apr. 3   Vladimir Lenin arrives in Petrograd from Switzerland, begins criticism of Provisional Government and Revolutionary Defensism.

Apr. 18–21   April Crisis over war and foreign policy.

May 2–5   Government crisis and reorganization to include Soviet leaders in the government: first "coalition government."

June 3–5	First All-Russia Congress of Soviets of Workers' and Soldiers' Deputies.
June 10	Ukrainian Central Rada issues First Universal.
June 18	Russian military offensive begins.
June 18	Soviet-sponsored demonstration in Petrograd turns into massive anti-war and anti-government demonstration.
July 1	Provisional Government delegation and Central Rada reach agreement on limited self-government for Ukraine.
July 2	Kadet ministers resign over Ukrainian issue; new government crisis begins.
July 3–5	July Days; Lenin and other Bolshevik leaders forced to go into hiding.
July 5	German counter-offensive and collapse of Russian offensive.
July 8	Alexander Kerensky becomes Minister-President.
July 18	General Kornilov appointed Supreme Commander of army.
July 20	Provisional Government extends right to vote to women.
July 21–23	Government crisis intensifies, second coalition government formed.
Aug. 27–31	Kornilov Affair; government collapses again.
Aug. 31	Bolshevik-sponsored resolution passes in Petrograd Soviet for first time.
Sept. 1	"Directory," a five-man government headed by Kerensky, established.
Sept. 5	Bolshevik-sponsored resolution passes in Moscow Soviet.
Sept. 14–22	Democratic Conference to find a base of support for Provisional Government debates forming an all-socialist government but fails to reach agreement.
Sept. 25	Trotsky elected chairman of Petrograd Soviet, Bolshevik-led radical bloc takes control.
Sept. 25	Third coalition government formed under Kerensky.
Oct. 7	"Preparliament" opens; Bolsheviks denounce it and walk out.
Oct. 11–13	Congress of Soviets of the Northern Region.
Oct. 10–16	Bolshevik leadership debates seizing power.
Oct. 21–23	MRC challenges military authorities over control of Petrograd garrison.
Oct. 22	"Day of the Petrograd Soviet" with rallies for "All Power to the Soviets."
Oct. 24	Kerensky moves to close Bolshevik newspapers, sparking the October Revolution.
Oct. 24–25	Struggle for control of key points in Petrograd between pro-Soviet and pro-government forces – the former prevail.
Oct. 25	Provisional Government declared deposed; Second Congress of Soviets opens.

Oct. 26	Second session of Second Congress of Soviets passes decrees on Land, on Peace and on formation of a new government – Council of People's Commissars.
Oct. 27	Decree establishing censorship of press.
Nov. 12	Elections to Constituent Assembly begin.
Nov. 28	Arrest of Kadet Party leaders ordered.
Dec. 2	Formal armistice with Germany and Austria-Hungary.
Dec. 7	Cheka (political police) established.
Dec. 12	Left SRs join the government.

1918

Jan. 5–6	Constituent Assembly opens and is closed by force.
Jan. 9	Ukrainian Rada issues "Fourth Universal" declaring independence.
Mar. 3	Treaty of Brest-Litovsk signed, formally ending World War I for Russia.
Mar. 8	Bolsheviks' name formally changed to Russian Communist Party.

INTRODUCTION

Rex A. Wade

The Russian Revolution of 1917 is, beyond question, one of the most important events of the modern era. The collapse of the Soviet Union in 1991 altered the prism through which we view the Russian Revolution, but did not change the basic reality of its events or the fact that the revolution profoundly shaped the history of the twentieth century. Moreover, its legacy continues to influence the modern world, in Russia and globally. Paradoxically, although the revolution's importance was recognized immediately and although there were scattered scholarly publications in the first half-century after the revolution, significant historical research in the form of a major body of scholarly writing emerged long afterwards, beginning only at the end of the 1960s. Since then scholarship on the revolution has expanded rapidly, producing a rich body of historical literature. Moreover, the collapse of the Soviet Union has made it easier to put the revolution into better historical perspective; writing about it no longer involves an implied judgment on an existing regime or on Cold War issues, as it often did during the era of the Soviet Union's existence. At the same time, the renewed struggle over democracy and political structures, class and socio-economic issues, the autonomy or independence of the non-Russian peoples, Russia's great power status, and other issues that have wracked the region since 1991 reaffirm the importance of the Russian Revolution of 1917, when these very issues were fought out but, as we now see, not settled.

Traditionally the Russian Revolution was described in mainly political terms, and primarily as the history of political parties and individual leaders, Vladimir Lenin and the Bolshevik Party most of all. This is not surprising given that the political actors of 1917 did most of the initial writing about the revolution. Indeed, competing versions of the events of 1917 were a part of post-revolutionary political struggle both within the Bolshevik Party and between the Bolsheviks and their political opponents, both Russian and foreign. Even the accounts of foreigners usually reflected an identification with one political faction or another. Both Western and Soviet histories, different as they were in their assessment

1

of events, were overwhelmingly political and concerned with political ideologies and the Bolshevik Party in particular.

The basic interpretation of the revolution took form in the early 1920s.[1] Especially important in this was Lenin's 1920 essay, "Left-Wing Communism," and the establishment that same year of an official party institution, the Commission on the History of the Russian Communist Party and the October Revolution (*Istpart*). *Istpart*'s function was to oversee the writing of a historical interpretation of the revolution based on Lenin's ideas and actions. It undertook to control all writing and source publication inside Soviet Russia about the revolution. As its name suggested, it blended the history of the revolution with that of the party, a tradition that continued in both Soviet and Western histories. For reasons having to do with then current politics as much as or more than actual past events of 1917, the regime-approved account that emerged in the early 1920s emphasized the leading and directing role of the Bolshevik Party and of Lenin in particular. Not only histories but memoirs and document collections were written or edited to fit the basic interpretation. An interpretation similarly focused on Lenin and the Bolsheviks developed in the West. Particularly important in shaping Western interpretations were the works of Leon Trotsky and William Henry Chamberlin in the 1930s. Trotsky, who had played a part in creating the basic Soviet interpretation in the 1920s, for reasons of his ongoing polemic with Stalin developed it further in his highly influential *History of the Russian Revolution* (1931). It became a very important source and basic interpretation for many Western writers. Chamberlin, whose *The Russian Revolution* (1935) remained the most authoritative history of the revolution in the West through most of the rest of the twentieth century, drew heavily on Trotsky and the by now standardized "sources" produced in the Soviet Union, as well as on émigré Russian accounts that in basics supported the Lenin-oriented account of the revolution (although Chamberlin did give more space to workers, peasants, and other social groups than most histories).

Throughout the long period from the revolution until the late 1960s or even later, both Western and Soviet historians saw the revolution in similar political terms, with the focus on a disciplined and monolithic Bolshevik Party under Lenin's unquestioned leadership. The October (or Bolshevik) Revolution in particular was seen as a political seizure of power (often termed a coup d'état) planned and engineered by Lenin, largely divorced from its broader political, social, and cultural context. For Soviet historians, this flowed naturally from the cult of Lenin worship as well as the demands of the Communist Party and Soviet state. Curiously enough, this Lenin-centered approach was congenial to anti-Communists, Russian and foreign, because it allowed an interpretation which, by largely ignoring other, especially social, factors, cast the

Bolsheviks as leaders of a coup with no popular support and thus illegitimate. In either approach, the "masses" were largely absent or inert, manipulated (or led) by unscrupulous (or farsighted) political figures, most importantly Lenin and the Bolsheviks. At the best the masses were "spontaneous," an ill-defined chorus chanting mindlessly in the background. They had no agency, no characterization as comprehensible interest groups or as actors. Institutionally, these histories focused primarily on the Bolshevik Party and Lenin's ideas and leadership, and secondarily on the Provisional Government formed after the overthrow of the monarchy (and within that on Alexander Kerensky and Pavel Miliukov, its two most prominent figures). Often the history of the revolution was reduced to Lenin's actions and to the assumption that what Lenin in his writings before and during 1917 said should happen, did happen. The story was framed to explain Communism and the Soviet Union, and thus focused on Lenin, the Bolsheviks, and their ideology. The difference was that Soviet histories saw that revolution as good and most Western historians saw it as bad. While pointing out their similar Lenin and "high politics" emphasis, it should be stressed that within that framework Western histories, Chamberlin especially, provided a much more complex and realistic picture of the revolution than did Soviet histories, where the Communist Party's control blighted the study of history.

The stereotypical account, reinforced during the Cold War era, prevailed largely unchanged until the late 1960s, and more particularly until the 1970s and 1980s. Questioning it came only after major scholarly research on the Russian Revolution was begun in the West in the 1960s (there had been scattered works before then), primarily by American and British scholars. This was a part of the post-World War II blossoming of Russian studies which was beginning to produce a significant body of research on Russian history generally. Then, between 1967 and 1969, Alexander Rabinowitch, Robert V. Daniels, Marc Ferro, and Rex A. Wade published books that, with a collection of essays edited by Richard Pipes and some articles appearing about the same time, represented the first cluster of new Western scholarship on the revolution.[2] Although still focused mainly on politics, these studies raised important questions about some of the traditional portrayals of a monolithic Bolshevik Party, the Provisional Government, non-Bolshevik parties, the interrelationship of the war and revolution, and the nature of the October Revolution. They even considered popular attitudes. Equally important, they made study of the revolution an important focus of scholarly research.

In the 1970s and 1980s scholarly studies of the revolution expanded rapidly, as a number of historians, mostly but not entirely younger historians coming out of graduate school, turned to examining the revolution "from below," producing a wide range of important new works. Most

3

REX A. WADE

notably, they introduced a "social history" that produced the most significant reinterpretation in the historiography of the revolution since the
1920s and which has remained central to subsequent scholarship on it.
They looked especially at the industrial workers but examined other
social groups as well. Although diverse in their approaches as well as
the sources of inspiration that led them into social history (they were
sometimes undifferentiatedly lumped together in both respects),
collectively they replaced the previous focus on political leadership,
ideology, and high politics with a greater emphasis on social groups,
their aspirations, and their self-directed and purposeful actions. They
found a deepening social polarization that undermined the Provisional
Government and its efforts at a Western-style parliamentary democracy.
Their work was criticized by some scholars, but the social history investigations invigorated the study of the revolution, deepened significantly
our understanding of it, set the ground for further investigation coming
from other angles, and became an important ingredient in most later
works. The selections by Smith and by Koenker and Rosenberg in this
collection typify this social history.[3]

Although social history was the most striking trend of the 1970s and
1980s, historians continued to produce important studies with primarily
political orientations or blending social and political history. These
included major new histories of the political parties, producing a better
understanding of the complexity of the internal conflicts and structures
of the parties, including the Bolsheviks. The period also saw the beginning of study of the revolution in the provinces and some study of the
nationality regions, as well as the publication of numerous articles and
several collections of essays and encyclopedias on the revolution. The
large outpouring of scholarly investigations enriched and made more
sophisticated our understanding of the process leading to the October
Revolution, especially the growing popular radicalization and support
for the Bolsheviks and other radical parties. Despite insights provided
by Robert V. Daniels in 1967 and Alexander Rabinowitch in 1976,[4] the
paradigm of the well-planned and well-organized Bolshevik seizure of
power (or coup d'état) under Lenin's direction proved powerful and
historians were slow to rethink the events of the October Revolution
itself and what happened during those fateful days. Only slowly, in the
1990s, did some scholars start to revise that picture, as reflected in
the White and Wade selections given here.

The late 1980s and 1990s witnessed a number of other important new
developments whose significance is still being played out and which
have created a much more complex historiographical scene. Some historians, influenced by the cultural and linguistic turns among historians
of Western Europe and the United States, began to apply those to the
study of the revolution. They examined how during revolutionary

4

upheaval new language and symbols are developed and utilized to analyze events and to achieve political, economic, or cultural goals. This "linguistic turn" flowed rather naturally from social history, since it is the culture and language of the lower classes with which it has been primarily concerned. Social and linguistic approaches merged to some degree, recognizing social classes and other groups as constantly developing and evolving, "constructed" by the events and language of the given point in time. Historians recognized how, for example, the new prestige of being a "worker" and the language used about class brought elements such as lower-level white-collar and other employees to self-identify as "workers," while forging a new meaning of what constituted "workers" and serving to help mobilize them as a political force.

• At the same time there has been a growing interest in provincial studies and in nationality issues. A dramatic expansion of the study of provincial Russia during the revolution has produced some of the most interesting recent work. A new awareness of nationality/ethnicity came with the collapse of the Soviet Union, leading to renewed interest in nationality issues during the revolution, when modern national assertiveness erupted vigorously among many peoples of the Russian empire (and future Soviet Union). The provincial and nationality studies have created a much larger spatial context for the revolution focused on the entire breadth of the country rather than just on Petrograd (and mostly on ethnic Russians).

The collapse of the Soviet Union contributed to two other trends, one that added little and one that probably over time will add much to the study of the revolution. The latter is new archival access; the former was a "triumphalist" mentality among some Western historians that led to an attempt to resurrect the old historiography that told the revolution in purely political terms, focused on Lenin and the Bolsheviks (and the evilness thereof). While this triumphalist approach found little favor with historians of the revolutionary period in the West, it did find a peculiar echo in the former Soviet Union. There historians, freed from Communist political control but not from its intellectual heritage, initially continued the old Lenin-centered history but joined the Western practice of assigning it a generally negative interpretation. These writings, Western and Russian, were a peculiar mirror image of the now-discredited Soviet histories. Most historians, however, eschewed this triumphalist or Lenin-as-demon approach. Instead, historians have continued to develop ever more sophisticated studies of the revolution, along lines indicated above, aided by new access to archives, the other post-Soviet new feature.

Archival access offers the prospect of increasingly important contributions, although it has not yet had as profound an influence on the general writing and interpretation of the history of the revolution as it has had for writing on the Soviet era, especially the Stalin period. The main reason for this is that the source base on the revolution was already so great, and thus the new archival access, especially at the Petrograd center, largely confirmed what was already known and filled in around the edges. Major reinterpretation thus far has come more from rethinking issues, asking different questions, and looking at long-existing sources anew than from wholly new sources. Archival access has, however, had a greater impact through allowing a flourishing of provincial and regional studies, which involved not only access to new kinds of materials, but letting Western historians have access to cities and regions that had been physically off-limits to all foreigners, including scholars, during the Soviet era. These flourishing provincial studies provide some of the most important contributions to the rewriting of the revolution, and are represented in this volume directly by the Hickey essay and indirectly by some others. Over time, archival access, coupled with freedom of research for Russian scholars, should make important contributions to our understanding of the revolution.

Writing in post-Soviet Russia and other countries of the former empire thus far has produced fewer new insights and approaches than many expected, despite a large output. Soviet historians were able to explore issues more extensively after Stalin's tight control was removed following his death in 1953, but still far from freely as the Communist Party's control remained strict. Many important Bolshevik leaders of 1917 still could not be mentioned by name, the policies and actions of other socialist parties and the liberals were grotesquely distorted, and many issues could not be explored (or only in distorted form), while the whole basic interpretation remained highly politicized. The revolution was seen as the founding event for the Soviet Union and a key source of its legitimacy, and therefore a "correct" interpretation was imperative. Mikhail Gorbachev's *glasnost'* (openness) after 1985 and then the collapse of the Soviet Union opened up what could be studied, but the task of producing quality new histories proved more difficult and slower than most expected. Old attitudes and explanations died hard, the old guard continued to hold key academic positions, and historians had to break free of old frameworks and ideological stereotypes. Only gradually did promising signs of a revitalized history in Russia begin to emerge, as represented by two of the scholars included in this volume (Kolonitskii and Protasov).[5]

It is too early to tell yet whether two other trends "on the horizon" will develop as major lines of research and scholarship on the revolution. One is a renewed interest in the revolution as part of some larger slice of Russian history and in looking at specific issues "across the revolutionary divide." This seeks to subsume the revolution of 1917 into a larger theme or time period (although even a cursory glance at books with the term "Russian Revolution" in their titles shows that it has long

6

been used for books with widely varying time-frames). The other possible trend is a revival of comparative history, especially fitting the revolution into a comparative European context. How much either approach will develop, and how much it will contribute to understanding the revolution itself (rather than the nature of the imperial or Soviet regimes), remains unclear.[6]

In contrast to these trends, gender, post-modernism, and some other approaches, especially the more theoretically based ones that have been popular in West European and American history, have played a minor role in the study of the Russian Revolution. They have been less prominent than in studies of the French Revolution, for example, or even than in some other areas of Russian history. Similarly, the original causes of the revolution have not been much debated during the past three to four decades, certainly not in the way they have been for the French and even the American and British revolutions. There is a rich literature on late Imperial Russia, the period between 1905 and 1914 (or February 1917) in particular, but this for the most part has not connected directly to the revolution itself in a debate on its causes and how prerevolutionary issues influenced 1917. A noticeable exception was the short debate over Leopold Haimson's mid-1960s articles about an intractable dual social and political polarization on the eve of the revolution, which did influence writing on 1917.[7] Recent writing about the revolution has centered more on the *process* of revolution, its dynamics during 1917 – how did it get from February to October (and beyond), how did the Bolsheviks manage to gain power, what was the role of various actors and of specific crises or issues in that process? This collection reflects that by focusing on the process of revolution after February rather than on the pre-1917 conditions that led to revolution.

Today there is no dominant paradigm or approach to writing the history of the Russian Revolution. "Social history" has influenced in varying degrees the work of almost all scholars working on the revolution. Although some charged the social historians with writing "history with the politics left out," politics was never really absent from social history simply because the question at the heart of all scholarship on the Russian Revolution has been and remains how did the Bolsheviks, a small minority party after February and largely excluded from participation in political power, manage to take power eight months later and then consolidate that into a dictatorship in another three months – less than a year altogether? Parallel is the reverse question: how did liberals and moderate socialists, who held power in the months after the February Revolution, lose it so quickly? Answering those questions adequately requires looking at popular aspirations and activity as well as party leaders and organizations, and in doing so social history never really moved away from pointing its studies toward answering that key, fundamentally political, question. Criticism that it "left the politics out," while never really accurate, did however lead those working in a mainly social vein to be more explicit about the political implications of social actions, about political factors as influences on social groups, and about the degree of autonomy of politics. At the same time, writers focused primarily on political issues now invariably give greater consideration to social factors. Accounts focused entirely on high politics, that take the writings and actions of political leaders as self-contained explanations for what happened, are rare, and the best political history (as perhaps the White piece in this collection demonstrates) considers the broader context of the event that it analyses and applies a critical scrutiny to the relationship between statements (at the time or later) of political figures and the reality of the historical event. Most typical today, especially when exploring the revolution broadly, is what might be called an "integrated" history, one that draws upon and integrates social, political, cultural, and linguistic approaches to produce more complex and richly textured accounts. This comes close to what some have called a "new political history," one that while still focused on questions of political power, brings in both the social-economic forces influencing those and the new language and symbolism that developed to express them.

This volume brings together the fruits of modern scholarship and current trends in interpretation of the revolution while also introducing readers to its basic history. It begins with two examples of the most important social history of the 1980s (Smith, Koenker and Rosenberg), and continues with an important newer type of social history (Hasegawa). It presents some of the recent cultural and linguistic approaches (Figes, Kolonitskii, and to a degree Hickey) that are affecting understanding of the revolution, and explores regional and ethnic/nationality issues (Hickey, Suny). Several of the essays (Melancon, Hickey, Wade) also represent the emerging "Integrative" and "New Political" approaches and the tendency to shift away from talking about the Bolsheviks alone to focusing more on a radical left. It ends with three essays (White, Wade, Protasov) that reexamine and explicitly ask for reconsideration of two major events that traditionally were often used to mark the end of the revolution in the specific sense of the word: the October (or Bolshevik) Revolution and the Constituent Assembly. Moreover, they (Protasov explicitly) pose the question of "alternatives," which has always been a subtext of writing on the revolution and which has been an important part of post-1985 writing in Russia.

The selections included here hardly exhaust the literature, and leaving out many fine works and authors who have made important contributions has been a wrenching process for this editor. These do, however, give a good representation of recent scholarship and issues. Moreover, while introducing readers to current writing and interpretation on the

revolution, care has been taken that the collection also add up to a sufficiently coherent picture and that readers will come away with a good
understanding of the history of the revolution, a grasp of the issues that
excited passions in 1917, and a sense of what it was all about and "what
happened." Not every important issue, event, or group can be covered
in a collection of reasonable length, but together these essays should
give a good sense of the revolutionary process and its meaning. To help
the reader who is approaching the revolution for the first time, aids such
as a glossary and chronology are provided.

NOTES

1   I am particularly indebted to James D. White for his accounts of the early
    writing of the history of the revolution: "Early Soviet Historical
    Interpretations of the Russian Revolution 1918–1924," *Soviet Studies* 37, no.
    3 (July 1985): 330–352, and his chapter on "The Lenin Legend," in his *Leninism,
    The Theory and Practice of Revolution*, London: Palgrave, 2001, pp. 178–201.
2   Robert V. Daniels, *Red October: The Bolshevik Revolution of 1917*, New York:
    Scribner's, 1967; Marc Ferro, *The Russian Revolution of February 1917*,
    Englewood Cliffs, NY: Prentice-Hall, 1972 (original French edition 1967);
    Alexander Rabinowitch, *Prelude to Revolution. The Petrograd Bolsheviks and the
    July 1917 Uprising*, Bloomington, IN: Indiana University Press, 1968; Rex A.
    Wade, *The Russian Search for Peace, February–October 1917*, Stanford: Stanford
    University Press, 1969; Richard Pipes, ed. *Revolutionary Russia: A Symposium*,
    Cambridge, MA: Harvard University Press, 1968.
3   Ronald Grigor Suny provided something of a manifesto for social history in
    "Toward a Social History of the October Revolution," *American Historical
    Review* 88 (1983): 31–52, which reviewed what he identified as an emerging
    social history of the revolution. Two important critical essays were David
    Longley, "Passionate Objectivity," *Revolutionary Russia*, 2 (1989): 153–60
    (which reviewed Daniel H. Kaiser, ed. *The Workers' Revolution in Russia, 1917.
    The View from Below*, an avowedly social history collection from which the
    Smith article in this collection is taken), and John Eric Marot, "Class Conflict,
    Political Competition and Social Transformation: Critical Perspectives on the
    Social History of the Russian Revolution," *Revolutionary Russia* 7 (1994):
    111–163. Marot's article, which focused on the Koenker and Rosenberg book
    on strikes from which an excerpt is taken as the second article in this collec-
    tion, sparked one of the relatively rare open debates in the form of rejoinders
    in later issues of the same journal by Steve Smith and William Rosenberg,
    and a concluding response from Marot. Ron Suny added to the debate in an
    article rethinking social history and its strengths and weaknesses in "Revision
    and Retreat in the Historiography of 1917: Social History and Its Critics,"
    Russian Review 53 (1994): 155–182.
4   Robert V. Daniels, *Red October: The Bolshevik Revolution of 1917*, New York:
    Scribner's, 1967; Alexander Rabinowitch, *The Bolsheviks Come to Power: The
    Revolution of 1917 in Petrograd*, New York: W.W. Norton, 1976.
5   Two essays that survey the development of writing in Russia are
    Elena Sargeant, "Reappraisal of the Russian Revolution in Contemporary
    Russian Historiography," *Revolutionary Russia* 10, no. 1 (1997): 35–54, and

V. P. Buldakov, "Scholarly Passions around the Myth of 'Great October': Results of the Past Decade," *Kritika, Explorations in Russian and Eurasian Studies* 2 (2001): 295–305.

6 A thoughtful attempt to look at directions writing on the history of the revolution might take after the collapse of the Soviet Union was made by Steve Smith in "Writing the History of the Russian Revolution After the Fall of Communism," *Europe-Asia Studies* 46 (1994): 563–578. Some of his projections have been realized, some have not.

7 Leopold H. Haimson, "The Problem of Social Stability in Urban Russia," *Slavic Review* 23 (1964): 619–642 and 24 (1965): 1–22.

Part I

THE VARIETIES OF
SOCIAL HISTORY

1

PETROGRAD IN 1917

The view from below

Steve A. Smith

"Social history" has been arguably the most important revisionist trend in writing about the history of the Russian Revolution. It had a major impact immediately and has remained extremely influential and an important ingredient in most current histories. It is thus the logical starting point for a book in a series called "Rewriting History." Studying history "from the bottom up" using the methods of "social history" began later for Russian history, and especially the history of the revolution, than it did in West European and American history. After a few scattered essays in the 1970s, it blossomed in the 1980s. Steve Smith's Red Petrograd *was one of the most important of the outpouring of social history works on the revolution. It focused on the industrial workers of the capital, Petrograd (St. Petersburg), who played a key role in both the February and October revolutions and in the process of popular political radicalization that led from the one to the other.*

Smith's main themes, as well as those of the social history research and writing of the 1980s in general, are conveniently summarized in the essay given here: the importance of the "revolution in the factories"; the workers as rational, self-motivated actors with concrete needs and expectations; that workers' actions grew out of their "own experience of complex economic and social upheavals and political events"; the importance of the workers' own organizations such as factory committees and Red Guards; their increasingly distrustful attitude toward the Provisional Government and their gradual alienation from the Revolutionary Defensist (moderate socialist) leaders of the Petrograd Soviet; the workers' political radicalization and turn toward the slogan of "All Power to the Soviets" when their expectations were not met; the growing correspondence between workers' aspirations and the politics of the Bolshevik party that prepared the ground for the October Revolution. Arguing that "it is clear that, rather than the Bolshevik party, the working class itself was the major factor in Petrograd politics in 1917," Smith (and the "social historians" generally) reject the older picture of workers (and soldiers and peasants) as an inert mass or mindless mob manipulated by the Bolsheviks. The Bolsheviks won, they conclude, because "their analysis [of events] and proposed solutions seemed to make sense" to workers, soldiers, and the lower strata of society in general.

This "social history" approach reshaped the conceptualization of the revolution and altered the writing of its history. It led to an appreciation of the growth of popular support for the radical parties, especially the Bolsheviks, as an important

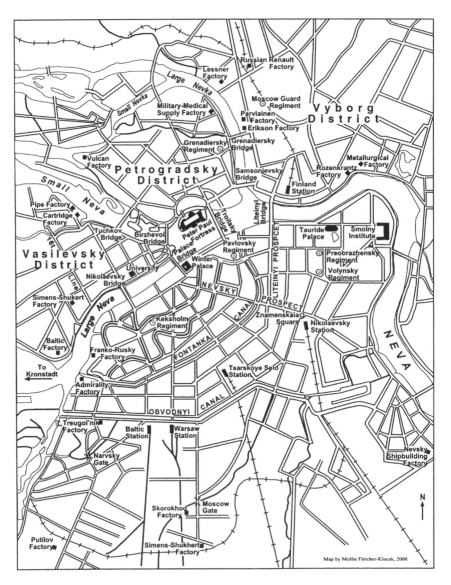

Map 1 Petrograd, 1917.

precondition for the October Revolution. Smith's conclusion that the October Revolution was "the political resolution of a long-drawn out social crisis" and of deep social divisions reflects the fundamentally new interpretation of the Bolshevik rise to power that social history provided (even though most social historians, like others, did not question the old notion of October as "a well-organized coup carried out by the Bolshevik party at the behest of Lenin"). The social historians were criticized, however, for writing "history with the politics left out"; the reader might reflect, while reading this and the next essay, on whether or not that was a fair criticism. This essay was written without source citations for the various quotations; interested readers can find these in Smith's Red Petrograd *(see Further reading) on which this essay is based.*

* * *

The city, its industry and workforce*

Petrograd was the capital of the Russian Empire and the foremost financial and industrial center in an overwhelmingly agrarian society. In 1917 it had a population of 2.4 million, making it by far the largest city in Russia. The city had been built by Peter the Great as Russia's "window on the West." Its Western architecture and layout symbolized the incorporation of Russia into Western culture and the European state system. Here was the seat of government, the court of Nicholas and Alexandra, the major institutions of learning and the arts, of law, commerce, and industry. In the central districts of the Admiralty, Kazan', and Liteinyi stood the palaces of the most eminent aristocratic families, the apartments of the gentry and wealthy bourgeois, elegant emporia, banks, and company offices. Yet just across the Neva River, to the northeast, were the slums and teeming factories of the Vyborg district; and encircling the city (moving in a clockwise direction) were the predominantly proletarian districts of Okhta, Nevskii, Moscow, Narva-Peterhof, and Vasil'evskii, where poverty, overcrowding, and disease were rife. Here there were few open spaces, and no proper roads, pavements, water supply, sewage system, or street lighting. Rubbish was piled up in the streets and open cesspools posed a mortal threat to public health.

With the outbreak of war in 1914, Petrograd became the major center of armaments production in Russia – meeting two-thirds of the nation's defense requirements. The industrial workforce grew by 60 percent to reach 392,800 by 1917 (or 417,000 if one includes factories in the suburbs of the city). Most of this expansion took place in industries producing directly for the war. By 1917 no fewer than 60 percent of the workforce were employed in the metal industries. compared to 11 percent in textiles and 10 percent in chemicals. About half of the workforce were newcomers to industry, made up of peasants drawn from their ailing villages by the

15

prospect of lucrative work in industry and of women responsible for the support of families now that husbands and brothers were at the front. Many of these newcomers had strong ties to the countryside and their experience of urban and factory life was limited. They were a different breed from the skilled men who had worked in industry for many years, whose wages were fairly good, and who were reasonably educated and politically aware. No fewer than 68 percent of the city's workforce worked in enterprises of more than a thousand workers – a degree of concentration unparalleled elsewhere in the world. The concentration of experienced, politically aware workers in large units of production was critical in facilitating the mobilization of the working class in 1917.

Under the old order, Russian workers had few of the rights that workers in the West enjoyed – the rights to strike, to form independent trade unions, and to negotiate collectively with employers. During the war the disciplinary regime within industry – especially those enterprises owned by the government itself – became especially repressive. Although the wages of most strikers in Petrograd rose until the winter of 1916–17, their conditions generally deteriorated. Working hours increased along with the intensity of work, resulting in a huge rise in industrial accidents. Those brave enough to challenge the situation courted transfer to the front, arrest, or dismissal. Workers known to have connections with the revolutionary underground were especially at risk. Yet in spite of the harsh reprisals of the employers and the state, the level of strikes and revolutionary activity rose steadily, as conditions of work deteriorated and as the level of carnage at the front mounted. Even so, in the winter of 1916, notwithstanding the vociferous protests at the dwindling bread supply, rising food prices, and the seemingly interminable war, few would have dared predict that within months the Romanov dynasty would come crashing down.

The February Revolution: dispensation in the factories

The revolution of February 1917 came unexpectedly. It began on February 23 [March 8], International Women's Day, when thousands of angry housewives and women workers, ignoring pleas from labor leaders to stay calm, surged onto the streets. A worker at the Nobel engineering works in the Vyborg district recalled:

> We could hear women's voices in the lane overlooked by the windows of our department: "Down with high prices!" "Down with hunger!" "Bread for the workers!" I and several comrades rushed at once to the windows. . . . The gates of No. I Bol'shaia Sampsonievskaia mill were flung open. Masses of women workers in a militant frame of mind filled the lane. Those who

16

caught sight of us began to wave their arms, shouting: "Come out!" "Stop work!" Snowballs flew through the windows. We decided to join the demonstration.

The next day 200,000 workers were on strike in Petrograd. By February 25 armies of demonstrators were clashing with troops, and the revolution had commenced. On February 27 the climax came when whole regiments of the Petrograd garrison deserted to the insurgents. The same day, the highly respectable leaders of the Duma refused to obey an order from the tsar to disperse and, with the reluctant support of the army generals, they declared themselves a Provisional Committee ("Government" from March 3). On March 3 Nicholas II finally agreed to abdicate, and Russia was free.

In 1905 the autocracy had withstood the revolutionary movement for nearly twelve months before finally moving to crush it; in February 1917 the autocracy succumbed in fewer than twelve days. The difference lay in the fact that in 1905 the army had basically remained loyal to the tsar, whereas in 1917, after three years of bloody and senseless war, the soldiers threw in their lot with the insurgents on the streets. Victory became assured once the liberal conservative opposition agreed to dispense with the tsar, believing that only thus could the war be won and the revolutionary movement halted.

The downfall of Nicholas "The Bloody" filled the workers and soldiers of Petrograd with joy and elation. They had no real sense of this as a "bourgeois" revolution, with all that that implied. Instead they believed that Russia was embarking on a democratic revolution that would bring enormous benefits to the common people. A general meeting at the Dinamo works declared:

> The people and the army went onto the streets not to replace one government by another, but to carry out our slogans. These slogans are: "Freedom," "Equality," "Land and Liberty" and "An End to the Bloody War." For us, the unpropertied classes, the bloody slaughter is unnecessary.

At this stage, a majority of workers, trusting implicitly in the Soviet as "their" representative, and unwilling to risk dissension in the revolutionary ranks, supported the policy of the moderate socialists in giving conditional support to the Provisional Government. They made no attempt, however, to hide their distrust of the latter. The common attitude was nicely summed up in a resolution from the Izhora works:

> All measures of the Provisional Government that destroy the remnants of the autocracy and strengthen the freedom of

the people must be fully supported by the democracy. All measures that lead to conciliation with the old regime and that are directed against the people must meet with decisive protest and counteraction.

From the beginning, therefore, workers were distrustful of the Provisional Government, which they felt to be bound by a thousand threads to landowning and business interests.

With regard to the burning question of the war, workers in Petrograd also tended at this stage to go along with the policy of the Soviet Executive Committee. In contrast to the Bolsheviks, who after April denounced the war as "imperialist" and called on workers to urge civil war against their own governments, the Mensheviks and Socialist Revolutionaries – although divided into "Defensist" and "Internationalist" wings – tended to put the accent not on opposing the war, but on working for peace. They pressed the new government to work earnestly for a democratic peace between the belligerents, who would renounce all indemnities and annexations of territory. The February Revolution strengthened support among Petrograd workers and soldiers for this policy. Lenin described their attitude as one of "revolutionary defensism" in that they were prepared to continue to fight until such time as peace was achieved, in order to defend revolutionary Russia from Austro-German militarism.

Revolution in the factories

On returning to their workbenches after the February strikes, workers proceeded to dismantle the autocratic structure of management in the factories, just as it had been dismantled in society at large. The creation of a "constitutional" factory was seen to be the prerequisite of an enhancement of the status and dignity of workers within society as a whole. Democratization of factory relations assumed a variety of forms. First, hated foremen and administrators fled or were expelled. At the giant Putilov works, for example, where some 30,000 workers were employed, workers thrust the one-time leader of the factory Black Hundreds, Puzanov, into a wheelbarrow, poured red lead over his head, and trundled him off to a nearby canal, into which they threatened to deposit him in punishment for his past misdemeanors. Second, the factory rule books, with their punitive fines and humiliating searches, were torn up. Third, and most important, factory committees were created to represent the interests of workers to management.

In the large state-run enterprises the new committees temporarily took over the running of the factories, since the old administration had fled. On March 13 committee members from factories belonging to the

Artillery Department defined the aim of the new factory order as being "self-management by workers on the broadest possible scale"; and the functions of the committees were specified as the "defense of the interests of labor vis-à-vis the factory administration and control over its activities." To our ears talk of control smacks of workers ousting management and running things by themselves, but in Russian the word *control* has the most modest sense of *supervision* or *inspection*. What these workers from the state plants envisaged was not that the committees should permanently run the enterprises, but that they should have full rights to oversee the activities of the official management and be fully informed of what was going on.

In the private sector the activities of the committees in the spring of 1917 were less far-reaching. There they functioned more or less as trade unions, for trade unions did not become properly established in Petrograd until the early summer. The first act of the committees was unilaterally to introduce an eight-hour working day, something that had eluded them in 1905, and to limit or abolish overtime work. Under enormous pressure, the Soviet and the Petrograd Society of Factory and Works Owners formally agreed to the introduction of an eight-hour day on March 10. The committee then proceeded to press for large wage increases to compensate them for the wartime rise in the cost of living. In the half-year prior to the February Revolution, wages had fallen in real terms by about 10 percent as a result of rocketing prices. Now a combination of action by the committees and spontaneous strikes persuaded the employers to agree to increases in monthly earnings of between 30 percent and 50 percent. Having achieved these increases, the committees then settled down to a wide range of activities, which included guarding factory property and maintaining law and order in the working-class districts; checking that workers had been legitimately excused from military enlistment; organizing supplies of food; maintaining labor discipline in the workshops; organizing educational and cultural activities; and campaigning against drunkenness.

Workers and the Provisional Government

The first sign of a growing rift between the masses and the Provisional Government came in April – over the question of the war. Although the government had affirmed its support for the peace policy of the Soviet Executive Committee, on April 18 the Minister of Foreign Affairs, P. N. Miliukov, sent a note to the Allies, which became public on the 20th, in which he reiterated Russia's determination to fight the war to a victorious conclusion and to stand by the treaties concluded with the Allies, whereby Russia stood to gain Constantinople and the Dardanelles. The publication of this note sparked an explosion of indignation in the factories and barracks. Workers and soldiers poured onto the streets on April 20 and 21, and there were violent clashes with bourgeois counter-demonstrators. The effect of the "April Days" was to deepen popular distrust of the government. Two thousand workers at the Siemens-Halske engineering works demanded the "strengthening of control over the government" by the Soviet Executive Committee, and the "exclusion of the supporters of an annexationist war, in particular, Guchkov [Minister of War under the first Provisional Government] and Miliukov." Other workers' resolutions demanded the renunciation of the secret treaties and the immediate formulation of peace terms.

In an effort to increase its popularity among the masses, the Provisional Government proposed to the Soviet Executive Committee that it join a new coalition government. At first, the Soviet leaders opposed the proposal, since they feared that as ministers they might become compromised in the eyes of the masses. The leader of the Executive Committee, I. G. Tsereteli, however, became convinced of the advantages of a coalition government, and on May 1 the Executive Committee agreed to the proposal by a vote of forty-four to ten with two abstentions. (The opposition came from Bolsheviks, Menshevik Internationalists, and Left Socialist Revolutionaries.) Six socialists thus took up seats in government alongside the ten "capitalist" ministers. It seems that a majority of workers considered that the Soviet Executive Committee had taken the right step in order, as the Admiralty workers put it, "to increase socialist influence over the organs of power." An ominously large minority, however, condemned the coalition as a "ministry of compromise with the bourgeoisie."

At the time of the February Revolution the Bolshevik party had been in considerable disarray. Its most able leaders were abroad or in exile; its membership had dwindled as a result of wartime persecution by the authorities; and the party organization was fragmented, both geographically (there was little centralized coordination of the regional organizations) and politically (factionalism was rife). The February Revolution took the Bolsheviks by surprise, and they divided in their attitude to the Provisional Government. It was only after Lenin returned from Switzerland on April 4 that a meaningful degree of political unity was restored in the party. Lenin's April *Theses* represented an extreme but perspicacious analysis of the political situation in Russia, which broke sharply with the orthodox Social-Democratic conception of a two-stage revolution. Lenin considered that the "old Bolshevik" formula that the "bourgeois revolution is not yet completed" was "obsolete." He argued that transition to socialism was on the agenda in Russia, since it was the weak link in the international chain of imperialism, and that revolution in Russia would precipitate revolution in the more advanced countries. Thus there must be absolutely no support for the capitalist

Provisional Government: power must pass instead into the hands of the proletariat and poor peasantry via a republic of soviets. Meanwhile, Lenin argued, the war remained one of "imperialist banditry," which the Bolsheviks must unbendingly oppose. The party accepted these new strategic perspectives at its April Conference only after considerable opposition had been overcome; the new views were concretized in the slogans "All Power to the Soviets!" and "Down with the War!"

These perspectives had a tremendous impact, since they accorded with the deepest aspirations of the most radical element within the Petrograd proletariat – the skilled metalworkers of the Vyborg district and, to a lesser extent, of Vasil'evskii Island. The attitudes of these workers found vivid expression in a resolution passed by general assemblies of workers at the Puzyrev and Ekval' factories during the "April Days":

> The government cannot and does not want to represent the wishes of the whole toiling people, and so we demand its immediate abolition and the arrest of its members, in order to neutralize their assault on liberty. We recognize that power must belong only to the people itself, i.e., to the Soviet of Workers' and Soldiers' Deputies as the sole institution of authority enjoying the confidence of the people.

Support for the Bolsheviks began to grow from this time, in reaction not only to political events but also to economic developments. By the summer the national economy was staggering under the crushing burdens of war. Production of fuel and raw materials plunged, leading to acute shortages in the centers of industrial production – shortages that the paralysis of the transport system aggravated. The result was that factories began to shut down, and the grim prospect of unemployment faced thousands of workers. Meanwhile the decline in grain production, combined with the chaos on the railways and waterways, led to a growing shortage of bread and basic foodstuffs in the cities. Finally, the dearth of primary items of subsistence, together with an ill-conceived financial policy by the government, fueled inflation to the point where the monetary system eventually collapsed. The Soviet historian Z. V. Stepanov reckons that by October 1917 the cost of living in Petrograd was 14.3 times higher than in 1913, and that the real wages of workers had fallen by anything from 10 percent to 60 percent from their January 1917 level. Some workers were already on the verge of destitution.

By the summer of 1917 the trade unions were reestablished, and it was they who led the battle to restore workers' living standards. Throughout 1917 they remained less influential than the factory committees, but they did become important mass organizations. Most were industrial unions, representing the interests of all workers in a given industry regardless of their trade. From the early summer, they began to negotiate with the appropriate section of the Society of Factory and Works Owners to achieve city-wide contracts regulating the wages of all workers in a given branch of industry. Despite acrimonious negotiations with the employers, most unions did succeed in winning such contracts; but although they appeared to grant sizable wage increases, especially to the low-paid, in real terms ravaging inflation devoured these increases almost before the ink had dried on the contract.

The deteriorating material condition of workers, especially of the low-paid, produced a radicalization in the political attitudes of the less skilled, less well-off peasant workers and women workers. This was especially apparent at the Putilov works, where low-paid workers vented their anger and frustration on trade union and factory committee leaders whom they felt to be too dilatory in promoting their interests. I. N. Sokolov, a Bolshevik at Putilov, reported:

> The mass of workers in the factory ... are in a state of turmoil because of the low rates of pay, so that even we, the members of the works committee, have been seized by the collar, dragged into the shops and told "Give us money!"

In general, however, economic distress tended to make workers receptive to Bolshevik attacks on the capitalist system, the imperialist war, and the bourgeois-landlord government. On June 20 S. M. Gessen informed the city committee of the Bolshevik party that:

> the Putilov works has come over decisively to our side. The militant mood of the factory has deep economic roots. The question of wage increases is an acute one. From the very beginning of the revolution the workers' demands for wage increases were not satisfied. Gvozdev [a Menshevik and deputy to the Minister of Labor] came to the factory and promised to satisfy their demands, but he did not keep his promises. On the demonstration of June 18 [organized by the Soviet Executive Committee, supposedly to rally support], the Putilov workers bore placards saying "They have deceived us!"

The rising tide of militancy among individual workers came to a head at the beginning of July.

The armed demonstrations of July 3–4, known as the July Days, occurred against a background of worsening economic difficulties, the dismal failure of the June offensive launched by Kerensky in order to impress the Allies, the attempt of the government to remove to the front regiments stationed in Petrograd, and the breakdown of the coalition government after the resignation of four Kadet ministers. The demonstrations were organized from the grass roots, but after initial wavering, the Bolshevik party agreed to assume leadership of them. The aims of the thousands of workers and soldiers who took to the streets were apparently straightforward – to force the resignation of the "ten capitalist ministers" and compel the Soviet Executive Committee (or more correctly, since the First All-Russian Congress of Soviets, the Central Executive Committee) to form a government. Events quickly took a nasty turn. Clashes broke out between demonstrators, counter-demonstrators, and government troops, in which as many as 400 were killed or wounded. On the night of July 4–5 the government – now under the leadership of Kerensky – in a determined effort to prove to the propertied classes its fitness to govern, arrested leading Bolsheviks, such as Trotsky and Lunacharskii, forced Lenin and Zinoviev to go into hiding, ransacked the Bolshevik party headquarters, closed *Pravda*, and rounded up arms in the possession of workers. Shortly thereafter the Kerensky government reintroduced the death penalty at the front and announced its intention of restoring discipline in the army. The July Days thus ended not in a soviet government, but in the Provisional Government taking a sharp turn to the right.

The July Days, even though dramatically illustrating the outright hostility of the majority of workers and soldiers to the government, highlighted their ambivalence toward the moderate socialists who controlled the national network of soviets. The demonstrators hoped to force the Central Executive Committee to take power; but the committee was determined not to do so and denounced the demonstrators as "counter-revolutionaries." This created confusion among the latter, evidenced in the speech of one of four workers allowed to address the Central Executive Committee on behalf of fifty-four factories:

> It is strange to read the appeal of the Central Executive Committee: workers and soldiers are called counter-revolutionaries. Our demand – the general demand of the workers – is all power to Soviets of Workers' and Soldiers' Deputies. . . . We demand the retirement of the ten capitalist ministers. We trust the Soviet, but not those whom the Soviet trusts. Our comrades, the socialist ministers, entered into an agreement with the capitalists, but these capitalists are our mortal enemies. . . . The land must pass immediately to the peasants! Control of production must be instituted immediately! We demand a struggle against the starvation that is threatening us!

"We trust the Soviet, but not those whom the Soviet trusts." In his fine study, David Mandel calls this the "paradox" of the July Days. The demonstrators had to believe that the Executive Committee could be persuaded to take power, since they could see no other alternative, yet the Central Executive Committee was prepared to lose popular support rather than assume power.

It is likely that a majority of workers still did not abandon hope in the Central Executive Committee, for the bloodshed and fraternal strife of the July Days strengthened a desire for unity against the openly mobilizing counterrevolution. For a short time, the Bolsheviks lost support as workers reacted against their divisive policies. Nevertheless, once everyone had time to take stock, workers – especially those in the metal industry – concluded that the members of the Soviet Central Executive Committee were "traitors" who had joined the ranks of the class enemy.

Workers' control and Bolshevism

Meanwhile, throughout the summer a movement for workers' control of production was built up. Workers' control is often depicted as an anarchist-inspired attempt by workers to seize the factories. In fact it originated as an eminently practical effort to stem the tide of economic disorder and to keep the factories running. The agents of workers' control, the factory committees, at first confined themselves to trying to procure fuel and raw materials and to keeping a general eye on management. During the summer, however, as the economic crisis deepened, the committees became convinced that the employers were deliberately exacerbating the crisis in order to quell workers' militancy and to make them "see sense." In a bid to stamp out "capitalist sabotage," the committees instituted more far-reaching forms of control. They took to intervening actively in management affairs, by examining order books and financial accounts, and insisted that all decisions made by the administration be ratified by the committees. In so doing, the committees sought to keep the factories open and to stave off mass unemployment. The Soviet historian, M. L. Itkin, estimates that by October 289,000 workers in Petrograd – or 74 percent of the industrial workforce – worked in enterprises under some form of workers' control. This should be kept in perspective, however, for Itkin calculates that workers' control operated in only ninety-six enterprises, which must mean that nearly 90 percent of Petrograd enterprises – mainly small and medium workplaces – were untouched by it.

The big employers could not tolerate such incursions on their "right" to manage as they saw fit. Consequently, they pressured Minister of Labor M. I. Skobelev to take steps to curb the factory committees' efforts at workers' control. Skobelev responded by issuing two circulars that forbade the committees to interfere in the hiring and firing of workers or to meet during working hours – a move that provoked howls of protest from the workers. The Langenzippen workers resolved:

Skobelev's circular has a purely political character and is counter-revolutionary. It prevents the labor movement from following an organized course and supports the organized march of the counter-revolution, which aims to sabotage industry and reduce the country to famine. We are forced to conclude that the Ministry for the "protection of labor" has been converted into the Ministry for the "protection of capitalist interests."

As a Menshevik, Skobelev believed that workers' control could only aggravate disorder in the economy, since it involved uncoordinated actions by atomized groups of workers. The moderate socialist argued that only planned centralized regulation of the economy by the state could begin to undo the damage wrought by the war. The Bolsheviks, too, believed that only action at the central level could restore the battered productive forces, but they argued that it was folly to trust this to a capitalist government, since any restoration of economic order would inevitably be at the expense of working people. They thus supported workers' control, essentially as a means of mitigating economic disorder until such time as a workers' government took power. Their support for workers' control was a major cause of the party's growing popularity. Indeed the factory committees were the first of the popular organizations to come out in favor of Bolshevik policies. As early as the end of May at the First Conference of Petrograd Factory Committees, a resolution drafted by Lenin "on measures to combat disruption in the economy" won by 297 votes to 21, with 44 abstentions. The opposition of the Menshevik and Socialist Revolutionary parties to workers' control, in turn, lost them a lot of grass-roots support.

As class conflict polarized ever more sharply, the Kerensky government was left stranded without any social support. Compared to the upheavals convulsing society, politics was increasingly reduced to a kind of shadow play. Hated by the radicalized masses, Kerensky's new coalition sought support from the Right, only to discover that the Right too was radicalizing. Army officers, industrialists, and middle-class liberals had now come to despise Kerensky for being weak, irresolute, and "soft" on the Left. After the failure of the June offensive they had begun to coordinate the search for a strong man who would crush "anarchy" in society, revitalize the army, and restore order to the economy. In August they found their "man on a white horse" in General Lavr Kornilov, recently appointed Supreme Commander-in-Chief by Kerensky. Kornilov made no secret of his desire for a military dictatorship that would crush the soviets, and plans were laid. The putsch, launched on August 28, failed almost as soon as it began, owing to poor organization, divisions within the counterrevolutionary ranks, and heroic resistance from railway and telegraph workers. In Petrograd the district soviets and factory committees helped to organize bands of armed workers to patrol the city or dig trenches and erect fortifications on the outskirts. Although Kornilov's forces never got within striking distance of the capital, the specter of counterrevolution frightened ordinary working people, who blamed Kerensky for allowing things to come to such a pass. Many were convinced that the extreme situation required an extreme solution.

After the Kornilov rebellion, support for the Bolsheviks grew in leaps and bounds. On August 31 the Petrograd Soviet passed a Bolshevik resolution for the first time, by 279 votes to 115 (with 51 abstentions). This resolution called for a government of representatives of the revolutionary proletariat and peasantry, for immediate peace negotiations, for confiscation of the large estates, and the introduction of workers' control in industry. On September 5 the Socialist Revolutionary–Menshevik presidium of the Soviet resigned, and Bolsheviks were elected to a majority of places in the new presidium with Trotsky as chairman. A majority of workers in the factories now supported the Bolshevik program. The Kerensky government – desperately trying to stitch together a new coalition – was deemed in the words of the Admiralty workers to be a "government of bourgeois-landlord dictatorship and civil war, which is conducting a policy of betrayal of the revolution and deception of the people." The moderate socialists of the Central Executive Committee, for their part, were unequivocally denounced for the "ruinous policy of compromise with the propertied classes, who seek to strangle the toiling masses with the bony hand of hunger." The Bolsheviks had dropped the slogan "All Power to the Soviets" after the July Days, since there was no chance of the soviets assuming power under moderate socialist leadership, calling instead for a "revolutionary government of the proletariat and poor peasantry." Some factories followed this change in tactics, and class hostility to the bourgeoisie and to capitalism became far more explicit. On August 10, for example, the Erikson workers demanded "the organization of a genuinely revolutionary power resting on the workers, soldiers, and poor peasants, i.e., a power which will be a dictatorship directed against the counterrevolutionary bourgeoisie." Not all factories followed suit: many continued to call for a government based on the soviets, or for a "homogeneous socialist government," or for a "homogeneous government of representatives of revolutionary democracy."

A new theme emerged within workers' discourse in September, namely, the need for workers to arm themselves in order to forestall a repetition of the Kornilov adventure. Alongside demands for the freeing of those Bolsheviks still in prison since the July Days, for the disbandment of the Kornilovite General Staff, for the abolition of the death penalty, and for the dispersal of the State Duma and State Council, there figured the demand "to give arms to the workers so that we can organize a Red

Guard." The Red Guards were armed detachments based on the factories, which consisted mainly of young men loyal to the Bolsheviks. The Red Guards described themselves as an "organization of the armed forces of the proletariat for struggle with the counter-revolution and defense of the conquests of the proletariat." But it became evident as September dragged into October, and Kerensky continued to cling to the vestiges of power, that the units training each evening in the factory yards were getting restive.

As support for the Bolshevik program grew, so workers flocked to join the party. In April the Petrograd organization had about 16,000 members; by October membership had risen to 43,000, of whom two-thirds were workers. Most of these recruits were young men (there were relatively few women) who were joining a political party for the first time. Some, however, joined from other parties. A Menshevik woman from the Siemens-Schuckert works asked to join the party, saying, "The Menshevik party leaders have forgotten their program and are not fulfilling the interests of the proletariat and poor peasantry. They have restored the death penalty and have locked up the best popular leaders in 'democratic jails'." A Socialist Revolutionary from the Aivaz works wrote to the newspaper *Rabochii* (The Worker), stating:

> Because of profound misunderstanding I joined the SR party which has now passed to the side of the bourgeoisie and lent a hand to our exploiters. So that I shall not be nailed to this mast of shame, I am quitting the ranks of the chauvinists. As a conscious proletarian, I am joining the Bolshevik comrades who alone are the genuine defenders of the oppressed people.

It is easy in retrospect to assume that from now on a Bolshevik victory was inevitable, but Lenin certainly did not believe this. His profound grasp of the social dynamics underpinning the system of "dual power" had allowed the party to turn to its advantage the successive political crises and to win an ever wider circle of popular support, but Lenin was convinced that power would not fall into the lap of the Bolsheviks. It would have to be seized. From the end of September, therefore, from his hiding ground Lenin relentlessly harried the Central Committee to prepare for an armed uprising.

The overthrow of the Kerensky government proved to be a relatively painless affair. At 10 a.m. on October 25 the Military Revolutionary Committee issued the following triumphant message:

> The Provisional Government is overthrown. State power has passed into the hands of the organ of the Petrograd Soviet of Workers' and Soldiers' Deputies – the Military Revolutionary

27

Committee, which stands at the head of the Petrograd proletariat and garrison.

The cause for which the people fought – an immediate proposal of a democratic peace, abolition of landlords' property rights in land, workers' control over production, the creation of a Soviet government – this cause is assured.

Long Live the Revolution of workers, soldiers and peasants!

The major factories of Petrograd and the main organizations of labor welcomed the new government. It is true that a minority of workers opposed what they saw as a violent and illegal seizure of power that threatened to engulf Russia in civil war. These consisted mainly of printers, about half the railway workforce, most white-collar workers (e.g., bank employees and draftsmen), and the odd factory such as the Pal' textile mill located in the mainly bourgeois Alexandro-Nevskii district of Petrograd. There is little doubt, however, that the majority of workers were pleased to hear that Kerensky had fled the city. They felt that at last a genuinely revolutionary government had come to power, representative of workers and peasants and based on the soviets. The immediate tasks of this government were clear: to bring an end to the war, to give land to the peasants, and to restore order in the economy. But regarding its longer-term tasks there was less agreement. Some resolutions passed by workers perceived the new government as merely a caretaker administration until the Constituent Assembly should meet. At the other extreme, some perceived the Bolshevik government as a proletarian dictatorship that would rapidly reorder society on socialist lines. The majority of resolutions in between were much vaguer: some talked of socialism, some of revolutionary democracy. The majority – at least initially – favored a coalition government comprising all the parties in the Soviet, since, in spite of massive disillusionment with the Mensheviks and Socialist Revolutionaries, they continued to be seen as legitimate democratic parties. At the beginning of November, however, no one foresaw that the country would soon be ruled by a one-party dictatorship and be poised on the threshold of civil war.

Conclusion

Until recently, much Western historiography has presented the October insurrection as a military coup carried out by a tightly knit minority party, led by a man with an almost Nietzschean will to power. There is an important grain of truth in this view. For the overthrow of Kerensky was indeed a well-organized coup carried out by the Bolshevik party at the behest of Lenin: To that extent, the October Revolution was quite unlike the February Revolution, when the masses themselves had directly precipitated the final crisis of the *ancien régime*. But to depict the October insurrection as a coup pure and simple is to fail to plumb its essence. The dominant characterization of the events of October 24–25 deserves closer scrutiny.

In October 1917 the Bolsheviks were still a minority party. In the national elections to the Constituent Assembly in November, they gained only a quarter of the vote, as against 38 percent for the Socialist Revolutionaries and 13 percent for the Kadets. Popular sentiment, however, was still shifting in the Bolsheviks' favor. In June only 105 Bolsheviks had been elected to the First All-Russian Congress of Soviets, as opposed to 283 Socialist Revolutionaries, 248 Mensheviks, and 73 nonparty delegates. At the Second All-Russian Congress of Soviets on October 25 – before the walkout of the moderate socialists – there were 390 Bolsheviks, 160 Socialist Revolutionaries, 72 Mensheviks, 14 Internationalists, 6 United Social Democrats, and 7 Ukrainian Social Democrats. By October support for the Bolsheviks was overwhelming in the large industrial centers, especially Petrograd, in the garrisons of the rear and at the front. Workers and soldiers were the most solid supporters of the party. Most groups of workers – with the exception of certain "labor aristocrats" and white-collar workers – had swung behind the party, beginning with the skilled metalworkers but quickly followed by unskilled peasant workers and women. It was in the vast rural areas that Bolshevik forces remained weak. But even there, the peasants who voted for the SRs in the Constituent Assembly elections voted for the policies of the left-wing of that party (which had already split from the "conciliationist" wing), and on the crucial questions of the land and the war, Left SR policies were not dissimilar to those of the Bolsheviks.

Until recently in the West, the workers, soldiers, and peasants were seen to have played an essentially destructive, anarchistic, and elemental role in the revolution. They were the "dark masses," able to tear down but not to build. Typical of this view is the comment by Theodore von Laue that "Russian politics from May 1917 to the spring of 1921 . . . must be viewed primitively in terms of Hobbesian social mechanics, in terms of crude violence among masses uprooted by war and revolution." The recent work of historians such as Diane Koenker, David Mandel, Ronald Suny, William Rosenberg, and Alexander Rabinowitch dissents from that view. The changing attitudes and activities of Petrograd workers, at least, are perfectly comprehensible in essentially rational terms, without resort to some Hobbesian model. The workers had very concrete needs and expectations that the Provisional Government failed to meet. They turned to the Bolsheviks because their policies seemed to represent the only viable political alternative.

Of course, rational self-interest does not exhaust the meaning of the revolution: In fact, it provides a rather jejune explanation of working-class conduct in 1917. Workers were motivated by more than mere calculations of means and ends. Their rationality was deeply imbued with morality and even utopianism. Revolutionary consciousness had emotional and moral, as well as rational, bases. Hope, a sense of justice, hatred, fear, and indignation all played a part in moving workers into action. Yet, in the final analysis, the radicalization of workers in 1917 can be explained quite simply: It arose from the fact that their hopes that the Provisional Government would uphold the interests of the common people, the status of workers in the workplace and in society, achieve a speedy peace settlement, and give land to the peasants, were bitterly disappointed. Instead the government appeared to uphold the interests of the privileged and the system of exploitation and militarism on which their power rested. As the employers and landowners were perceived deliberately to prolong the war, to perpetrate sabotage in industry, and artificially to create the food shortages, so working-class hostility to the propertied classes grew and support for the Bolsheviks increased.

Related to the view of the "dark masses" is the notion that the Bolsheviks won their following by "manipulating" the base instincts of the masses by a fearsome combination of demagogy and lies. To be sure, Bolshevik agitation and organization played a crucial role in radicalizing the masses. But the Bolsheviks themselves did not create popular discontent or revolutionary feeling. This grew out of the masses' own experience of complex economic and social upheavals and political events. The contribution of the Bolsheviks was rather to shape workers' understanding of the social dynamics of the revolution and to foster an awareness of how the urgent problems of daily life related to the broader social and political order. The Bolsheviks won support because their analysis and proposed solutions seemed to make sense. A worker from the Orudiinyi works, formerly a bastion of defensism where Bolsheviks were not even allowed to speak, stated in September that "the Bolsheviks have always said: 'It is not we who will persuade you, but life itself.' And now the Bolsheviks have triumphed because life has proved their tactics right."

In respect of the same issue, it is clear that, rather than the Bolshevik party, the working class itself was the major factor in Petrograd politics in 1917. Workers created a gamut of organizations and a huge variety of revolutionary practices that to some degree constituted the embryo of a new social order. Not only was a national network of soviets set up, first by workers and soldiers and later by peasants, but also factory committees (probably the most important of the proletarian organizations), trade unions, workers' militias, Red Guards, consumer cooperatives, and educational and cultural organizations. Measured against this powerful grid of interlocking organizations, the Bolshevik party apparatus was puny. The Bolsheviks were not, therefore, in any real position prior to October to manipulate or control these popular organizations. Instead the Bolsheviks won support from the organizations by taking up their concerns as the party's own, and gradually rose to positions of leadership within the organizations, largely by democratic means. By successfully relating to the popular movements, the Bolsheviks had, in a sense, already "come to power" even before the overthrow of the Provisional Government.

Finally, the notion of the Bolshevik party as the "manipulator" of the masses has another source in a stereotyped image of the party itself. This view projects the party in 1917 as being an exact replica of the model party outlined by Lenin in 1902 in *What Is To Be Done?*. In this pamphlet Lenin argued for a vanguard party of professional revolutionaries, highly disciplined and centralized, and conspiratorial in its methods. In 1917, for better or worse, the reality of the Bolshevik party was very different. In the first place, it was a mass party, with perhaps as many as 300,000 members by October, working openly. Second, it was a loosely structured organization, in which the Central Committee had astonishingly little control over provincial and city organizations. Third, the much-vaunted discipline of the party was a fiction. On every major question of the day there were sharp disagreements and factions that did not stop short of frontal challenges to the leadership of Lenin himself (most dramatically, the opposition of Kamenev and Zinoviev to the October seizure of power). The party in 1917 was thus characterized by vigorous debate, a measure of internal democracy, and considerable flexibility with regard to its relations to the masses. Relative to its rivals (which had suffered fatal splits and a massive hemorrhage of members), it is true that the Bolshevik party was more unified and centralized, but it was a far cry from the "organizational weapon" beloved of some political sociologists.

In making a final assessment of the October seizure of power one is forced to conclude that the events of October 24–25 were far more than a military coup. They were the political resolution of a long-drawn-out social crisis, the origins of which go back at least as far as 1905. The war released the accumulated tensions within Russian society, and the February Revolution once more opened up a divide between the popular masses and propertied society. This divide ran so deep through society that the possibilities for bridging it, even in March 1917, were very limited. The Provisional Government, aided by the Soviet Executive Committee, for several months attempted to do so, but it failed to tackle with the necessary speed and nerve the issues that were of pressing concern to the masses. It thus lost any potential social base that it might have had. Instead, it devoted itself to one end – the preservation of the alliance with society – and failed even at that. When in October the Bolsheviks overthrew the government of Kerensky, it appeared to the suffering masses to be less a lethal deathblow to the body politic than an act of euthanasia.

NOTES

Reprinted from Daniel H. Kaiser, ed., *The Workers' Revolution in Russia, 1917: The View from Below* (Cambridge: Cambridge University Press, 1987), 59–79.

* I wish to acknowledge my debt to the authors of the following works on whose fine scholarship I have drawn freely: Marc Ferro, *The Russian Revolution of February 1917* (London: Routledge and Kegan Paul, 1972); Marc Ferro, *October 1917: A Social History of the Russian Revolution* (London: Routledge and Kegan Paul, 1980); Tsuyoshi Hasegawa, *The February Revolution: Petrograd 1917* (Seattle: University of Washington Press, 1981); David Mandel, *Petrograd Workers and the Fall of the Old Regime* (London: Macmillan, 1983); Alexander Rabinowitch, *The Bolsheviks Come to Power* (New York: W. W. Norton, 1976).

2

STRIKES AND REVOLUTION IN RUSSIA, 1917

Diane P. Koenker and William G. Rosenberg

Diane Koenker and William Rosenberg both have contributed important works to the history of the revolution and are usually numbered among the more influential social historians. Their joint study of strikes is especially significant, exploring the nature and meaning of this, one of the most important and publicly visible features of the revolution. Like Smith, Koenker and Rosenberg argue that the months between March and October were in large part a workers' revolution. They go on to add that "the nature and import of strike activism in 1917 has largely escaped serious historical scrutiny," even though strikes affected workers, management, political leaders, and the general population in significant ways. Strikes were not simply a workers' activity, central as they were to workers' efforts to fulfill their aspirations ("the central experience of more workers than any other form of participatory politics"). Rather, strikes helped shape a whole range of attitudes toward the new order not only for workers themselves, but also for plant owners and managers and for "state and soviet officials struggling . . . to build a democratic regime." Koenker and Rosenberg emphasize the interconnectedness of strikes with broader political, economic, and social developments. After the February Revolution, strikes became not merely a legitimate and even routine labor-management tool, but also were an instrument for political as well as social change and posed a threat to the Provisional Government's effort to create a functioning new democratic order. Koenker and Rosenberg also raise the important question of social identities and polarization that has been a central part of the social history of the revolution: strikes not only helped social groups develop their own self-identities and self-perceptions, but also were an important part of how others perceived them and they perceived others.

Koenker and Rosenberg reflect a central tenet of the social historians in their last sentences, when they emphasize that the revolutionary process cannot be fully understood simply through emphasis on Lenin's leadership or Kerensky's failures, but must also consider the "powerful forces emanating from the rank and file of the Russian labor force, the depth of their grievances, and the logic of their participation in the revolutionary struggle." This brief selection comes from the introductory chapter and the concluding pages of the book; in between is an extremely rich, if dense, work of historical research and writing. This selection has the added benefit that it opens with a discussion of a group of women workers, for women in general and women workers in particular have been little studied and poorly represented in the literature of the revolution.

* * *

Understanding strikes in 1917

On Monday, May 1, 1917, by the old calendar, the Executive Committee of the Petrograd Soviet voted in emergency session to send official representatives to the Provisional Government. The margin in favor was 43 to 19.[1] Dual power, formerly shared uneasily between the Provisional Government and the Petrograd Soviet, now became institutionalized in a coalition government, and the attention of national and international political figures focused on Petrograd to see how the new coalition would handle the burden of revolutionary power. Not many noticed another event, in its own way as symbolic as the formation of the coalition. Also on May 1, several thousand Petrograd laundresses in over 100 small and large shops declared a strike against their employers. By the next day, three-quarters of all the city's washerwomen had left their jobs; soon, 5,500 women in nearly 200 firms had joined the strike.

The laundresses spoke through their trade union, which had been organized in the heady days after the February revolution. They demanded a package of reforms: an eight-hour workday, minimum daily wages of four to six rubles, the introduction of a pay book for accurate calculation of pay, required two-week notice for dismissals, recognition of the union, polite address on the part of employers, more and better quality food, improved sanitary conditions in the shops, two weeks' annual paid vacation, and one month's sick leave with jobs to be held for six additional months.[2]

Almost immediately after the May 1 walkout, employers began to resort to that "common Western European practice," as *Pravda* described it, the use of scab labor and the formation of an alternative, "yellow" trade union.[3] Tempers flared on both sides, and so did the use of force. When two union leaders failed to convince women in one shop to join the strike, they doused the stoves and hot irons with water, virtually forcing the recalcitrant laundresses to join the walkout. Management retaliated: in this shop, the activists were chased away with hot flatirons. Elsewhere, shopowners poured boiling water on strikers, and reportedly went after the "damned vipers" and "unbelieving filth" with pokers and revolvers.[4]

In the face of this hostility, working-class Petrograd rallied around the laundresses. Contributions to the union strike fund poured in from district soviets and individual factories, amounting by May 21 to nearly 16,000 rubles. The laundresses held mass meetings around the city, where political activists like Alexandra Kollontai encouraged them in their solidarity. Within a week, owners of 40 small laundries had agreed to the strikers' demands; by May 16, 80 laundries were back to work, with more owners settling each day. On May 28, the strike ended triumphantly for the strikers with an agreement worked out in arbitration.[5]

The Petrograd laundry workers' strike was one of many in revolutionary Russia involving not muscular proletarians toiling at fiery furnaces but workers in nonindustrial and service occupations, often women previously unorganized and unheard from. In other features, as well, this strike typified the emerging themes of labor protest in the spring of 1917. It reflected the depth of workers' grievances and their conviction that the revolution would finally right past wrongs. It demonstrated the ways in which even unskilled and politically inactive groups of workers scattered throughout an entire city could mobilize, if they had to, in support of common goals. It also engendered strong expressions of moral and material solidarity from other workers in the metropolis, the experience in arbitration of the dignity of the workers' cause, and a sense of vindication as employers capitulated even to the demand for pay to be awarded for the time on strike. In its course and aftermath, moreover, the strike also undoubtedly raised consciousness about class position.

Also typical of the strike was the lack of response generated in the non-socialist press and in subsequent recollections of the events of 1917. The fact that most of the city's laundries had shut down was commented upon only once or twice in liberal or conservative newspapers, whereas socialist papers reported almost daily on the events surrounding the strike. Nikolai Sukhanov recalled this particular strike in his invaluable memoir of the revolution published in 1922: "Notwithstanding the fact that the contingent of strikers was backward, unaccustomed to struggle and dispersed among masses of enterprises, the conflict was distinguished by the utmost persistence and it spun out over several weeks."[6] But aside from Sukhanov, this and other individual strikes were rarely mentioned by eyewitnesses, even though the press regularly demonstrated how much they had become part of the daily experience of the Russian revolution. Unruly street demonstrations and political strikes such as those of the February Days and the July Days alone seem to have stuck in the memories of participants in 1917. Of strikes, some memoirists recalled only the general phenomenon, "the excessive and increasing demands of the workers,"[7] or how at the same time as the Petrograd laundresses' strike, the Minister of Trade and Industry, A. I. Konovalov, "was faced with the threat of total stoppage of all Russian industry as a result of the steadily growing demands of the 'proletariat'."[8] Alexander Kerensky denied the significance of strikes altogether; once work resumed after the fall of the tsar, "what problems remained were caused not so much by poor relations between workers and management as by the blockade."[9] In short, strikes and workplace unrest remained for outsiders part of the background hum of revolution, unremarkable in itself and unremarked upon in the historical record.

The indifference of contemporaries has subsequently shaped historical assessments of strikes. With little descriptive evidence on which to draw, both Western and Soviet historical schools have portrayed labor activism in broad generalities, mythologizing strikes without clarifying them as phenomena or analyzing their integration with other aspects of the revolutionary process. Historians have referred to the 570-odd strikes reported by the Factory Inspectorate from March to October 1917 as evidence, simply, of worker unrest and have offered various unsubstantiated interpretations.[10] To most of our Soviet colleagues, reality was close to the cinema images of Sergei Eisenstein's 1925 film, *Strike* – miserable workers, brutal managers, and repression by an unsympathetic, "bourgeois" regime. Trotsky describes a "wave of big strikes and other conflicts" in response to the industrialists' political offensive against the revolution.[11] The senior Soviet academician I. I. Mints describes strikes in equally heroic terms:

> The strike struggle in May–June contributed to the class-based political education of the proletariat, to its consolidation around the Bolshevik party, to the strengthening of the unity of the working class, to the growth and authority of its vanguard – the proletariat of Piter, Moscow, Kharkov, the Donbass, and the Urals.[12]

In the only historical monograph devoted to strikes in 1917, A. M. Lisetskii sees the strike process in terms of the Bolsheviks leading workers toward October.[13] Others, like the Soviet historian L. S. Gaponenko, regard strikes essentially as the "deepest manifestations" of ongoing class struggle in 1917, a "characteristic of all capitalist societies."[14]

Nor have Western accounts offered a substantive alternative, although the general interpretation is far from the Soviet view. Here strikes have signified essentially anarchic impulses among workers: a blind and insatiable lashing out for selfish gains or an irrepressible urge to settle old scores with no regard for consequences. A principal cause of Russia's shattered economy, strikes left economic and social devastation in their wake and paved the way for political extremism. These interpretations follow from the views of Russian emigres and Western eyewitnesses like the Englishman R. H. Bruce Lockhart, who wrote, "Wage-earners made exorbitant demands upon their employers and frequently ceased work or interfered arbitrarily in the working of their factories. This behavior, together with the lack of fuel and raw materials, hastened the decline of industrial output."[15] As one historian puts it, "A rampage of strikes swept the country from March 1917. . . . The workers struck over any grievance without hesitation. No one – trade unions, Soviet leaders, or Bolsheviks – could control them."[16] Irrational strikers and irresponsible strikes were thus a principal cause of the Provisional Government's collapse and the onset of Bolshevik authoritarianism.[17]

The weaknesses of both Soviet and Western interpretations lie most of all in their failure to recognize the complexity of strikes as a form of collective action, one involving difficult objective tasks of organization and mobilization as well as subjective elements of attitude and conscious- ness. They also ignore significant difference in strike behavior among different industrial and service sector workers, as well as differences in the possible causes of strikes. They show little recognition of how inter- actions between workers and management might have affected the strike process or how strikes in turn affected the relations between labor and management and representatives of state or local governments, including the soviets. And they fail in their analysis of 1917 to appreciate either the vast array of strike goals and demands that emerged between March and October or their possible implications in terms of workers' relations to Russia's new order.

Thus, although the months between March and October were in large part a workers' revolution, the nature and import of strike activism in 1917 has largely escaped serious historical scrutiny. Strikes clearly shaped a whole range of attitudes toward the new state order on the part of workers themselves, for plant owners and managers, and for state and soviet officials struggling in various ways to build a democratic regime. They also played a central role in the mobilization of labor and in the ways in which shop owners and managerial associations organized themselves to resist change. They articulated workers' goals far more comprehensively and clearly than any other activist form, and are thus a way to explore the difficult and important question of workers' "consciousness," of what workers thought they wanted from the new revolutionary order. Strikes were therefore central to Russian politics and society in 1917, far more so than historians and others have appreciated. They constitute a critical point of entry into the complex historical rela- tionships between social activism and political change. . . .

Strikes and revolution

. . . We must therefore set two distinct but related objectives in exploring strikes in revolutionary Russia. One is to analyze the strike process as a social phenomenon in its own right in 1917, and to understand in this way its relationship to broader and common patterns of labor activism in other times and places. This will require us to explore such elements as the scope, intensity, and degree of organization of strikes in 1917, as well as their duration and outcome, and to explain them, at least in part, in terms of Russian and European labor history generally. The second must be to relate strikes as a specific element of labor activism to the political and socioeconomic evolution of the Russian revolution itself. Here our focus has to be on the ways that elements common to the strike process generally, in Russia before 1917 and elsewhere, both affected and were affected by the particular elements of Russia's revolutionary conjuncture and the fundamental sociopolitical relationships that defined it.

Problems of identities, perceptions, and interpretations

Defining these sociopolitical relationships is no easy task in the dynamic and fluid context of revolution, and one must recognize some of the conceptual problems involved in identifying the relevant attributes of labor activism in such a period. First among these is what Leopold Haimson has identified as the "problem of social identities": the ways in which an individual's sense of his or her place in Russian society corresponded to political outlook and the nature of collective action in general. As Haimson has argued, all social actors clearly brought multiple identities into the revolutionary period, and those actors most involved in the struggle for change in the years leading up to 1917 are identifiable not by any single characteristic of social position, but by combinations of indices related in each case to the inability of extant institutions and socioeconomic relations to accommodate their needs.[18] As we begin to analyze 1917, however, one central issue clearly relates to the difficult question of social group or class coherence: the degree to which the patterns and pressures of aggregate identities may have come to dominate tendencies toward social differentiation. The revolutionary process as a whole, in fact, may well be correlated in some important ways to the moments when aggregate identities like "worker" or "bourgeois," "gentry" or "peasant," began to overwhelm the more particularistic identities of trade or profession, geography, or traditional social status.

In terms of Russian labor, the question of how or why these unifying identities may have come to dominate particularistic ones cannot be separated from the changing nature and form of labor activism, especially strikes. In other words, the question of identities cannot be divorced from the actual experience of conflict. Strike activism in 1917 must thus be analyzed, at least in part, in terms of the ways in which it might have contributed to the complex process of class formation.

38

Second, one must also recognize the centrality here of social interactions themselves: those between labor and management that emerged in the course of specific conflicts, but also the triangular patterns of interaction between workers, employers, and both official and unofficial agencies of the regime (including, in some instances, the soviets). This dimension of the problem is very much complicated by variations among localities and industries, but everywhere in 1917, at the center or on the periphery, it was the nature of these interactions themselves rather than slogans or more elaborate forms of ideology that gave many workers (and others) a sense of who they were, or at least of who they were not, with equally significant consequences.

Finally, there are the closely related and extremely complex problems of representation and perception: the ways in which various social groups and political formations presented themselves to others and were perceived by them, and the ways, further, in which activist behavior actually signified values or other elements of sentiment and belief (consciousness) that may have underlaid political inclinations. These issues, too, are complex, but also central to our understanding of the revolutionary period both in the ways they affected expectations and judgments and in the manner they contributed to the formation of both class and political outlooks. To approach them, and to understand in particular their relation to strikes, we must consequently explore what might be called the language of strikes, expressed in both formal and informal demands, and determine as well as we can the ways in which language may have reflected underlying commitments. And to evaluate the degree of complementarity in perceptions and outlooks between different social groups and political contenders, it is also essential to examine carefully the ways in which strikes were reported and represented in the press.

In this respect, the most fundamental labels concerning strikes must be carefully understood and even more carefully qualified. Strikes in Russia, whether before, during, or after 1917, are conventionally dichotomized as "economic" or "political." Before 1917 there was a clear distinction in law and practice between economic and political strikes in Russia. Economic strikes related directly to the workplace. Strictly speaking, they were legal, although "fomenting," "instigating" or "organizing" them was illegal.[19] Political strikes were always against the law, but took place frequently anyway. These were generally demonstrative strikes, occurring massively in the 1905 revolution and recurring on the anniversaries of important events like Bloody Sunday (the firing by troops outside the Winter Palace on demonstrating workers in January 1905) or the 1912 massacre of Lena gold-field workers. Political strikes were thus a substitute for demonstrations and other forms of mass politics. They were carefully monitored by tsarist police, and during the war years in particular they were brutally repressed. In August 1915, for example, over 25,000 textile workers struck in Ivanovo-Voznesensk to protest the war. A crowd advancing on the city square was repeatedly fired upon by police, leaving 25 dead and more than 30 wounded.[20]

In recording strike statistics both before the revolution and after, factory inspectors always distinguished between the two categories. Strikes were recorded as either political or economic, depending on the overt object of protest. As we have already suggested, however, at one level all strikes were (and are) struggles over power, whether inside the factory or out. Hence in one sense, the distinction between political and economic has little meaning.

But the distinction nonetheless has descriptive merit. Despite the vital, dialectical relationship between strikes and the process of revolutionary change in 1917, one cannot assume there is always an overt link between any given strike and the broader political process. Strikers themselves often acted without reference to politics, and much of their behavior is only comprehensible in these terms. Life in the factory had its own momentum, its own timetable, its own issues and agendas, even in 1917. Despite appearances to the contrary, strikes occurring even in the midst of major political events like the April demonstrations or the July Days sometimes had nothing directly to do with these external occurrences.

Hence it is important to understand strikes over workplace issues in 1917 as fundamentally economic in character, continuing the Factory Inspectorate's distinction. Doing so will enable us to look as closely as possible at those structural elements of labor activism that might have had a direct and independent effect on strikes: who struck; what they believed they were striking for; how strikers mobilized in support of their goals; the strike process itself, from organizational meetings to demonstrations and walkouts; the particularities of labor–management negotiations; and the nature of settlements and their impact on subsequent labor unrest. It is here that we need to concentrate our effort to understand Russian strikes in 1917 as events in themselves.

In terms of interpretation, however, we must put these economic strikes back into the political context of 1917. No strike in Russia between March and October was merely economic. Overt political strikes occurred, of course, especially around the July Days and the Kornilov mutiny, and we must pay attention to these in due fashion, distinguishing them by their specific political content. But even ordinary economic strikes were themselves conditioned in some ways by the political context in which they occurred. Few workers leaving their shops or factories in the course of 1917 could fail to develop some awareness of how their actions might relate to broader political events around them. Regardless of goals, in other words, the act of striking was itself a part of the process of developing political consciousness in 1917, in ways it is essential to explore.

40

Economic strikes must also be considered carefully within the context of political relationships within enterprises themselves. Some workplace issues are quite central to issues of power and political relations. They touch directly the question of who (or which groups) will control whom, who will have what power to manage the processes of production. Here, of course, the Factory Inspectorate's bipolar schema of strikes breaks down. In order to realize our objective of understanding both the overt and subliminal political implications of strikes in revolutionary Russia, we therefore need to replace the economic-political dichotomy with new categories that distinguish strikes over wages or conditions from those that challenge managerial authority, and that distinguish both of these from political strikes whose target is the state rather than the enterprise.

By challenges to managerial authority we have in mind strikes that indicate a rejection of managerial prerogatives normally associated with a free-enterprise economy. Strikes over workers' rights to have a role in hiring and firing, for example, directly challenge managerial authority in the workplace in ways quite different from, say, strikes over higher wages, in which the right of management itself to set wages is not specifically in question. Similarly, strikes in which workers demand that plant owners share profits, guarantee a certain number of work days per month regardless of actual production, cancel cutbacks in production, or replace foreign directors also indicate a clear challenge to the power of management to control production, even if the challenge appears in less explicit fashion.

Strikes that test the good faith of management by demanding that past agreements be honored are also political challenges, since what is at stake is the viability of legal forms like contracts or court orders. These might be thought of as "secondary" strikes, since workers are demanding not that their primary demands be granted, but that promises to grant them be upheld. The outcome of such strikes might thus have a direct bearing on the ways in which workers think about political issues or the possibility of alternative political structures. . . .

Strikes and revolution in Russia [Conclusions]

Throughout this discussion, we have avoided the term "strike movement" in describing strike activity in 1917.[21] The word "movement" implies a linearity, a uniformity, a teleology of events moving toward an October climax that obscures the complex and multivalent nature of strikes in the revolution of 1917. We have stressed rather two parallel conceptualizations of these strikes: they must be seen both as routine tools of labor–management relations in a system with mutually acceptable rules, and as instruments for revolutionary change outside established social and political boundaries. Strikes functioned in both ways and further contributed to the very definition of these boundaries. The malleability of the rules of the game was of course a characteristic feature of the revolutionary situation.

The term "movement" is also inappropriate to describe the process of mobilization and strike participation. There were many paths to a strike, many different histories that formed the critical background to a particular conflict, many ways of mobilizing fellow workers around a cause. Factory workers in large plants with a single entrance through a courtyard mobilized differently from sales clerks in sprawling covered markets or waiters, waitresses, and cooks in resort hotels. Metalworkers, with their history of political activism, also possessed prior networks and resources with which to mobilize more readily than workers with less past experience in protest. Mobilization brought conflict, too, between impatient rank-and-file strikers and their leaders who worked to mobilize for the longer haul, or between fearful laundresses and their aroused leaders who put out the stoves so the workers would have to quit work. Mobilization took different forms, as well; the strike was not the only outcome of labor mobilization. And as we have stressed, workers were not always the masters and mistresses of their own fates: their decision when, how, and whether to strike was often forced or influenced by the actions of management and the intervention of state or other superordinate mediating agencies.

Finally, the term "movement" obscures the richness of the workers' goals as well as their experience. The agenda of strikers in 1917 appeared to be predominantly economic, certainly predominantly directed toward the workplace. Higher pay was a central issue of most strikes, regardless of the specific economic or political context. But money was not the only issue at stake: workers' demands reflected longstanding and deepseated grievances about factory order and human dignity. The explosion of labor protest ignited by the fall of the old regime in 1917 must be seen in part as the product of many years of pent-up labor–management conflict. The extent and spread of demands about job control and about defining the boundaries of managerial authority signified an effort to establish new patterns of routine workplace relations, patterns that would parallel the democratization occurring in political life outside the factories. And still, although workers' demands focused on relations within the workplace, a number of Russian workers continued to use strikes – withdrawal of labor – to signify grievances against the state and the political order. Such political strikes erupted sporadically, if in great force, and between March and October they did not have the same instrumental effect on state power that strikes had in the February revolution. If the massive strikes in September and October helped to undermine the Provisional regime, they were still, in the main, directed against the entrepreneurial class rather than the regime itself.

These diverse patterns of strike experience make it difficult and perhaps pointless to create a single set of postulates about strike behavior, about revolutionary strikes, or about a single strike movement. At the same time, we can argue for the formation in the course of 1917 of a working class largely conscious of its identity, a class formed in the process of these struggles in the workplace. We reject the notion of a teleological and mass movement, in other words, but we embrace the notion of class and the role of strikes in class formation. We have argued that all social actors in 1917 possessed multiple social identities and allegiances. Workers possessed regional, shop, and trade loyalties that often produced stronger ties than classwide identities; economic divisions between workers in favored, well-paying industries and workers in unfavored sectors of the economy also loomed large during the war. But in the economic conditions of 1917, with a massive decline in productivity and utter uncertainty about Russia's economic future, distinctions between favored and unfavored sectors tended to disappear. All workers, however privileged or unprivileged, began to see themselves as common partners in the struggle against this collapse.

Added to this material component of a developing class identity for workers was the subjective experience of strikes and labor relations in 1917. We have shown how the process of conflict encouraged both sides to coalesce around common positions identified early in the spring as class positions. The very patterns of mobilization – appeals for and pledges of outside support, press reports of the justice of the workers' cause, and, of course, the principled resistance of management – contributed to the formation of a cohesive working class in Russia, conscious of its collective position in the social order. Each strike, whether directly experienced or only shared through the press, contributed to this sense of cohesion.

We have shown also how the language of the press reports and the various representations of strike activism in the socialist and bourgeois press shaped perceptions of class identity and class struggle. And we have argued that class identities took firm shape on both sides of the labor–management divide. The threat of socialization that seemed to underlie the claims of workers and their leaders surely helped to undermine deep-seated differences among entrepreneurs, the divisions between Petrograd and Moscow industrialists, between small owners and industrial giants. The language of class was increasingly the language of both management and workers in 1917.

Bolshevik programs and politics have been largely absent from this discussion, but this is certainly not to minimize that party's role in the unfolding revolutionary process as a whole in 1917. The Bolshevik press, like that of other socialist parties, was active in promoting news of strikes and labor organizations, and Bolsheviks were influential in mobilizing some of the largest political strikes in the March–October period, the July Days, and the Moscow Conference protests. And although many party leaders rejected the utility of strikes, especially after July, individual Bolsheviks, as well as Mensheviks and SRs, dominated many factory committees, strike committees, and trade union organizations. But in relation to strikes, they served largely as workers and as socialists rather than as party agitators. Party labels were significantly absent from strike activity. They also cannot be found to any extent in strike reporting, where this form of protest was collectively represented as a symbol of class solidarity rather than partisan policy.

Strikes were consequently central to the course of Russia's revolution. Their changing contours did not merely track its path or illustrate processes of revolutionary conflict. Strikes were the central experience of more workers than any other form of participatory politics. They thus served as the central conduit of labor mobilization and, to a large extent, of management mobilization as well. The strike was also the flash point of labor–management relations, and these relations constituted the core of the process of struggle for power in the revolutionary arena. Above all, this process of struggle itself conditioned relations in other arenas, in the Provisional Government, in municipal dumas and soviets, and in the streets. To understand fully Russia's revolutionary process, one cannot, therefore, simply recognize the importance of Lenin's leadership qualities, Kerensky's failure to strengthen the army, the power of socialist ideology, or the very real social pressures in the countryside that propelled peasants to appropriate private property for themselves. One must also recognize the powerful forces emanating from the rank and file of the Russian labor force, the depth of their grievances, and the logic of their participation in the revolutionary struggle.

NOTES

Selected from Diane P. Koenker and William G. Rosenberg, *Strikes and Revolution in Russia, 1917* (Princeton: Princeton University Press, 1989), pp. 3–8, 14–18, 326–329.

1 *Rabochaia Gazeta*, May 2, 1917.
2 *Pravda*, May 16, 20, 1917 (n.s.); *Delo Naroda*, May 10, 1917; *Edinstvo*, May 11, 1917.
3 *Pravda*, May 25, 1917 (n.s.).
4 S. S. Goncharskaia, "Profsoiuz prachek v 1917 goda," in *V ogne revoliutsionnykh boev (Raiony Petrograda v dvukh revoliutsiiakh 1917 goda)* vol. 1 (Moscow, 1967), p. 48; *Edinstvo*, May 11, 1917; *Novaia Zhizn'*, May 12, 1917; *Pravda*, May 25, June 1, 1917 (n.s.); *Rabochaia Gazeta*, May 14, 18, 1917.
5 *Pravda*, May 23, 27, 29, 30, June 1, 3, 8, 13, 1917 (n.s.); *Delo Naroda*, May 10, 28, 1917; *Zemlia i Volia*, May 10, 1917; *Izvestiia Petrogradskogo Soveta Rabochikh Deputatov* (hereafter *Izvestiia* (Petrograd)), May 9, 11, 16, 17, 19, 21, 30, 1917;

Novaia Zhizn', May 13, 17, 1917; *Rabochaia Gazeta*, May 14, 17, 18, 24, 26, 28, 1917; *Raionnye sovety Petrograda v 1917 godu*, 3 vols. (Moscow and Leningrad, 1964–66), vol. 2, p. 156.

6 N. Sukhanov, *Zapiski o revoliutsii* (Berlin, 1922–23), vol. 4, p. 143.

7 V. D. Nabokov, *V. D. Nabokov and the Russian Provisional Government, 1917*, ed. Virgil D. Medlin and Steven L. Parsons (New Haven, Conn., 1976), pp. 97–98.

8 Paul Miliukov, *Political Memoirs, 1905–1917*, ed. Arthur P. Mendel (Ann Arbor, Mich., 1967), p. 463.

9 Alexander Kerensky, *Russia and History's Turning Point* (New York, 1965), p. 324.

10 The aggregate reports of the Factory Inspectorate, collected in TsGAOR SSSR, f. 6935, op. 8, d. 349, were published by K. N. Iakovleva in 1920, and variously reprinted in Soviet document collections. See K. N. Iakovleva, "Zabastovochnoe dvizhenie v Rossii za 1895–1917 gody," in *Materialy po statistike truda*, vyp. 8 (Moscow, 1920), and the six volumes in the series *Velikaia oktiabr'skaia sotsialisticheskaia revoliutsiia. Dokumenty i materialy*, ed. A. L. Sidorov *et al.* (Moscow, 1957–62). These are cited by their individual titles, *Revoliutsionnoe dvizhenie v Rossii.* . . .

11 Leon Trotsky, *The History of the Russian Revolution*, trans. Max Eastman, 3 vols. (New York, 1980), vol. 2, p. 266.

12 I. I. Mints, *Istoriia velikogo oktiabria*, 3 vols. (Moscow, 1967–72), vol. 2, p. 434.

13 A. M. Lisetskii, *Bol'sheviki vo glave massovykh stachek (mart–oktiabr' 1917 goda)* (Kishinev, 1974). Lisetskii's study is qualitatively rich, however, and contains a wealth of interesting material, as do his principal articles. . . . [List of articles follows in original, ed.]

14 L. S. Gaponenko, *Rabochii klass Rossii v 1917 godu* (Moscow, 1970), p. 376.

15 R. H. Bruce Lockhart, *The Two Revolutions: An Eye-Witness Account of Russia, 1917* (Chester Springs, Pa., 1967), p. 83.

16 Jay B. Sorenson, *The Life and Death of Soviet Trade Unions, 1917–1928* (New York, 1969), p. 36.

17 See, e.g., William H. Chamberlin, *The Russian Revolution*, 2 vols. (New York, 1935), vol. 1, p. 275; W. S. Woytinsky, *Stormy Passage: A Personal History through Two Russian Revolutions to Democracy and Freedom, 1905–1960* (New York, 1961), p. 260; John M. Thompson, *Revolutionary Russia, 1917* (New York, 1981), pp. 73–74; John L. H. Keep, *The Russian Revolution: A Study in Mass Mobilization* (New York, 1976), pp. 73–75.

18 Leopold H. Haimson, "The Problem of Social Identities in Early Twentieth Century Russia," *Slavic Review* 47, no. 1 (1988), pp. 1–20.

19 Law of December 2, 1905, *Polnoe sobranie zakonov Rossiiskoi imperii*, sobranie 3, vol. 25, no. 1 (1905), pp. 850–52. N. N. Polianskii, "*Russkoe ugolovnoe zakonodatel'stvo o stachkakh" i drugiia stat'i po ugolovnomu pravu* (Moscow, 1912), pp. 1–130, and M. I. Tugan-Baranovsky, *The Russian Factory in the Nineteenth Century*, trans. Arthur and Claora S. Levin (Homewood, Ill., 1970), pp. 327–31, elaborate on this law and 1886 legislation on strikes. In practical terms, the distinction was impossible to enforce. Strike leaders were frequently arrested.

20 M. G. Fleet, ed., *Rabochee dvizhenie v gody voiny* (Moscow, 1925), pp. 89, 214–15; K. F. Sidorov, "Rabochee dvizhenie v Rossii v gody imperialisticheskoi voiny," in *Ocherki po istorii oktiabr'skoi revoliutsii*, ed. M. N. Pokrovskii (Moscow and Leningrad, 1927), vol. 1, pp. 283–85.

21 In this we were much encouraged by Lewis Siegelbaum.

3

CRIME, POLICE, AND MOB JUSTICE IN PETROGRAD DURING THE RUSSIAN REVOLUTIONS OF 1917

Tsuyoshi Hasegawa

"How did people live during the Russian Revolution of 1917? What were their immediate daily concerns? What did they think and how did events change their attitudes?" These are the questions, largely ignored by historians of the revolution, that Tsuyoshi Hasegawa raises in this essay on crime in Petrograd in 1917. In looking at the relationships between crime and society, Hasegawa moves social history away from its focus on social-economic classes (workers especially) to how people experienced the revolutionary days across social and economic class lines. In particular, he uses the issue of crime to examine how such matters affected daily life and how they shaped the revolutionary process. Hasegawa chronicles the dramatic surge in crime following the collapse of the old regime's police force along with its political structure in the February Revolution. In Petrograd, crime increased throughout the year and this increase, especially the violent crimes, alarmed the citizenry. Crime contributed power-fully to the sense of crisis, the feeling that society was collapsing, and to the demand for a radical change of political regimes embodied in the call for "all power to the soviets." An important expression of public insecurity, as well as a sign of breakdown of faith in the system and perhaps a harbinger of the brutality to come in the civil war, was the appearance of samosudy *– mob justice, lynch law. While acknowledging the important contributions of the social historians in advancing the study of the revolution, Hasegawa criticizes their concentration on the political implications of mass movements and on these as explanations for the October Revolution. He seeks a different kind of social history, although he does not abandon searching in it for explanations of the revolutionary process that led to the Bolshevik triumph.*

The original article contained four tables on crime before the revolution. These have been deleted and only the fifth table, focused on 1917, has been included here. The text has been altered throughout to label that Table 3.1 instead of table 5.

* * *

How did people live during the Russian revolutions of 1917? What were their immediate concerns? What did they think and how did events change their attitudes? Oddly, historians have rarely asked these questions. For a long time the main focus of historical research on the revolutions of 1917 was the major characters in revolutionary politics. The ideologies, organizations, strategies, and tactics of these elites were the dominant topics. During the last decade or so, many Western historians have finally begun to study mass movements. The result has been several excellent monographs on workers, soldiers, sailors, and peasants, and on the revolutionary process in the provinces. Despite this shift of emphasis, these historians have concentrated on the political implications of mass movements; implicitly or explicitly, they seem to seek in the mass movement the explanations for the October Revolution.[1]

The problem with this approach is that the complex social dimensions of everyday life, considered politically unimportant, tend to be excluded from analysis. The more immediate, direct changes in daily life during 1917 are not studied in their own right. The consequence of this rejection of "social history with politics left out" is, ironically, the failure to appreciate the real extent of the social polarization that developed within spheres normally considered nonpolitical.[2]

This essay examines the relationship between crime and society in Petrograd during the Russian revolutions of 1917 as the first step toward broader issues in the social history of this period. Immediately after the February Revolution, Petrograd was plagued with a phenomenal increase in crime, not only numerically but in degree of violence. Since the newly created law enforcement agencies could not cope with the rising crime rate, the populace was forced to defend their security and property themselves – in turn further contributing to the erosion of order and authority. Crime was thus one of the most important causes for rapid disintegration of social cohesion in Petrograd in 1917. But crime did not affect social classes equally. The well-to-do and the urban poor were the hardest hit, while the working class, which managed to maintain social cohesion, was least affected. The workers' militia proved to be more effective than the city militia in combating crime, and became an important basis on which the Bolshevik regime established the police system after the October Revolution.

This essay presents a picture of city life increasingly threatened by crime, and citizens and various organizations attempting to cope with it. While it cannot contain all elements of the mosaic, it conveys a part of the reality of life in Petrograd in 1917, and may serve as a starting point to further our understanding of social disintegration in urban centers in Russia in 1917.[3]

On the whole, Russian cities, and Petrograd in particular, were free from violent crimes during World War I. . . . The most common crimes committed in Russian cities during the war were thefts, followed by such economic crimes as embezzlement, extortion, and swindling. Murder, armed robbery, and arson ranked only ninth, tenth, and fifteenth in nineteen types of crime. As the largest economic and population center in the empire, Petrograd led all other cities in number of people arrested and number of thefts and other economic crimes. But when the number of arrests is considered in proportion to the population, Petrograd ranked only eighth. ... In the rank order of violent crimes in different cities, Petrograd was low in murders, armed robberies, and attempted murders. ... The number of murders in Petrograd in 1914 was fourteen, and only nineteen in 1915. Armed robberies were almost nonexistent, with only three cases in 1915. Unarmed robberies even decreased, from 207 in 1914 to 60 in 1915. These figures reveal an extremely low crime rate in a city of more than two million people.[4]

All this was changed by the February Revolution of 1917, which contributed in three fundamental ways to a rise in crime. First, all prisoners formerly incarcerated in Petrograd's prisons were freed during the insurrection. Soviet archives indicate that as of February 26 the city's prisons held 7,652 prisoners.[5] The records do not indicate how many of these were political prisoners, but we can assume that a large majority were common criminals. Second, a large number of weapons were given out in great quantities to the insurgents, and presumably some of them fell into the hands of criminals as well. Easy access to weapons after the revolution led to crime being more violent and easier to commit.[6] Third, the tsarist police force was annihilated during the February Revolution, and the newly created militia was ineffective.

Thefts and robberies

Despite expectations by the new government and citizens alike that increased crime was merely a by-product of confusion arising from the revolution, crimes did not subside even after the new political system was established under the Provisional Government. Robberies, in the guise of searches allegedly authorized by the militia or the military authority, took place so frequently that newly installed Mayor (gradonachal'nik) Iurevich felt compelled to issue an order strictly forbidding illegal searches. But it was relatively easy to forge documents.[7] In some cases, soldiers' uniforms or militiamen's armbands were enough to silence the frightened property owners. Often illegal searches were committed by professional criminals.[8] The number of illegal searches reported in newspapers suddenly decreased after April, but this did not mean that order was gradually restored in Petrograd. On the contrary, by then criminals had learned how to get what they wanted without bothering to disguise themselves as militiamen.

In late April and early May, the number of thefts and robberies showed a sharp increase. Several spectacular bank robberies were committed.[9] Newspapers did not even bother to report petty thefts. But major thefts and robberies were so frequent that *Petrogradskii listok* began a special column called "Thefts in the Capital" ("Stolichnye khishchniki"), in which it listed several major thefts and repeated at the end, like a ritual, "And many more were also reported." On June 16 it reported that in the previous twenty-four hours more than forty cases of theft and robbery had been filed. With a sense of alarm the press complained that this was unprecedented anarchy.[10] But this was merely the beginning.

The political crisis of the July Days was fully exploited by criminals to conduct illegal searches. It is estimated that at least fifty stores were attacked by robbers and two to three million rubles' worth of goods were stolen during the crisis.[11] On July 15, ten reports of theft were filed, including six major ones ranging from 15,000 to 100,000 rubles in value of stolen property.[12] On July 27, about twenty soldiers in uniform arrived at the Chernigov Refrigeration Company in an official vehicle and executed with military precision a heist worth 230,000 rubles.[13] On August 15, a major theft was committed at the Historical Museum of property worth five million rubles.[14] On August 29, more than thirty thefts and robberies were reported.[15]

In the last two months before the October Revolution the crime rate rose so high that Petrograd was on the verge of collapse. Statistics of thefts and robberies show an exponential leap. On September 13, twenty thefts were registered,[16] but on October 4 the total rose to 250, and on October 7 to 310. On October 14 *Petrogradskii listok* reported that in the previous forty-eight hours more than 800 thefts and robberies had been registered.[17] We should remember that only five months earlier, the press had been alarmed by the sharp increase in thefts and robberies to forty per day. Nothing remained sacred. Thefts took place in Spasskaia Church in Sennaia Square, Volkov Cemetery, the Museum of Jewelry, and even in the Petrograd Soviet in the Smol'nyi Institute. The apartment of Vera Figner, the legendary populist revolutionary, was burglarized. At least one professional thief was robbed.[18]

Armed robberies

The numbers of armed robberies reported in the papers show that Petrograd was becoming extremely violent. Compared to 1915 when only three armed robberies were reported, eighty-seven cases were reported in Petrograd newspapers from March through October in 1917 (see Table 3.1). Even this figure is extremely conservative, since almost certainly an equal number of cases were simply not sufficiently newsworthy to be printed in newspapers or were not even reported to police.

Table 3.1 Crimes in Petrograd

Crime	1914	1915	March–October 1917				
			Mar.–Apr.	May–June	July–Aug.	Sept.–Oct.	Total
Murder cases	14	19	13	21	30	26	90
per day*	0.038	0.052	0.24	0.45	0.55	0.58	0.448
Armed robberies	0	3	23	26	24	14	87
Samosudy cases			1	12	29	33	75
per day**			0.02	0.26	0.53	0.82	
Missing days			2	15	7	5	29

*The murder rate per day = (Number of murder cases) / {(Number of days of the month) – (Number of missing days)}.
**The rate of mob acts per day = (Number of mob acts) / {(Number of days of the month) – (Number of missing days)}.

In response to the increase in armed robberies, citizens began to arm themselves for protection.

One interesting twist was that in numerous incidents, particularly in May and June, self-proclaimed anarchists attempted to "expropriate the expropriators." They raided the apartments and villas of property owners and robbed them under the banner of anarchism. The anarchists' occupation of the dacha owned by the family of the late P. N. Durnovo, formerly minister of interior, and the Provisional Government's attempt to reconquer it are too well known to be repeated here.[19] The Durnovo case was merely one of many attempts by genuine or pseudo-anarchists to dispossess the privileged. On April 28, the palace of the duke of Likhtenberg was expropriated by eighteen "anarchists" armed to the teeth, some of whom turned out to be professional criminals with prison records.

On May 7 "anarchists" raided the apartment of a former high tsarist government official, and stole all his valuables. The same day the home of Count Ruge was attacked by armed anarchists who took away 5,000 rubles' worth of property. On May 18, three men in soldiers' uniforms calling themselves anarchists and communists – they later turned out to be ex-convicts – broke into the home of K. K. Grigoriev on Kalinin Square, and shot the owner and a servant. On May 21, two well-dressed men and a young woman attacked a house in Soldatskii Lane. After seriously wounding a doorman, they ransacked the apartment and made off with all the valuables.[20] We do not know how many such incidents were carried out by politically committed anarchists as opposed to criminals who wrapped the anarchist banner around themselves. But clearly "anarchism" was becoming a favored "political doctrine" for criminals. A cartoon published in *Petrogradskaia gazeta* on April 23 shows a militiaman approaching the scene of a crime where a thief is about to run off with a big sack of loot. The militiaman says to the thief: "I think you are a thief." To this the thief replies: "What a reactionary you are, comrade. The tsarist police thought the same."[21]

Arsons

In July and August, newspapers reported several fires, some of mysterious origin. On July 21, sabotage was suspected in an explosion at the "Dinamo" factory. Four days later the "Respirator" factory was burned. Donetsko-Iurievsky factory caught fire under suspicious circumstances on July 30. A week later Electric Station No. 76 was burned to the ground. On August 16 a large portion of the Westinghouse complex was destroyed by fire; a week later another fire burned one of the buildings at the Putilov factory.[22] By far the largest fire in 1917 was the spectacular one on August 11 that raged for more than ten hours, burning four factories in Okhta, destroying some barges on the Neva River, and claiming twenty lives. The fire was so intense that it spread to the other side of the Neva. Immediately after the fire started, pillaging and looting began in the evacuated apartment buildings, and more than fifty looters were arrested.[23]

Undoubtedly, declining worker discipline and inadequate security measures at factories contributed to some of these fires. But arsons and alleged arsons might also have been the result of rapidly deteriorating labor relations. When industrialists began a militant counteroffensive against the workers' demands after the July Days, the workers became more combative.[24] Although arson was not a standard weapon in the labor movement, the increased number of arsons might be a sign of workers' growing radicalism. Or, considered from the opposite angle, these boulevard newspapers, which took a strong stand against the workers' movement, might have used the fires to cast a negative image on the labor movement.

Murders

The most important feature of crime in Petrograd after the February Revolution was the frightening increase in murders. Table 3.1 shows monthly statistics for murders from March through October as reported in the newspapers. During that period, at least ninety murder cases were reported. Compared with the prewar statistics, this number may not seem significant, but compared with fourteen murders in 1914 and nineteen in 1915, this was an alarming increase.[25] In addition, this number is definitely conservative. First, deaths caused by mob justice are excluded, since the number of victims is unknown. Second, I was unable to read all the newspapers, and for a total of twenty-nine days between March and October 10, I could not use even one newspaper. But even with these incomplete data, we see the rise in daily average number of murders as follows: 0.038 for 1914, 0.052 for 1915, but 0.448 from March 5 through October 10, 1917. This means an average of one murder every two or three days in 1917. Table 3.1 shows that during the same period, the murder rate per day also increased: 0.24 in March–April, 0.45 in May–June, 0.55 in July–August, and 0.58 in September–October.

Two types of newspaper murder reporting can be contrasted: the Schlossberg murder and the Sezakh-Kulero case. On March 10, a barrister named Schlossberg was attacked on Kazan Street by three men, wearing sailors' uniforms, who had just left a house of prostitution. The innocent victim offered everything he owned, but the attackers stabbed him with knives several times, continuing to attack him even after he had fallen to the ground. Militiamen rushed to the scene, but by the time the assailants were subdued and arrested, Schlossberg had died.[26]

The second type is represented by the most sensational murder of the period, on April 16. Two men in officers' uniforms escorted a French singer, Margarette Sezakh-Kulero, and her live-in friend, Mariia Popova, to their apartment on Kamenoostrovskii Prospekt in a plush residential area in the Petrograd District. After they were properly entertained with sumptuous dinner and wine, the guests suddenly attacked the hostess, brutally cutting her head with their sabers, and proceeded to hack to death Mariia Popova and the servant who came to rescue her mistress. The assailants ransacked the apartment and stole valuables worth 30,000 rubles. One turned out to be none other than Baron von Schrippen, who in 1916 had pulled off a daring illegal search of the apartment belonging to the wealthy industrialist Zhitovskii. For this crime he had been serving a term in a Petrograd prison until he escaped amid the confusion of the February Revolution. After gaining unexpected freedom, he had openly joined the circles of money and pleasure which the French night club singer and her friend frequented.[27]

The tone of the reporting on the Schlossberg murder was indignation at the senselessness of the violence and fear that such a fate could befall anyone. The report on the Sezakh-Kulero case demonstrated the typical sensationalism of these boulevard papers, appealing to the readers' appetite for details of violent acts. This sensationalism, reminiscent of the coverage of some murder cases and famous trials prior to the February Revolution, was a departure from the norm in reporting violent crimes in 1917. Two factors explain the difference. First, this case dealt with a crime in which both the victims and the assailants belonged to a small circle of pleasure seekers, far removed from the common readers of these newspapers. The existence of such circles was indicative of the chaos of the times in which people of privilege were driven into the world of decadence. The newspapers reported widespread use of cocaine among members of these circles and the presence of high-class prostitutes. Unlike the Schlossberg murder, which was frightening to the general readers because anyone could be a potential victim, the premeditated murder in the Sezakh-Kulero case was far removed from the general reader's experience. Second, this incident aroused the curiosity of the general reader because the main culprit, von Schrippen, had acquired notoriety by raiding Zhitovskii's apartment. Although newspaper reports of the raid had a tone of admiration for his daring and precise execution, the reports also had a note of apprehension and confusion about the violence committed by this counterculture former hero.

The boulevard papers, of course, continued to report grisly details of murder cases to satisfy their readers. For instance, they reported that on May 18 a woman's dead body was found in Ekaterinogofki River with her hands tied at the back and a deep wound in her head.[28] On May 24, a young Chinese woman, an apparent rape victim, was found dead. Her eyes were cut out, her throat slit open, and many knife wounds were on her breast and other parts of her body.[29] Boulevard papers did not forget to include, amid the news of the Kornilov affair, the discovery of a headless torso with severed legs and arms wrapped in three separate packages and found in different parts of the city.[30] In August they reported news of a psychopath in Lesnoi. In grisly detail, sometimes accompanied by illustrations (no photographs were printed in newspapers in those days and even illustrations were rare), they described how the authorities dug up body after body in his backyard.[31]

One senses, however, that the general tone of even these usually sensational boulevard papers was gradually becoming one of fear and anger at extreme violence grown out of control, particularly regarding murders committed against common people. Two such murders occurred in Lesnoi. Once a quiet residential suburb of Petrograd, Lesnoi became the site of several nightmarish murders. The fact that violent crimes had spread to previously quiet residential districts was another frightening aspect of 1917. For instance, on May 2, two deserters broke into a house in Lesnoi, strangled to death a servant, beat a thirteen-year-old boy into unconsciousness, and stole money and valuables worth approximately 20,000 rubles.[32] An even more frightening murder was committed in Lesnoi on October 1. A father and his three small children were brutally murdered in the very building that housed the Lesnoi militia headquarters. Out of anger and frustration, irate Lesnoi residents sacked the militia headquarters.[33]

Two additional comments should be made with regard to murders in 1917. First, after the July Days an increasing number of murders occurred as a result of political argument. This reflected the temper of the times, when the means to settle political differences were rapidly shifting from persuasion and compromise to physical violence. The civil-war mentality has its origin in this period.[34]

Second, the Chinese ethnic question became enmeshed with the question of crime in Petrograd in 1917. At least five Chinese were murdered during July and August, and the murder suspect arrested for the Lesnoi family murder was also Chinese. During the war, Russian industrialists had brought Chinese laborers to Petrograd to combat the serious labor shortage.[35] It is estimated that by 1917 more than 10,000 Chinese had arrived in Petrograd, where they worked primarily on construction projects and as unskilled laborers in factories. Working virtually as slave laborers, and unable to speak the language, they were usually the first to be thrown into the streets when recession hit the economy. Unemployment became a serious problem among the Chinese. They formed segregated communities in Novaia Derevnia and Peski in the Rozhdestvenskii district of Petrograd, where they lived in crowded, unsanitary hovels. They practiced the habits they brought with them of opium-smoking and gambling.[36] In the summer, with no work available and no possibility of returning home, some of them formed into gangs of robbers. Presumably the murdered Chinese were victims of infighting among various gangs. But there were disturbing signs that Chinese gangs were beginning to commit crimes in Russian communities. Although Chinese crimes were no more vicious than the norm for Petrograd, outraged residents of Novaia Derevnia demanded their deportation from Petrograd.[37]

The February Revolution opened the floodgate of crime in Petrograd. Extremely safe during the war, Petrograd increasingly became a dangerous place to live after February. The crime rate rose sharply as social disintegration continued, and the increase in crime, in turn, contributed to further social disintegration. It would not be an exaggeration to say that on the eve of the October Revolution, Petrograd was on the verge of collapse, threatened by waves of crime. This opinion was expressed vividly by former Petrograd Okhrana Chief K. I. Globachev, who had been arrested after the February Revolution and released from prison at the end of August:

> In the entire month of September and October, anarchy essentially ruled over Petrograd. Criminals multiplied to an unimaginable extent. Every day robberies and murders were committed not only at night, but also in broad daylight. Residents could not but be disturbed for the safety of their own lives. The populace, seeing that it would be impossible to expect any help from the nominally existing authority, began to organize themselves and form house guards or take other security measures in case of attack by robbers. In every residential house armed guards were posted every night. But this did not help and robberies did not decline.[38]

Criminals and deserters

The most alarming source of lawlessness in Petrograd was the presence of numerous criminals and deserters. The Provisional Government passed decrees favorable to criminals, such as the abolition of the death penalty on March 12.[39] On March 17, it decreed a reduction and cancellation of the penalties for those who had committed criminal offenses under the old regime. According to this decree, death sentences were commuted to hard labor in exile not exceeding fifteen years. Those who had been sentenced to hard labor in exile had their term reduced by half, with a maximum of twelve years. All sentences of exile were reduced to three years. Prisoners who were serving their terms in prison were freed. Those who were supposed to be in prison but had been freed during the February Revolution were ordered to turn themselves in by May 1, 1917. They would be rewarded for such good behavior by having their sentences cut in half.[40] Needless to say, few prisoners responded to the new government's offer to return to prison. In an additional appeal to former prisoners, Kerensky issued another decree shortly after Easter freeing criminals who were willing to serve at the front.

According to Globachev, who shared prison experience with criminals in the Kresty Prison, almost all criminals volunteered to go to the front. They openly admitted: "You think we are fools to fight in war? We will be clothed and fed, and at the first railway stop, we will disappear."[41] To paraphrase Lenin's famous expression, Russia had suddenly become the freest country in the world for criminals, and they certainly took full advantage of that freedom. *Petrogradskii listok* attributed the sharply rising crime rate to the presence of criminals. In a tone of alarm, it editorialized:

> If Petrograd is now being robbed and plundered, it should not surprise us, since as many as 20,000 thieves were let go from various prisons. Robbers, enjoying full civil rights, are now freely walking the streets of Petrograd. Officers of the Criminal Militia often encounter thieves in the streets, but there is nothing they can do. Among them there are many who were deprived of their rights by the previous courts, but they now ignore such decisions.[42]

Deserters presented another problem. Some insurgent soldiers who had left their barracks during the February Revolution never returned. They were soon joined by deserters from the front who arrived in the capital looking for better opportunities. Brutalized by the war, these armed deserters contributed significantly to the rising crime rate in Petrograd. With no attachment to an official institution, the sine qua non for getting food rations, they had only crime as a means of survival. It was estimated that some 50,000 to 60,000 deserters were in Petrograd in July.[43]

Gradually, criminals and deserters formed their own colonies into which not even a militiaman dared set foot. Such colonies existed around the Olympia amusement park on Zabalkanskii Prospekt; in Village Volkovo in the Narva District; Galernaia Gavan; Gavanskoe Pole, and Golodai on Vasilevskii Island, Ligovki, Peski, and Poliustrovo.

During March and April the militia conducted periodic raids on cafes, restaurants, and cheap hotels in these colonies. Among those apprehended were well-known ex-convicts, who had fled jail during the February Revolution.[44] Such raids, however, did not prevent a frightening increase in the criminal population in Petrograd, for the new criminal system contained fatal weaknesses, which will be explained below. Against this tidal wave – swollen daily by newly arriving professional criminals, deserters from the front, and restless urban youths – sporadic raids by the militia could hardly be effective. By summer, criminals and deserters no longer meekly surrendered to the militia. In several instances they actively counterattacked. In fact, some of the militia's raids can better be described as military operations, sometimes assisted by military detachments. Such operations occurred, for example, against the robbers' colony in Volkovo at the end of July. In response to the militia detachment's first raid, the criminals defended themselves by firing back. In crossfire that lasted more than half an hour, one militiaman was seriously wounded. All but three criminals escaped. It was not until the end of August that the militia, this time joined by a few detachments of the Izmailovskii Regiment and the Fourth Don Cossack Regiment, carefully laid siege to Volkovo and arrested 150 deserters and criminals. Such incidents were by no means isolated. Of twenty-four raids reported in July and August, the militia were attacked in at least eight instances.[45]

On occasion, residents in these colonies rioted when the militia arrested one of their comrades. One such riot took place in Olympia amusement park. Arrests of several hooligans and suspicious characters in the park occasioned a group of deserters, criminals, hooligans, and others to gather in protest. Shouting "Pharaohs! Oppressors!" – reminiscent of shouts heard during the February Revolution among demonstrators against the tsarist police – they attacked the militia headquarters. Several militiamen were caught and brutally beaten, and one was thrown from the third floor to the ground, where a mob lynched him.[46]

The new criminal justice system

As Leonard Schapiro has observed, the men in the Provisional Government were motivated by "innocent faith in the perfectibility of man" and "detestation of violence and coercion."[47] This was particularly true of the two ministers who were directly responsible for the criminal justice system: Minister of Internal Affairs Prince G. E. L'vov and Minister of

Justice Alexander Kerensky. These predilections explain the abolition of the death penalty and the decree on March 17 granting amnesty to criminals. Moreover, the Provisional Statute on the Militia, issued by the Provisional Government on April 17, imposed heavy restrictions on the militia's treatment of persons arrested. For instance, Article 28 stipulated that the militia had no right to detain the arrested for more than twenty-four hours without specific criminal charges. Thus the majority of those apprehended in periodic raids of criminal colonies were back on the street the following day.[48]

Furthermore, the newly created Temporary Court (*Vremennyi sud*), presided over by a justice of the peace assisted by two mandatory assistant justices (representing the soldiers and the workers), was far from effective in instilling a sense of justice among the populace. Originally designed as an emergency measure to "remove misunderstandings" between the insurgents and the privileged class during the February Revolution, when the tsarist legal and court system ceased to function, the Temporary Court became virtually the only court in Petrograd handling both criminal and civil cases.[49] Arbitrariness was one of its distinct characteristics. V. Menshutkin, who wrote a valuable, sympathetic record of this court, states that it was allowed to impose a wide variety of punishments for theft ranging from a warning to a maximum fine of 10,000 rubles. He admitted that in general the Temporary Court was lenient in punishing thieves. On the other hand, apartment-house owners were often found guilty for not keeping sanitary conditions, and had to pay the maximum fine. Despite its original intention to remove misunderstandings between the privileged and those who had participated in the February Revolution, this court system probably contributed to intensifying antagonism between the two classes. Furthermore, the new court, which handled cases ranging from wives' complaints about their husbands' extramarital affairs and illegal brewing of alcoholic beverages to serious murder cases, could not possibly handle the deluge of criminal cases. In March alone the Petrograd Temporary Court dealt with 5,237 cases, but the astonishing increase in the rate of crime surely precluded the court from rendering justice even for crimes where the perpetrators were apprehended and brought before the court.[50]

The destruction of the old police system paralyzed one important prerevolutionary crime-prevention device. Although not formally integrated into the police system, the doormen (*dvorniki*) – those men who guarded virtually every public building, kept watch over those who came and went, and maintained close contact with the police – performed an essential security function before the February Revolution. But resenting the allegation that they were a part of the tsarist police, the doormen organized themselves into a trade union and refused to perform security duties.[51] On May 9, in the face of a sharp rise in crime, Mayor

Iurevich ordered obligatory night duty for doormen under penalty of law. The offended doormen declared that they would not obey an order issued without prior consultation with them, and on May 15 Iurevich was forced to rescind the decree. In return, the doormen agreed to do the night watch on a voluntary basis.[52] Consequently, most of Petrograd's buildings were left without guards.

Finally, even if thieves and robbers were caught, tried, and sent to prison, there was no guarantee that they would stay there. The February Revolution caused a serious breakdown in security at prisons as well. The Provisional Government carried out a prison reform, the first step of which was to fire prison wardens and guards.[53] They were replaced by untrained former soldiers and other volunteers hired on the spot. Globachev described the condition of the Kresty Prison, which was ostensibly one of the tightest security prisons in Petrograd: guards often fell asleep, abandoned their posts, or left their rifles behind within easy reach of prisoners, and they often left prisoners totally unguarded during the periods they were allowed to walk in the yard. Of course, many prisoners escaped. The only reason Globachev did not escape was that he felt safer behind bars than in the street, given his former status as Okhrana chief.[54] Prison security became particularly lax in the summer. During the July days, many political prisoners were incarcerated, but after the Kornilov affair they were either freed or escaped, often with the connivance of prison guards. On August 30, for instance, 208 prisoners ran away from the Kresty Prison, and 150 prisoners fled the Peterhof Commissariat.[55] Not all of these were political prisoners; common criminals also took advantage of the opportunity. Only thirty of those who broke from Kresty on August 30 were political prisoners.

The new criminal justice system, created by Kerensky with so much goodwill and idealism, simply did not work. On the contrary, criminals fully exploited it, crime spread rapidly, and the criminal population swelled. Threatened by crime, people surely felt frustrated, powerless, and frightened.

Ineffectiveness of the militia

A major reason that crime increased was the ineffectiveness of the newly created militia. It was divided into a dual power structure composed of the city militia and the workers' militia.[56] Organized by the Petrograd City Duma, the city militia was based on democratic principles in the sense that the organization was to include all classes and serve the entire population, transcending class differences. Its function was to ensure security of life, property, and public order. In contrast, the workers' militia was a class organization, serving only the working class, and composed only of members of that class. Its primary function was the political task of protecting the gains of the revolution from anticipated counterrevolutionary actions by its class enemies.[57] If combating crime became also a function of the workers' militia, it resulted from necessity.

Although the authority of the city militia was nominally recognized by the workers' militia, the latter maintained itself as an autonomous organization. On the whole, the workers' militia exerted exclusive control in the outlying workers' districts, while the city militia was predominant in the center of the city. But as Rex Wade points out:

> This neat dichotomy . . . breaks down on close examination. Some factory-based workers' militia units accepted directions from and subordinated themselves to the City Militia authorities, although they retained varying degrees of autonomy. Others rejected all subordination. Within the City Militia there were units made up largely of workers but operating strictly within the City Militia framework. Many districts were divided between workers' militia and City Militia commissariats by subdistricts. In some subdistricts even further division took place as certain streets, buildings, and areas were patrolled by autonomous workers' militia units while other streets and buildings were guarded by the City Militia. In such areas there were parallel militia structures, with an ad hoc territorial division of the subdistrict. Finally, though these lines of division and authority generally followed those established during the February Revolution, there was some shifting and reorganizing, as well as recurring efforts by city officials to close down or more tightly control worker units.[58]

The basic principle on which both the city militia and the workers' militia functioned was that of local self-determination.[59] Specifically, they insisted on local autonomy and election of their chiefs. Neither the Provisional Government's Ministry of Justice nor the City Administration controlled the local militia organizations, and their attempts to reorganize them on the principle of centralization met effective resistance by both the city militia organizations and the workers' militia.[60]

Another reason why the militia was so ineffective was the poor quality of militiamen, particularly in the city militia. In the beginning, the city militiamen were volunteers, predominantly students and others from the middle class – including, at the very beginning, boy scouts.[61] Later, each district militia head, called commissar, became more selective in hiring militiamen, but the new men also usually lacked basic training as police officers. The condition was not much better for the workers' militia, since turnover was extremely high. Faced with rising crime and the ineffectiveness of the militia, the City Administration and the Ministry of Justice recognized the need to establish a criminal division by recruiting former tsarist police officers. The problem was that almost all veteran police officers of the criminal division had been arrested and locked up in the city's prisons. After the Petrograd mayor created the Criminal Investigation Division on March 9, two men who had been agents of the former tsarist Criminal Police (*Syskaia politsiia*) were released from prison to serve in the new institution. But Kirpichnikov, the former head of the Criminal Police, remained under arrest for a while longer before he was made head of the new institution. Eventually, all the members of the former Criminal Police joined the Criminal Militia, which was directly subordinated to the Ministry of Justice.

Among all other amateur militiamen, these experienced investigators were the only effective agents in dealing with hard-core criminals. However, they had to work against tremendous odds; they were poorly paid (mostly 100 to 200 rubles a month), understaffed, and overworked. The Criminal Police was headed by a chief, and staffed by two assistant chiefs, ten inspectors, and 200 junior inspectors. It was hamstrung by the Supervisory Commission, which included representatives from the Petrograd Soviet, the City Duma, and the military authorities.[62] The stigma of having served in the former tsarist police also hampered these investigators' effectiveness.

Another weakness was lack of financial support for militia organizations and militiamen. The city militia was financed by the City Administration, whose financial base rapidly deteriorated. The workers' militiamen received their wages from the factory management, but as antagonism between labor and management intensified, the issue of the factory managers' obligation to finance the workers' militia became contentious. The City Administration's failure to provide financial support for the city militia had dire consequences for its effectiveness. First of all, it resulted in a lack of firearms. Amazingly, not all city militiamen were armed. The shortage of weapons posed a serious threat to the militiamen on duty, who were often attacked by criminals and hooligans. In one instance a militiaman was seized by a gang of young hooligans and forced at gunpoint to crawl on all fours and bark like a dog.[63] The insufficient funds for the militia also caused a shortage of boots and uniforms. But most important, it necessitated low wages, and significantly contributed to gradual demoralization.

This situation led the city militiamen to organize their own trade union, and through it they, ironically, requested official affiliation with the Petrograd Soviet. Their major complaints focused on the shortage of uniforms, boots, and weapons and the low wages. Their demand for a wage increase was supported by the conservative Criminal Militia, which sent a petition to the Ministry of Justice, complaining that they had received no salary since July. One can imagine their frustrations, knowing that well-armed thieves and robbers were living in expensive apartments, keeping permanent rooms in luxury hotels, and being served by their own entourage and chauffeurs. Having received no satisfactory answer to their demands from the City Administration, the militiamen held a general conference in which they decided to go on strike unless they received satisfactory settlement to their wage demands from the City Administration by October 11. Frustrated by the City Administration's inaction on their demands, some of the city militiamen brought their complaints to the district soviets and sometimes to the factory committees.[64] The City Administration was still negotiating with the militia representatives to avert a strike, and was simultaneously beginning to plan a sweeping reorganization of the militia forces, when the October Revolution began.[65]

The alarming increase in the crime rate led the public to criticize the ineffectiveness of the militia. Already in the spring, newspapers had begun criticizing the militia, and carried articles exposing militiamen engaged in criminal acts. These criticisms also found an echo in the City Duma.[66] Whereas the spring newspaper articles had focused on isolated cases of militiamen committing disgraceful acts or former criminals infiltrating the militia organizations, by fall the tone had shifted to a complete denunciation of the militia organization itself.[67] The changing attitude of the press toward the militia was vividly illustrated in a cartoon in *Petrogradskii listok* on October 24. A couple walking on a deserted street are about to be attacked by a mugger from behind, and in front of them a militiaman is patrolling at the corner. The caption reads: "How horrible! A robber behind, and a militiaman in front!"[68]

Mob justice (*Samosudy*)

Threatened by sharply increasing crimes, and deserted by the doormen who had protected their buildings, the city's residents began to organize themselves to protect their homes from criminals. As early as April, residents had already organized many apartment house committees (*domovye komitety*) in residential buildings. Some of these committees decided to lock all the gates day and night, issue a pass to all residents, and organize compulsory guard duty for residents. Others went a step farther by creating a private apartment house (*domovaia*) militia.[69] By autumn, when it had become clear that residents could not rely on the city militia, many apartment house committees began hiring military guards and soldiers from nearby barracks. The City Administration, which was reluctant to give weapons to its own militia, handed out weapons to such vigilance groups organized by apartment house committees![70]

It is against the background of increasing lawlessness and a sense of powerlessness that acts of mob justice (*samosudy*, literally "self-made trials") – one of the most frightening practices of 1917 – became commonplace in the city's major streets.[71] On May 13, *Petrogradskii listok* reported: "Incidents of minor mob justice against thieves have been observed earlier, but yesterday they took a sharp turn." It then described three incidents of such justice in graphic detail.[72] From then on, such incidents began to fill the pages of the boulevard newspapers. In broad daylight at the busiest intersection of the city, Sadovaia and Nevskii streets, two pickpockets were lynched. An angry crowd broke into a store and beat the shop clerks suspected of hoarding goods. Whenever a crowd gathered, it was enough for someone to shout "Beat him! I know he did it!" to turn the angry mob against the accused. No evidence was necessary; a voice counseling moderation was invariably drowned out, and often the person objecting was himself attacked by the angry mob.[73] Incidents of mob justice were so numerous that *Gazeta-Kopeika* began to carry a column called "Today's mob trials [*samosudy*]."

During May and June a total of twelve acts of mob justice were reported. In July and August the number rose to twenty-three, and in September and October to thirty-three. The average number of acts of mob justice reported daily in newspapers shows clearly a sharp increase from March to October: 0.02 in March–April, 0.26 in May–June, 0.53 in July–August, and 0.82 in September–October. (See Table 3.1.) A typical case transpired on August 19 at the intersection of Smolenskaia and Lubenskaia streets. A group of people caught a thief. A crowd gathered. Not wishing to turn him over to the militia, they decided to hold a public trial on the spot. "A people's court is the most just and quickest!" someone shouted. "Thieves will run away from the militia!" others responded. Discussions were brief, and the unanimous verdict was the death sentence. Immediately, they began beating him with shoes, sticks, fists, and stones. When militiamen arrived to rescue him, the crowd reacted with hostility, and threw stones at them. The thief, bleeding heavily and already unconscious, was brought to a hospital, where his condition was pronounced hopeless.[74] In another instance, three unknown men fired shots from a moving automobile at soldiers standing at the entrance of the People's House, near Aleksandr Garden, killing a bystander and wounding two soldiers. The snipers were caught by angry soldiers, and literally torn limb from limb. The militiamen, who came to the scene too late, had to pick up pieces of their bodies.[75]

Whereas in the previous months acts of mob justice had been directed mainly against thieves, during the summer such acts began to be reported more frequently against merchants. Often these mob actions bore a character of anti-Semitism. A Jewish leather merchant, who was pulling his cart on Sennaia Square, was attacked by the angry crowd that suspected him of hoarding goods. Despite intervention by a militiaman and despite the merchant's innocence, the crowd of over a thousand discussed what to do with him. Some suggested killing him on the spot, while others recommended drowning. But "more reasonable" elements prevailed and the crowd decided to tie him to the cart and deliver him to the Petrograd Soviet. They pushed the cart all around the city, beating him constantly on the way. The innocent victim was in a state of delirium when he was finally freed from the ordeal at the Smol'nyi Institute.[76] At the end of August and the beginning of September, a sudden upsurge of food riots began in various parts of the city. Particularly in the Kolomenskii District, several food riots were accompanied by pogroms against Jewish merchants.[77]

The ugly specter of mob justice raged violently as the October Revolution approached. An inmate of a mental institution escaped into the streets on September 14, claiming that he had been beaten by nurses. An outraged crowd attacked the hospital and subjected the administrator to a mob trial. A week later a crowd brought about swift justice by beating to death a thief who stole an apple on Sennaia Square.[78] On October 15 two shoplifters were caught in a store at the corner of Sadovaia and Apraksin streets – one in a soldier's uniform and another an elegantly dressed woman. Such a huge crowd gathered at the corner that it halted all streetcar traffic. A militia detachment rushed to the scene, but confronted by the extremely hostile crowd demanding that the shoplifters be handed over for a mob trial, the militia had to request assistance from soldiers stationed nearby at the state bank. The soldiers arrived at the scene and cordoned off the store, separating the criminals from the crowd. The angry crowd shouted at the soldiers. "You are like militia, hiding the thieves!" Some, pushing their way, broke into the store and dragged the male shoplifter out into the streets. Immediately the crowd began pounding him. The frightened female accomplice escaped into a telephone booth in the store. One militiaman stood on a table in front of the telephone booth with a revolver in his hand to protect the woman. The mob pulled him off the table and began beating him also. The mob then pulled the young woman out of the telephone booth and beat her severely. One person in the crowd shouted "What are we waiting for?" Pulling a revolver, he fired two shots into the male shoplifter, killing him instantly. A few minutes later, the mob executed the woman also.[79]

Alarmed by a sudden upsurge in mob justice, criminals sent out an ultimatum, declaring that they would "kill anybody we meet at the dark corner of streets. . . . Breaking into a house, we will not simply loot, but will murder everyone, even children, and won't stop our bloody revenge until acts of mob justice are stopped."[80] It seemed as though another "class struggle" was in progress in Petrograd – between criminals and the public.

Nothing indicates more clearly the ugly mood of the citizens than these instances of mob justice. Citizens were angered and frustrated by creeping lawlessness, the inability of the militia to prevent crime, and the uselessness of the criminal justice system. Every day, insolent crimes were committed directly under the nose of the militia, sometimes with the complicity of the militiamen themselves. Even if burglars and rubbers were caught, they either received lenient sentences in the Temporary Court or escaped from jail. Mob trials were thus the public's attempt to bring swift justice. By inflicting the death penalty even for a minor offense, they were also venting their frustration and anger. Renderings of mob justice were visible expressions of the general social breakdown, but they contributed to the further erosion of order and authority.

Sociology of crimes

Who were the victims of crime? Should crime be considered in the context of the deepening social chasm between the wealthy and the poor, and interpreted as an act of revolt by the downtrodden against their oppressors? Or did crime affect all segments of the population indiscriminately? Who committed crime? Was it committed mostly by criminals and deserters, or were other segments of the population drawn into the criminal population? Can regional differentiations be discerned in the crime rate?

Reading the boulevard newspapers, one immediately notices the heavy concentration of reported crimes and acts of mob justice in the center of the city, in such districts as Kazan, Kolomenskii, Moscow, Narva, Rozhdestvenskii, and Aleksandr-Nevskii. These districts were characterized by a mixed population consisting of the privileged and the urban poor and by the absence of large contingents of factory workers. Partly, the concentration of reported crimes in these districts can be explained by the bias of the boulevard papers, which drew the majority of their readers from the lower class outside the organized proletariat. It is possible, therefore, that crimes committed in the outskirts of the city, where the factory workers were heavily concentrated, were simply not reported.

Nevertheless, the concentration of reported crimes in the center of the city cannot be explained only by the bias of the newspapers. It was also the result of the sociology of crime during this period of revolution. Two segments of the population were most deeply affected by crime. First was the propertied class – the class that owned something worth stealing. They were the first to desert the city. According to reports, some 6,000 Petrograders had arrived in the Crimea in July, far more than the usual summer vacationers.[81] For some, emigre life started long before the Bolshevik seizure of power. Obviously, crime was not the only cause for the mass exodus of the privileged and the middle class, but no doubt it provided a powerful motivation.

Second, crime deeply affected the lower classes. They included those who belonged, at least in consciousness if not income, to the lower middle class, such as civil servants at the lowest ranks, small merchants, pharmacists, and owners of small restaurants, taverns, and tearooms. A segment of the working class not included in the organized working class movement – such as workers in small factories and workshops, carpenters, street sweepers, plumbers – were also in this group. Also affected were the artisans (*remeslenniki*), including shoemakers, watchmakers, locksmiths, carpenters, painters, and others; and the servants and service employees (*sluzhashchie*), including house servants, doormen, porters, butlers, shop clerks, waiters and waitresses, laundresses, office workers, and others. We must also consider their wives, who had to shop in the crime-ridden streets. These urban poor bore the brunt of economic and social dislocation. Mostly uneducated, disoriented by changing values, not united by a class-consciousness, and unorganized by any class-based organizations, they were deeply affected by crime. The boulevard papers expressed, above all, the fear and anger felt by these people. Those who participated in acts of mob justice came from these urban poor. They represented simultaneously ideologically reactionary and revolutionary elements. On the one hand, they expressed strong anti-Semitic sentiments, and engaged in anti-Jewish pogroms. On the other hand, some of the groups affiliated themselves with the Petrograd Soviet, and showed intense class hatred of the privileged. Probably the urban youths coming from the urban poor were drawn into the city's criminal element.

The attitudes of soldiers toward crime varied. Some were active participants in crimes; others were the ultimate authority to be relied on to combat crime. After the Kornilov affair, demoralization and disintegration took root in the reserve forces in the city. With the exception of a few reserve units that maintained political cohesion, the masses of soldiers were probably turning into potential criminals.

Compared with all other classes in Petrograd, the working class alone maintained social and political cohesion. More important, it maintained coherent, effective organizations through which it could enforce discipline and combat the spread of crime into the working-class districts. No doubt, crimes did take place in the working-class districts as well, but the crime rate in these districts was markedly lower than in the center of the city. Among the workers' organizations that played an important role in preventing and combating crime were the factory committees, the district soviets, and especially the workers' militia and the Red Guards. The main purpose of the workers' militia and the Red Guards was political, and aimed at organizing the workers militarily to prepare for expected counterrevolutionary attacks against the working class. But in the absence of an effective police force in the working-class districts, the workers' militia had to assume the task of security duties as a matter of necessity. For instance, the Militia Commission of the Vasilevskii district soviet included, among the tasks assigned to the workers' militia, security of life and property as well as investigation of murders, robberies, and thefts.[82] While it is true, as Rex Wade argues,

that the Red Guards were to arm the workers to combat counterrevolution, it is also interesting that the draft statutes of the "Workers'
Guards," adopted by the Vasilevskii district soviet, included as one of
their tasks "security of life [and] property of all citizens without regard
to sex, age, and nationality."[83]

After the July Days, the Provisional Government attempted to abolish
the workers' militia by issuing the new statutes on the militia, which
aimed to create a centralized militia organization. But this attempt did
not succeed. Although weakened in strength, the workers' militia
continued to exist.[84] This was partly because it functioned as the most
effective, and in some districts the sole, instrument to maintain order.
For instance, despite the Provisional Government's directive, the
managers of the Pipe Factory refused to discontinue paying salaries to
the workers' militia on the grounds that its abolition would endanger
the security and discipline of the factory.[85]

As the city militia became ineffective and demoralized, the workers'
militia and the Red Guards served an increasingly important security
function, not only in the working-class districts but also in the center
of the city. The First City District Soviet, which included the most
crime-ridden former Liteinyi, Rozhdestvenskii, Aleksandr-Nevskii, and
Moscow districts and also included Ligovki and the Olympia amusement
park, had to be concerned with crimes in the district. In August, the soviet
decided to close down the Olympia, to increase the patrol duties of the
workers' militia in Ligovki and other troubled areas, and in general to
assume increased responsibility for security duties in the district.[86]

As the October Revolution approached, the conflict between political
struggle against counterrevolution and security duty became a subject of
intense discussion among the activists of the district soviets and the factory committees. Generally, the Vyborg, Vasilevskii, and Peterhof district
soviets took the stand that the workers' militia and the Red Guards were
an instrument of class struggle, and should not waste time in doing security duties. This position coincided with the policy of the Bolshevik Party.
On the other hand, the Petrograd, Rozhdestvenskii, and First City district
committees (where crime rates were higher) tended to accept security
duties as a necessary part of their functions.[87] Despite these differences,
the workers' militia and the Red Guards fulfilled the function of security
duty even in those districts where the district soviet leaders rejected it as
a proper function of the workers' armed organizations.

Conclusion

Crime contributed to the disintegration of society in Petrograd in 1917.
A society that is reduced to anomie cannot exist for long, and such a
situation dictates the emergence of a strong power that can restore order,

even if it must use an iron fist. In 1917 only the working class possessed the social cohesion and effective instruments needed to restore order. And only the Bolsheviks, who were riding the crest of working-class support, had the will to exercise violence to impose order. Crime did not stop suddenly when the Bolsheviks seized power. On the contrary, violent crimes and acts of mob justice even increased after October. The Bolsheviks, who had stood aloof from the problem of crime throughout 1917 until their seizure of power, declared that crimes were instigations by the bourgeoisie to overthrow the proletarian regime. The Bolsheviks used the presence of crime as justification to create a repressive police system. Increase in crime resulted from more than the causes discussed in this essay. A profound change in people's consciousness was also a cause. The old regime was gone, and with it many of the values of the old world. Everything was questioned, and much was rejected. Old notions of right and wrong were reversed, and the line that separated criminal acts from legality became blurred. The notion of inviolability of property and life came under assault. The political ideology that was gaining popularity among the masses further contributed to undermining this concept. Moreover, the downtrodden and the oppressed had gained a sense of self-respect – a consciousness that they had now become the master. At the same time, this sense of self-respect was closely mixed with a sense of revenge against the privileged. It might be said, therefore, that revolution conceals within itself an element of criminality.

NOTES

This essay is reprinted from *Religious and Secular Forces in Late Tsarist Russia. Essays in Honor of Donald W. Treadgold*, ed. Charles E. Timberlake (Seattle: University of Washington Press, 1992), 241–271. Four tables on crime before 1917 have been omitted and table 5, on crime during 1917, is given here as Table 3.1.

1 For the recent monographs on social aspects of the October Revolution, see Ronald Grigor Suny, "Toward a Social History of the October Revolution," *American Historical Review* 88 (1983): 31–52. In his provocative article, Suny argues that the social history of the October Revolution cannot exist independently of political history. In his opinion, the social history of the revolution "has been more concerned with the movement and movements of social groups and classes than with patterns of fertility or mortality." The task of social historians, he declares, is to examine the deepening social polarization between those at the top (*verkhi*) and those at the bottom (*nizy*) of society, with sufficient attention paid to the political implications.

2 A good example is Rex A. Wade's *Red Guards and Workers' Militias in the Russian Revolution* (Stanford: Stanford University Press, 1984). This excellent study examines the conflict between the workers' militia and the city militia in Petrograd and the growing radicalization of the working class, accompanied by the rapid development of the Red Guards. Wade's primary approach is precisely what Suny proposes as the only method applicable for social

historians of the Russian revolutions: to examine the militia organizations from the point of view of deepening social polarization. In this it is exceptionally successful. But since crime is a nonpolitical issue not directly related to the main focus of social history, it is excluded from Wade's study. This omission is serious in two respects. First, the militia organizations' effectiveness in dealing with crime had an important bearing on the relationship between the workers' militia and the city militia. Second, as I will show in this essay, politics had a tendency to be enmeshed with the question of crime. By excluding crime from his range of analysis, therefore, Wade fails to see the extent of the politicization of society that affected even what were considered to be nonpolitical areas.

3 In dealing with this question, one is faced with a serious problem of sources. As society began to break down in 1917, the systematic collection of criminal records was seriously disrupted. The highly meticulous statistical data compiled by the Ministry of Justice ceased to be published in 1917. There must be a wealth of material in Soviet archives, but it has not been examined systematically. My request to use archival material was rejected during my stay in the Soviet Union in the early 1980s. We do not have to wait, however, until the Soviet archives become open to have a general picture of crime in Petrograd during the revolution. One source that gives us a clue to the relationship between crime and society is contemporary newspapers, particularly the boulevard newspapers. Historians have ignored these papers as a serious source of evidence until recently. The boulevard newspapers contain a wealth of information on daily life in Petrograd during these turbulent days in 1917, particularly with regard to crime. Recent works that have imaginatively used these newspapers include: Jeffrey Brooks, *When Russia Learned to Read: Literacy and Popular Literature, 1861–1917* (Princeton: Princeton University Press, 1985); Louise McReynolds, "Images of Crime in the City: Crime Reporting in the St. Petersburg Tabloid *Gazeta-Kopeika*," a paper presented at the AAASS Convention, November 1984, Washington, D.C.; Joan Neuberger, "Hooliganism and the *Mirovoi Sud* in St. Petersburg, 1900–1914" (Ph.D. diss., Stanford University, 1985).

4 In mid-1914, the population of Petrograd and its suburbs was 2,103,000; by the end of 1915 it had risen to 2,347,850. By the beginning of 1917 it was 2,420,000, but after the February Revolution it began to decline. By autumn 1917 it had diminished to 2,300,000. But the most drastic decline occurred only after the October Revolution. By June 1918, it had shrunk to 1,468,000. See Z. G. Frenkel', *Petrograd perioda voiny i revoliutsii: sanitarnye usloviia i kommunal'noe blagoustroistvo* (Petrograd, 1923), 9–13.

Actually, the crime rate, which sharply declined at the outbreak of World War I, began to increase in the second half of 1916. Particularly important was the increase in juvenile crimes. See E. N. Tarnovskii, "Voina i dvizheme prestupnosti v 1911–1916 gg.," *Sbornik statei po proletarskoi revoliutsii i pravu* (Petrograd, 1918), 100–104; M. N. Garnet, *Revoliutsiia, rost prestupnosti i smertnaia kazn'* (Moscow, 1917), 2.

5 TsGAOR, f. DPOO, d. 341, ch. 57/1917, listy 24, 29; Tsuyoshi Hasegawa, *The February Revolution: Petrograd, 1917* (Seattle: University of Washington Press, 1981), 289.

6 Hasegawa, *The February Revolution*, 287–88.

7 For Iurevich's order, see *Petrogradskaia gazeta* (hereafter *PG*), March 5, 1917. Robberies in the guise of searches were reported in *Petrogradskii listok* (hereafter *PL*), March 5, 16, 17, 21, 26, and 28, April 28, 1917; *PG*, March 8, 19, 1917.

8 *PL*, March 16, 1917.
9 *PL*, April 7, 20, 23, and 25, May 9, 17, 1917.
10 *PL*, April 27, 29, May 10, 17, 18, 19, and 21, June 8, 9, and 17, 1917. "Stolichnye khishchniki" first appeared in *PL* on April 26. According to *Gazeta-Kopeika* (hereafter *GK*), the number of reported thefts and robberies on June 15 was 60.
11 *PL*, July 7, 1917; *GK*, July 6, 11, 1917.
12 *PL*, July 16, 1917; *PG*, July 16, 1917.
13 *PL*, July 28, 1917.
14 *PL*, August 17, 1917; *GK*, August 15, 1917.
15 *GK*, August 30, 1917.
16 For thefts in September see *GK*, September 2, 6, 7, and 9, 1917; *PL*, September 12, 14, 1917.
17 *PL*, October 1, 14, and 18, 1917; *GK*, October 3, 4, and 8, 1917.
18 *PL*, September 12, 14, 17, 19, 20, and 11; October 4, 1917.
19 Alexander Rabinowitch, *Prelude to Revolution: The Petrograd Bolsheviks and the July 1917 Uprising* (Bloomington: Indiana University Press, 1968), 64–66; Michael M. Boll, *The Petrograd Armed Workers' Movement in the February Revolution* (Washington, D.C.: University Press of America, 1979), 146–52.
20 *PL*, April 29, May 7, 20, 21, and 30, 1917
21 *PG*, April 23, 1917.
22 *PL*, July 20, 21, and 25, August 30, 1917; *PG*, August 6, 17, 1917.
23 *PL*, August 12, 13, 1917.
24 S. A. Smith, *Red Petrograd: Revolution in the Factories, 1917–1918* (Cambridge: Cambridge University Press, 1983), 168–71; David Mandel, *The Petrograd Workers and the Soviet Seizure of Power: From the July Days 1917 to July 1918* (London: Macmillan, 1984), 264–86.
25 Murder statistics reported in *Ves' Peterburg* are as follows:

Year	St. Petersburg	Suburbs
1896	117	10
1899	127	17
1900	178	11
1902	156	16
1903	206	24

These figures were given to the author by Joan Neuberger.
26 *PL*, March 11, 1917; *Rech'*, March 11, 1917.
27 *PL*, April 17, 20, 1917; *PG*, April 18, 1917. Von Schrippen's raid on Zhitovskii's apartment was reported in *GK*, November 4, 16, and 20, 1916.
28 *PL*, May 19, 1917.
29 *PL*, May 25, 1917.
30 *PL*, August 29, 1917.
31 *PL*, August 12, 13, 1917.
32 *PL*, May 3, 1917.
33 *PL*, October 2, 4, 1917.
34 *PL*, July 13, 1917.
35 See Lewis Siegelbaum, "Another Yellow Peril? Chinese Migrants in the Russian Far East and the Russian Reaction before 1917," *Modern Asian Studies* 12 (1978): 307–30; *Vestnik gorodskogo samoupravleniia*, July 4, 1917.
36 *PL*, April 25, May 2, 1917; *PG*, July 26, 1917.
37 *PL*, September 23, 1917.
38 K. I. Globachev, "Pravda russkoi revoliutsii: vospominaniia byvshego nachal'nika Petrogradskogo okhrannogo otdeleniia," manuscript, Bakhmeteff Archives, Columbia University, 131–32.

39 Robert P. Browder and Alexander F. Kerensky, *The Russian Provisional Government 1917. Documents*, 3 vols. (Stanford: Stanford University Press, 1961), 1:199–200.

40 *PL*, March 18, 1917.

41 Globachev, "Pravda russkoi revoliutsii," 117–18.

42 *PL*, April 24, 1917.

43 *PL*, July 28, 1917.

44 *PL*, March 10, 16, 22, and 30, 1917.

45 *PL*, July 26, August 24, 1917; *PG*, July 26, 27, 29, and 31, August 24, 1917; *PG*, July 26, 1917; *GK*, August 5, 8, and 20, 1917.

46 *PL*, July 25, 1917; *GK*, July 25, 1917.

47 Leonard Schapiro, "The Political Thought of the First Russian Provisional Government," in Richard Pipes, ed., *Revolutionary Russia* (Cambridge: Harvard University Press, 1968), 113.

48 Browder and Kerensky, *Provisional Government*, 1:220.

49 For the Temporary Court in Petrograd, see V. Mantushkin, "Vremennye sudy v Petrograde," *Zhurnal Ministerstva iustitsii, 1917*, no. 4:184–92. For the Statutes of the Temporary Court, see ibid., 190–92. For a reaction to the Temporary Court, see *PL*, August 8, 1917.

50 Mantushkin, "Vremennye sudy," 189.

51 *PL*, May 22, 1917.

52 *PL*, May 9, 16, 17, 1917.

53 Browder and Kerensky, *Provisional Government*, 1:205–6.

54 Globachev, "Pravda russkoi revoliutsii," 124.

55 *GK*, August 31, 1917; *PL*, August 31, 1917. For other prison escapes see *PL*, July 2, August 2, 9, 1917; *GK*, July 27, 1917.

56 See Tsuyoshi Hasegawa, "The Formation of the Militia in the February Revolution: An Aspect of the Origins of Dual Power," *Slavic Review* 32 (June 1973): 302–22; Wade, *Red Guards and Workers' Militias*, chaps. 2 and 3.

57 The existence of two competing political principles – the democratic principle and the class principle – and the eventual triumph of the latter are important aspects of the October Revolution not thoroughly examined at either the national or the local level. Valuable suggestions are made, however, in monographs by Rosenberg, Startsev, Raleigh, and Wade. Particularly, Wade describes the contradiction of the working-class demand. While insisting on democracy, the workers rejected any all-people body or solution that might result in a nonworking class or nonsocialist majority. The contradiction, Wade insists, presaged a civil war (*Red Guards and Workers' Militias*, 64–65).

58 Ibid. 68.

59 The principle of local self-determination is one of the important aspects of the October Revolution often ignored by historians. This aspect has recently been emphasized by Donald J. Raleigh, *Revolution on the Volga: 1917 in Saratov* (Ithaca: Cornell University Press, 1986).

60 Wade describes the workers' protest against I. G. Tsereteli's attempt to centralize the militia structures (*Red Guards and Workers' Militias*, 124–26). But Tsereteli's attempt provoked equally vigorous protests among the district militia organization under the city militia. On this topic, see *Vestnik gorodskogo samoupravleniia*, July 19, 20, 21, 25, 29, and 30, August 2, 4, 8, 11, and 22, 1917.

61 Z. Kel'son, "Militsiia fevral'skoi revoliutsii," *Byloe* 29 (1925): 163.

62 *PL*, April 1, 7, 1917; *PG*, April 13, 1917.

63 *PL*, October 19, 1917.

64 The city militiamen's demands were discussed in some district soviets and factory committees. See *Raionnye sovety v Petrograde v. 1917 godu: protokoly, rezoliutsii, postanovleniia obshchikh sobranii i zasedanii ispolnitel'nykh komitetov* (hereafter *RSP*), 3 vols. (Moscow and Leningrad, 1964), 2:278; *Fabrichnoza-vodskie komitety Petrograda v 1917 godu: protokoly* (Moscow, 1917), 456–59, 605.
65 *GK*, September 28, October 5, 7, 1917.
66 *PL*, May 14, 19, 29, and 30, June 2, 1917. For the City Duma's discussion on the city militia, see *PL*, May 11, 1917.
67 *PL*, September 12, 14, 17, 19, 20, and 22, October 4, 1917.
68 *PL*, October 20, 1917.
69 *PL*, April 28, 1917.
70 *PL*, October 19, 1917.
71 Mob justice, or trial by the mob (*samosud*, plural is *samosudy*), was rooted in the Russian criminal tradition. For some examples of *samosudy* in villages, see Valerii Chalidze, *Ugolovnaia Rossiia* (New York: Khronika, 1977), 23–32.
72 *PL*, May 13, 1917.
73 *GK*, June 25, 1917. Also see Garnet, *Revoliutsiia, rost prestupnosti i smertnaia kazn'*, 27–30; A. Askii, "Samosud: Pis'mo ochevidtsa," *Vestnik gorodskogo samoupravleniia*, August 6, 1917.
74 *PL*, August 20, 1917.
75 *GK*, July 9, 1917. Other cases of trials by the mob were reported in *PL*, July 20, 26, August 2, 3, and 10, 1917; *GK*, July 9, August 3, 19, 1917.
76 *PL*, July 16, 1917; *GK*, July 16, 1917.
77 *PG*, July 16, 29, 1917; *PL*, July 16, 1917; *GK*, July 16, 1917.
78 *PL*, October 2, 4, 5, 7, 8, 10, 11, 12, and 17, 1917.
79 *GK*, October 16, 1917.
80 *PL*, July 9, 1917.
81 *GK*, July 14, 1917. Those who left the city were not merely the well-to-do. By fall of 1917 approximately 120,000 had left Petrograd. Frenkel', *Petrograd perioda voiny i revoliutsii*, 13.
82 *RSP*, 1:72; 3:186, 189.
83 Ibid., 1:135.
84 Wade, *Red Guards and Workers' Militias*, 121–32. For the new militia statutes issued by Tsereteli, see *Vestnik gorodskogo samoupravleniia*, July 19, 1917.
85 Wade, *Red Guards and Workers' Militias*, 126–27.
86 *RSP*, 1:225–26.
87 See *RSP*, 1:234–36; 3:120, 338; *Fabrichno-zavodskie komitety Petrograda v 1917 godu* (Moscow, 1979), 390, 450, 491.

Part II

LANGUAGE AND IDENTITY

4

"DEMOCRACY" IN THE POLITICAL CONSCIOUSNESS OF THE FEBRUARY REVOLUTION

Boris Ivanovich Kolonitskii

Historians and social scientists recently have looked more closely at language and how use of language defines groups and issues. This "linguistic turn" has influenced writing on the Russian Revolution as historians have given more attention to language and the way it was used and helped shape events. Boris Kolonitskii has taken a leading role in exploring the role of language and symbolism in the revolution. One of the most striking features of the revolution was the influx and use of Western-derived political and social terms, terms that often were unfamiliar to their users or were used in special ways. These terms had to be defined in the process of revolutionary turmoil and in turn influenced the revolutionary process. In this essay Kolonitskii explores the meanings and use of one such word, "democracy," as self-identification and in the political and social struggles of the revolution.

*All groups and political actors, from left to right, sought to identify themselves as democratic. Democratization was seen as the way to solve all problems. At the same time, however, the meaning of "democracy" and who was "democratic" was contested ground. In many usages it was limited to "the people" (*narod*) in the sense of the laboring masses of workers and peasants. Terms such as "democratic strata," "democratic classes," "democratic elements," "revolutionary democracy," or simply "the democracy" became a part of daily language and gave a distinct class coloration to the political and social debates in which they were used. "Democratic" often was used as the opposite not of dictatorship or autocracy, but of the upper and even middle classes, toward whom it was antagonistic. In this meaning, used by almost all socialists, even Bolsheviks were included as democratic, while liberals such as the Kadets as well as almost all propertied elements were excluded. Indeed, the distinction between "the democracy" and "the bourgeoisie" became central in political discourse, especially by socialist parties and by the urban lower classes.*

75

Thus used, it reflected and contributed to the tendency toward a simple twofold class and political division, we/they, us/them, nizy/verkhi *(lower strata/upper strata). Kolonitskii here, as in his research on other symbols and terms, such as the use of the word "bourgeois," is dealing with the relationship between dramatic changes in political vocabulary and symbolism and the continuity or change in deep-seated mental structures of the populace.*

* * *

Historians of quite diverging orientations have interpreted the February revolution of 1917 in Russia as a "democratic" revolution. Several generations of Marxists of various stripes (*tolk*) have called it a "bourgeois-democratic revolution." In the years of perestroika, the contrast between democratic February and Bolshevik October became an important part of the historical argument of the anticommunist movement. The February revolution was regarded as a dramatic, unsuccessful attempt at the modernization and westernization of Russia, at its democratization. Such a point of view was expressed even earlier in some historical works and in the memoirs of participants in the events – liberals and moderate socialists. For example, just such a description of the revolution is given by Aleksandr Kerenskii, whose last reminiscences are especially significant. Kerenskii thought that "the overwhelming majority of the Russian population . . . were wholeheartedly democratic in their beliefs."[1]

In many respects, this viewpoint is correct. For the most part, both the legislation of the February revolution and the practical activity of the Provisional Government were directed toward creating democratic, elected institutions, toward securing human rights and democratic freedoms. Democratization was seen as a universal means to solve any kind of problem. After February, people strove to democratize the theater, church, and schools (in the latter case one might mean labor education and the creation of self-management). During the revolution a unique experiment was conducted in the democratization of the army, which Kerenskii himself called "the freest in the world" (*samaia svobodnaia v mire*) (soldiers of the 12th Army, for example, were proud of the fact that it was "the most democratic" of the Russian armed forces). Troop committees of elected representatives were created in the army and were able to exercise significant rights; soldiers of many units and subdivisions chose their commanders; even the decision to initiate an attack was occasionally subject to a vote.[2]

Democratic ideology and phraseology influenced the language of revolution. The term *democracy* (*demokratiia*), which gave way in popularity to the concepts of "the people" (*narod*), "freedom" (*svoboda*), and "socialism" (*sotsializm*), was absolutely "politically correct," ideologically fashionable, and emotionally attractive. The *guberniia* [provincial] dioceses congress in Kursk concluded that the republican democratic structure "corresponded most closely" to evangelical law. The battleship *Imperator Nikolai I* was to take the name *Democracy*. But ships were not the only things changing names. On 8 (21) April 1917, one soldier, Sergei Romanov, made a special request: like many who shared his surname, he wanted to be rid of the Romanov name because it was considered "monarchist" and "unpleasant" (some Rasputins and Sukhomlinovs also aspired to change their surnames). Romanov wrote, "A wounded soldier, I consider it shameful at the present time to bear the surname Romanov, and therefore request that you permit me to change my name from Romanov to Demokratov" (his request was denied).[3] If the renaming of military ships testifies to the inclusion of a political term in the new government ideology, then the anthroponymic reaction to the revolution (changes in surnames and the decline in popularity of the name Nikolai were unusually widespread after February) indicates a distinctive politicization of private life. For neophytes of political life the term *democracy* had a positive meaning; one must suppose that the soldier Romanov (he was never allowed to change his name) thought that he, his family, and his descendants would be proud of the new name.

Including the term *democracy* in one's own political lexicon became a must for practically all political forces – from Bolsheviks to Kornilovites. Thus, Nikolai Berdiaev called Lavr Kornilov* an "indubitable democrat" and Boris Savinkov considered the general "a true democrat and unwavering republican."[4] To combat German propaganda in Russia, British and French missions, in cooperation with Kornilov's entourage, created a special publishing house in Petrograd, turning out no fewer than 12 million leaflets. Significantly, the publisher was called Demokraticheskaia Rossiia (Democratic Russia). Evidently, it was assumed that printed matter from such a source would be in demand.[5]

On the other hand, even the leader of the Bolsheviks was seen by his supporters as "the leader of democracy." In May 1917 front-line soldiers wrote to the editorial office of a Bolshevik newspaper: "We send a warm greeting to the leader of Russian democracy and the defender of our interests, comrade Lenin." A Bolshevik poet proclaimed on the pages of *Pravda* [Russian original omitted here and below – ed.]:

I sing the family of my people,
Which is called democracy,
For her instinctive battle
With darkness and apathy.[6]

* General Lavr Kornilov, leader of a military counterrevolutionary move against the Provisional Government in August – ed.

And so, representatives of nearly the entire political spectrum thought they should call themselves "democrats." This facilitated the multiple meanings of the term *democracy* and lent the advantages of political mimicry to those who used it. The satirist D. N. Semenovskii had good reason to describe the situation in the following way:

> All of Russia is newly decked out,
> A devilishly motley masquerade!
> A thug pretends to be a Kadet,
> And who's not a democrat now?[7]

One distinctive piece of evidence concerning the popularity of the term *democracy* in revolutionary Russia was the emotional statement made by Lord Charles Hardinge, the permanent undersecretary of state for foreign affairs of Great Britain. On 13 (26) April, Hardinge wrote to Sir George Buchanan, the British ambassador in Petrograd:

> How I hate the word democracy at the present time: if we do not win the war, as it should be won, it will be thanks to the Russian revolution and the absurd nonsense talked about the democracies of the world.[8]

An official of conservative convictions, Hardinge questioned, not without foundation, the battle readiness of the Russian revolutionary army, at the same time that many of his compatriot liberals wrote enthusiastically of a unified battle pitting the "democratic countries" against Prussian militarism and absolutism.

The most democratic country

Active participants in the Russian revolution not only strove toward democratic transformations in their country, they thirsted to make Russia "the most democratic" government in the world: "We won't create some kind of English or German structure, rather a democratic republic in the full sense of the word," Kerenskii declared on 15 (28) May in Helsinki. He called Russia "the freest country in the world," "the avant-garde of the democratic socialist movement in Europe," "the most democratic government in Europe," and declared that Russia "had become the leader of the democratic governments." Russian politicians sometimes even infected foreigners with their enthusiasm. After a meeting with Kerenskii, Harold Williams, an influential British journalist, wrote, "If all went well Russia might actually prove to be an even freer country than England."[9]

Kerenskii turned out to be emotionally similar in one respect to his political opponent V. I. Lenin, who called post-February Russia "the freest" country. A comparable point of view was expressed in agitational brochures: "If the Russian republic will be the youngest in the family of nations, then, we hope, it will be the best, the most perfect."[10] Concerning belief in the miracle "of the transformation of a half-Asian despotic state into nearly the freest country in the world," the Menshevik-defensist A. N. Potresov wrote with sarcasm:

> As if even a backward country that until recently aroused mixed feelings of apprehension and pity in a foreigner, even a country with a dispersed populace that was submissive to the Cossack's whip, might actually be able, not only to jump in one bound across the abyss that has separated it from the cultural level of the European west since time immemorial, but also to disgrace that west and reveal heretofore unknown patterns of democratism and unseen forms of citizenship.

P. A. Sorokin called these attitudes "inside-out slavophilism." Revolutionary messianism was inherent to both the radicalized masses and the liberal members of the Provisional Government:

> By its very nature, the soul of the Russian people turned out to be a democratic soul of the world. This soul is prepared not only to unify with democracy all over the world, to stand before it, but also to lead democracy along the path of the development of humanity toward the beginnings of freedom, equality, and brotherhood.

So declared the prime minister-chairman Prince G. E. L'vov, expressing a worldview strongly influenced by the Slavophiles.[11]

Ideas of Russian messianism, inherited by the Bolsheviks, were intrinsic even to some leaders of democratic February. Occasionally "revolutionary-democratic" messianism was already combining at that time with ideas about "exporting the revolution." So, for example, I. G. Tsereteli, the leader of the Mensheviks and minister of the Provisional Government, stated that the task of revolution "is the final victory of democracy inside the country and beyond its borders." Kerenskii expressed similar ideas. In April 1917, he announced:

> We can play a colossal role in world history if we manage to cause other nations to travel our path, if we make our friends and enemies respect freedom. But for that they must see the impossibility of fighting the ideas of Russian democracy.[12]

Of course, such statements above all provided the ideological basis for the need to continue the war against German militarism, "the bulwark of monarchism in Europe." Correspondingly, in their propaganda leaflets, Russian soldiers called on their opponents to follow their example and overthrow their ruling dynasties. Allies could also become the target of the export of revolution, however, and calls to bring about an anti-monarchist revolution in Romania were widely circulated among Russian soldiers deployed in that country. Anti-Shah and antifeudal sentiments were spread in the north of Persia by Russian soldiers who wanted to "democratize" that country.

Legislative practice also reflected attempts to become the "most advanced democracy." For example, a law on elections to the Constituent Assembly put into place electoral norms that appeared only a decade later in countries with more developed legal rights.

"Democracy" as identification

The term *democracy* was understood in various ways in 1917. Different interpretations of the idea are given by numerous dictionaries that were intended to facilitate the acquisition of the language of contemporary mass politics. (Contemporaries spoke of the need for a corresponding "translation" of the newspapers and leaflets.) In many cases "democracy" was understood as "people's power" (*narodovlastie*).[13] Sometimes the real target was not existing governments, however, but rather some kind of sociopolitical ideal. Thus, a dictionary published by the Moscow publishing house Narodnaia mysl' (People's thought) stated that the United States and France "are entirely bourgeois republics; tiny Switzerland is drawing much nearer to the model of a democratic republic, but it is still far from a fully unconstrained democracy." Such a formulation seemed to suppose that a "bourgeois republic" could not be democratic. Sometimes the arming of the populace as a replacement for a standing army was considered the most important indication of a democratic republic.[14] The legal understanding of the term *democracy* could also harbor antibourgeois sentiments: a democratic "people's" republic was seen as a way to limit the power of the "upper classes" (*vysshie klassy*).[15]

But the concept of democracy as "people's power" was not the only one. P. Volkov, the author of a dictionary issued by the Moscow publishing house Ideia, aptly noted:

The word *democracy* is now used either in the sense of "rule by the people" (*pravlenie naroda*) or "power of the people" (*vlast' narodu*) or denotes the broad masses of people, the aggregate of democratic parties, or a government based on a democratic foundation.[16]

And so, in some cases "democracy" was understood as a synonym for the concept of the "people" (*narod*) and, correspondingly, a "democrat" was defined as a "populist" (*narodnik*).[17] However, sometimes not the entire people but only the "democratic strata" (*demokraticheskie sloi*) and the "laboring classes" (*trudiashchiesia klassy*) were given this name. Polemicizing from a similar point of view, N. A. Arsen'ev, the author of a dictionary published by the Moscow publishing house D. Ia. Makovskii, wrote: "Democracy is the whole people, the poor and the rich, men and women, and so on. Presently democracy refers only to the poor, to people without resources, that is, workers and peasants; but this is incorrect." The opposite position was taken, for example, by the authors of a *Guide to Political Terms and Politicians* who distinguished between the terms *democratic republic* and *democracy*: "Democracy is all classes in a country who live by their own labor: workers, peasants, servants, intelligentsia."[18] It is significant that this last dictionary was issued by an extremely moderate liberal publishing house, Osvobozhdennaia Rossiia (Liberated Russia), which was created by the Provisional Committee of the State Duma.

As we see, the term *democracy* had quite specific connotations in 1917; it often expressed a certain type of self-identification. "Democracy" was opposed, not to "dictatorship" (*diktatura*), "police state" (*politseiskoe gosudarstvo*), and the like, but rather to "privileged elements" (*tsenzovye elementy*), "the ruling classes" (*praviashchie klassy*), and, quite often, "the bourgeoisie" (*burzhuaziia*).[19] The terms *democracy* and, especially, *revolutionary democracy* often served as synonyms for the ideas of "democratic classes," "democratic strata" ("people"), "democratic organizations" (as Soviets and committees were considered in 1917), and "democratic forces" (here the socialists considered only themselves to be democrats). In the minds of the socialists (especially in the first months of 1917), the terms *democracy* and *democratic camp* (*demokraticheskii lager'*) meant the aggregate of the working masses and the socialist intelligentsia supporting the Soviets.[20]

The position of the socialists sometimes influenced even the language of liberal publications. Thus *Birzhevye vedomosti* called the Executive Committee of the Soviet of Workers' and Soldiers' Deputies "the managing organ of democracy." The equating of "democracy" with the socialists could be found also in I. G. Tsereteli's [Menshevik and Soviet leader] speeches to the Constituent Assembly. He said that "the internecine civil war of democracy, which with the hands of one part destroys the achievements of all of democracy, even surrenders it trussed by the arms and legs of the bourgeoisie." As we see, "democracy" was contrasted to the "bourgeoisie," and even at this time and in this situation he unconditionally included the Bolsheviks in the camp with "democracy": "The part of democracy represented by you," Tsereteli would say to the Bolsheviks.[21]

So deeply rooted was this interpretation that one finds similar use of the term, not only in texts from 1917, but also in memoirs by émigrés. And in I. G. Tsereteli's memoirs we find echoes of a similar approach, although they were written many years later. He uses the term in various meanings. In some cases he writes about "socialist" democracy and "purely bourgeois" democracy. In this way, he points to the components of "democracy," which included a "bourgeois" element. And in other places he writes about the "united front of all democratic forces." In this case he does not talk exclusively about socialists. However, additionally, he sometimes contrasts "democracy" and "bourgeoisie." Sometimes he examines Bolshevism, "left maximalism," as the opponent of "democracy," and sometimes, describing the conflict of the Bolsheviks with the moderate socialists, he speaks about "internecine strife in the ranks of democracy," that is, he includes Bolsheviks in the "camp of democracy."[22] In this case, Tsereteli as a memoirist uses the socialist jargon of 1917.

Even such a staunch advocate of cooperation with the "bourgeoisie" as A. N. Potresov grouped the Bolsheviks in the "camp of democracy": "Lenin's furious ideology is only a concentrated and perhaps exaggerated expression of those thoughts and feelings that partially ferment in the heads of a significant portion of democracy," he wrote in 1917.[23]

For Tsereteli, Potresov, and many other moderate socialists of 1917, "democracy" meant the forces represented in the Soviets, in the committees and by socialists of various types. This understanding of "democracy" also had an effect, for example, on the composition of the Democratic Conference 14–22 September (27 September–5 October) – representatives of the "bourgeoisie" were not invited to participate. Activists did not let the families of landowners take their places for the elections for the new zemstvo – it would have been "undemocratic."[24]

In his memoirs, Kerenskii criticized the language of the Russian socialists and contrasted it to his own supposedly purely democratic western position. Kerenskii the memoirist often distorts the true picture of Kerenskii the politician of 1917, however; his formal self-portrait is modernized and westernized. In actuality such socialist language was also his own; at least he used it in many of his important speaking appearances. In his famous speech of 2 (15) March at the Soviet he announced:

> I am a representative of democracy, and the Provisional Government must see me as someone expressing the demands of democracy and must especially take account of the opinions that I will uphold as a representative of democracy, by whose efforts the old regime was overthrown.

In other words, he considered only himself a representative of "democracy." In another speech he proclaimed: "In the name of the Provisional

Government of the country, I can convey greetings and a bow to all democracy: to workers, soldiers, and peasants."[25] The "minister-democrat" (and this is exactly how Kerenskii presented himself) gave the impression that he did not consider other members of the government – representatives of the Constitutional Democratic [Kadet] Party and other liberals – as "democrats." Even in Kerenskii's early émigré works one sees the oppositions between "bourgeoisie" and "democracy" and between "Russian bourgeoisie" (*russkaia burzhuaziia*) and "laboring democracy" (*trudovaia demokratiia*).[26]

The opposition between "bourgeoisie" and "democracy" became an important instrument for classifying political forces. The language of the Russian revolution also influenced reports by foreigners. Thus, for example, the famous English journalist Arthur Ransome also wrote about the conflict between the Bolsheviks and the "other part of democracy," indicating a split among the socialists. In a survey put together for the War Ministry of Great Britain, there was talk of a compromise between the "bourgeois" and "democratic" parties in Russia. Even the British ambassador, George Buchanan, used the concepts of the "bourgeoisie" and "democracy" to describe the opposing camps.[27]

Throughout history, the concepts "democracy," "democrat," and "true democrat" have been used fairly often for self-identification; correspondingly, political opponents are thereby as if excluded from the political process. In this connection the Russian revolution of 1917 was no exception. A special aspect of this revolution was the contrast between "democracy" and "bourgeoisie" proposed by socialists of various tendencies. Not everyone, of course, agreed with this approach; there were even attempts to contrast democracy and socialism. However, in Russia's political life the language of class dominated; the concept of "democracy" was included in this language and subjected to specific changes. We find a distinctive confirmation of this in reports by the British vice-consul in Khar'kov: "Class hatred had been intensified by ill use of foreign terminology, such as 'bourgeois,' 'proletariat,' 'democrat,' 'citizen,' and 'comrade.'"[28] And N. A. Berdiaev wrote: "A new creation of idols has begun, many idols and earthly gods have appeared – 'revolution,' 'socialism,' 'democracy,' 'internationalism,' and 'proletariat.'"[29] It is significant that both authors place the term *democracy* among the concepts of a socialist vocabulary.

Mass democratic consciousness and the cult of the leader

The interpretation of "democracy" proposed by the socialists was reflected in mass consciousness; "democracy" was equated with the "people" – "We are democracy" (*demokratiia – eto my*). The people, however, developed the ideas of "democracy" and "the republic" according to their own traditional conceptions of power (mass consciousness also gave its interpretations to other concepts borrowed from the language of contemporary politics – "socialism," "bourgeoisie," "Bolsheviks," and so on). Here we encounter the problem of the translation from the bookish language of the February revolution by the less educated and sometimes illiterate activists. Research into this little studied borderland between oral and printed culture is a complex task.

Buchanan recalled that in the first days of the revolution one Russian soldier noted: "Oh, yes, we must have a republic, but we must have a good tsar at the head." Such an example could serve to corroborate the ambassador's own views with respect to the Russians' low level of political culture: "Russia is not ripe for a purely democratic form of government," he stated. And we see echoes of similar sentiments in other sources: "We want the Republic . . . but with a good Tsar," wrote a French diplomat, de Robien, on the views of Russian soldiers. An American historian and Slavicist, Frank Golder, who was in Petrograd in 1917, also noted:

> Stories are being told of soldiers who say they wish a republic like England, or a republic with a Tsar. One soldier said he wanted to elect a President and when asked "whom would you elect?" he replied, "The Tsar." From all accounts many of the soldiers do not grasp and do not understand what the Revolution means.[30]

One may, of course, suppose that these authors wrote about the same soldiers – foreigners often socialized together, met regularly at gatherings, told each other new anecdotes and political news. Yet even in reports by the Russian military censorship office we encounter analogous excerpts from soldiers' letters: "We want a democratic republic and a tsar-father for three years"; "it would be good if they gave us a republic with a tsar who can get things done." One of the censors reported, "in nearly all letters, the peasants express the desire to see a tsar as the leader of Russia. Obviously, monarchy is the only method of governance compatible with peasant conceptions."[31]

It is possible that officials of the military censorship office were of a conservative disposition and chose examples that reflected their political biases. But it is unlikely that all peasants and soldier-peasants who made such statements in March and April about the tsar were convinced monarchists (as we see, some of the soldiers wanted to limit the tsar's term in office). Rather, they saw the concepts of "state" (*gosudarstvo*) and "tsardom" (*tsarstvo*) as synonyms; they could not imagine a state without a "sovereign" (*gosudar'*). It is well known that soldiers often refused to swear allegiance to the Provisional Government; the mention of the word "state" in the text of the oath was seen as a counterrevolutionary advocacy of monarchism. The soldiers shouted, "We do not have a state, but we do have a republic."[32]

A striking example of the combination of antimonarchist sentiment and monarchist mentality was given in the memoirs of a Menshevik, a deputy of the Moscow Soviet of Workers' Deputies. He described his speech at a rally of reserve regiments near Vladimir at the beginning of March 1917:

> in the middle of a field stood a podium with two or three soldiers on it, and all around stood a crowd of thousands – it was black from all the people. I spoke, of course, about war and peace, about land – "land to the people" – and about the advantages of the republic over the monarchy. But when I had finished and the excited "hurrahs" and applause had ceased, a powerful voice shouted "We want you as tsar," which brought more applause. I declined the crown of the Romanovs and left with a grave feeling from the realization of how easy it would be for any adventurist or demagogue to take control of this simple and naive people.[33]

In this case there was an interesting relationship between the "enlightened western" socialist speaking the language of contemporary politics, and the "dark," uneducated soldier-peasants, who did not understand the "correct" language of the democratic socialists. Yet this incident also clearly testifies to the fact that the adherents of democracy and "the people" often spoke in different political languages. The use of the same words – *democracy, republic, tsar, socialism,* and so on – created only an illusion of mutual understanding.[34]

As we see, from the beginning the concepts of "democracy" (which could serve as a synonym for "new life" – "bright future") and "good tsar" could peacefully coexist in mass consciousness. However, this was evidently characteristic only in the first months of revolution. The "Rasputiniad," the destruction of the symbols of the empire, the mass antimonarchist propaganda – these all led to the words *tsar* and *monarchy* becoming taboo to the point where they were almost completely excluded from the political lexicon (although in the fall of 1917 one can note some rebirth of monarchist sympathies, reflected, for example, in the views of individual peasants).

Even an attempt to distribute brochures describing the state structure of England led to unrest in one regiment – even the mention of the term *constitutional monarchy* was taken as malicious monarchist propaganda. However, mass consciousness, having stopped using some of the concepts of the language of monarchy, preserved a monarchic mentality; democratic ideology could be superimposed on traditional authoritarian-patriarchal culture – the place of the tsar or the "sovereign" comes to be occupied by the "true fighters for freedom," by the "true leaders of democracy."

The chief "leader of democracy" became Kerenskii, the most popular leader in February. In 1917 a real cult of the "leader of the people" (*vozhd' naroda* – precisely this term was used) developed that in many ways exceeded the corresponding cults of the Soviet period. Resolutions called him "the true leader of Russian democracy," "a symbol of democracy," and so on. The Russian intelligentsia played a large role in creating the cult of Kerenskii.[35] The leader's name itself became an important political symbol. Kerenskii the "minister-democrat" was also called "a symbol of democracy": "For us, Kerenskii is not a minister, not a people's tribune; he is even simply no longer a human being. Kerenskii is a symbol of the revolution," wrote admirers of the "people's minister" in 1917, subjectively considering themselves supporters of democracy.[36] The atmosphere at the meetings with the "democratic minister" is significant: after his speeches, many soldiers kissed his clothing, cried, prayed, and knelt.[37]

Kerenskii may have been correct when he stated that the absolute majority of the population of Russia were supporters of democracy. Nevertheless, the various admirers of "democracy" pursued completely different goals. As we have seen, the word *democracy* itself was understood in completely different ways. The mention of this term in the 1917 sources constantly demands a qualified translation by historians (and admittedly a translation cannot always be given). From our contemporary point of view, the understanding of "democracy" exhibited by many socialists, soldiers, and peasants was often "incorrect." However, such a judgment can hardly be considered historical (by this standard even the understanding of democracy in Aristotle's *Politics* would be "incorrect"). Indeed, the very fact that several different political languages were functioning simultaneously objectively impeded the country's democratic development.

The language of democracy in 1917 was strongly influenced by the language of class, by the language of the socialists, which dominated during the revolution.[38] On the other hand, the deep authoritarian-patriarchal tradition often facilitated the creation of a new style of ideological construct, but sometimes also deformed the existing constructs, endowing them with new meaning. Thus, mass "democratism" of the 1917 type could be combined with the cult of the leader who was "of the people" and "democratic." One must then state that during the creation of the model of "Soviet" democracy, the Bolsheviks used several ideological structures created after February. In this sense their politics represented a radical continuation of the past, and not a revolutionary break with it.[39] Obviously the influence of radical political upheavals on mass consciousness should not be exaggerated – a dramatic change in political symbolism need not be accompanied by the overthrow of deep-seated mental structures.

Translated by Christopher K. Cosner

NOTES

Essay reprinted from *Slavic Review* 57, no. 1 (Spring 1998): 95–106.

1 A. F. Kerensky, *Russia and History's Turning Point* (New York, 1965), 326.

2 V. V. Shul'gin claims, with reference to the testimony of German officers, that soldiers sometimes voted in the middle of an attack, before each charge. It is difficult to believe this, but the very existence of anecdotes on the theme of "democratized battles" is symptomatic. V. V. Shul'gin, "1917–1919," in A. V. Lavrov, ed., *Litsa: Biograficheskii almanakh* (Moscow, 1994), 5:143.

3 *Russkaia volia*, 1 (14) June 1917; *Russkoe slovo*, 21 April (4 May) 1917; Rossiiskii gosudarstvennyi istoricheskii arkhiv, f. 1412, op. 16, d. 532. On changing surnames, see Andrew M. Verner, "What's in a Name? Of Dog-Killers, Jews and Rasputin," *Slavic Review* 53, no. 4 (1994): 1046–70.

4 N. A. Berdiaev, "O svobode i dostoinstve slova," *Narodopravstvo: Ezhiniedielnyi zhurnal*, 1917, no. 11:6; House of Lords Record Office, Historical Collection, no. 206: The Stow Hill Papers, DS 211 (G).

5 B. I. Kolonitskii, "Izdatel'stvo 'Demokraticheskaia Rossiia,' inostrannye missii i okruzhenie L. G. Kornilova," in I. L. Afanas'ev, A. U. Davydov, V. I. Startsev, eds., *Rossiia v 1917 godu: Novye podkhody i vzgliady: Sbornik nauchnykh trudov*, 2nd edn. (St. Petersburg, 1994), 28–31.

6 *Pravda*, 11 (24) May and 19 May (1 June) 1917.

7 *Russkaia stikhotvornaia satira 1908–1917 godov* (Leningrad, 1974), 568.

8 Cambridge University Library, Hardinge Papers, vol. 31, p. 311.

9 *A. F. Kerenskii ob armii i voine* (Odessa, 1917), 10, 32; *Rech' A. F. Kerenskogo, voennogo i morskogo ministra, tovarishcha predsedatelia Petrogradskogo Soveta rabochikh i soldatskikh deputatov, proiznesennaia im 29 aprelia, v soveshchanii delegatov fronta* (Moscow, 1917), 3; H. Pitcher, *Witnesses of the Russian Revolution* (London, 1994), 61.

10 R. Grigor'ev [R. G. Lemberg], *Demokraticheskaia respublika* (Petrograd, 1917), 19.

11 A. N. Potresov, *Posmertnyi sbornik proizvedenii* (Paris, 1937), 230; *Volia naroda*, 17 (30) September and 25 September (8 October) 1917; *Rech'*, 27 April (10 May) 1917.

12 I. G. Tsereteli, *Vospominaniia o Fevral'skoi revoliutsii*, bk. 1 (Paris, 1963), 147, see also 119; *Rechi A. F. Kerenskogo* (Kiev, 1917), 8.

13 See *Narodnyi slovar'* (Petrograd, 1917), 11; *Narodnyi tolkovyi slovar'* (Petrograd, 1917), 8; *Politicheskii slovar': Obshchedostupnoe izlozhenie inostrannykh i drugikh slov, voshedshikh v russkii iazyk* (Petrograd, 1917), 8ff.; *Politicheskii slovar'*, comp. V. I. (Piriatin, 1917), 14; *Kratkii politicheskii slovar' c prilozheniem svedenii o glavneishikh russkikh politicheskikh partiiakh: Posobie pri chtenii gazet i knig po obshchim voprosam*, comp. I. Vladislavlev (Moscow, 1917), 14.

14 *Politicheskii slovar'*, comp. Pr. Zvenigorodtsev (Moscow, 1917), [column 6] 16; *Tolkovatel' neponiatnykh slov v gazetakh i knigakh* (Odessa, 1917), 8.

15 Grigor'ev, *Demokraticheskaia respublika*, 8–9.

16 P. Volkov, *Revoliutsionnyi katekhizis (Karmannaia politicheskaia entsiklopediia)* (Moscow, 1917), 7.

17 *Politicheskii slovar'* (Piriatin, 1917), 22.

18 N. A. Arsen'ev, *Kratkii politicheskii slovar' dlia vsekh* (Moscow, 1917), 9; *Tolkovnik politicheskikh slov i politicheskikh deiatelei* (Petrograd, 1917), 22.

19 For example, on 19 August, I. G. Tsereteli announced: "At the Moscow Conference, organized democracy resisted privileged Russia for the first time," *Mensheviki v 1917 g.*, vol. 2, *Ot iiul'skikh sobytii do kornilovskogo miatezha* (Moscow, 1995), 337.

20 Z. Galili, *Lidery men'shevikov v russkoi revoliutsii: Sotsial'nye realii i politicheskaia strategiia* (Moscow, 1993), 421.

21 *Birzhevye vedomosti*, 22 April (5 May) 1917; *Pervyi den' Vserossiiskogo Uchreditel'nogo sobraniia* (Petrograd, 1918), 36, 45.

22 I. G. Tsereteli, *Vospominaniia*, bk. 1, pp. 61, 121; bk. 2, pp. 194, 394, 402.

23 Potresov, *Posmertnyi sbornik proizvedenii*, 299. Potresov linked Bolshevism to "revolutionary democracy" even in 1926; see S. Ivanov, *A. N. Potresov: Opyt kul'turno-psikhologicheskogo portreta* (Paris, 1938), 211.

24 S. E. Trubetskoi, *Minuvshee* (Moscow, 1991), 172–73.

25 Kerensky, *Russia and History's Turning Point*, 411; *Petrogradskii Sovet rabochikh i soldatskikh deputatov v 1917 godu: Protokoly, stenogrammy i otchety, rezoliutsii, postanovleniia obshchikh sobranii, sobranii sektsii, zasedanii Ispolnitel'nogo komiteta i fraktsii 27 fevralia–25 oktiabria 1917 goda* (St. Petersburg, 1993), 77–78.

26 *Vserossiiskoe soveshchanie Sovetov rabochikh i soldatskikh deputatov: Stenograficheskii otchet* (Moscow, 1927), 68; A. F. Kerenskii, *Izdaleka: Sbornik statei (1920–1921)* (Paris, 1922), 93, 164, 165.

27 Pitcher, *Witnesses of the Russian Revolution*, 117; Public Record Office, War Office, 158/964; G. Buchanan, *My Mission to Russia and Other Diplomatic Memories* (London, 1923), 2:128.

28 Public Record Office, Foreign Office, section 371, box 3015, N 225904, p. 250.

29 N. A. Berdiaev, "Pravda i lozh' v obshchestvennoi zhizni," *Narodopravstvo* 4 (1917): 7; N. A. Berdiaev, "Kontrrevoliutsiia," *Russkaia svoboda*, 1917, nos. 10–11:6.

30 Buchanan, *My Mission to Russia*, 2:86, 114, see also 2:111, 128, 216–17; L. de Robien, *The Diary of a Diplomat in Russia, 1917–1918* (London, 1969), 24; Terence Emmons and Bertrand M. Patenaude, comps, and eds., *War, Revolution and Peace in Russia: The Passages of Frank Golder, 1914–1927* (Stanford, 1992), 46.

31 Rossiiskii gosudarstvennyi voenno-istoricheskii arkhiv, f. 2003, op. 1, d. 1494, l. 14; Otdel rukopisei Rossiiskoi Natsional'noi biblioteki (formerly Gosudarstvennaia Publichnaia biblioteka im. M. E. Saltykova-Shchedrina), f. 152, op. 1, d. 98, l. 34.

32 See D. P. Os'kin, *Zapiski praporshchika* (Moscow, 1931), 110–11.

33 St. Antony's College (Oxford), Russian and East European Centre, G. Katkov's Papers; *Moskovskii Sovet rabochikh deputatov (1917–1922)*, 10.

34 The testimony of the eminent historian N. I. Kareev is significant in this regard. He spent the summer in the countryside, where a local blacksmith told him: "I would like ... our republic to be socialist." It turned out that the blacksmith, who had separated his farm from the commune, was in favor of a guarantee of private property and against a presidential form of governance. N. I. Kareev, *Prozhitoe i perezhitoe* (Leningrad, 1990), 268.

35 Gosudarstvennyi arkhiv Rossiiskoi federatsii, f. 1778, op. 1, d. 83, l. 92; d. 85, l. 7; d. 90, l. 50; on the cult of Kerenskii, see A. G. Golikov, "Fenomen Kerenskogo," *Otechestvennaia istoriia*, 1992, no. 5; on the relationship between

Kerenskii and the intelligentsia, see B. I. Kolonitskii, "A. F. Kerenskii i Merezhkovskie," *Literaturnoe obozrenie*, 1991, no. 3.

36 Gosudarstvennyi muzei politicheskoi istorii Rossii (Sankt-Peterburg), f. 2, N. 10964: see also A. Kulegin and V. Bobrov, "Istoriia bez kupiur," *Sovetskie muzei*, 1990, no. 3:5–6.

37 Richard Abraham, *Alexander Kerensky: The First Love of the Revolution* (London, 1987), 200. It is interesting that Kerenskii himself gradually changed his image. At first he emphasized his democratism – handshakes, black jacket. As "the people's minister," however, he demonstrated an imperial style – moving into the tsar's apartments, using the imperial automobiles, assuming the pose of Napoleon. This created the basis for many rumors connecting Kerenskii to the tsar's family.

38 On the "language of class," see Diane P. Koenker, "Moscow in 1917: The View from Below," in Daniel H. Kaiser, ed., *The Workers' Revolution in Russia, 1917: The View from Below* (Cambridge, 1987), 91–92.

39 A similar conclusion was reached by William Rosenberg after studying another problem with different sources. See Rosenberg, "Sozdanie novogo gosudarstva v 1917 g.: Predstavleniia i deistvitel'nost'," *Anatomiia revoliutsii: 1917 god v Rossii: Massy, partii, vlast'* (St. Petersburg, 1994), 97.

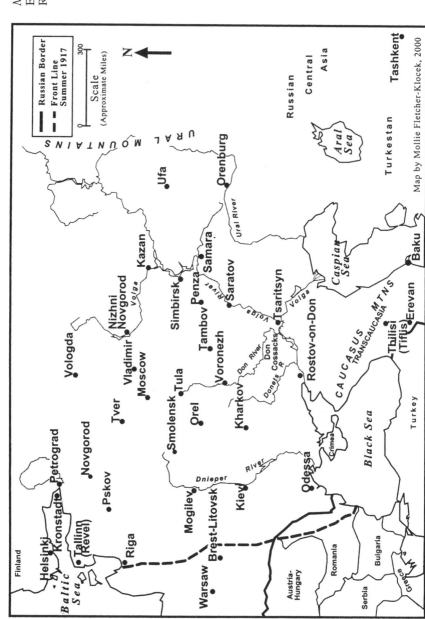

Map 2
European
Russia, 1917.

Russian Border

Front Line
Summer 1917

Scale
(Approximate Miles)

0 300

N

Finland

Baltic Sea

Helsinki

Kronstadt

Tallinn (Revel)

Petrograd

Riga

Pskov

Novgorod

Warsaw

Brest-Litovsk

Mogilev

Kiev

Smolensk

Tver

Vologda

Vladimir

Moscow

Nizhni Novgorod

Kazan

Ufa

URAL MOUNTAINS

Orenburg

Simbirsk

Tula

Orel

Tambov

Penza

Samara

Saratov

Voronezh

Kharkov

Dnieper River

Don River

Donets R.

Don Cossacks

Tsaritsyn

Volga River

Volga

Ural River

Odessa

Crimea

Rostov-on-Don

Black Sea

Caspian Sea

Aral Sea

CAUCASUS MTNS

TRANSCAUCASIA

Tbilisi (Tiflis)

Baku

Erevan

Turkey

Russian Central Asia

Turkestan

Tashkent

Austria-Hungary

Romania

Bulgaria

Serbia

Greece

Map by Mollie Fletcher-Klocek, 2000

5

THE RUSSIAN REVOLUTION OF 1917 AND ITS LANGUAGE IN THE VILLAGE

Orlando Figes

Orlando Figes here combines an exploration of the uses of symbolism and language with his study of the often ignored peasants. He sketches the political worldview of the peasants – their ideas about democracy and monarchy, their idea of citizenship and equality, the ways they viewed the role of the state and nation, and their understanding of class and "socialism." While concerned with the view "from below," Figes also looks at the problem "from above." The Provisional Government believed that one of its primary responsibilities was to "educate the people in their civil rights and duties." Like revolutionaries in France in 1789, their task was to create a new political nation, and they saw the integration of peasants into this as especially important to this goal. In this as in other tasks they had to depend on the power of the word to establish the government's authority. Yet there was a vast gulf between the vocabularies and concepts of the educated/urban and the uneducated/rural worlds. The intelligentsia, from all parties as well as non-party individuals, set out to break down the linguistic barriers with a wide variety of publications, orators, congresses, and discussion circles, all of which sought to connect the urban revolution and ideas of educated society to the peasant world. The peasants, however, digested that information and news of events from the perspective of their own values and experience. They took ideas, words, and concepts and fitted them into their own worldview and interests, often significantly altering them in the process. It is this complex world of the peasant, and the role of symbols and language, especially the new Western-derived political and social vocabulary, that Figes explores. In doing so he also points our attention away from the traditional focus on peasant actions such as land seizure – important as those were – to peasants as political actors and to how they understood the revolution in all its complexity.

* * *

The Provisional Government was a government of persuasion. Not having been elected by the people, it depended largely on the power of the word to establish its authority. It was a government of national confidence, self-appointed during the February Revolution with the aim of steering Russia through the war-time crisis toward democracy, and as such its mandate had to a large extent to be created by propaganda, cults, and festivals, fostering consensus and national unity. There was little else the government could do, since it lacked the power to enforce its will by any other means. And yet many of its liberal leaders also saw a virtue in this necessity. They rejected the traditions of the tsarist state, emphasized the need to govern by consent, and, in the words of Prince G. E. Lvov, the prime minister, placed their faith in the "good sense, statesmanship and loyalty of the people" to uphold the new democracy.[1]

Their optimism was based on the assumption that the primary duty of the February Revolution was to educate the people in their civic rights and duties. Like the French revolutionaries of 1789, they understood their task as nothing less than the creation of a new political nation. The peasants, above all, who made up more than three-quarters of the population, had to be transformed into active citizens. They had to be brought out of their cultural isolation and integrated into the national political culture. Upon that hung the Revolution's fate – and not just because it depended on the peasants to fulfill their civic duty by supplying food-stuffs and soldiers for the nation, but even more importantly because, as the vast majority of the electorate, it required them to vote as citizens, free from the domination of their former masters (landowners, priests, and monarchist officials), in the elections to the Constituent Assembly and the other institutions of the nascent democracy.

The "darkness" of the peasants – and its inherent dangers for the Revolution – was the constant refrain of democratic agitators in the countryside during 1917. "The peasants do not understand anything about politics," wrote one soldier from Penza Province to the Petrograd Soviet on 25 April. "Although there were deputies [that is, Soviet agitators], the peasants soon forgot what they had told them about freedom, a republic, and a monarchy."[2] As one provincial propagandist concluded:

> The peasant is still very easily deceived by monarchist officials and other dark forces in his midst. He has never been acquainted with the most elementary political questions, he has never received the education of a citizen. But the peasants, whose votes will decide the political and socioeconomic structure of the Russian state, have to become citizens, with an understanding of the different forms of rule and an ability to make rational choices between different political points of view, immediately![3]

Language was the key to this cultural integration of the peasantry. The dissemination of the Revolution's rhetoric to the countryside – the development of a national discourse of civic rights and duties – would create the new political nation dreamed of by the leaders of democracy. Here again there were clear parallels with France. For just as in France there was an enormous gulf between the French written culture of the Revolution and the patois oral culture of the peasantry, so in Russia there was an equal divide between the political language of the towns and the terms in which the peasants couched their own moral and political concepts.

The terminology of the Revolution was a foreign language to most of the peasants (as indeed it was to a large proportion of the uneducated workers) in most parts of Russia.[4] Of course, there were important variations. The younger, richer, and better-educated peasants tended to be more politically aware, as did those living closest to the towns or in regions with a well-developed network of party and peasant organization (in parts of the North, the middle Volga, or western Siberia, for example).[5] But in general the peasants and their spokesmen in 1917 were painfully aware of the linguistic gulf that separated them from the Revolution in the towns. "We can't understand many of your words," complained one peasant to the SR leaders of the Kurgan' peasant congress during a debate on the structure of the state – "you have to speak in Russian."[6] Imported words ("republic," "constitution," "federation," "democracy," "regime," "annexation," and even "revolution") were misunderstood and mispronounced by peasants. Thus the word "republic" (*respublika*) appeared as *despublika* and *razbublika* in various peasant letters; "regime" (*rezhim*) became *prizhim*; "constituent" (*uchreditel'noe*) was transformed into *chereditlel'noe* (on the basis that the Constituent Assembly would decide everything "in its turn," or *cheredom*); "revolution" (*revoliutsiia*) was pronounced and written *as revutsia, levoliutsiia*, and *levorutsia*; the "Bolsheviks" (*bol'sheviki*) were confused with a party of *bol'shaki* (peasant elders) and of *bol'shie* (big people); while "annexation" (*anneksiia*) was thought by many peasant soldiers to be a small Balkan kingdom neighboring *kontributsiia* (the Russian word for "indemnity") and at least on one occasion was confused with a woman called "Aksinia." "Who is this Aksinia?" one peasant asked another who had heard about her from an "oratater" (*oratel'* instead of *orator*). "God knows who she is. They say that because of her there will be a great harm, and that if there is Aksinia there will be another war against us after we have made peace with the Germans." "Ooh she must be bad: over one woman there is war again!" ("Ish' ved' kakaia vrednaia: ot odnoi baby i opiat' voina!").[7]

Equally, the new institutions of the state appeared strange and alien to many of the peasants. For example, a group of wounded peasant soldiers in a Petrograd hospital wrote through a scribe a series of petitions to the Tauride Palace in September. Each one started with the clumsy words: "I have the honor humbly to ask the Tauride Palace not to refuse me an extraordinary pension as a wounded veteran of the war." None of the petitions was addressed to an official body – indeed the palace was empty by this time, the Duma having closed its offices and the Soviet having moved to the Smolny – and it seems the soldiers had no idea of who was in the building. The Tauride Palace – perhaps because of the connotations of the word "palace" or perhaps because it had become a symbol of the Revolution (which frequently appeared in propaganda posters) – simply meant to them the seat of power.[8]

Such misunderstandings were a major hindrance to the democratic cause in the countryside. Its propaganda had to cross a huge linguistic gulf to communicate with the peasantry. The first pamphlets for the rural population were mostly reprints of editions written during the 1905 Revolution. According to a valuable report by the Temporary Committee of the Duma during May, they had been written "in a language which the people do not speak. . . . They needed translators." The report concluded that "it played a major role in the rapid alienation of the peasantry from the intelligentsia."[9]

A related problem was the peasants' inclination to believe naively in every printed word. Long starved of an open press, they were hungry for any printed news, especially about the war and the latest events in the capital, and as a result they tended to believe that whatever was printed must be true. The Duma report thought that, as a rule,

> The less literate a peasant is, the more he believes in the written word. He has a conviction that if something is printed in a book then it is the truth. He reads one newspaper – and that is one truth; then he reads another – where there is another, even if it is directly contrary to the first. He sits there and tries to work it out "freely" – until his head begins to spin.[10]

Such credulity could make the peasant vulnerable to demagogues, as Kerensky warned in his famous "rebellious slaves" speech to the soldiers' delegates at the end of April, when he spoke of those who "even now take every printed word for truth."[11] One may well ask in this context whether there was any extra persuasive power in the newspaper of the Bolsheviks because it was called *Pravda*.

Oral forms of propaganda had the same problems. Too many agitators spoke in terms the peasants could not understand, especially in the early months before they had been trained for their rural trips. Too many talked at them in long and boring speeches rather than engaging them in lively conversations. The educative purpose of the peasant congresses was similarly lost, especially in the early months, because of the tendency of the congress leaders, most of whom were SR *intelligenty*, to speak in abstract terms far above the heads of the peasant delegates. At the Kurgan' peasant congress during April, for example, the SR leaders of the congress became embroiled in a long debate about the relative merits of various federative principles. The peasant delegates became restless, and at last one intervened: "I have been listening for two hours and can't understand: is this an assembly for peasants or for speech-making? If this is a peasant assembly, then the peasants ought to speak." There was a general hum of approval so that, while insisting on the need to discuss such important questions, the SR leaders felt obliged to explain the meaning of a federation to the delegates in terms that were more comprehensible to them. They chose to compare the federal division of the state to the division of the communal land. But this merely gave rise to more misunderstandings. One group of delegates said they did not want to "divide Russia," while another suggested "taking away the land of the nobles and dividing it between the peasants" – only to be told, "that is not the question."[12] The all-too-frequent consequence of such abstract debates was that the peasant delegates forgot what had been said. As the Duma report put it:

> There are occasions when a deputy returning from Petrograd, where he has been deluged by noisy rhetoric and the storm of party arguments and debates, replies to the question about what he had heard there: "I have forgotten! I've forgotten everything I heard. I heard so much that in the end I could remember nothing." He has become confused and forgotten all. And his fellow-villagers put him into jail because they have paid him to travel to the city and he has told them nothing.[13]

Bridging the linguistic gulf?

The democratic intelligentsia set out with the passion of civic missionaries to break down these linguistic barriers and communicate the gospel of their revolution to the peasantry. It was like another "Going to the people" – the propaganda mission of the Populists in the 1870s – only now the government was on their side. Dictionaries were published to explain the Revolution's strange vocabulary.[14] And there was a whole new range of pamphlets for the peasants telling them what they should know to become citizens.[15] The new rural press also took upon itself the political education of its peasant readers. Many papers had a column such as "Letters from the Village," or "Answers to Your Questions," in which issues raised by peasants were explained. Most of these were technical concerns to do with the land and property, yet they often touched on politics as well. Many of the SR papers, in particular, also published so-called letters "From a Soldier" which were thinly disguised propaganda. The "soldier" (a party activist in the ranks) would call on his peasant "brothers" to help in the defense of their freedom and their farms by giving up their harvest surplus to the government. Such appeals were often couched in religious terms: "Your conscience says it's sinful to think about yourself while your brothers spill their blood. ... Make a sacrifice, as we soldiers are doing to defend you. We are just to say this."[16]

There was also a small number of newspapers specifically intended for the political education of the peasants, such as the tabloid *Narodnaia gazeta* put out twice a week in the Kerenskii district of Penza Province between May and September. "The aim of our newspaper," its editors declared, "is to help the people understand the events of the war, national and local political life, and to enable every citizen to play a conscious role in the construction of a new life." It printed explanations of political terms and articles with titles such as "What is freedom and why has it been given to us?" or "What is socialism and will it arrive soon?"[17]

The supply of this literature could not keep up with demand. Of course, there were places where the peasants were indifferent to politics, and where any propaganda was torn up by them for cigarette paper. But in general there was a huge demand for news and explanatory literature. The war had opened up the peasants' world and made them more aware that their own daily lives were closely connected with national and international affairs. The publications of the peasant unions and provincial peasant assemblies often had to be reprinted several times. Hand-printed and mimeographed copies were also distributed in huge quantities. A second stenographic edition of the 1905 All-Russian Peasant Union Congress, published in the spring of 1917, carried on its title page a warning from the Main Committee of the Union that there were so many of these unofficial versions that it could not be held responsible for them.[18] The Petrograd Soviet, in particular, but also the Duma and the Provisional Government received hundreds of peasant appeals for political literature. As the Duma report put it, the phrase "we are dark people" (*my temnye*), which the peasants had used ironically, now contained a message of "sincere regret: there is so much the peasants want to know but cannot understand." It cited the moving words of one peasant from Pskov: "There are no words to explain the shame and pain that engulf a man when he realizes that even what has been given to him is too hard for him to understand, and is like a stone instead of bread."[19]

In addition to pamphlets and newspapers the peasant leaders appealed for agitators, often specifically to help them counteract the influence of the local priests or monarchist officials, or to help them dispel rumors undermining confidence in the Revolution.[20] The demand for such people was increased by the flight of the rural intelligentsia from the countryside during 1917.[21] Impoverished, demoralized, and threatened by the violence of the peasant revolution, many teachers, vets, and doctors fled to the towns. Yet these were the very people who in former years had read the newspapers to the peasants, explained to them the meaning of the news, interpreted decrees, and acted as their scribes to the authorities.

A wide range of public bodies – from working-class organizations to sailors' and soldiers' delegations – dispatched agitators to the countryside. Teachers' bodies were particularly active.[22] One of their main professional journals carried a regular article entitled "For the aid of teachers in their conversations with the population on current affairs," in which they were advised on how best to engage the attention of their peasant audience.[23] Many of the provincial peasant congresses, and even some of the district ones, organized their own teams of rural propagandists to acquaint the peasants with their resolutions or to counteract the influence of local monarchists.[24] In Perm, Nizhegorod, Vladimir, Saratov, and Viatka the provincial zemstvos and public committees trained and paid for "lectors" and "translators" (*perevodchiki*) from the local intelligentsia to go to the peasants and explain to them the main issues of the day.[25]

In Moscow, Petrograd, and Kaluga there was a religiously oriented group called the Union for the Free Person which set up lecture and discussion circles for the peasantry.[26] Democratic priests and seminarians also doubled up as propagandists, the priests often using the church service to preach about the "Christian mission of the revolution" to their peasant worshipers. For example, the chaplain of the 105th Orenburg Regiment gave a speech in the church of Slipki village on Trinity Sunday (21 May) in which he compared the revolutionaries to Jesus Christ, the "liberator of poor and oppressed peasants and the proletariat" from their "enslavement" to the "Roman tsars."[27] Finally, there was a Society for the Political Education of the Army and Wide Sections of the Population, set up by the zemstvos and cooperatives in several provinces, which trained volunteers (mainly teachers and students) for propaganda work among the peasantry and sent them out to the villages and army units to explain to them the duties of a citizen.[28]

All these missionaries faced the same problem: how to talk to the peasants about politics so that they would listen and understand. It was an old problem, going back at least to the 1870s and the "Going to the people," but it was now more urgent since upon it hung the fate of the democracy.

Many books and articles were published on this problem during 1917. E. N. Medynskii's *How to Conduct Conversations on Political Issues* was perhaps the best known of these manuals, selling 50,000 copies in its first edition, and up to 40,000 more in two further editions of 1917.[29] But close behind came his *The Revolution and Education Out of School*, which sold up to 70,000 copies in its two editions of the same year.[30] Both gave advice on how to talk with peasants on political issues. The agitator should speak in the language of the peasants and avoid using foreign words. It was important not to give a "dry and official speech" but to have a "conversation" with the audience and to ask them questions from time to time. The agitator was to illustrate his arguments with examples drawn from peasant daily life. The war, for example, might be compared with a village fight, in which one side (Russia) fights fairly and the other (Germany) unfairly. To explain the advantages of a republic over a monarchy the speaker might say:

> Would it be good if you could not judge the chairman of your cooperative or your *volost'* [district] elder? If he spends your money, or loses it, or rules the *volost'* badly – he is always right. You cannot replace him or take him to court. "Do not dare to touch me, to judge me is a sin," he says to you. The same happens with a monarchy. The tsar, however bad, is always right.[31]

One can detect the same philosophy in the rhetoric of the democratic leaders. They made a conscious effort to explain the abstract concepts of democracy in simple concrete terms for the peasantry. The February Revolution was often portrayed as an enormous *physical* effort – comparable to the peasants' own back-breaking toil. "The Russian people has pulled itself free . . . [and] thrown off the heavy chains of tsarist slavery."[32] Notions of statehood and civic duty were couched in metaphors from peasant daily life. The postrevolutionary state was depicted as a "beautiful new house" whose construction, like a village house, required the participation of all its inhabitants.[33] The purpose of the Constituent Assembly was explained by analogy with the cooperatives, which were normally organized at a "constituent assembly" of their members where the administration was elected and the rules of the society defined.[34] Where there were no cooperatives, and the word "constituent" was foreign to the peasants, agitators used the word *narodnoe* ("people's") instead, since this was familiar. Thus one peasant leader in Olonets Province ended a speech with the rallying cry: "Long live Land and Freedom and the People's Assembly! (*narodnoe sobranie*)."[35] The word *narodnyi* was also substituted for other foreign words (for example, "democratic" and "national").[36] Similarly, the "nationalization" of the land was frequently explained as the transfer of the land to the "people's" property.[37]

Family metaphors for society – which were a staple of the political rhetoric of the nineteenth-century revolutionaries – featured prominently in the language of the democratic leaders of the peasantry. "The Russian people wants to be and must be a single family of brother-laborers," wrote the peasant propagandist Alexander Os'minin in his brochure for the first-time rural voter.[38] Two fundamental ideas of democracy were contained in this metaphor: that the people's victory as a brotherhood was incompatible with their domination by patriarchal figures like the "father tsar"; and that its success depended on the expression of that brotherhood as a sense of duty to the nation as a whole. The peasants' obligation to supply the army was often couched in these familial terms of national unity. "If the village does not give its harvest," declared the *Izvestiia* of the Peasant Soviet, "then the ones to suffer will be the poor people and the soldiers, the brothers of the peasantry by blood and destiny."[39] The need for the officers and soldiers to unite was similarly described in familial terms – as in this telegram to the Soviet: "The soldiers and the officer-citizens of the 16th Irkutsk Hussar Regiment, united in a single compact family, send their heart-felt greetings to the Soviet of Workers' and Soldiers' Deputies in celebration of 1 May."[40] Last but not least, the democratic leaders also used the metaphor of the family to assert their status as "the best sons of the nation" because they had "sat in tsarist jails and suffered for their brothers, the peasantry."[41]

How effective was this rhetoric? How far, and in what forms, did the peasants understand the political concepts of the democratic revolution in the towns? It is always difficult to know what peasants think. They may speak in one language to each other, address outsiders in another, and, as far as they are able, write or dictate petitions to the authorities in a third "official" language.[42] Peasants often adopt the language of a politically dominant urban culture without necessarily believing in its values – indeed they may do so to dissimulate conformity to it, to legitimate their own aims and actions, or to ridicule and subvert it. In short, behind the public discourse of any peasantry there may be (and often is) what J. C. Scott has called a "hidden transcript," carried through the language of village songs and jokes, rumor and gossip, largely impenetrable to the outside world.[43] In 1917 the peasants would write humble petitions to the Provisional Government, prefacing them with stock phrases of religious thanks, deferential greetings, and heart-felt declarations of loyalty – and then go on to demand the release of their sons from the army or the right to confiscate the landowners' land. Or they would pretend that "we are dark people" – echoing the urban myth about the peasantry – to explain and justify their own neglect or contravention of the law. But it would be mistaken to conclude from this that the peasants were indifferent to – and remained untouched by – the new democratic political culture spreading down toward them from the towns. The peasants had their own forms of politicization, their own *prise de conscience politique*, in which certain aspects of the public discourse might be adopted to articulate their own political ideals and traditions, while other aspects of it might be consciously ignored because they could not be "peasantized."

The remainder of this essay shall attempt to sketch the political world-view of the peasants – their construction of the state and the nation, their ideas of citizenship and equality – insofar as these may be inferred from their village resolutions and petitions, their private letters and recorded conversations, and the statements of peasant delegates at provincial assemblies. Of course, the reader should bear in mind that sometimes these records have come down to us through nonpeasant intermediaries – scribes, officials, schoolteachers, and other spokesmen for the peasants – and hence may be couched in a language that reflects the intelligentsia's construction of the peasantry ("dark," "dependent," "pious," and so on) rather than the discourse of the peasantry itself. But in the absence of any other sources, and with the proviso that those used below are approached critically, it seems appropriate to proceed.

Peasant monarchical attitudes

The idea that the peasant was at heart a monarchist remains one of the most enduring myths of Russian history.[44] Yet throughout Russia in 1917 the peasantry rejected the monarchy. As the Duma report wittily concluded:

> The widespread myth that the Russian peasant is devoted to the tsar and that he "cannot live" without him has been destroyed by the universal joy and relief felt by the peasants upon discovering that in reality they *can* live without the tsar, without whom they were told they "could not live." The scandal of Rasputin, which is known in even the remotest villages, has helped to destroy the status of the tsar. Now the peasants say: "The tsar brought himself down and brought us to ruin."[45]

Of course, not all the peasants were equally decided. Many were afraid to speak their minds until the land captains and police were removed – which in some provinces (Mogilev and Kazan, for instance) was not completed until April – and even then they were hesitant in case the Revolution was reversed.[46] Many of the older peasants were confused by the downfall of the tsar.[47] "The church was full of crying peasants," one witness recalled. "'What will become of us?' they constantly repeated – 'They have taken the tsar away from us.'"[48] Some of these older peasants had venerated the tsar as a god on earth (they crossed themselves whenever his name was mentioned) and saw his removal as an attack on religion – a fact exploited by many priests and monarchist officials in their counterrevolutionary propaganda. Even among the more rural workers the tsar's removal could give rise to religious doubts. The American Frank Golder talked with one such worker, "an old muzhik," in mid-March, who "said it was a sin to overthrow the emperor, since God had placed him in power. It may be that the new regime will help people on this earth, but they will surely pay for it in the world to come."[49] The patrimonial conception of the tsar – as the "master (*khoziain*) *of* the Russian land" – also found expression in these fears. "How can Russia survive without its master?" one old Tambov peasant asked.[50]

But generally the news of the tsar's abdication was welcomed joyously. "Our village," wrote one peasant, "burst into life with celebrations. Everyone felt enormous relief, as if a heavy rock had suddenly been lifted from our shoulders." Another wrote: "People kissed each other from joy and said that life from now on would be good. Everyone dressed in their best costumes, as they do on a big holiday. The festivities lasted three days."[51] Many villages held religious processions to thank the Lord for their newly won freedoms, offering up prayers for the new government. The Revolution thus attained the status of a religious cult, while those who had died fighting for freedom (*bortsy za svobodu*) were venerated as modern saints. The villagers of Bol'she-Dvorskaia *volost'* in Tikhvinsk district, for example, held a "service of thanksgiving for the divine gift of the people's victory and the eternal memory of those holy men who fell in the struggle for freedom."[52] To reciprocate this sacrifice many villages sent donations of money, often amounting to several hundred rubles, to the authorities in Petrograd for the benefit of those who had suffered losses in the February Days.

What is striking here is the extent to which the peasantry identified itself with the ideas and the symbols of the republic. There was of course a precedent here. The establishment of a republic had been a basic demand of the peasant unions and the rural socialists ever since the 1905 Revolution. And events since then ("Bloody Sunday" and the suppression of the peasant disorders during 1905–7; the gross mismanagement of the war campaign and its criminal wastage of human life; the scandal of Rasputin and the rumors of treason at the court) had already shaken many of the peasants from their old belief in the tsar's benevolence and the sacred sources of his power. Nonetheless, it is still remarkable how far and how fast the idea of the republic took root among certain sections of the peasantry. The most educated peasants and those living closest to the towns readily adopted the rhetoric and metaphors of the new republican propaganda in their petitions to the authorities. The form of the republic was heatedly debated at most provincial peasant congresses. Hundreds of villages passed formal resolutions in favor of a republic and sent them to the authorities. Some of them took part in the "Festivals of Freedom" and the "Peasant Days," sponsored respectively by the Provisional Government and the Peasant Soviet, where the symbols and the public rituals of the nineteenth-century republican tradition (planting "Trees of Liberty," singing the "Marseillaise," and constructing memorials to those who had died in the struggle against the monarchy) played a major role in the celebrations.[53]

For many peasants, however, the idea of the republic remained confused with the idea of the monarchy. The British ambassador, George Buchanan, was told by one peasant soldier in the spring: "Yes, we need a republic, but at its head there should be a good tsar."[54] Similarly, Frank Golder noted during March: "Stories are being told of soldiers who say they wish a republic like England, or a republic with a tsar. One soldier said he wanted to elect a president and when asked, 'Whom would you elect?' he replied, 'The tsar.'"[55] Many soldiers' letters voiced the same confusion. "We want a democratic republic and a *tsar-batiushka* for three years," declared one regiment. "It would be good if we had a republic with a wise tsar," concluded another.[56] It seems that the peasants found it difficult to distinguish between the person of the sovereign (*gosudar'*) and the abstract institutions of the state (*gosudarstvo*). Hence many peasant soldiers were confused by the new oath of allegiance to the Provisional Government, with some even refusing to swear it because it contained the word *gosudarstvo*. "We are not for a gosudarstvo," the soldiers reasoned, "we are for a republic."[57] They conceived of the state as embodied in a monarch, and projected their ideals onto a "peasant king" or some other authoritarian liberator, come to deliver their cherished land and freedom. Here, at least in part, were the popular roots of the cults of Kerensky, the "people's champion," and of Lenin, too. Both were attempts to fill the space left by the myth of the tsar-deliverer. Indeed, at times it seemed that almost anyone could perform the role of the peasants' king, such was their demand for outside leadership. A few weeks after the February Revolution a Menshevik deputy of the Moscow Soviet went to agitate at a regimental meeting near Vladimir. He spoke of the need for peace, of the need for the land to be given to the peasants, and of the advantages of a republic over monarchy. The peasant soldiers cheered loudly and one of them called out, "We want to elect you as tsar," whereupon the other soldiers burst into applause. "I refused the Romanov crown," recalled the Menshevik, "and went away with a heavy feeling of how easy it would be for any adventurer or demagogue to become the master of this simple and naive people."[58]

This monarchical republicanism mirrored in some ways the philosophy and practice of the village assembly, where there was a strange mix between the principles of democratic self-rule by open debate and patriarchal rule by the village elders. During 1917 it was reflected in the way that many peasants believed the new democratic institutions ought to operate. Thus it was common for the peasants to declare that the

Constituent Assembly should "take complete power in its hands" or "become the master (*khoziain*) of the Russian land" in the manner of an autocrat.[59] Two old peasants were heard in conversation in a railway carriage during the autumn, and although this version, printed in the press, may have been exaggerated to amuse the reader, it conveys the spirit of their words:

> *First peasant.* The Constituent Assembly, brother, will be the master; and because we the peasants will be voting, it will be a peasant one (*budet muzhitskim*). The peasant cannot stand disorder. Our business is a serious business: we feed everyone. And for our work we need peace and order. We have not had that. There have been too many changes . . .
>
> *Second peasant.* Too many! We don't like changes! Under the tsar everything was normal, but now it is hard to keep up with the changes.
>
> *First peasant.* Our rulers today – they have thought of everything, but they don't have any real strength. They are unable to rule the people strictly as they ought to do. But the Constituent Assembly – that, my friend, will be the real master. It will put everyone in their place. Do not disobey! Do not shout! Wait for us to give you your land and freedom! Great deeds cannot be achieved in a single day. The peasantry has waited a long time for their land and freedom. It has to be done properly – not just for us but also for our children and grandchildren – and for that we need a master's hand (*khoziaiskaia ruka*).[60]

The need for a "master's hand" to maintain order and defend their interests was a frequent theme in the peasants' statements on politics. This authoritarianism was, at least in their view, quite compatible with the democratic goals of the Revolution. So much for the notion of most historians that the Russian peasant was at heart an "anarchist" and rejected the need for a strong authority. On the contrary, many peasant resolutions spoke out in support of a "firm power" (*tverdaia vlast'*) to end the disorder in the country and force the other classes to accept their revolution on the land.[61] The sociologist S. S. Maslov, paraphrasing what the peasants had told him during 1917, claimed that they distinguished between the need for a strong government at the national level and the right of self-rule in the localities:

> There can be no order without a stable power A stable power needs a single person in whose hands are concentrated force and many rights. Such a person ought to be a president but under no circumstances a tsar. A president is elected by the people, he

is temporary and can be supervised, but a tsar is like a *volost'* elder who would rule the *volost'* all his life and on his death would pass on his power to his children. With such an elder one could not live. The Russian state should be unified, but it must not oppress the people – let everyone think, believe and speak as they wish, as their mother and father taught them. Local matters must not be left to bureaucrats from Moscow or Petrograd. The people should be given complete freedom to organize their own local affairs.[62]

But some peasants also advocated running local government on the same authoritarian lines as it had been run under the tsarist regime, albeit now in the revolutionary interests of the people. At the Tambov provincial peasant congress in mid-September one delegate argued:

The Soviets do not need the sort of power which the Bolsheviks are foisting upon them – the power to appoint and mix ministers: that is not power but powerlessness. No, give them the power to make people listen, as they once listened to the [provincial] governors. Surely if we are not fully organized for power and cannot use it, then it will be the cause of our downfall. Our enemies will say – they are good for nothing!

Another peasant took up the same theme: "What was the strength of the old regime? It had autocrats at every level – Nicholas, the governor, and the policeman. Let us arrange things so that today there is a people's autocracy (*samoderzhavie narodnoe*)!"[63]

Peasant notions of citizenship

During the course of 1917 the word *grazhdane* spread throughout the countryside as a term of peasant self-identity. Village resolutions and petitions tended increasingly to begin with the words, "We the citizens" (*My grazhdane*) of such and such a village, rather than the old phrase, "We the peasants" (*My krest'iane*).[64] Delegates to peasant congresses referred to each other as "citizens" during the debates. This new self-identification was no doubt a source of pride for many peasants. It was a badge of equality with the other classes of society, a society from which they had always been excluded by a comprehensive range of legal discriminations against them. The abolition of the old class system of legal estates (*sosloviia*), a legacy from serfdom which guaranteed the privileged position of the landed nobles, had long been a demand of the peasant movement. The announcement of the Provisional Government's plans to abolish the *sosloviia* ("on the principle of equal rights for all citizens")[65] was hailed by many peasants – and especially by those in the army, where the privileges of the noble officers was still a source of bitter resentment among the peasant soldiers – as a new emancipation. As one soldiers' resolution put it (with a rhetorical flourish that gave expression to their euphoria), the abolition of the estate system "will bring our freedom to full liberation (*raskreposhcheniia*) from the heavy yoke of slavery, from the eternal prison, and the shameful servitude in which we have lived."[66]

But within the village what did "citizenship" mean? Clearly, it did not mean equal rights for everyone: the peasant revolution was itself class-based and directed against groups outside "peasant society" (landed nobles, townsmen, the intelligentsia, and so on). The peasants' language of citizenship was thus clearly different from that of other classes. One noble officer understood this well when he wrote to his father on 11 March:

> Between us and the soldiers there is an abyss that one cannot cross. Whatever they might think of us as individuals, we in their eyes remain no more than *barins* (masters). When we talk of "the people" (*narod*) we have in mind the nation as a whole, but they mean only the common people (*demokraticheskie nizy*). In their view what has taken place is not a political but a social revolution, of which we are the losers and they are the winners. They think that things should get better for them and that they should get worse for us. They do not believe us when we talk of our devotion to the soldiers. They say that we were the *barins* in the past, and that now it is their turn to be the *barins* over us. It is their revenge for the long centuries of servitude.[67]

One way to review this question is in terms of who was given land and voting rights within the village community (*mir*). Generally, the peasants drew up their own circle of "insiders" and assigned a certain set of rights and duties to each subgroup of the community according to their perceived social value. Peasants who farmed with their own family labor – and former landowners who turned themselves into "peasants" by doing the same – were assigned an equal share of the communal land and full voting rights at the village assembly (*skhod*). The younger peasants, in particular, gained a larger influence at the assembly – partly because the astronomic rate of household partitioning in 1917 created a large number of young household heads (with rights to attend the assembly), and partly because the prestige of the younger peasants increased as a result of their service in the army and the growing need for literate village leaders after the collapse of the old regime and the flight of the rural intelligentsia. Peasant women, too, gained rights at the *skhod*, often as the heads of households in the absence of their husbands on military service. But it was not just the peasants who were given land or rights at the assembly. Nonfarming groups deemed of value to the village (for example, craftsmen who manufactured goods demanded by the peasants, democratic priests and teachers, agronomists and vets, and sometimes landless laborers) were also deemed to be citizens, with a right to share in the benefits of the community. On the other hand, those who were a burden on the village's resources (such as migrants and townspeople without relatives in it) might be given temporary aid "as human beings" but were rarely given land or rights at the *skhod* as "village citizens."[68]

It was common for the peasants to define their own tightly knit community in familial terms. The "peasant family" (*krest'ianskaia sem'ia*) was a stock phrase in their rhetoric, and within the village they addressed each other as if they were kin. A child, for example, would call the men "uncle" or "grandfather," and all the women "auntie" or "grandmother," whether they were related or not. At one level, then, the familial metaphor for society used by the democratic leadership found an echo in the traditional language of the peasantry. But it would be mistaken to conclude from this that the official usage of the metaphor – to define a nation of civic rights and duties – was also adopted by the peasantry. On the contrary, the peasants used the family metaphor to reinterpret these rights and duties so that they would not undermine the traditions and interests of the village.

Take, for example, the question of elections, where the peasants were to exercise their civic rights. The peasants did not vote as individuals but as families or whole communities (that is, the household or village elders decided how to vote and the rest of the peasants followed suit, or, alternatively, the household or the village decided collectively how to vote). This sort of "herd voting," to adopt the phrase of O. H. Radkey, was widely noted in the three main elections of 1917: to the *volost'* zemstvos, the *volost'* soviets, and the Constituent Assembly.[69] There were obvious reasons to vote in this way. It was very hard, if not impossible, to arrange a secret ballot in the Russian village, where voting had always been done in the open (either by shouting or standing in sides) and where, in any case, everybody knew how everybody else was intending to cast their vote. In this context it was more important for the villagers (or household members) to maintain their unity by voting together than it was for them to exercise their voting rights as individual citizens and yet run the risk of becoming divided on party lines. Unity had always been the main priority at the village assembly – its resolutions were by custom passed unanimously – and it was enforced by the patriarchs. Equally, most peasants were quick to condemn the fighting between the socialist parties, which, to extend the familial metaphor, they blamed for the "war of brothers" (*bratoubiistvennaia voina*), the peasant term for the Civil War.[70]

On the issue of taxation, where they were to exercise their civic duties, the family concept of society was similarly interpreted by the peasants to suit their own best interests. Nearly all the peasants recognized the need to give food to the army, where their sons and brothers were fighting for the defense of the motherland, but very few agreed with the need to give food to the workers in the towns. Despite the efforts of the urban propagandists, they felt no kinship with the workers, whose strikes and eight-hour days they held responsible for the problems of the army and the growing shortages of manufactured goods.[71]

Peasant constructions of power and the state

"For hundreds of years the Russian peasant has dreamt of a state with no right to influence the will of the individual and his freedom of action, a state without power over man." Thus wrote Maxim Gorky in 1927.[72] His view of the peasantry as anarchists has been shared by many historians since. Indeed the idea that the peasants wanted nothing to do with the state, that their only aim was to free themselves completely from its influence and to rule themselves in their own villages, has become the dominant conception of the rural revolution in the Western historiography of 1917.

It is, of course, true that among the peasantry there was a marked preference for localist solutions to the social problems of 1917 (land and food distribution above all), and that this formed part of a general peasant drive toward autonomy from the state.[73] But this does not mean that the peasants were indifferent to the structures of the state or that they did not want a state at all. The peasant idea of autonomy was not the same thing as anarchy: it was a demand for a state in their own image, one that would enforce their own agenda of the Revolution and compel the other classes to submit to it. Judging from the fat files of their letters and petitions lying in the archives from 1917, the peasants had a lot to say about the power question. The First World War had politicized the village – literally so during 1917 as the peasant soldiers, revolutionized by their military service, returned home. Thousands of villages passed formal resolutions on the future structure of the state. Many of these mandates were imbued with a solemn rhetoric, such was the seriousness with which they were viewed, and nearly all contained a long list of political demands. The villagers of Vyshgorodetsk in Pskov Province, for example, signed a petition to the Soviet entitled "Our Demands," in which they called for the establishment of a democratic republic, universal suffrage, more rights of local self-government, school education in the local tongue, equal rights for women and all national groups, court reforms, progressive taxes, and the prohibition of all vodka sales.[74] Such resolutions hardly suggest a parochial peasantry, one with its back to the outside world and preoccupied with its own village affairs, as so often depicted in the literature on 1917. Nor could one conclude this from the long and heated debates about the power question which so often dominated peasant congresses, and even less from the high turnout of peasant voters in the elections to the Constituent Assembly. This was not a peasantry indifferent to the state but, on the contrary, one that, for the first time in its history, was becoming aware of its power to reshape it.

Following the February Revolution the Provisional Government and the Petrograd Soviet received hundreds of peasant greetings and declarations of support. Many of these were couched in religious terms. The villagers of Tetrin in Arkhangel'sk Province wrote to express their "devout gratitude" to the Provisional Government for Russia's liberation from "the sinful tsarist regime" and to "pray to it to lead Russia onto the just path of salvation and truth."[75] A group of peasant soldiers from XI Army was even more explicit in its religious greeting to the leaders of the Soviet: "You have been blessed by Jesus our Savior and are leading us to the dawn of a new and holy fraternal life. May the Lord help you!"[76] Many peasants saw the February Revolution in religious terms, or at least gave that impression in their correspondence with its official bodies. They described the old regime as sinful and corrupt, praised the revolutionary "freedom fighters" as Christ-like saviors of the people, and projected their religious hopes and ideals onto the new government. The words *pravda* ("truth" or "justice") and *pravitel'stvo* ("government") are – uniquely to the Russian language – derived from the same root. These two religious concepts were intimately linked in the Russian peasant mind: the only true form of government (and the only one the peasants recognized) was the administration of *pravda* (meaning it gave land and freedom to the peasantry). By embracing it in these religious terms the peasants sought to imbue the new order with their own ideals of government. As the peasant propagandist Os'minin concluded:

> We are standing for the people to become the masters of their own lives, for our country to become a single family of brother laborers, without rich or poor – in short for the Kingdom of God to come to our land.[77]

The peasantry projected its own religious ideals of social justice onto the new order – and in this way they inverted (or perhaps subverted) the whole state structure to suit peasant goals. Thus in the peasants' view any public body sanctioning their revolution on the land was to have the status of an organ of the state with the power to pass its own "laws"; whereas the laws of any other body, including the Provisional Government, that opposed their revolution were not to be recognized at all. This is neatly illustrated by the All-Russian Peasant Congress during May, and the peasant assemblies convened in most central Russian provinces during the spring.[78] Despite the warnings of the Provisional Government, which had pledged to protect the gentry's property rights until the convocation of the Constituent Assembly, most of these assemblies gave what the peasants took to be a legal sanction for their confiscation of the gentry's land. The peasant delegates, in the words of one observer at the All-Russian Congress,

> did not clearly understand the difference, firstly, between a declaration of some principle and the implementation of it as a law, or, secondly, between a resolution by the congress, expressing its opinion, and a law by the government, which has a binding force.[79]

The peasants seemed to believe that their own assemblies' resolutions already carried the status of "laws," and that in order to "socialize" the land it was enough for a large peasant assembly to pass a resolution to that effect. Their expectations transformed their assemblies into pseudo-governments promulgating "laws" by simple declaration – "laws" that then took precedence over the statutes of the Provisional Government. As one of the government's provincial commissars complained, "The peasantry has got a fixed opinion that all civil laws have lost their force, and that all legal relations ought now to be regulated by peasant organizations."[80]

It was precisely in this sense that the peasants came to see their local soviets as sovereign state organs, implementing and legitimizing their own revolution on the land, as the Bolsheviks encouraged them to do through the slogan "All power to the soviets!" In the peasant view their soviets were the only legitimate organs of state power in the countryside, and if they resolved to seize the gentry's land against the orders of the Provisional Government, they did so with the idea that they were acting with the sanction of a national state authority (the All-Russian Soviet Assembly) and as such their actions were "legal." A strong soviet, with the coercive means to enforce this peasant revolution and compel the other classes to submit to it, was thus seen by the peasants as a necessity, at both the local and the national levels. Nearly all the peasant soviets had their own Red Guard or armed detachment, not to mention police and judicial institutions, precisely for this purpose.

Similarly, the peasants tended to regard the Constituent Assembly as a national body giving legal force to their own revolution on the land. They saw it as "the spokesman of the peasants' will," as the "deliverer

ORLANDO FIGES

of land and freedom," which, by "getting all the people to agree" to it, would make their revolution binding and irreversible.[81] At times the peasants expressed the naive belief that as long as the assembly had a wise old peasant at its head, like some elder at a giant "people's *skhod*," or that as long as it contained enough peasants who were known and trusted by their fellow villagers, then it could not fail to bring them land and freedom.[82]

Finally, to finish with this theme of the peasants' reconstruction and inversion of the state, it was common for them to propose remedies to national problems that they might have applied in their own village. So, in April 1918 the peasants of Trostian *volost'* in Samara Province suggested resolving the industrial crisis by a repartition of all town property, just as the repartition of the land had "resolved" the crisis in agriculture.[83] Similarly, many peasants believed that the war with Germany could and should be resolved like a village brawl. A group of mainly peasant soldiers in II Army appealed to the Petrograd Soviet in April: "Once the German people and their Social Democrats have over-thrown their Terrible Wilhelm we should hold out to them a brotherly hand and firmly conclude a people's peace (*narodnyi mir*)."[84] And in the same month a peasant from Samara Province wrote to a newspaper: "We should talk things over with the German people; let them overthrow their Wilhelm, as we overthrew the tsar, and then we will hold out a hand to them, and we will all go back to our homes."[85]

The peasants and the language of socialism

There were four aspects of the "Russian peasant ideology" that could loosely be described as "socialist" in content: the belief that all the land should be held collectively and that every person had a right to work it using his own labor; the custom of the land commune (in most parts of Russia) of redistributing the plots of land in accordance with house-hold size; the welfarism of the village (for example, provision for widows and orphans); and the not infrequent custom of collective labor for communal ends (building irrigation schemes or harvesting communal grain stores, for instance). Yet this does not mean that the peasantry was ripe for "socialism" in the usual understanding of that term. The peas-ants may have assimilated some of the ideas of the socialist movement in the towns, but they added to them a traditional peasant gloss, informed by the egalitarian values of their own political culture, and the result was a strange hybrid creation, in part peasant and in part socialist.

The socialists in Russia had always found it hard to get across their abstract ideas to the peasantry. As one Populist concluded from the failure of the "Going to the people" in the 1870s, the peasants "were left cold by socialism, and yet they debated heatedly those questions that

110

affected their immediate concerns and which did not go beyond their customary ideas of a better peasant life."[86] Most of the peasants were easily confused by the abstract jargon of the socialists – all their talk of "classes," of successive "stages of development," and their "ism" this and their "ism" that. At the Shatsk district peasant congress in July 1917 one muddled peasant, obviously outraged by the exploitation of the capitalist system, argued that no socialist should be elected to the Constituent Assembly "because socialism grew from capitalism."[87] Even those peasants who had learned to speak this "scientific" language, mostly in the army, and who liked to speak it as a sign of "education," sometimes betrayed a ridiculous confusion about the meaning of its words. The memoirist Okninskii, in his remarkable account of rural life in Tambov Province during the Civil War, recalls the visit of some Soviet propagandists in the summer of 1920. Among them was a young local peasant from the Red Army who, to the delight of the villagers, also gave a speech, from which Okninskii quotes:

> Comrades! Can you tell in diameters what you know of the internal size of our victorious Red Army? I am sure that diametrically-perpendicularly you cannot say anything about its internal size. Our victorious Red Army on a scale always beats our enemies in parallel. To understand the axiom, you ought to think not in straight lines, like women, but perpendicularly like men. Then two radiuses will be equal to a diameter.

As the peasant spoke, his fellow villagers were increasingly amazed: "See how clever he has become! All those words! Where did he learn them! He is completely educated!"[88]

The socialists' theoretical language of class was almost entirely alien to the peasants – and was soon transformed by their use of it. The word *burzhooi* – which was roughly synonymous with "bourgeois" in the propaganda of the socialists, yet, as Boris Kolonitskii has so brilliantly shown, had no set class connotations for the urban masses and was used by them as a general form of abuse for virtually any perceived social enemy – became in the language of the village a term for all forces hostile to the peasantry.[89] Many peasants used it to describe all townsmen, thought to be hoarding the manufactured goods so badly needed in the countryside. Some confused the word *burzhooi* with *barzhui* (the owners of a barge) and *birzhye* (from the word *birzh* for the Stock Exchange) – perhaps on account of this association with the towns.[90] But by far the most common peasant understanding of the term *burzhooi*, at least during 1917, was that he was a supporter of the monarchy and was perhaps plotting for its restoration, along with the power of the gentry on the land. For example, two peasants from Viatka Province wrote in May to the Peasant Soviet claiming that in their district "no new laws have been introduced because all the *burzhooi* support the old regime and do not permit our village committees."[91] In Penza Province the word *borzhuki* (a misspelling of *burzhooi*) was used by the peasants "for all monarchists," who they said had committees called *khameteti* – a compound of *komitety* (committees) and *khamy* (hooligans).[92]

Later, in the summer of 1918, when the Bolsheviks attempted to divide the "rural poor" against the "kulaks" or the "rural bourgeoisie," this language of class was equally rejected by the peasantry. The Committees of the Rural Poor (*kombedy*), which were supposed to ignite this class war in the village, spectacularly failed to get any of the peasants, let alone the poorest, to think of themselves as "proletarians" or of their richer neighbors as a "bourgeoisie." In most villages the peasants thought of themselves as a community or "family" of farmers (*krest'ianskaia sem'ia*), tied together by their common links to the village and its land, and the notion of a separate body for the village poor, especially when the whole village was united behind the soviet, seemed both strange and unnecessary. The villagers of Kiselevo-Chemizovka in the Atkarsk district of Saratov, for example, resolved that a *kombed* was not needed,

> since the peasants are almost equal, and the poor ones are already elected to the Soviet ... so that the organization of separate committees for the poor peasants would only lead to unnecessary tensions between the citizens of the same commune.[93]

Most villages either refused to elect a *kombed*, thus leaving it to outside agitators, or established one which every peasant joined on the grounds that all of them were equally poor. The following resolution, from the Serdobsk district of Saratov Province, was typical of this linguistic subversion:

> We the peasants of Commune No. 4 welcome the committees of the rural poor, for in our commune no one speculates and no one is rich. We are all middle peasants and poor peasants and we will do all we can to help the poor peasants.[94]

"Socialism," recalled Ivan Nazhivin, a Tolstoyan peasant from Vladimir Province, in his entertaining *Notes on the Revolution*,

> appeared to us as some mystical method – mystical because it was unclear to us and we could not imagine what it might consist of in practical terms – of dividing all the property and money of the rich; according to our village tailor, this would mean that every peasant household would be given 200,000 rubles. This, it seems, was the biggest number he could think of.[95]

Nazhivin meant this as a condemnation of the socialists, and of the naive peasants who believed them. Yet there is no doubt that the propaganda of socialism was most effective when communicated, if not explicitly in religious terms, then at least in terms of the peasantry's traditional community values, which they saw as "just" and "willed by God." If socialism became the dominant political language of 1917, then it was largely because it provided the peasants with an idiom in which to formulate their own revolutionary ideals. The old peasant conception of the "toiling people" (*trudovoi narod*) gave the socialist parties an ideological *point d'appui* for the dissemination of a class-based rhetoric of politics – a rhetoric that increasingly undermined the language of democratic citizenship promoted by the Provisional Government as this came to be seen by the peasantry to signify the defense of the gentry's landed rights.

It was a well-established practice of the socialists to couch their propaganda in religious and peasant terms. The populists of the 1870s had often used the ideas of Christian brotherhood to preach socialism to the peasantry. And the same theme was taken up by the socialist parties in 1917. Pamphlets for the peasants presented socialism as a sort of religious utopia: "Want and hunger will disappear and pleasure will be equally accessible to all. Thieving and robbery will come to an end. In place of compulsion and coercion there will be a kingdom of freedom and fraternity."[96]

It was the Bolsheviks, however, who made the most political capital out of socialism's religious resonance. S. G. Strumilin, in a pamphlet for the rural poor, compared socialism to the work of Christ and claimed that it would create a "terrestrial kingdom of fraternity, equality and freedom."[97] The cult of Lenin, which took off in August 1918 after he had been wounded in an assassination attempt, carried explicit religious overtones. Lenin was depicted as a Christ-like figure, ready to die for the people's cause, and, because the bullets had not killed him, blessed by miraculous powers.[98] Even the Red Star, the emblem of the Red Army, had religious connotations deeply rooted in peasant folklore. A Red Army leaflet of 1919 explained to the servicemen why the Red Star appeared on the Soviet flag and their uniforms. There was once a beautiful maiden named Pravda (Truth) who had a burning red star on her forehead which lit up the whole world and brought it truth, justice, and happiness. One day the red star was stolen by Krivda (Falsehood) who wanted to bring darkness and evil to the world. Thus began the rule of Krivda. Meanwhile, Pravda called on the people to retrieve her star and "return the light of truth to the world." A good youth conquered Krivda and her forces and returned the red star to Pravda, whereupon the evil forces ran away from the light "like owls and bats," and "once again the people lived by truth." The leaflet made the parable clear:

So the Red Star of the Red Army is the star of Pravda, And the Red Army servicemen are the brave lads who are fighting Krivda and her evil supporters so that truth should rule the world and so that all those oppressed and wronged by Krivda, all the poor peasants and workers, should live well and in freedom.[99]

The democratic revolution in the towns spoke a foreign language to the peasantry. Its leaders were acutely aware of the problem – many even thought that the whole success of their democratic mission would depend on finding a common discourse with the peasantry – and they went to great lengths to explain their ideas in terms they thought the peasants might understand. To some extent they succeeded with that small section of the literate peasantry among whom the urban culture of democracy was most developed. But in their communication with the peasant masses these ideas were soon translated (almost beyond recognition) into specific peasant forms. The idea of the republic became in the village a monarchical idea, a demand for order and a "master's hand" to direct the Revolution, shaped less by the democratic culture of the towns than by the patriarchal culture of the peasantry. The new language of citizenship was reinterpreted to suit the peasants' own revolutionary and social needs. The idea of the state and its coercive power, far from being negated by the peasants, was reconstructed and inverted by them to serve their own interests and religious ideals of social justice. Finally, the language of socialism was similarly understood in these religious terms.

Language, then, was still a fundamental problem for the democratic mission in the village, even after eight months of trying to construct a national political culture. The leaders of the February Revolution had initiated a public discourse of democracy, to which the peasants had been exposed through newspapers, pamphlets, and oral propaganda, but the peasants' "hidden transcripts" of this public discourse gave a different meaning to many of its terms. Whereas the main purpose of this discourse had been to break down class distinctions, resolve social conflicts, and create a nation of citizens, the way it had been received by the peasantry merely served to reinforce these social divisions. Language, more than ever, defined the peasants' self-identity and united them against the educated classes of the towns.

NOTES

Reprinted from "The Russian Revolution and its Language in the Village," *Russian Review* 56, no. 3 (1997): 323–345.

1 *The Kerensky Memoirs: Russia and History's Turning Point* (London, 1965), 228.
2 Tsentral'nyi gosudarstvennyi arkhiv Sankt-Peterburga (TsGASP), f. 7384, op. 9, d. 209, l. 17.

3 E. N. Medynskii, *Revoliutsiia i vneshkol'noe obrazovanie: S prilozheniem konspektov besed c krest'ianami nad temama sviazannymi c revoliutsiei* (Moscow, 1917), 4–5.

4 In Ukraine, the Baltic lands, and the Caucasus, where the urban elites were ethnically different from the native peasantry, it was literally a foreign language. But my concern here is exclusively with Russia.

5 For a discussion of these variations see my *A People's Tragedy: The Russian Revolution, 1892–1924* (London, 1996), 92–95, 182–84.

6 *Pervyi kurganskii krest'ianskii s"ezd (8–9 aprelia 1917 g.)* (Kurgan', 1917), 3.

7 TsGASP, f. 7384, op. 7, d. 11, l. 57. op. 9, d. 254, l. 217, and f. 1000, op. 74, d. 13, l. 147; A. M. Selishchev, *Iazyk revoliutsionnoi epokhi: Iz nabliudenii nad russkim iazykom poslednikh let (1917–1926)* (Moscow, 1928), 215; A. Okninskii, *Dva goda sredi krest'ian': Vidennoe slyshannoe, perezhitoe v Tambovskoi gubernii s noiabria 1918 goda do noiabria 1920 goda* (Riga, 1936), 32; Rossiiskii gosudarstvennyi voenno-istoricheskii arkhiv (RGVIA), f. 162, op. 2, d. 18, l. 12: *Volia naroda* (26 May 1917): 2.

8 Rossiiskii gosudarstvennyi istoricheskii arkhiv (RGIA), f. 1278, op. 10, d. 18, ll. 206, 209, 211, 213, 215, 217, 219. 222, 224, 226, 228. 229, and so on.

9 RGIA, f. 1278, op. 10, d. 4, ll. 257–58. The report was compiled from information provided by local correspondents in more than a dozen provinces for the period between the start of March and the end of April. Some thirty pages long, it is an important, yet hitherto neglected, source on the February Revolution in the provinces.

10 RGIA, f. 1278, op. 10, d. 4, l. 257.

11 R. P. Browder and A. F. Kerensky, eds., *The Russian Provisional Government, 1917: Documents*, 3 vols. (Stanford, 1961), 2: 915.

12 *Pervyi kurganskii krest'ianskii s"ezd*, 3.

13 RGIA, f. 1278, op. 10, d. 4, l. 249.

14 See, for example, *Tolkovnik politicheskikh slov* (Petrograd, 1917); *Karmannyi slovar' revoliutsonera* (Petrograd, 1917); and N. G. Berezin, *Novyi sotsial'no-politicheskii slovar': Sputnik svobodnogo grazhdanina* (Odessa, 1917). Over a dozen such dictionaries were published, with a total print-run of half a million copies, between March and October.

15 See, for example, N. Petrovich, *Chto nuzhno znat' krest'ianinu* (Kiev, 1917); idem, *Krest'ianskaia pamiatka* (Moscow, 1917); S. Zaiats', *Kak muzhiki ostalis' bez nachal'stva* (Moscow, 1917); I. Shadrin, *Blizhaishchie zadachi (krest'ianinu-grazhdaninu)* (Kazan', 1917); and A. Os'minin, *Chto dolzhno dat' narodu uchreditel'noe sobranie* (Petrograd, 1917).

16 *Izvestiia vserossiiskogo soveta krest'ianskikh deputatov*, 20 July 1917.

17 *Narodnaia gazeta*, 28 July 1917.

18 *Uchreditel'nyi s"ezd vserossiiskogo krest'ianskogo soiuza* (Moscow, 1917).

19 RGIA, f. 1278, op. 10, d. 4, l. 258.

20 See, for example, TsGASP, f. 7384, op. 9, d. 176, l. 184, and d. 209, l. 10.

21 On this see my *Peasant Russia, Civil War: The Volga Countryside in Revolution, 1917–1921* (Oxford, 1989), 35, 147–51.

22 See N. N. Smirnov, *Na perelome: Rossiiskoe uchitel'stvo nakanune i v dni revoliutsii 1917 goda* (St. Petersburg, 1994), 243–50.

23 *Dlia narodnogo uchitelia*, 1917, no. 8: 29–32, no. 10: 29–31, and so on.

24 See, for example, TsGASP, f. 1950, op. 1, dd. 10, 13.

25 RGIA, f. 1278, op. 10, d. 4, l. 257.

26 *Otchet deiatel'nosti soiuza vospitaniia svobodnogo cheloveka za 1917–18 (pervyi) god* (Petrograd, 1918).

27 RGIA, f. 806, op. 5, d. 10313, l. 131.

28 *Biulleten' obshchestva politicheskogo prosveshcheniia armii i shirokikh sloev nase-leniia*, 1917, no. 1: 1–3, no. 2: 1–4.
29 E. N. Medynskii, *Kak vesti besedy po politicheskim voprosam: Metodicheskie ukaza-zniia, konspektyi i spiski literatury dlia lektorov, uchitelei i pr.* (Moscow, 1917). Medynskii (1885–1957) later became a well-known Soviet educationalist.
30 Medynskii, *Revoliutsiia i vneshkol'noe obrazovanie.*
31 Ibid., 23; Medynskii, *Kak vesti besedy*, 4, 7.
32 G. Korelin, *Gotovtes' k uchreditel'nomu sobraniiu* (Ketch, 1917), 2.
33 See, for example, the speeches of Uspenskii and Nabatov in *Zhurnal shatskogo uezdnogo s"ezda krest'ianskikh deputatov, 23–25 iiulia 1917 goda*, 2, 5.
34 Shadrin, *Blizhaishchie zadachi*, 7.
35 TsGASP, f. 446, op. 1, d. 15, l. 26.
36 *Tikhvinskii uezdnyi krest'ianskii s"ezd 29–30 aprelia 1917g.* (Tikhvin, 1917), 6.
37 S. P. Rudnev, *Pri vechernikh ogniakh: Vospominaniia* (Kharbin, 1928), 96–99.
38 Os'minin, *Chto dolzhno dat' narodu*, 15. Os'minin is a fascinating figure in the history of the February Revolution. A peasant from Osvishi village in Tver Province, he fought at the Front for thirty months and rose to the rank of a sergeant. On 7 March 1917 he was sent by his village to the capital with a gift of bread and salt and 60 rubles for Rodrianko, chairman of the Duma, in gratitude for "the blessing of the people's victory" (RGIA, f. 1278, op. 10, d. 11, l. 332). There he became involved in politics – figures of his type were in high demand. He wrote for the newspapers *Trud i volia* and *Soldatskaia mysl'* before becoming editor of *Soldatskoe slovo*, a paper oriented toward peasant soldiers like himself. It is thought that he joined the SRs and became a leader of the soldiers' veteran organization. I am grateful to Boris Kolonitskii for this information.
39 *Izvestiia vserossiiskogo soveta krest'ianskikh deputatov*, 22 August 1917.
40 TsGASP, f. 7384, op. 9, d. 158, l. 29.
41 Shadrin, *Blizhaishchie zadachi*, 10–11.
42 See M. Bakhtin, *The Dialogic Imagination* (Austin, 1981), 295–96.
43 J. C. Scott, *Domination and the Arts of Resistance: Hidden Transcripts* (New Haven, 1990).
44 The most recent statement of the view is in R. Pipes, *The Russian Revolution, 1899–1919* (London, 1990), 118–19.
45 RGIA, f. 1278, op. 10, d. 4, ll. 241–42.
46 Ibid., l. 241.
47 Many propagandists commented on this generational divide. See, for example, TsGASP, f. 1950, op. 1, d. 10, ll. 7–8, f. 7384, op. 9, d. 176, ll. 177–80, and d. 209, l. 5; and Tsentral'nyi gosudarstvennyi arkhiv istoriko-politicheskikh dokumentov (TsGAIPD), St. Petersburg, f. 1, op. 1, d. 228, l. 46.
48 F. Iusupov, *Pered izgnaniem, 1887–1919* (Moscow, 1993), 187.
49 T. Emmons and B. Patenaude, eds., *War, Revolution, and Peace in Russia: The Passages of Frank Golder, 1914–1927* (Stanford, 1992), 50.
50 Okninskii, *Dva goda*, 28.
51 *1917 god v derevne: Vospominaniia krest'ian* (Moscow-Leningrad, 1929), 40, 64.
52 TsGASP, f. 8558, op. 1, d. 5, l. 30.
53 RGIA, f. 794, op. 1, d. 17, l. 23, and f. 1278, op. 10, d. 4, l. 83; *Izvestiia vserossi-iskogo soveta krest'ianskikh deputatov*, 14 and 15 March 1917.
54 G. Buchanan, *My Mission to Russia and Other Diplomatic Memories*, 2 vols. (London, 1923), 2: 86, 114.
55 Emmons and Patenaude, *War, Revolution, and Peace*, 46.
56 RGIA, f. 1278, op. 10, d. 4, l. 243.

57 D. Os'kin, *Zapiski praporshchika* (Moscow, 1931), 110–11. See further A. Wildman, *The End of the Russian Imperial Army: The Old Army and the Soldiers' Revolt (March–April 1917)* (Princeton, 1980), 241–42.

58 "Moskovskii sovet rabochikh deputatov (1917–1922)," p. 10, George Katkov Papers, Russian Centre, St. Antony's College, Oxford University, England.

59 *Tret'ii s"ezd vserossiiskogo krest'ianskogo soiuza v Moskve*, 11; *Gubernskii s"ezd krest'ianskikh deputatov tomskoi gubernii, sostoiavshchiisia v g. Tomske 14–22 sentiabria 1917 g.* (Tomsk, 1917), 27.

60 *Delo derevni*, 3 November 1917.

61 *Sel'skii vestnik*, 5 July 1917.

62 S. S. Maslov, *Rossiia posle chetyrekh let revoliutsii* (Paris, 1922), 149.

63 *Delo derevni*, 20 September 1917. The phrase *samoderzhavie narodnoe* was sometimes used in propaganda – and so may have been picked up by him in this way.

64 Sometimes a village resolution might begin: "We the citizens of peasant origin" (*My grazhdane iz krest'ianskikh proiskhozhenii*).

65 *Izvestiia*, 12 March 1917.

66 TsGASP, f. 7384, op. 7, d. 11, l. 32.

67 "Iz ofitserskikh pisem c fronta v 1917 g.," *Krasnyi arkhiv*, 50, no. 1 (1932): 200.

68 See my "Peasant Farmers and the Minority Groups of Rural Society: Peasant Egalitarianism and Village Social Relations during the Russian Revolution (1917–1921)," in *Peasant Economy; Culture and Politics of European Russia, 1800–1921*, ed. E. Kingston-Mann and T. Mixter (Princeton, 1991), 378–401.

69 RGIA, f. 1278, op. 10, d. 4, ll. 247–48; *Sel'skii vestnik*, 23 and 30 September 1917; Rudnev, *Pri vechernikh ogniakh*, 83–85; Figes, *Peasant Russia*, 64–66; *Delo naroda*, 19 December 1917; O. H. Radkey, *Russia Goes to the Polls: The Election to the All-Russian Constituent Assembly, 1917* (Ithaca, 1989), 65–71.

70 Figes, *Peasant Russia*, 175–76, 309.

71 RGIA, f. 1278, op. 10, d. 4, l. 255; TsGASP, f. 446, op. 1, d. 1, ll. 11–12; *Sel'skii vestnik*, 9 July 1917.

72 M. Gorky, "On the Russian Peasantry," in *The Russian Peasantry 1920 and 1984*, ed. R. E. F. Smith (London, 1977), 12.

73 On this see my *Peasant Russia*, chaps. 2 and 3.

74 TsGASP, f. 9, d. 255, l. 11.

75 RGIA, f. 1278, op. 10, d. 4, ll. 192–93.

76 TsGASP, f. 7384, op. 9, d. 255, l. 24.

77 Os'minin, *Chto dolzhno dat' narodu*, 15.

78 On the peasant assemblies in the Volga provinces see my *Peasant Russia*, 40–46.

79 V. Ia. Gurevich, "Vserossiiskii krest'ianskii s"ezd i pervaia koalitsiia," *Letopis' revoliutsii*, 1923, no. 1: 191. See similarly the Duma report in RGIA, f. 1278, op. 10, d. 4, l. 248 ("the peasants take as a law any resolution in the newspaper. . . . And usually they take to be 'the most correct law' those parts of the parties' resolutions . . . in which their own ancient ideals are expressed").

80 L. Trotsky, *The History of the Russian Revolution* (London, 1977), 882.

81 TsGASP, f. 446, op. 1, d. 1, ll. 2, 5, 8, and f. 7384, op. 9, d. 255, l. 11.

82 See, for example. TsGASP, f. 8558. op. 1, d. 5, l. 24; *Zhurnal shatskogo uezdnogo s"ezda*, 7; and *Gubernskii s"ezd krest'ianskikh deputatov tomskoi gubernii*, 25.

83 Gosudarstvennyi arkhiv Kuibyshevskoi oblasti, f. 81, op. 1, d. 199a, l. 171.

84 TsGASP, f. 7384, op. 7, d. 11, l. 33.

85 *Sel'skii vestnik*, 13 April 1917.

86 O. V. Aptekman, *Obshchestvo "zemlia i volia" 70-kh gg.* (Petrograd, 1924), 178.

87 *Zhurnal shatskogo uezdnogo s"ezda*, 7.

88 Okninskii, *Dva goda*, 247–48.

89 B. Kolonitskii, "Antibourgeois Propaganda and Anti-'Burzhui' Consciousness in 1917," *Russian Review* 53 (April 1994): 183–96.

90 I. Nazhivin, *Zapiski o revoliutsii* (Vienna, 1921), 15; Gosudarstvennyi arkhiv Rossiiskoi Federatsii (GARF), f. 551, op. 1, d. 108, l. 2; TsGASP, f. 7384, op. 9, d. 255, l. 25.

91 *Izvestiia vserossiiskogo soveta krest'ianskikh deputatov*, 20 May 1917.

92 Ibid., 20 October 1917.

93 Cited in G. A. Gerasimenko and F. A. Rashitov, *Sovety nizhnego povolzh'ia v Oktiabr'skoi revoliutsii* (Saratov, 1972), 266.

94 GARF, f. 393, op. 3, d. 340, l. 70.

95 Nazhivin, *Zapiski*, 14.

96 *Chto takoe sotsializm?* (Minusinsk, 1917), 9.

97 S. Petrashkevich (Strumilin), *Pro zemliu i sotsializm: Slovo sotsialdemokrata k derevenskoi bednote* (Petrograd, 1917), 1–2.

98 See N. Tumarkin, *Lenin Lives! The Lenin Cult in Soviet Russia* (Cambridge, 1983), 82–95.

99 R. Stites, *Revolutionary Dreams: Utopian Vision and Experimental Life in the Russian Revolution* (New York, 1989), 110; and Tumarkin, *Lenin Lives!*, 71–72.

6

NATIONAL REVOLUTIONS AND CIVIL WAR IN RUSSIA

Ronald Grigor Suny

Nationality, ethnicity and national assertiveness were among the relatively ignored issues of the history of the Russian Empire/Soviet Union until recently, despite the fact that ethnic Russians (Great Russians) made up under half of the country's population in 1917. Moreover, traditional writing tended to posit a strict division between class and national identity, between Marxism and nationalism as ways of thinking and behaving. The breakup of the Soviet Union into fifteen independent states has led people to reassess nationalism and ethnicity in the region. Ironically, however, 1991 was not the first time that the Russian state disintegrated and broke into a large number of independent or would-be independent states – it happened first in 1917–1918 during the revolution.

Ron Suny has played a leading role in exploring the nationality issue during the revolution and after. In this selection from his larger book, Suny discusses the conjunction between two of the most powerful forces of 1917, two of the key ways people identified themselves and others and acted accordingly: by nationality and by class. Students of nationality tend to divide into two schools, the "essentialists" who argue that peoples naturally see themselves in terms of distinct national characteristics and inherently possess a sense of national identity, and "constructivists" who see national identity as socially and intellectually constructed. Suny's analysis rests with the latter approach. In his emphasis on the social construction of identity, his work is broadly connected to the issues of language and symbols that were raised in the previous two essays, in this case their role in national/ethnic identity as against other identities, especially class. The essay also ties in to at least two other themes of this collection: it brings some of the issues of social history (which focused on the major cities) to the borderlands and minorities, and it presents another facet of the tension between the interests of peasants and those of urban intellectuals attempting to mobilize them.

Suny divides nine larger ethnic groups of the Russian Empire into five categories based on their degree of national identity and political behavior in 1917–1918. This selection, for reasons of space, includes only two of them, the

Ukrainians and the Latvians. The Ukrainians are selected because they were the second largest ethno-linguistic nationality after Great Russians, because of Ukraine's economic and geographic importance, and because the complexity of the issues of nationality and class in Ukraine sheds light on so many of the fundamental questions about nationality at this time. Latvians are chosen because they represented a different important category, one quite different from Ukrainians (but similar to Georgians, across the country in the Caucasus Mountains). Moreover, the Latvian and Baltic region was important to the development of the revolution, especially in the period leading up to the October Revolution. These two peoples allow us to explore important questions of national, class, and other competing identities, including the circumstances under which national movements might or might not be successful. In the process Suny cautions us about the importance of distinguishing "between cultural or ethnic awareness and full blown political nationalism," but also warns that sometimes (in 1917 certainly) "social and ethnic are so closely intertwined that separation of the two can be artificial and misleading." There may well be no definitive answer to the question of the relative importance of nationality and class identities (and other identities) in motivating people to action, whether in the Russian Revolution or in many of the other important social and political upheavals of the modern world, but addressing the question is important both to history and to understanding our own times.

* * *

Because many of the peoples of the Russian empire, after five or six decades of Soviet or independent development, had forged national-cultural identities with established state structures and powerful nationalist political discourses, historians have often viewed the revolutionary years as if that future had already existed in 1917. The nationalist representation of an essential if concealed national consciousness, ever present and ready to emerge when opportunity knocked, seemed borne out by subsequent events and was easily read back into an earlier age. The appeal of this nationalist construction, its success in mobilizing populations at the end of the 1980s in political struggles for sovereignty, has obscured a much more complex, if less melodramatic, story of nation-building, and even nationality formation, which for many peoples of the empire belongs more appropriately to the Soviet period than to the years before the civil war.[1] The dramatic narratives of uneven evolution from ethnic and religious communities into conscious nationalities and the complex relationship with class formations – all taking place in the swirling vortex of war and economic collapse – need to be recovered.

Unless one simply assumes that ethnicity always and everywhere has a greater power than class, or vice versa, the particular contexts in which one or the other emerges paramount must be part of the story. How the

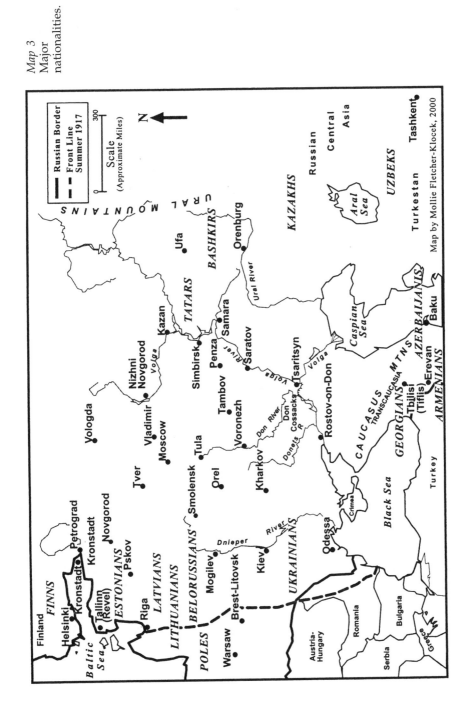

Map 3
Major nationalities.

Map by Mollie Fletcher-Klocek, 2000

larger political context – public policies, oppressive laws, public education, recruitment into armies, interstate conflicts, and other political
interventions from states and powerful elites – contributes to the kinds
of discourse that find resonance in social groups is a question that has
to be particularized in microstudies of class and nationality formation.
Access to state institutions or isolation from them profoundly influences
the generation of identities. Moreover, the direction from which the major
danger to a social formation comes – from above, in the form of state
oppression, or from below, in the claims of other classes, or from outside,
in a foreign threat or alien ethnicity – determines what solidarities are
forged. The intensity with which commitment to class or nationality (or,
indeed, to religion, region, gender, or generation) is felt at a given time
is highly dependent on specific political relations and the depth and
ferocity of the social and political conflicts of the moment.

Class and nationality in the Russian empire

Looking through the exclusive prisms of Marxism or nationalism,
theorists and political activists in the late nineteenth and early twentieth
centuries structured their understandings of social reality and political
antagonisms by positing a strict division between class and nationality.
The rival discourses of nationalism and Marxism radically simplified the
complex, overlapping relationships between ethnicity and social structures and limited each movement's appeal among significant populations.

As many writers have pointed out, in Eastern Europe and the Russian
empire, class and ethnic identities existed simultaneously and with little
separation. Sometimes ethnic loyalties were paramount, often preventing
or delaying class solidarity; at other times horizontal social links thwarted
vertical ethnic integration. In particular configurations, ethnicity and class
coincided, tying specific groups together in opposition to other ethnically
homogeneous groups. In central Transcaucasia, for example, Georgian
nobles and peasants, who shared an ethnic culture and values based on
rural, precapitalist traditions, faced an entrepreneurial Armenian urban
middle class that dominated their historic capital, Tiflis (Tbilisi), and
developed a way of life alien to the villagers. To the east, in and around
Baku, the peasantry was almost entirely Azerbaijani, and urban society
was stratified roughly along ethnic and religious lines, with Muslim
workers at the bottom, Armenian and Russian workers in the more
skilled positions, and Christian and European industrialists and capitalists dominating the oil industry.[2] Whereas ethnicity conferred social
privilege on some and disadvantages on others, thus reinforcing differ-
ential social positions, vertical linguistic, cultural, and religious ties that
united different social strata in a single "ethnic" community affected the
horizontal class links in complex ways.

Though sometimes ethnicity reinforced class and vice versa, at other times ethnic loyalties cut across class lines and prevented horizontal solidarities. Muslim workers in the Baku region, for example, were separated from the more skilled Armenian workers, not only by wage differentials and class cultures, but also by their memories of the "Armenian–Tatar War" of 1905.[3] The bonds of religion and custom tied the Muslim workers to their Muslim compatriots, even to a Muslim capitalist. Both Muslim workers at the bottom of the labor hierarchy and Muslim industrialists near the top experienced condescension, not only from Russian officials and foreign capitalists, but also from Armenian entrepreneurs, engineers, and skilled workers.[4] In colonial Transcaucasia, the tsarist regime treated Christian Armenians more favorably than Muslims, and both Russians and Armenians, even sympathetic Social Democrats, viewed the Muslims as *temnye liudi*, unenlightened "dark people."

Which ties, ethnic or class, bound most tightly were contingent on the particular political and economic conjuncture and the intervention of intellectuals and activists. In moments of economic stress, in 1905, 1914, and 1917, workers of all ethnicities joined in broad strike movements and common political endeavors, with Russians active earlier and more enthusiastically than Armenians and Muslims. The links between them were always fragile and provisional, and by early 1918 ethnosocial fractures overwhelmed the best efforts of the Marxists and exploded in a new round of Armeno-Azerbaijani violence.

The peculiarities of Russian imperialism, still inadequately explored in both Western and Soviet scholarship, had a highly differentiated influence on the development of nationalities within the empire. . . .

As the seigneurial economy gave way to market relations and new forms of the exploitation of labor replaced more traditional and paternalistic ones, radical intellectuals articulated the sufferings of newly minted workers in the idiom of Marxism. But the interconnection of ethnic and social discontents made it difficult, even for those peoples who entered industrial and city life, to separate class from ethnic experience. The embryonic working classes of Russia's peripheries remained ambivalent about nationalism in most cases and expressed their political consciousness through ethnic socialist movements. Peasantries, though ethnically cohesive, were also generally indifferent to the nationalists' programs.

The discourses of class (socialism) and nationality (nationalism) were largely urban phenomena in prerevolutionary Russia. No matter how sincerely patriots extolled the virtues of the peasantry, making actual converts among villagers proved to be as difficult for the followers of the Ukrainian patriotic poet Taras Shevchenko as for the disciples of Marx. In part, this difficulty was the result of the perceptual limitations of those nationalists who tended to emphasize the unity of the "nation" and neglect social conflicts and divisions, and of those socialists who promoted class divisions and were dismissive of, if not hostile to, ethnic solidarities. Nationalists and socialists alike failed to appreciate the complex meshing of social and ethnic grievances in situations where class and ethnicity reinforced individual and collective positions in the hierarchy of power and powerlessness.

Socialism and nationalism in the revolution

Although most of the non-Russian peoples of the tsarist empire were overwhelmingly peasant, they differed radically from one another in their internal class structures and in the degrees of their national consciousness. It is useful to cluster nine major nationalities in the Russian empire at the time of the revolution – four Baltic peoples, three Transcaucasian peoples, and two Western Slavic peoples – into five subgroups, based on their identifications with class or nationality. The first group, distinguished by their almost completely peasant composition and low level of national consciousness, includes the Belorussians, Lithuanians, and Azerbaijanis. The second, marked by social and geographic divisions and a profound ambiguity in their national and class orientations, involves the Ukrainians and the Estonians. A third group, consisting of the Georgians and the Latvians, resolved the tension between nationality and class through socialist-oriented national movements. The fourth group – the Finns – divided into fiercely opposing camps, one socialist, the other nationalist, that resolved their conflict through bloody civil war. The Armenians, who comprise the fifth group, subordinated class divisions to a vertically integrating nationalism. This typology illustrates the variety of socially and ethnically generated responses to the new opportunities offered by the revolution. . . .

Group II: Ukrainians and Estonians

Ukrainians

A far more complex and ambiguous relationship between nationality and other social identities existed among the Ukrainians and Estonians, in whom national consciousness was more developed than in the nationalities of Group I, though not strong or widespread enough to overwhelm competing identities.

Scholars agree that in Ukraine nationality coincided to an unusual degree with economic class. Except for a small intelligentsia, Ukrainians were almost entirely peasants; the landowners and officials were Poles or Russians, whereas the commercial bourgeoisie was largely Jewish.[5] Steven L. Guthier writes:

Class and ethnic cleavages were closely related. ... Russians manned the oppressive bureaucracy and were heavily represented among the principal landowners. Poles dominated the *pomeshchiki* [noble landlord] class in the right bank provinces of Kiev, Podolia, and Volhynia. Petty trade, commerce, and much of industry on the right bank were controlled by Jews who were therefore the peasantry's most visible creditors. As a consequence, the ethnic and socioeconomic grievances of the Ukrainian peasant proved mutually reinforcing and provided the foundation for a political movement which combined nationalism with a populist social program.[6]

Ukraine had developed a distinct ethnic culture and language in the long period from the fall of Kiev to the Mongols (1240) through the Polish dominion (1569) to the union with Russia (1654). Early in the nineteenth century, nationalist intellectuals articulated a notion of Ukrainian distinctiveness, and the Romantics Taras Shevchenko and Panko Kulish formed a Ukrainian literary language from the vernacular of the southeast.[7] The brief flourishing of Eastern Ukrainian intellectual culture in the first two-thirds of the nineteenth century was curtailed after the Polish insurrection of 1863, however, particularly in 1876, when the tsarist state prohibited public expression in Ukrainian. With the restrictions on "Russian" Ukrainian culture, Galicia, which contained the Western Ukrainian regions under Austrian rule, became the center for literary expression and a popular nationalism.[8] In contrast, "Russian" Ukraine, a vast territory with non-Ukrainians dominating urban centers and state-imposed constraints on ethnic intellectual life, developed neither a coherent mass-based national movement nor even a widely shared sense of a Ukrainian nation in the decades before the twentieth-century revolutions.

Ukrainian peasants were very active in 1905–7, though the movement in the first revolution had only superficially nationalistic characteristics. Largely a protest over land shortages, which were blamed on the large holdings by noble landlords (most of them Polish and Russian), social discontent led to violence, but with minimal ethnic expression. Even the supposedly traditional Ukrainian anti-Semitism was largely absent, and Jewish revolutionaries were welcomed as supporters of the peasant movement.[9] Peasant grievances were sufficient to generate protests without consistent intervention from outsiders, though "Spilka" (the Ukrainian Social Democratic Union) was active on the right bank, and the SRs and the Peasants' Union were active on the left bank[10] [western and eastern sides of the Dnieper River, respectively].

Historians differ in their evaluations of Ukrainian nationalism in 1917–18. Without question, an articulate and active nationalist elite, made up of middle-class professionals, was prepared to confront both the Provisional Government (March–October 1917) and the *Sovnarkom* (Lenin's Council of People's Commissars) with its demand for autonomy and self-rule.[11] John Reshetar, the author of the first major scholarly monograph on the Ukrainian Revolution, writes:

> Immediately after the March Revolution, leadership in the Ukrainian national movement was assumed by the democratically inclined petite bourgeoisie, the intelligentsia with nationalist sympathies, and the middle strata of the peasantry which supported the cooperative movement. The peasant masses, the soldiers, and the urban proletariat were not participants at this early period, and it cannot be said that the national movement permeated their ranks to any significant extent in the months that followed since it was competing with more urgent social and economic issues.[12]

The *Rada* [Ukrainian nationalist council] was committed to finding a democratic solution to the political crisis, to remaining within a federated Russian state, and to launching a radical program of land reform. Its support in the cities was minimal. In the elections in July to the municipal *duma* [city council] in Kiev, Ukrainian parties won only 20 percent of the vote, whereas Russian parties garnered 67 percent (Russian socialists, 37 percent; "Russian voters," 15 percent; Kadets, 9 percent; Bolsheviks, 6 percent), but the Ukrainian politicians were backed by Ukrainian soldiers, who were particularly interested in the formation of ethnic military units.[13]

Far more problematic, however, is the estimate of the level of national cohesion among Ukrainians and the degree of support for the national program among the peasants. For Reshetar, nationalism is a middle-class movement and the peasant "was enslaved by his locale and regarded the inhabitants of the neighboring villages as a species of foreigner." The absence of a Ukrainian bourgeoisie of any weight and the

> essentially agrarian character of late nineteenth-century Ukrainian society, with its emphasis on the locale, tended to retard the development of that sentiment of group cohesiveness which transcends localism and is termed national consciousness. The peasant, because of his conservatism, was able to retain his language, peculiarities of dress, and local customs despite foreign rule, but initially he resisted the notion that all Ukrainians, whether living in Kharkiv [Kharkov] province, in Volynia, or in Carpatho-Ukraine, belonged to the same nation.

Though this peasant parochialism was partially broken down by the spread of a money economy, the building of railroads, and the dissemination of newspapers and periodicals, the protracted process of nationality formation "had not been consummated as late as 1917." Reshetar points out that even in 1917, peasants in Ukraine referred to themselves not as a single collective but with regional terms: Rusins (sons of Rus), Galicians, Bukovinians, Uhro-rusins, Lemkos, and Hutsuls. Russophilia was still strong in many parts of the country, even among the peasantry, and the middle and working classes were largely Russified.[14]

In his encyclopedic study of nationalism in the revolutionary years, a work sympathetic to the aspirations of the nationalists and repelled by the opportunism and centralism of the Bolsheviks, Richard Pipes repeatedly demonstrates that social environment – the isolation of the nationalists from urban society and the working class, and their dependency on and difficulties in mobilizing the peasantry – confounded the plans of the Ukrainian ethnic parties.[15] Agreeing with Reshetar that "the weakest feature of the Ukrainian national movement was its dependence on the politically disorganized, ineffective, and unreliable village," Pipes emphasizes the village's "political immaturity, which made [it] easily swayed by propaganda, and ... strong inclinations toward anarchism." Nevertheless, for Pipes, nationalism was a reality in Ukraine, "a political expression of genuine interests and loyalties," which had its roots in

> a specific Ukrainian culture, resting on peculiarities of language and folklore; a historic tradition dating from the seventeenth-century Cossack communities; an identity of interests among the members of the large and powerful group of well-to-do peasants of the Dnieper region; and a numerically small but active group of nationally conscious intellectuals, with a century-old heritage of cultural nationalism behind them.

But "the fate of the Ukraine, as of the remainder of the Empire, was decided in the towns, where the population was almost entirely Russian in its culture, and hostile to Ukrainian nationalism."[16] Contingent factors, such as the inexperience of the national leaders and the shortage of administrative personnel, are mentioned as part of the toxic mix that destroyed the Ukrainian experiment in independence. Pipes takes nationalism as a natural and admirable development, whereas he sees communism as an artificial implant forcibly imposed upon non-Russians.

Though one might hesitate to accept Reshetar's firm requirement that a middle class must exist for a nationalist movement to succeed, or Pipes's assumption that there was a conscious community of interests between intelligentsia and peasantry in 1917, the argument that the movement would stand or fall on the backs of the peasantry seems compelling.

In a most intriguing article, Steven L. Guthier argues, in contrast to Reshetar, that the Ukrainian peasantry was nationally conscious in 1917, as demonstrated in the November elections to the Constituent Assembly, in which the peasantry overwhelmingly supported Ukrainian parties. In the eight Ukrainian provinces (Kiev, Poltava, Podolia, Volhynia, Ekaterinoslav, Chernigov, Kherson, and Kharkov), "55 percent of all votes cast outside the Ukraine's ten largest cities went to lists dominated by the UPSR [Ukrainian Party of Socialist Revolutionaries] and 'Selians'ska Spilka' [All-Ukrainian Peasants' Union]; another 16 percent went to Left PSR/UPSR slates."[17] The cities, on the other hand, went for Russian and Jewish parties, though a heavy turnout of Ukrainian soldiers gave substantial backing to Ukrainian parties.

Guthier concludes that "Ukrainian nationalism as a substantial political force was a one-class movement," but one in which identification between peasant aspirations and the programs of the national parties was quite close.[18] He assumes that peasants voting for the Ukrainian peasant parties were aware of and accepted the national planks in their programs. "The peasants were committed to the creation of a Ukraine which was both autonomous and socialist. They wanted land rights to be reserved for those who farmed the land with their own hands."[19]

A useful distinction might be made, however, between cultural or ethnic awareness and full-blown political nationalism – that is, an active commitment to realizing a national agenda. Although the 1917 election results show that peasants in Ukraine preferred parties and leaders of their own ethnicity, people who could speak to them in their own language and promised to secure their local interests, these results do not provide sufficient evidence either that the peasantry conceived of itself as a single nationality or that it could be effectively mobilized to defend ideals of national autonomy or independence. Though the mentality of the Ukrainian peasants in 1917 needs to be explored further, they seem to have been ethnically aware, preferring their own kind to strangers, but not yet moved by a passion for the nation, and certainly not willing to sacrifice their lives for anything beyond the village. Defeated nationalists, as well as "class-conscious" Bolsheviks, considered the peasants of Ukraine to be "backward," "unconscious," unable to be mobilized except for the most destructive, anarchistic ends. But one might more generously argue that rather than being backward, Ukrainian peasants had their own localistic agenda in the chaos of the civil war, one that did not mesh neatly either with that of urban intellectuals, nationalist or Bolshevik, or with that of workers, many of whom despised those living in the villages.

Guthier may be closer to the mark when he sees the momentary coincidence of peasant voters and Ukrainian populists as the specific conjuncture when "national autonomy was seen as the best guarantee that the socioeconomic reconstruction of the Ukraine would reflect local, not all-Russian conditions."[20] Here once again both the contingent and evolving character of nationalism (and class, for that matter) and the closeness of ethnic and social factors become clear. At least in 1917–18, the Ukrainian peasants were most concerned about the agrarian question and their own suffering in the years of war and scarcity.[21] They thought of themselves as peasants, which for them was the same as being "Ukrainian" (or whatever they might have called themselves locally). Their principal hope was for agrarian reform and the end of the oppression identified with the state and the city. Russians, Jews, and Poles were the sources of that oppression, and it is conceivable that for many peasants the promise of autonomy was seen as the means to achieving an end to the onerous and arbitrary power of those groups. But ethnic claims had no priority over social ones in these early years of revolution, and alliances with nationalists (or, more frequently, with ethnic populists) could easily be replaced by marriages of convenience with more radical elements.[22]

When the nationalist *Rada* was unable to resist effectively the Bolshevik advance in January 1918, it turned as a last resort to the Germans, who requisitioned grain and terrorized peasants. When the nationalists failed to back up their own agrarian reform, support rapidly evaporated. As a consequence of the German occupation, the nationalist forces in Ukraine splintered into competing groups. The nationalist cause was identified by many as linked to foreign intervention; to antinationalist elements, particularly in towns, the only viable alternative to social chaos, foreign dependence, and Ukrainian chauvinism appeared to be the Bolsheviks. A German report of March 1918 gives a sense of the fragmentation in Ukraine at the time, the uncertainty of nationalist influence, and the relative strength of the Bolsheviks:

> It is not true that the Bolsheviks are supported only by the Russian soldiers who remained in the Ukraine. . . . They have a large following in the country. All the industrial workers are with them, as is also a considerable part of the demobilized soldiers. The attitude of the peasants, however, is very difficult to ascertain. The villages that have once been visited by Bolshevik gangs . . . are, as a rule, anti-Bolshevik. In other places Bolshevik propaganda seems to be successful among the peasants.
>
> The peasants are concerned chiefly with the dividing up of the land; they will follow the Rada if it allows them to take the estates of the landlords . . . as proclaimed in the Third and Fourth Universals. . . . Otherwise they will go with the Bolsheviks. Although the Bolsheviks lost out in many places because of their system of terror, their slogan "Take everything, all is yours" is too attractive and tempting to the masses.

> The Ukrainian separatist movement, on which the Rada is relying, has no true roots in the country and is supported only by a small group of political dreamers. The people as a whole show complete indifference to national self-determination.[23]

Sadly for the nationalists and happily for the Bolsheviks, the peasantry proved to be an unsteady social base for a political movement. A British observer in May 1918 confirmed to the Foreign Office the lack of national consciousness among the Ukrainian peasants.

> The peasants speak the Little Russian [Ukrainian] dialect; a small group of nationalist *intelligentsia* now professes an Ukrainian nationality distinct from that of the Great Russians. Whether such a nationality exists is usually discussed in terms in which the question can receive no answer. Were one to ask the average peasant in the Ukraine his nationality he would answer that he is Greek Orthodox; if pressed to say whether he is a Great Russian, a Pole, or an Ukrainian, he would probably reply that he is a peasant; and if one insisted on knowing what language he spoke, he would say that he talked "the local tongue." One might perhaps get him to call himself by a proper national name and say that he is "russki," but this declaration would hardly yet prejudge the question of an Ukrainian relationship; he simply does not think of nationality in the terms familiar to the *intelligentsia*. Again, if one tried to find out to what State he desires to belong – whether he wants to be ruled by an All-Russian or a separate Ukrainian Government – one would find that in his opinion all Governments alike are a nuisance, and that it would be best if the "Christian peasant-folk" were left to themselves. . . .[24]

Group III: Latvians and Georgians

Latvians

Speaking a language that belongs to the Baltic branch of Indo-European languages (along with Lithuanian and Old Prussian), the ancestors of the Latvians inhabited the Baltic littoral in the ninth century. German merchants and missionaries arrived in the mid-twelfth century, and soon after, the "treacherous Livs" were converted to Christianity. The establishment of German rule obliterated the tribal structure of the indigenous peoples, and Latvians existed as a subject peasant population until the tsarist period. As with the Estonians, the German clergy dominated learning in the region and initiated scholarly interest in Latvian folk culture. A German cleric translated the Bible into Latvian in the late seventeenth century, and secular literature, written by Germans, appeared in the eighteenth. A "national awakening," that is, the development of significant secular writing by Latvians, dates from the mid-nineteenth century. Much of the ethnic "revival" actually occurred outside Latvia proper, as the title of the first Latvian newspaper, *Peterburgas avizes* (St. Petersburg Newspaper), indicates.

By the last decade of the nineteenth century, young Latvians were joining the Russian revolutionary movement – first the populists, then, after 1893, the fledgling Marxist circles. With high levels of literacy and urbanization (in 1897, 79.4 percent of the people of what would become Latvia lived in cities), as well as growing labor discontent, the Social Democrats found a ready response among both radical intellectuals and workers. Latvian parishioners resented the protectorate of the German barons over local churches and allowed the churches to be used as fora for political agitation. In Kurzeme, for example, local Social Democrats distributed socialist appeals in rural churches and developed strong ties with agricultural workers.[25]

By 1905, the Latvian Social Democratic Labor Party (LSDLP) boasted 10,000 members. Over 1,000 schoolteachers, deeply influenced by Social Democracy, met late that year and demanded instruction in the mother tongue, a more democratic curriculum, and the separation of church and education. The national struggle against the German lords combined with a broad political struggle against autocracy, led by Marxists. In the words of one veteran of the movement, "The strength of the movement was not the result of political and social factors alone ... the 1905 Revolution in Latvia was also a *nationalist* revolution – a Latvian revolution against Russian–German oppression."[26]

Whereas Estonians, like Ukrainians, vacillated between nationalism and other social movements, Latvians, like Georgians, combined their ethnic and social grievances in a single, dominant socialist national movement. As Andrew Ezergailis has shown in two monographs, Social Democracy, particularly Bolshevism, had exceptionally strong support in 1917 among Latvian and other workers and among the famous Latvian riflemen. In the August elections to the municipal council of Riga, Bolsheviks won 41 percent of the vote (60 percent among ethnic Latvians).[27] A week later, Bolsheviks won 63.4 percent of the vote to the major rural institution, the Vidzeme Land Council, and in November they carried the elections to the Constituent Assembly in those parts of Latvia (Vidzeme) not yet occupied by the Germans, winning 71.85 percent of the vote. Among the *strelki* (riflemen), Bolsheviks won 95 percent of the vote.[28]

This extraordinary showing stems from a number of factors: the general Latvian alienation from the Germans and the relatively less hostile attitude toward Russians; the high proportion of landless peasants (more than 1,000,000 in 1897) that favored Social Democracy and opposed the "grey barons" (Latvian smallholders) almost as much as they did the German nobles; the support of Social Democracy by a militant working class that had experienced a bloody baptism in 1905, as well as by intellectuals, schoolteachers, and students; the particularly devastating experience of the World War, which had brought the fighting deep into Latvia, dividing the country, causing great hardship, and radicalizing the population; and finally, the ability of the Bolsheviks to develop and propagate a program that attempted to deal with both social and ethnic grievances.[29] Many Latvians in 1917 saw the solution to their national future within a Russian federation, but one that had moved beyond the bourgeois revolution. The brief experiment in Bolshevik rule after October, the Iskolat, collapsed when the Germans moved into unoccupied Latvia in February 1918. In all likelihood, Bolshevism would have been the eventual victor in Latvia save for the German intervention, which gave the nationalists a chance to create their own republic. . . .

Conclusion

The revolution of 1917 and the subsequent civil war were interpreted by the Marxists as a civil war of class against class, worker against peasant and bourgeois, city against country. Many Bolsheviks and other Russian socialist and nonsocialist parties viewed events as a single, gigantic revolutionary process engulfing the whole of the now-defunct empire. Nationalists, in contrast, interpreted the struggle as a national war of Russians against minorities, the center against the peripheries. They viewed the experiences of the borderlands as unique events that fulfilled and justified the natural historical evolution to national independence.

The nationalists' example, followed by most of the monographic studies of individual nationalities in the West, has produced histories of the non-Russian peripheries sharply distinguished from those of central Russia. Whereas much of the new social history depicts the revolution in the central Russian cities as a struggle between increasingly polarized social classes, or at least an intense pulling-apart of the *verkhi* (top) and the *nizy* (bottom) of society, historians of the revolution in the borderlands have traditionally emphasized ethnic rather than social struggles.[30] Yet woven through the monographic literature on the non-Russian regions, both Soviet and Western, is a red thread of social conflict of great intensity in the national borderlands, obscured at times by the ethnic coloration, but in fact made all the more ferocious by cultural as well as class cleavages. Here the social and the ethnic are so closely intertwined that separation of the two can be artificial and misleading.

When we acknowledge the provisional and contingent nature of nationality and class and the volatility with which people moved from social to ethnic identities and loyalties, the revolution and civil war, both in the center and in the peripheries, appear much more related than divorced. It was not two kinds of revolution, but one gigantic social upheaval that engulfed the whole of the Russian empire in the third year of the World War, bringing down the integrating imperial authority and launching a crisis of authority that continued well into the civil-war years. For that period, economic disintegration shredded the social fabric of the old order. Everyone everywhere was affected, and physical survival became the primary goal for tens of millions of people. Ethnically distinct peasants and workers, whatever their particular experiences, shared the general experience of the collapse of state authority and economic order. The sundering of political and economic ties opened the way for some parts of the empire, most immediately Finland and Poland, to opt for a viable independence (though not without dissenters and, in the case of Finland, bloody civil war); other areas, fatally linked to the whole history of Russia, were simply set adrift (like Azerbaijan and Armenia) or found neither the opportunity nor the will to break with revolutionary Russia (for example, Tataria).

The story of national formation and nationalism in the revolutionary years is seen here as part of the intricate mosaic of the Russian Civil War, with social and ethnic conflicts inextricably mixed. The civil war in the disintegrating Russian empire was a civil war everywhere, right up to pre-World War I borders, and though in the national peripheries the conflict took on aspects of national wars, the social struggles between workers and industrialists, *tsentsovoe obshchestvo* (propertied society) and *demokratiia* (the lower classes), city and countryside were powerfully present. From this "civil-war perspective," Soviet power or Bolshevism never simply meant Russia, and the extension of its power was not simply a Russian conquest of other peoples. Bolshevism, for better or worse, was the actual achievement of the revolution of the *demokratiia* of the central Russian cities as that revolution stood after October 1917; Russian and Russified Ukrainian workers in Kiev and Kharkov, Russians and Armenians in Baku, and Russians and Latvians in Riga supported local soviet power (and even Bolshevism) in preference to a national independence promoted by a small nationalist elite in the name of a peasant majority. The difficult choice before both the Russians and the non-Russian peoples was whether to support the central Soviet government and the revolution as now defined by it, or to accept a precarious existence in alliance with undependable allies from abroad with their own self-aggrandizing agendas. In making that choice, social structure, past experience, and the relative advantages of the options available were often much more significant than ethnic considerations.

Almost everywhere, the nationalist movements were either strengthened or fatally weakened by the nature of their class base. Because ethnic
solidarity, activism, Russophilia, or Russophobia were very often
primed by social discontents, where nationalist leaderships were able to
combine social reform with their programs of self-definition, autonomy,
or independence, their chances for success were increased. Where social,
particularly agrarian, reform was delayed or neglected, ethnic political
aspirations alone did not prove strong enough to sustain nationalist
intellectuals in power. For ethnic leaders who faced a peasant majority
indifferent to their claims to power and caught up in an uneven struggle
with the Bolsheviks, an appeal to the Great Powers of Central and
Western Europe became the last resort. And the intervention of foreigners,
particularly the Germans in the crucial first months after the October
Revolution, radically altered the developmental lines of the first revolutionary year. Geoff Eley writes,

> By interposing itself between the peoples of the Russian Empire
> and their practical rights of self-determination at a crucial moment
> of revolutionary political rupture – after the old order had
> collapsed, but while the new was still struggling to be born (to
> adapt a saying of Gramsci) – the German military administration
> suspended the process of democratic experimentation before it
> had hardly begun. The Germans' essentially destructive impact
> explains some of the difficulty experienced by the competing
> political leaderships in the western borderlands of Russia during
> 1918–20 in creating a lasting relationship to a large enough coali-
> tion of social support. The various political forces – Bolshevik,
> left-nationalist, autonomist, separatist, counter-revolutionary –
> operated more or less in a political vacuum in a fragile and inde-
> terminate relationship to the local population, not just because
> the Belorussian and Ukrainian societies were so "backward" (the
> explanation normally given), but because the cumulative effects
> of war, Imperial collapse, and German occupation had radically
> dislocated existing social organization, strengthening old antago-
> nisms between groups and inaugurating new ones.[31]

Nationalism, like class consciousness, was a disturbingly ephemeral
phenomenon among most non-Russians in these turbulent years, especially once the revolution outgrew the cities. Whatever their cultural and
ethnographic preferences, non-Russian peasants did not automatically
opt for the national programs of their urban ethnic leaders. Mobilized
in the aftermath of the October Revolution, the peasantry was, in Eley's
words, "a class restlessly *in motion*."[32] Neither nationality nor class had
an a priori claim on the loyalties of its potential constituents.

The mixed fates of nationalism and socialism in the whirlwind of the Russian Revolution and the subsequent civil war are illustrative of the relationships of class and nationality, both to the historical social locations of peoples and to the social and intellectual activities that harmonize internal discordances within groups and imagine interconnections between members of the group and the distance from the "other." Neither "objective" in the sense of existing outside the constitutive practices of its members and its opponents, nor completely "subjective" in the sense of existing only when perceived to exist by members or opponents, a nationality or a social class is here understood to be both socially and discursively constituted.

In the great sweep of the revolution and civil war, nationalism was for most nationalities still largely concentrated among the ethnic intelligentsia, the students, and the lower middle classes of the towns, with at best a fleeting following among broader strata. Among Belorussians, Lithuanians, and Azerbaijanis, the paramount identification was not with one's nation, but with people nearby with whom one shared social and religious community. Neither nationalism nor socialism was able to mobilize large numbers of these peoples into the political struggles that would decide their future. For several other nationalities, among them the Latvians and the Georgians, class-based socialist movements were far more potent than political nationalism. Socialism as presented by the dominant intellectual elite answered the grievances of both social and ethnic inferiority and promised a socio-political solution to the dual oppression. For still other nationalities, like the Ukrainians and the Estonians, nationality competed with class for the primary loyalty of the workers and peasants, with neither winning a dominant position. In Finland, a deadly polarization between social groups led to a civil war between parts of a population relatively united on the question of national independence and commitment to Finnish culture. For the Armenians, a rather unique case of a people divided between two empires, without a secure area of concentration, and facing imminent extermination, a nonclass, vertically integrating nationalism overwhelmed all competitors.

The reasons for the relative weakness of nationalism and the strength of local and social identities in 1917–18, and even further into the civil war, require further attention by scholars, but tentatively one might suggest that the social distance between villagers and townspeople, between peasants and intellectuals, militated against the supraclass appeal of nationalism. The most successful appeals were populist or even socialist, especially when they were enhanced by ethnic arguments. Furthermore, long-established trade patterns and complex economic relations tied most of the non-Russian peoples of the old empire to the center (the Finns and the Poles are perhaps exceptions here); these were powerful forces for integration with the rest of Russia rather than for the development of separate nations. Separation from Russia was almost always a political decision based on a need for support by an outside power – at first Germany and Turkey, later the Entente powers – and had far less intrinsic appeal among the various nationalities than has been customarily assumed.

The ebbs and flows of socialism and nationalism were tied to the tides of war and revolution, to the relative fates of the Great Powers and their ability to act within Russia. In the twentieth century, intervention became an unwelcome but ubiquitous guest at the revolutionary table. When the Bolsheviks were relatively weak and the Germans strong, separatism and the fortunes of the nationalists rose; when the Germans were defeated and the Entente withdrew, the appeals of the Bolsheviks for social revolution, land to the peasants, and even a kind of greater "all-Russia nationalism" found supporters. Not to be discounted as a factor in the Bolshevik victory was their own confidence in their reading of history, their sensitivity to the social dynamics within the revolutionary crises, their readiness to compromise with popular nationalism in the formation of the Soviet federation, and their willingness to use their military and political power ruthlessly to achieve their historic goals.

Lenin's estimation that national separatism would be reduced by central Russian tolerance and a willingness to allow national self-determination to the point of independence has appeared, understandably, to be either a utopian fantasy or an example of political dissimulation. Yet Lenin appears to have understood that for many ordinary people, neither nationalism nor a sense of class was an end in itself as often was the case for intellectuals. If, in fact, nationalism was far weaker than most nationalists have allowed; if in Russia it was almost invariably connected with concrete social and political discontents caused by years of discrimination and hardship under tsarism; and if, indeed, significant groups within the non-Russian peoples responded well to the socialist programs of social transformation and national self-determination; then perhaps Lenin's notion that non-Russians would be willing to remain within a multinational state was less a fantasy than another example of his political style, an uneasy combination of hard-nosed realism and the willingness to take extraordinary risks.

NOTES

Abridged selection from Ronald Grigor Suny, *The Revenge of the Past: Nationalism, Revolution and the Collapse of the Soviet Union* (Stanford: Stanford University Press, 1993), pp. 20–23, 29–30, 43–51, 55–58, 76–83.

1 This, indeed, is the argument I have tried to develop in my work on the republics of Transcaucasia. See, for example, Ronald Grigor Suny, *Armenia*

in the Twentieth Century (Chico, Calif.: Scholars Press, 1983); idem, *The Making of the Georgian Nation* (Bloomington: Indiana University Press, 1988); idem, "Nationalist and Ethnic Unrest in the Soviet Union," *World Policy Journal* 6, 3 (Summer 1989): 503–28.

2 Ronald Grigor Suny, "Nationalism and Social Class in the Russian Revolution: The Cases of Baku and Tiflis," in Ronald Grigor Suny, ed., *Transcaucasia, Nationalism and Social Change: Essays in the History of Armenia, Azerbaijan, and Georgia* (Ann Arbor: Michigan Slavic Publications, 1983), pp. 239–58; idem, "Tiflis, Crucible of Ethnic Politics, 1860–1905," in Michael F. Hamm, ed., *The City in Late Imperial Russia* (Bloomington: Indiana University Press, 1986), pp. 249–81; idem, *Making of the Georgian Nation*; idem, *The Baku Commune, 1917–1918: Class and Nationality in the Russian Revolution* (Princeton: Princeton University Press, 1972).

3 In 1905, Armenians and Azerbaijanis in and around Baku fought and killed each other. In February, Azerbaijanis attacked first, alarmed by rumors of Armenians arming themselves, and Armenians, led by the leading nationalist party, the *Dashnaktsutiun*, retaliated fiercely. A second round of mutual massacre occurred in August. Rioters set fire to the oil fields. Both the Social Democrats and the oil industrialists worked to reconcile the Armenian and Azerbaijani communities. The passivity of the government inspired suspicions that tsarist authorities had instigated, or at least favored, the riots.

4 Suny, *Baku Commune*, p. 14.

5 John Armstrong, *Ukrainian Nationalism* (New York: Columbia University Press, 1963), p. 10.

6 Steven L. Guthier, "The Popular Base of Ukrainian Nationalism in 1917," *Slavic Review* 38, 1 (Mar. 1979): 32. In 1897, Ukrainians made up only 35 percent of the population in the 113 towns in Ukraine; the larger the town, the smaller the Ukrainian proportion. In Kiev, Ukrainians made up 22 percent of the population, Russians 54 percent, Jews 12 percent, and Poles 7 percent; in Kharkiv, Ukrainians accounted for 26 percent of the population, Russians 53 percent, Jews 6 percent, and Poles 0.3 percent. Steven L. Guthier, "Ukrainian Cities During the Revolution and the Inter-war Era," in Ivan L. Rudnytsky, ed., *Rethinking Ukrainian History* (Edmonton: Canadian Institute of Ukrainian Studies, University of Alberta, 1981), p. 157; Patricia Herlihy, "Ukrainian Cities in the Nineteenth Century," in Rudnytsky, ed., *Rethinking Ukrainian History*, p. 151.

7 On the formation of the Ukrainian literary language, see George Y. Shevelov, "Ukrainian," in Alexander M. Schenker and Edward Stankiewicz, eds., *The Slavic Literary Languages: Formation and Development* (New Haven: Yale Concilium on International and Area Studies, 1980), pp. 143–60.

8 John-Paul Himka, *Galician Villagers and the Ukrainian National Movement in the Nineteenth Century* (Basingstoke: Macmillan, 1988); idem, *Socialism in Galicia: The Origins of Polish Social Democracy and Ukrainian Radicalism (1860–1890)* (Cambridge, Mass.: Harvard Ukrainian Research Institute, 1983).

9 In Austrian Galicia, the economic and political grievances of Ukrainian peasants and the anti-Jewish editorial policy of the leading nationalist newspaper contributed to widespread anti-Semitism. "The Ukrainian nationalism that took root in rural Galicia had a distinctly anti-Jewish component," writes John-Paul Himka in his study, "Ukrainian–Jewish Antagonism in the Galician Countryside During the Late Nineteenth Century," in Peter J. Potichnyj and Howard Aster, eds., *Ukrainian–Jewish Relations in Historical Perspective* (Edmonton: Canadian Institute of Ukrainian Studies, University of Alberta, 1988), pp. 111–58.

RONALD GRIGOR SUNY

10 On the peasant movement in Right Bank Ukraine (Kiev, Podolia, and Volhynia provinces), see Robert Edelman, *Proletarian Peasants: The Revolution of 1905 in Russia's Southwest* (Ithaca, NY: Cornell University Press, 1987).

11

> Most of the men who undertook the propagation of the national idea in Ukraine were intellectuals with a middle-class background although many of them were of peasant stock. Hrushevsky was the son of an official in the Russian ministry of public instruction, and Dmitro Doroshenko was the son of a military veterinarian. Colonel Eugene Konovalets and Volodimir Naumenko were the sons of teachers. Nicholas Mikhnovsky, Volodimir Chekhovsky, Valentine Sadovsky, Serhi Efremov, and Colonel Peter Bolbochan were the sons of priests.
>
> (John Reshetar, *The Ukrainian Revolution, 1917–1920: A Study in Nationalism* [Princeton: Princeton University Press, 1952], pp. 320–21)

12 Ibid., p. 48.
13 See the resolutions of the First Ukrainian Military Congress in May 1917 in S. M. Dimanshtein, ed., *Revoliutsiia i natsional'nogo voprosa v Rossii i SSSR v XX veke* (Moscow: Izdatel'stvo Kommunisticheskoi akademii, 1930); Richard Pipes, *The Formation of the Soviet Union: Communism and Nationalism, 1917–1923* (Cambridge, Mass.: Harvard University Press, 1954; reprinted 1964), p. 63; Reshetar, *Ukrainian Revolution*, pp. 50–51, 102n–103n.
14 Reshetar, *Ukrainian Revolution*, pp. 319–23.
15 See particularly the conclusion in Pipes, *Formation*, pp. 283–86.
16 Ibid., p. 149.
17 Guthier, "Popular Base," p. 40.
18 Ibid., p. 46.
19 Ibid., p. 41.
20 Ibid.

21

> The Central Rada and the Directory failed to solve the agricultural problem; the hetman government did worse. It was constantly a step behind the revolutionary spirit of the peasants. Its policy was to carry out the land reform legally for approval by a future Constituent Assembly. For this reason it was not able to compete with the Bolsheviks, who were promising the land to the peasants immediately, or even with Makhno, who was giving the land to the peasants as soon as it was captured. For the peasants, the land was a primary question and those forces that would not interfere in the division of land would get their support.
>
> (Michael Palij, *The Anarchism of Nestor Makhno, 1918–1920: An Aspect of the Ukrainian Revolution* [Seattle: University of Washington Press, 1976], pp. 54–55)

22 For another point of view on Ukrainian nationalism and the peasantry, see Andrew P. Lamis, "Some Observations on the Ukrainian National Movement and the Ukrainian Revolution, 1917–1921," *Harvard Ukrainian Studies* 2, 4 (Dec. 1978): 525–31. Lamis argues that Ukrainian nationalism from Taras Shevchenko on had a dual nature: glorification of the homeland and a demand for social reform. Often these two components remained separate and in a state of dialectical tension (p. 528). He takes issue with Arthur Adams, who

claimed that Ukrainian peasants revolted during the German occupation primarily because of the grain requisitions and fear for their land. Lamis contends that the jacquerie was nationalist, aimed at both national and social freedom, even though the peasants and the intelligentsia did not act in concert (p. 530). For Adams's argument, see his essay, "The Great Ukrainian Jacquerie," in Taras Hunczak, ed., *The Ukraine 1917–1921: A Study in Revolution* (Cambridge, Mass.: Harvard Ukrainian Research Institute, 1977), pp. 247–70.

23 The report, authored by the German writer Collin Ross, was first published in *Arkhiv russkoi revoliutsii* (Berlin: Slovo, 1922–37), 1: 368–76, and translated and reprinted in James Bunyan, *Intervention, Civil War, and Communism in Russia, April–December 1918: Documents and Materials* (Baltimore: The Johns Hopkins University Press, 1936), pp. 4–5.

24 [Colonel Jones], "The Position in the Ukraine," Public Records Office, London, Cab 24/52, ff. 117–18. I would like to thank Professor George Liber for a copy of this document, which was – to my knowledge – first referred to by Professor David Saunders in his paper, "What Makes a Nation a Nation? Ukrainians since 1600," presented at the Conference on Premodern and Modern National Identity, University of London, March 30–April 3, 1989.

25 I. G. Ozol, "The Revolution in Latvia, 1905–1907," unpublished typescript in the Boris I. Nicolaevsky Collection, Hoover Institution Archives, ser. 67, box 121, folders 1–2, pp. 58, 70–71.

26 Bruno Kalnins, "The Social Democratic Movement in Latvia," in Alexander and Janet Rabinowitch, eds., with Ladis K. D. Kristof, *Revolution and Politics in Russia: Essays in Memory* of B. I. *Nicolaevsky* (Bloomington: Indiana University Press, 1972), p. 137.

27 Andrew Ezergailis, *The 1917 Revolution in Latvia* (Boulder, Colo.: East European Quarterly, 1974), p. 145; idem, *The Latvian Impact on the Bolshevik Revolution, The First Phase: September 1917 to April 1918* (Boulder, Colo.: East European Monographs, 1983), p. 75.

28 Ezergailis, *Latvian Impact*, pp. 79, 87, 89.

29 For an attempt to deal with the different choices of the Estonians and the Latvians in 1917, see Stanley W. Page, *The Formation of the Baltic States: A Study of the Effects of Great Power Politics upon the Emergence of Lithuania, Latvia, and Estonia* (Cambridge, Mass.: Harvard University Press, 1959; reprinted New York: Howard Fertig, 1970), pp. 83–85.

30 For a review of Western writing on 1917 in Russia proper that emphasizes the importance of deep social polarization as an explanation for Bolshevik victory, see Ronald Grigor Suny, "Toward a Social History of the October Revolution," *American Historical Review* 88, 1 (Feb. 1983): 31–52.

31 Geoff Eley, "Remapping the Nation: War, Revolutionary Upheaval and State Formation in Eastern Europe, 1914–1923," in Potichnyj and Aster, eds., *Ukrainian–Jewish Relations*, pp. 205–46.

32 Ibid., p. 232.

Part III

REVISITING THE PROVISIONAL GOVERNMENT AND THE FAILURE OF THE MODERATES

7

FROM RHAPSODY TO THRENODY

Russia's Provisional Government in Socialist-Revolutionary eyes, February–July 1917

Michael S. Melancon

Michael Melancon has written widely on the revolution and has been especially important in developing an appreciation for the role of the non-Bolshevik and non-Marxist socialists, the Socialist Revolutionary Party (SRs) in particular. He has also stressed the provisional *nature of the Provisional Government, its temporariness. Here he brings the two themes together, arguing that if the majority of SRs never stood solidly behind the government, even after leading SRs entered it, this alters the traditional picture of political and social dynamics in 1917. Most SRs, he contends, viewed the government from the beginning with "suspicious tolerance," and the tolerance half of that phrase soon evaporated. The famous agreement of the Petrograd Soviet during the February Revolution to support the new Provisional Government "in so far as" it pursued policies of which the Soviet approved had real meaning not only for Soviet leaders, but for their rank and file followers. Moreover, he emphasizes, people took the planks of the various programs announced by successive Provisional Governments seriously and expected them to be fulfilled; the government's very legitimacy rested on their doing so. He also stresses that suspicion of or open hostility toward a "bourgeois" or coalition government arose not as a result of Bolshevik agitation, but because of initial skepticism reinforced by government failure to meet expectations, and grew with the disasters of 1917. One result was a surprisingly early call for the soviets to take power. The ingredients for a radical shift left among SRs were there from the beginning, he suggests, and once it materialized it produced the radical left blocs and alliances that played such an important role in the October Revolution and attainment of "soviet power" across the country. The Provisional Government, Melancon concludes, "did not founder on the rocks of Bolshevism but on the shoals of a socialist and revolutionary popular culture." He proceeds to marshall evidence to prove this through analysis of SR actions and resolutions on power. Although the theme is primarily political history, he relies heavily on analysis of "discourse" and language and on examination of a substratum of social relationships, reflecting how various ways of approaching the revolution often merge and how a new political history now incorporates social and linguistic approaches.*

A note might be made about Melancon's discussion of the debate over stages of revolutionary development. It is easy to forget, from the contemporary viewpoint, that this idea permeated thought at the time. Marxist ideology about stages of revolution, and especially a "bourgeois" stage that must precede any "proletarian" or socialist stage, was extremely influential and profoundly influenced the thinking and actions of political actors in 1917.

* * *

In a 1993 article, I argued that resolutions of local soviets and other low-level bodies throughout 1917 contained language suggesting that large segments of the politically activized population took seriously the "provisional" segment of the new government's title.[1] They viewed it as caretaker, with a limited mandate to create the conditions necessary for Constituent Assembly elections and to summon the Constituent Assembly itself, after which, as befit its "temporary" nature, it should withdraw from the scene. We should recall here that the original agreements between the provisional committees of the State Duma and Petrograd Soviet that gave birth to the Provisional Government contained quite distinct and restrictive language highly reminiscent of the formulations in the above-noted resolutions. This suggests that, regardless of what the Provisional Government and its close supporters thought, a solid basis existed for viewing the government's mandate as quite limited.

This article will analyze various Socialist-Revolutionary (SR) outlooks on the Provisional Government, with special emphasis on the first half of 1917. Its goal is to ascertain what relationship they had to the problem raised in the article about common understandings of the Provisional Government's proper functions and longevity. The matter takes on more than minor significance since one prominent SR entered the government from the outset, others entered it after the April crisis, and by July the party had practically taken over the government in terms of leading personnel and, thereby, virtually identified itself with it. If indeed large numbers of SRs always had highly circumscribed views of the government's temporal mandate and power, then this would constitute a matter worth pondering. After all, one can assume that most Constitutional Democrats [Kadets] stood behind the government that was in a real sense their brainchild. Likewise, whatever reservations Mensheviks had about the entry of socialists and, especially, of *their party* into the government, the prolonged existence of a bourgeois phase of development with a liberal-oriented government was very much part of their theoretical outlook. These two movements had no other type of government to turn to.

In several respects, for the SRs the matter stood somewhat differently.[2] Classical populist and neo-populist (SR) theory allowed for no prolonged bourgeois-capitalist phase or accompanying liberal political regime. SR entry into the Provisional Government was therefore even more fraught with awkward theoretical and programmatic consequences than was the case for the Mensheviks, for whom it was also quite uncomfortable. Furthermore, when the SRs came to predominate in the government after the July Days, the party's enormous peasant, worker, soldier and *intelligenty* [members of the intelligentsia] following found itself drawn unwillingly into the midst of the whole drama of the government's specific policies and its very legitimacy. Most commentary has assumed that from April 1917 on SR and Menshevik organizations, as well as most of those parties' cadres and followers (with the partial exceptions of the Left SRs and Left Mensheviks), stood solidly behind the government, whereas only the Bolsheviks opposed it. If this was never the case, then we have badly distorted the entire socio-political dynamic of the 1917 revolutions and, more to the point, misjudged the nature and durability of the Provisional Government's support.

The title's duality, "from rhapsody to threnody," may suggest to readers a temporal evolvement: after initial hesitation, the PSR [Party of Socialist Revolutionaries] came behind the government and then only much later, after heavy disappointments, began, in some of its elements, to criticize and even reject it (one might call this the "Chernov maneuver"). To the contrary, the title here suggests that from the outset SR views, if plotted on a graph, would have spread across it all the way, so to speak, from enthusiasm to fear and loathing, with an initial heavy weight toward suspicious tolerance or indifference that rather quickly edged toward impatience, anger, and contempt. In other words, to the extent that Provisional Government members and backers counted on SR support in real historical time or that historians have posited that support in reconstructed past time, both have skated on thin ice.

Before turning to SR words and actions about this important question, we must briefly recreate the ideological context in which they occurred, the discursive world occupied by living SRs. Unfortunately, SRs of the period lived in two worlds since by 1910 the party (like other parties between the 1905 and 1917 revolutions) had split. The main body of the party under the leadership of Chernov, Rakitnikov, and Natanson retained its adherence to neo-populist thought that foresaw no evolution toward socialism through a capitalist-liberal phase; however, a sizable group of party leaders and intelligentsia cadres (Gots, Breshko-Breshkovaskaia, Bunakov, Argunov, Avksentiev, and Sletov) had followed the earlier example of the Popular-Socialists and the Menshevik Liquidators in espousing reformist development within the bourgeois state. The latter group had little mass following, for which it partially compensated by its talented intelligentsia ranks well positioned in party and social organizations throughout the country. When World War I broke out, the Chernov–Rakitnikov–Natanson cadres, who had maintained their revolutionism intact, opposed the war, which they viewed as cause and basis of revolution. Having already renounced revolution, the reformist Gots–Argunov–Avksentiev wing found unthinkable any change of the wartime government; only much later did they move into serious opposition to the tsarist regime, which they wished to remove in order to create a Duma-based government better able to defend the nation and win the desired victory. As for so many Kadets, Mensheviks, and Popular-Socialists, for many Right SRs the war had become the *ultima ratio*.

Naturally, the two wings of the PSR, unsuccessfully reunited after the February Revolution, viewed the events of the February Revolution and thereafter in very different ways.

Right SRs, like centrists and leftists, for the most part adhered to hallowed socialist doctrine in opposing socialist entry into bourgeois governments. Nonetheless, on his own Kerensky entered the government and a small group of moderate populists (Right SRs, Trudoviks, and Popular-Socialists) began to see an advantage to socialist entry into the government. Regardless, all the moderate SRs – joined by many Mensheviks – perceived the Provisional Government as a logical and desirable development under the circumstances. Meanwhile, the vast majority of party leaders and cadres were adamantly opposed to socialist entry into the government. Furthermore, as noted, many SRs evinced suspicion toward this particular gathering (i.e., the Provisional Government) of Kadet and Octobrist politicians, with one SR-Trudovik; for them, it seemed by nature hostile to the aspirations of most workers, peasants, and soldiers, not to mention the laboring intelligentsia. Just after the February Revolution, however, the question did not pose itself in an especially sharp manner. After all, the government was temporary, Kerensky could serve as a (loudly self-proclaimed) source of information and control for "democracy," and the elections to the Constituent Assembly loomed in the near future. The people, after all, would soon have their opportunity to speak.

What were SRs saying about the government? Even as Kerensky and other moderate socialist members of the provisional executive committee of the Petrograd Soviet were laying the groundwork for the Provisional Government on February 27 and 28, SR worker contingents, under the leadership of Aleksandrovich (sent during 1916 to Petrograd from Switzerland by the Chernov–Natanson leadership) were attempting to subvert these efforts in favor of a popular soviet-based government. On the 27th and on following days, the internationalist SRs, in cooperation with the like-minded Mezhraionka [a socialist group], issued leaflets that bear on this matter. Two SR-Mezhraionka leaflets appearing late on the 27th called for a "provisional revolutionary government" based upon the workers and soldiers and one of them praised the formation of the soviet; neither so much as mentioned a liberal-oriented government, provisional or otherwise.[3]

On March 1, the radical SR-Mezhraionka alliance made their anti-Provisional Government stance even clearer in a leaflet that not only told soldiers and workers to elect their own deputies to the soviet, out of which should arise the real "Provisional Revolutionary Government," but heaped scorn on the newly formed liberal-oriented government: "the workers and soldiers have already held Petrograd in their hands for two days, while the pitiful State Duma chooses a Provisional Committee and calls it a provisional government" and so forth.[4]

Later that same day, soldier SRs in the soviet played a considerable role in drafting the famous Order No. 1, which not only helped democ-ratize the armed forces but also, like the SR–Mezhraionka leaflet, attempted to cut the ground out from under the new government in favor of the soviet: "in all political matters," stated the soviet's first decree, "the military branch is subordinated to the soviet of workers' and soldiers' deputies." The joint Petersburg SR–SD student organiza-tion also issued a leaflet specifically calling for a government based upon the soviets. Meanwhile, when news of the events in Petrograd reached SRs in the emigration, the newspaper *Na chuzhbine*, organ of the SR Committee Abroad, darkly noted the rise of the bourgeois-oriented Provisional Government but reassured readers that, after all, the rise of the soviets at least held promise for the future.[5] In essence, SR activists representing workers, soldiers, students, and underground party struc-tures all displayed a clear early preference for soviet power over the liberal-oriented Provisional Government.

The intra-SR struggle over the new government had of course only just begun. The very next evening after the inflammatory March 1 leaflet, the SRs held their first city-wide conference of the new era, followed two days later by a provincial conference. Although *Delo naroda*'s account of the March 2 conference, published two weeks later, claimed that the delegates had unanimously supported the creation of the government, at the time Aleksandrovich told Sukhanov that the pro-government forces had won with only a bare majority. The pertinent resolution insisted that "no one should disturb the Provisional Government's exercise of power"; the March 4 provincial conference passed a similar resolution by an even larger majority (Aleksandrovich complained that "the devil knows who they sent there"). Even so, both conferences displayed ambivalence about the vexed question of power by staunchly espousing the soviets. The provincial conference even issued a call for the "creation of an All-Russian soviet of workers, peasants, and soldiers deputies," the first origin of this idea (on March 4 Molotov reported to the Bolshevik Petersburg Committee about the SR plan for an all-Russian soviet, which Bolsheviks had as yet not mentioned). If brought to reality, a national soviet could not help but challenge the authority of the Provisional Government. Attending these hastily summoned conferences were sizable numbers of *intelligenty*, who, on the one hand, supported Kerensky's pro-governmental stance and, on the other, outspoke and outvoted the hapless leftists such as Aleksandrovich and his radical worker, soldier, and student contingents (most radical spokespersons were either in internal or foreign exile or in prison or *katorga* [penal servitude in exile, usually Siberia]).[6] Similar processes occurred in Moscow and numerous other localities, as moderate intelligentsia party forces, over vociferous leftist objections, quieted the doubts of rank-and-file cadres by referring to Kerensky's presence in the government and to the "insofar as" formula that seemed to give the soviets control over the government's actions. In the minds of numerous SRs, even the qualified (insofar as) support they gave to the government reflected their faith in the soviets as protectors of democracy's interests, a matter reflected, as we shall see, in their later resolutions and speeches.

The concealment from historiographical view of the radical implications of much post-February SR discourse reflects the extent to which the moderate party *intelligenty* seized control of numerous city and provincial, as well as the national, organizations, including most SR newspapers; many of these individuals also took prominent positions in soviet executive committees. Two additional factors contributed to the distortion: (a) Chernov's temporary inclination to the right upon his return home in April and (b) contemporary Leninist and later Soviet-era historiographical tendencies to write off the entire SR and Menshevik movements as virtually reactionary. Regardless, information is not lacking about the real situation. On March 4, just after their defeats in the city and provincial conferences, worker, soldier, and student cadres under Aleksandrovich's guidance established an "informational bureau" to coordinate their activities as an early opposition to the tack taken by the party leadership and by the Petrograd Soviet executive committee in legitimizing the Provisional Government. Their problem lay not in lack of cadres or will but in insufficiency of persuasive speakers and authoritative leaders. Aleksandrovich kept awaiting the return of Chernov, Gots, and Natanson, only the last of whom actually fulfilled Aleksandrovich's hopes.[7]

By the time of the All-Russian Convocation of Soviets during late March, the situation had improved for radical tendencies in the party in that Kamkov, evidently the very first of the major emigres abroad to return home, had gotten back to Petrograd through Denmark. At the conference, several moderate Mensheviks and SRs made the case for the Provisional Government, whereas the Pskov Trudovik delegate even recommended, for the first time in a public sphere, significant socialist entry into the government in order to "strengthen its resolve and heighten its authority." This incident points up the reality that right-wing populism provided much of the impetus for socialist entry into a coalitional Provisional Government. Some SRs (and Mensheviks) praised this idea, while others condemned it. For example, the Ufa SR delegate called for "our leaders in the executive committee to enter the Provisional Government, where ... we will offer them our unconditional support," whereas the Chita SR Pumpianksii scorned a "coalitional ministry," which would signify a "weakening of revolutionary resolve." For the leftist SRs proper, Kamkov argued at length for power based upon democratic elements in the soviet: "Do you believe," he concluded after criticizing the government's inaction on the eight-hour day, "that a Provisional Government of this composition will be able to resolve the land question in a manner that the revolutionary *narod* [the people] will demand?"[8]

One may dismiss this latter position as that of an evidently small minority in the party; yet, as we shall see, this was not necessarily the case. The earliest suggestions about socialist entry into the government focused not on compromise with the bourgeoisie but on a strengthening of socialist control over the government. The theme of "control" over the government found support in many low-level SR groups in Petrograd. Already on March 10, the worker and soldier SRs of Petrograd's Kolpino district (Izhorsk armaments plant) passed a resolution asserting that "we are subject to the soviet and recognize the Provisional Government only as long as ... it does not abandon the [soviet's] program." Ten days later, a meeting of 1,000 SRs in the capital's Moskovskii district found the "central revolutionary task [to be] to exert pressure on the Provisional Government." Throughout the balance of the month a series of SR factory and district *massovki* [mass meetings] passed resolutions calling for the soviets and other worker–soldier organizations to "pressure" the government to end the war and carry out other tasks.[9]

Throughout the late winter and early spring of 1917, such attitudes were a commonplace in local SR organizations nationwide and, perhaps even more interestingly, in social organizations dominated by SRs. For instance, on March 10 the Helsinki SR organization, which was far less radical than that in nearby Kronshtadt, expressed support only for the soviets while bitterly criticizing the Provisional Government on several scores (in dealing with members of the old regime, as regards ending the war, and so forth). This set the stage for the Helsinki soviet, with its dominating SR contingents, to pass resolutions in April increasingly condemnatory of the government, culminating in an April 21 resolution stating that "since it is not fulfilling the will of the people, the Provisional Government should retire." With its SR majority, the Helsinki soviet then pledged to "support the Petrograd Soviet with armed force at any moment," not exactly a soviet power resolution but rather close. During early April, at the first congress of the western front, which, according to Bolshevik memoirists, took place under SR domination, when one speaker criticized the Petrograd Soviet for interfering in the Provisional Government's affairs, the delegates shouted him down and then passed a resolution expressing support "for the soviets" rather than "any reactionary institutions." The late March congress of the Special Army (southwestern front), even more heavily dominated by SRs, instructed the Provisional Government to "be guided in its actions by policies worked out with the Petrograd Soviet."

Even more striking was the resolution passed during early March by the Kharkov SR organization, admittedly one of the most radical in the nation. This document called for extreme pressure against the "bourgeois" Provisional Government and threatened to summon the "revolutionary people to overthrow it and establish a provisional revolutionary government" if it did not remain "under democratic control." More surprisingly, later in March the regional conference of eleven Volga SR provincial organizations voted in favor of this resolution utterly hostile to the existing government. When the Kiev workers' soviet debated the question of governmental power during April, it passed a resolution that offered support for the government "as long as it fulfills the desired programs and when it does not, it will confront our [the soviets'] control." During the debate, the SR chair of the soviet, Nezlobin, a quite moderate worker in the printing profession, stated that "we have organized control of the Provisional Government in the person of the soviets and the Provisional Government now obeys the demands of the EC [executive committee] of the Petrograd Soviet." Of interest here is not the literal accuracy or inaccuracy of the statements but their language and tendency.

During late March, the Tsaritsyn SR organization voted for "conditional trust . . . for now in the Provisional Government [which] must fulfill the needs of the workers. . . . who must [however] watch out for their own interests." On March 10, the Ufa soviet, which had an SR majority, called for workers and soldiers to unite around the soviets: "only in this way will we ensure the future form of government in the interests of the broad mass of the population." When later in the month the Ufa soviet provided its delegates to the upcoming all-Russian Soviet Convocation with instructions regarding the Provisional Government, it referred only to the resolution of March 10, which in essence signified soviet power in the near future.[10] Clearly, during the first two months of the new era, numerous SRs, activists and cadres, as well as supporters, admired the conditions, qualifications, and controls applied to Provisional Government power more than that power itself, which, in effect, hung by a trip-wire.

The April crisis deepened suspicions and led some SR organizations to abandon even the "conditional support and trust" they had formerly, albeit reluctantly, offered. The foundation for this potential transition to full distrust was laid before the crisis. For example, the Petrograd SRs held their second city-wide conference during early April, just before the return of Lenin and Chernov and Miliukov's infamous note, all of which farther roiled the revolution's waters. The conference witnessed severe clashes over the war but not about the Provisional Government because, in essence, the centrist *intelligent* N. S. Rusanov handled the conference resolution on power in a way so heavily weighted against the government and in favor of the soviets that it handily garnered centrist, left centrist and leftist votes (real rightist support was in short supply). As at the recent soviet convocation, Kamkov, joined by Trutovskii and several others, made a strong case for soviet power; a composite of these speeches runs like this: "SRs should not support the bourgeois Provisional Government" but rather "should support only a government that would carry out the socialist maximum program"; the government had "displayed anti-narod tendencies from the outset" and "would soon take action to rid itself of the soviets," as a result of which SRs should abandon "even the insofar as" formula and "trust only the soviets," and so forth. The successful Rusanov resolution simply emphasized the government's bourgeois nature (*de rigueur* in 1917 socialist parlance), called for unceasing pressure upon it to ensure that it governed "in a manner appropriate for laboring democracy," and proclaimed socialist entry into it "impermissible." The essence of Rusanov's position became clearer in his accompanying speech: because of its make-up the government could hardly govern in the required manner. If and when the government failed to fulfill its tasks, laboring democracy had two choices: enter into it and "truck with the bourgeoisie" or throw its weight behind the soviets; "the SRs," proclaimed Rusanov with little prescience, "will not go into a coalitional government." Rusanov had so clearly outlined the case for a shift toward soviet power at the government's first misstep that the Right SR Gukovskii protested that he had "falsely" described a Provisional Government that "betrayed the people every hour."[11] Of importance here, as had been the case in Kiev, is that, to gather votes from rank-and-file party members, resolutions expressing even the most qualified support for the government had to be couched in terms hostile to the government and favorable to the soviets.

The April crisis sharply harshened the atmosphere in the capital and throughout much of the country. In Petrograd, many factories, district *massovki*, and military units made increasingly sharp demands of the government and even of the soviet executive committee in the matter of controlling the government. In virtually every case, the dominant political groups were the SRs and Mensheviks, with Bolsheviks at this point playing little role. (We should recall that Lenin's April theses were not readily accepted even by most Bolsheviks and had little influence in the crisis. In truth, Bolshevik mass-level influence was as yet so low that even in Petrograd's Vyborg district, often described as a veritable Bolshevik stronghold, the Bolsheviks could not even call *massovki* and depended on making speeches at meetings summoned by the SRs and Mensheviks.)[12] Most striking is the April 13 resolution issuing from the Staryi Parviainen plant, where the SRs, under the leadership of S. Ustinov, Miasnikov, and I. Teterkin, wielded predominant influence. This document abandoned entirely the idea of merely controlling the government; its first plank read: "remove the Provisional Government ... and pass power ... to the soviet." The entire resolution appeared in *Pravda* and *Izvestiia* over the signature of the Staryi Parviainen factory collective head, S. Ustinov, a prominent worker-SR.[13] Russia's first factory-level soviet power resolution came from the SRs (casting our glance forward a month, the Kronshtadt SR organization offered the first soviet power resolution passed by a soviet). Various factories and military units in Petrograd and elsewhere began to pass resolutions obviously modeled on the Staryi Parviainen document, while others simply sharpened their rhetoric, as when the SR-dominated executive committee of the 11th Army (southwestern front) "entrusted control over the [Provisional Government] to the soviet of worker and soldier deputies as the only representatives of organized democracy."[14] The phrase "trust only the soviets" or analogues now wove their way through hundreds of resolutions as non-Bolshevized precursors to the later "all power to the soviets."

Meanwhile, debate in the Petrograd Soviet about Miliukov's note matched the tumultuous discourse in the districts. Left Mensheviks, Bolsheviks and radical SRs all led a withering attack not only against the Provisional Government but against the soviet executive committee for supporting it. For example, the soldier-SR I. Borisov, himself a member of the executive committee, denounced soviet support for the government as "an unnatural union of revolutionary democracy with counter-revolution" and accused the majority in the executive committee of "shirking its duties and groveling in fear" at the prospect of the government's collapse.[15] A day later, the SR soldier Shapiro asserted that already "by March 1 it was clear that all of Russia had united behind the soviets but we were not yet ready [to take power]. ... Now the moment has arrived for us ... to have our own government."[16] During the crisis, the newspaper *Zemlia i volia* of the SR Northern Regional

Committee noted the numerous demonstrators with banners saying "We trust only the soviets!," a sentiment seconded by the editors: "only the soviet," said one editorial, "will protect the freedom of the citizenry."[17] A sign of how far things had gone not only among the general laboring elements but among many SRs comes from the resolution of SR soldiers at the Petrograd military warehouse, not usually known as a center of radicalism:

> We 300 members of the party . . . state the following: Russia . . . should be a democratic republic . . . [with] one legislative body. . . . We . . . express our full trust in the soviet of workers and soldiers as the guardian of the interests of the laboring masses.[18]

Notwithstanding the deep misgivings of many party activists and followers and Rusanov's confident prediction to the contrary, by early May several SR leaders, joined by one Menshevik, had taken the fateful step of entering the Provisional Government. Chernov motivated his stance and his personal entry on the role that socialists in charge of key social and economic positions in the government could, he hoped, play in quickly preparing the soil for socialism. The flaws in his reasoning, which he himself had recognized by August, leading to his withdrawal from the government, are here beside the point. The fact was that, although predominant party opinion had been against entry into the government, SR party leaders, like those of the Mensheviks, now brought their weight to bear in persuading the party to do the unthinkable. A special joint city and provincial party conference and a meeting of SR delegates to the Petrograd Soviet both now voted for entry, with significant but insufficient opposition from Left SRs (the votes for entry were respectively 172–34, 5 abstentions, and 64–25, 5 abstentions). The immediate background to this remarkable turnaround lay in the debates in the Petrograd Soviet executive committee, where moderate SRs and Popular-Socialists led the charge for a coalitional government. Chernov pointed out that only two options existed: overthrow or entry, of which he favored the latter since he did not yet feel that socialists were in a position to form the government themselves. The Right SR Fillipovskii recognized the dangers for socialists in entering a government in alliance with bourgeois elements (something Chernov seems to have overlooked entirely at this point) but felt that no other real alternative existed; but, he stated, "if we enter, let's dominate [the government]." Indeed, a certain shift in sentiment within the PSR for entry was predicated on a socialist majority in the coalitional government. At all of these meetings, Left SRs warned against the new policy; for example, at the above-mentioned city and provincial SR conference Kamkov argued that "only the soviet . . . can set out on a path of breaking imperialist war policies and [initiating] democratic reorganization of the country. ... All the rest is useless compromise." Avksentiev's successful motion in favor justified entry "in order to make [the government] more responsible [to democracy]."[19]

Somewhere along the way, the party leaders simply dropped the demand for a socialist majority in the government (presumably, liberals would not have agreed to such a composition). The pseudo-radical rhetoric of the pro-entry campaign aside, many Right SRs (and Right Mensheviks) simply wanted to shore up with socialist support and prestige the liberal-oriented Provisional Government to enable it to continue its current policy of fighting and winning the war (the first real fruit of socialist entry, after all, was the attack at the front). Regardless, the rhetoric was "democratic" and "radical," creating the impression of forward momentum toward socialism. As SRs accustomed themselves to the fact that their party was now prominently represented in the Provisional Government, their speeches and resolutions emphasized the role they foresaw for the socialists in the government, trust in whom they now proclaimed. Even the radical *Zemlia i volia* attempted to find merit in the new situation by noting on May 6 that Guchkov and Miliukov were out and by listing the six new socialist ministers now representing democracy.[20] Zhiva Galili has similarly argued that resolutions from rank-and-file Menshevik workers also viewed the new coalitional government in this light: not as a compromise with liberals or a shoring up of a liberal government but as the entry of trusted socialists into the government with the goal of protecting workers' rights.[21]

This helps explain the numerous letters, telegrams, resolutions, and instructions arriving at the center between May and August from worker, soldier, peasant, and white-collar organizations – still overwhelmingly dominated by SRs and/or Mensheviks – that offered support and trust to the socialist ministers, who were now expected to accomplish certain tasks: rapid elections to the Constituent Assembly, land reform, and steps toward peace. The documents associated with the rise of the May and July coalitional governments specifically pledged the Provisional Government to carry out such tasks.[22] Historical commentary has failed to note that at the ground level members of all the socialist parties, as well as innumerable rank-and-file laborers of all types, understood and took quite seriously, literally even, the planks that from February on established the various versions of the Provisional Government; for ground-level Russia fulfillment of those planks was the prime criterion of the government's legitimacy.

At the May SR party congress, the June congress of soviets, and thereafter, SRs continued to approach the question of power from within parameters already laid down from the very beginning of the revolution – that is, from rhapsody to threnody. Right SRs, using as always radical-sounding turns of phrase about the soviets, continued to warn about the dangers of counterrevolution, and to extol the merits of the socialists in the government, which was now portrayed as fulfilling the needs of democracy or, at least, laying the groundwork for fulfilling those needs.[23] Leftists continued to warn about the danger of counterrevolution, which, however, it associated with the bourgeois elements represented in the Provisional Government; Left SRs also noted the rise of Bolshevik mass support and, later, the fall in support for the SRs, both of which they connected directly to the association of the party with the Provisional Government's policies: the attack at the front, the constantly postponed Constituent Assembly elections, and the utter lack of concrete progress on land reform and relief for workers.[24] More to the point, like many rank-and-file Mensheviks, numerous ordinary SRs, that is, the large majority throughout these months, placed their hopes in the socialist ministers in the Provisional Government, which they hoped, under pressure from those socialists and from soviets and other laboring organizations, would carry out its assigned tasks.[25] Let us consider the attitudes displayed by a small number of pertinent resolutions. At mid-year, a *volost* [rural district] soviet of Novgorod province offered

> sympathy and support to the soviets, as the only democratic revolutionary organs that stand on the side of the people's inter-ests. ... We will support the soviet ... and the Provisional Government to the extent that it acts for the good of the people.

During July the Iziumsk SR organization offered support to the Provisional Government "with its present socialist majority" and "to VtsIK" [All-Russian Central Executive Committee of the Congress of Soviets]. Many SRs, as well as the soviets and other peasant, soldier, and worker collectives they dominated, understood the July composition of the government, with a socialist majority, as a sign that the soviet and the government had merged or that the all-Russian executive committee had "taken over" and now "controlled" the government, which in a sense was true. For example, the Iziumsk peasant soviet sent a message to the center with the same emphasis as the Iziumsk SR organization.[26]

As the summer proceeded with its well-known list of calamities – the failed offensive, the Provisional Government–Right SR oppression of leftist socialists, and finally the Kornilov episode – innumerable SRs (not to mention Mensheviks) and their followers responded by finally giving up on all hope in the coalitional Provisional Government and in their own Right SR leadership. This explains defections toward the Bolsheviks and, even more so, the rapid advance of outright Left SR influence. Left SRs began to take over organization after organization, while many osten-sibly centrist SR organizations passed resolutions against the Provisional Government, in favor of either entirely socialist or soviet power. Even more threateningly for the Provisional Government's prospects, by September a rapidly growing majority of provincial peasant soviet executive committees, formerly Right SR bastions, had turned against the coalitional government in favor of a purely socialist one.[27] The authentic voice of most SR activists, cadres, and followers about the Provisional Government is captured by the message sent during early fall by the Penza SR organization, as yet not especially distinguished for radicalism, to Kerenskii as head of the government: "Are there no limits to your . . . retreat from revolutionary positions? Who is dearer to you: the laboring people or the bourgeoisie? Are you with us or against us?"[28]

The information and analysis presented in this essay suggests needed revisions in the history of the PSR during 1917. It simply will not do to continue writing off the PSR as hopelessly conservative, except for a small leftist group commonly portrayed as virtually outside the party. To the contrary, it was the Right SRs, with the truly inexplicable temporary but crucial help of Chernov, who were foreign to SR theory, program, practice, and majority attitudes, as some Right SRs such as Argunov later admitted. At the same time, it also suggests that our understanding of the radicalization process that all comment upon during the year is highly flawed. Suspicion toward or outright opposition to a bourgeois-oriented government or a coalitional socialist-bourgeois government did not arise in association with Bolshevik agitation but existed from the outset as part of the outlook of most socialists and their laboring constituencies. Bolshevik agitation's role was in placing that party in a position to reap organizational benefits from the existing popular attitudes toward the Provisional Government when it failed to live up to what were perceived as minimal demands made upon it and when SR and Menshevik leaders disastrously associated themselves and their parties with it. This was an important accomplishment but not one of the scale that we normally credit the Bolsheviks with.

As regards the Provisional Government itself, this essay's findings indicate that we have misunderstood early popular conceptions of its mandate and appropriate longevity and therefore exaggerated its viability. Of course, numerous Octobrists, Cadets, and Right Socialists placed high hopes in the government, veritably as an incipient new state that would usher in the bourgeois capitalist era; but we cannot attribute such attitudes to the large majority of the Russian population. The Provisional Government did not founder on the rocks of Bolshevism but on the shoals of a socialist and revolutionary popular culture, by no means to be identified with Bolshevism. For better or worse, this culture could not visualize potential benefit from cooperation with the upper segments of society. Indeed, whatever small chance the upper middle segments of society had, even with the help of much of the socialist intelligentsia, of producing palpable, concrete benefits for workers, peasants, soldiers, and laboring *intelligenty* fell victim to their implacable desire to pursue the war to victory. But then, that is another story.

NOTES

Reprinted from *The Soviet and Post-Soviet Review*, 24:1–2 (1997), 27–42.

1 Michael Melancon, "The Syntax of Soviet Power: The Resolutions of Local Soviets and other Institutions, March–October 1917," *The Russian Review*, 52, no. 4 (Oct. 1993), 486–505.

2 Information and evaluations pertaining to general SR history prior to and just after the February Revolution reflect in part my research published in the following: M. Melancon, "'Stormy Petrels': The Socialist-Revolutionaries in Russia's Legal Labor Organizations, 1905–1914," *The Carl Beck Papers in Russian and East European Studies*, no. 703 (Pittsburgh: University of Pittsburgh Center for Russian and East European Studies, 1988); *The Socialist Revolutionaries and the Russian Anti-War Movement, 1914–1917* (Columbus: Ohio State Univ. Press, 1990); "Who Wrote What and When? The Proclamations of the February Revolution," *Soviet Studies*, 40, no. 3 (July 1988); "The Socialist-Revolutionary Party," "The Left Socialist-Revolutionaries," "Chernov," in *Critical Companion to the Russian Revolution, 1914–1921*, eds E. Acton, V. Cherniaev, W. Rosenberg (Bloomington and Indianapolis: Indiana Univ. Press, 1997); "The Left Socialist Revolutionaries and the Bolshevik Uprising," in *The Bolsheviks in Russian Society: The Revolution and the Civil Wars*, ed. Vladimir Brovkin (New Haven, CT: Yale Univ. Press, 1997).

3 Melancon, "Who Wrote What and When," pp. 493–94.

4 A. Shliapnikov, *Semnadtsatyi god*, 4 vols. (Moscow and Petrograd: Gosizdat, 1922–23), 1: 339–40.

5 *Izvestiia*, no. 1, Febr. 28, 1917, no. 3, March 2, 1917; *Na chuzhbine*, no. 14, March 17, 1917, no. 15 (April 1917).

6 *Delo naroda*, no. 1, March 15, 1917, no. 6, March 21, 1917; *Zemlia i volia*, no. 1, March 21, 1917; N. Sviatitskii, "Voina i predfevral'e," *Katorga i ssylka*, no. 75 (1935), pp. 40–42; S. Postnikov, "V gody mirovoi voiny," unpublished manuscript in Hoover Institution Archives, Boris I. Nicolaevsky Collection, Box 11, file 8, 23.

7 *Izvestiia*, no. 7, March 6, 1917; N. Sukhanov, *Zapiski o revoliutsii*, 7 vols. (Berlin, Izdatel'stvo G. I. Grzhebina, 1922) 2: 96–97, 140–41, 270, 289–90; Shliapnikov, *Semnadtsatyi god*, 1: 243–44.

8 *Vserossiiskoe soveshchanie sovetov rabochikh i soldatskikh deputatov. Stenograficheskii otchet* (Moscow and Leningrad: Gosizdat, 1927), pp. 131–40.

9 *Delo naroda*, no. 4, March 18, 1917, no. 6, March 21, 1917, no. 6, March 29, 1917; *Zemlia i volia*, no. 5, March 28, 1917, no. 7, March 30, 1917; *Izvestiia*, no. 24.

10 *Izvestiia* (Helsinki), no. 21, April 9, 1917, no. 22, April 11, 1917; Gosudarstvennyi arkhiv Rossiiskoi Federatsii [GARF], f. 6978, op. 1, d. 350, l 2; d. 1021, ll. 12–13; *Pravda*, no. 14, March 21, 1917; GARF, f. 6978, op. 1, d. 77; *Zemlia i volia* (Kharkov), no. 3, March 11, 1917; GARF, f. 6978, op. 1, d. 478, l. 8; *Zemla i volia* (Petrograd), no. 17, April 14,1917; *Delo naroda*, no. 28, April 15, 1917.

11 *Delo naroda*, no. 17, April 6, 1917, no. 23, April 18, 1917.

12 *Pervyi legal'nyi Petrogradskii komitet bol'shevikov v 1917 g.* (Moscow: Gosizdat, 1927), pp. 113–17.

13 *Izvestiia*, no. 41, April 15, 1917; *Pravda*, no. 35, April 18, 1917.
14 *Pravda*, no. 33, April 15, 1917, no. 36, April 20, 1917, no. 37, April 21, 1917.
15 *1917 god. Petrogradskii sovet rabochikh i soldatskikh deputatov ot fevralia k oktiabriu* (Moscow and Leningrad: Gosizdat, 1931), pp. 383–84.
16 F. P. Matveev, *Iz zapisnoi knigi deputata 176 pekhotnogo polka Petrogradskogo soveta rabochikh i soldatskikh deputatov, mart–mai 1917* (Moscow and Leningrad: Gosizdat, 1927), pp. 93–94.
17 *Zemlia i volia*, no. 24, April 22, 1917, no. 25, April 23, 1917.
18 Ibid., no. 26, April 25, 1917, no. 29, April 28, 1917, no. 30, April 29, 1917.
19 *Petrogradskii sovet rabochikh i soldatskikh deputatov. Protokoly zasedanii ispol-nitel'nogo komiteta i biuro ispolnitel'nogo komiteta* (Moscow and Leningrad: Gosizdat, 1925), pp. 130–31; *Novaia zhizn'*, no. 13, May 2, 1917; *Delo naroda*, no. 40, May 4, 1917; *Zemlia i volia*, no. 33, May 3, 1917, no. 34, May 4, 1917.
20 *Zemlia i volia*, no. 36, May 6, 1917; *Izvestiia*, no. 59, May 6, 1917.
21 Zhiva Galili, *The Menshevik Leaders in the Russian Revolution: Social Realities and Political Strategies* (Princeton: Princeton Univ. Press, 1989), pp. 186–87.
22 Melancon, "Syntax," pp. 489–90, 499.
23 *Tretii s"ezd partii sotsialistov-revoliutsionerov* (Petrograd: n.p., 1917), pp. 206–14.
24 Ibid., pp. 214–19.
25 Melancon, "Syntax," pp. 499–500.
26 Ibid., p. 500.
27 Michael Melancon, "The Left Socialist Revolutionaries and the Bolshevik Uprising," in *The Bolsheviks in Russian Society*, pp. 63–65.
28 Ibid., p. 62.

8

THE RISE AND FALL OF SMOLENSK'S MODERATE SOCIALISTS

The politics of class and the rhetoric of crisis in 1917

Michael C. Hickey

Michael Hickey shifts our attention to the provinces, a focus of study long neglected but now increasingly popular as a means to better comprehend Russian history. In doing so, he brings together many important issues, especially the complex role of politics and class rhetoric, the role of everyday life (not just major factory conflict), the moderate versus radical socialists division, shifting popular allegiances, and the fundamental dilemma and weakness of the moderate socialists. If Michael Melancon looks at the SR party and its suspicious attitude toward the Provisional Government, Hickey traces the process of the rise and fall of the moderate socialists – the SRs and Mensheviks – in power. This – why did the moderates fail? – is the reverse side of the question: why were the Bolsheviks successful? The moderate socialists, he argues, politicized the problems of daily life and framed them within a politics of class that initially won mass support. They then, however, failed to solve the very economic, crime, and other daily life issues that they had politicized. At the same time they became defenders of the new state structure and political system. The combination undermined their support as those very workers, soldiers, and lower-class elements they had helped politicize turned to the radical left for leadership. A similar trajectory of moderate socialist rise and fall was found in most cities of Russia, and thus Hickey's discussion is of a nationwide, not merely local Smolensk, process. His account also illustrates the role of a radical left bloc, not just Bolsheviks, in the rise of the radical left in the name of power to the soviets. At the same time, by pursuing this in a provincial setting such as Smolensk, freed from the national politics in Petrograd, many of the important issues can be seen more clearly.

A particularly important contribution is his discussion of "social geography" as he considers crime, the economy, sanitation, living conditions, and class inequalities as these were reflected geographically and socially. These are essential, but little studied, aspects of life in the revolutionary milieu of 1917 that were important in radicalizing public opinion and pushing it to look for alternative leadership and explanations of their condition, which the Bolsheviks and radical left provided (one might compare his to Hasegawa's essay earlier in this collection). Hickey notes how "social geography," the way the population was physically separated in living districts, helped create the broad "us" versus "them" identity and mentality that was so important in the revolution. This goes beyond other studies that have noted that division, but which focus on its class roots without considering geographic features. The two are not mutually exclusive, but by stressing geography Hickey introduces an important new consideration, one that every person in 1917 would have been aware of. His article also shows how close attention to "discourse," in the sense of the specific words selected and used, can be important to understanding political trends, as illustrated by the switch from "working class" to "masses" in speeches and writings of moderate socialists as the year progressed. In analyzing the factors that undermined the moderates, he nicely illustrates the blending of political, social, and linguistic approaches.

*   *   *

Research on Petrograd and Moscow during the Revolution of 1917 has cast light on political party organizations, factory-based labor conflict, workers' militias, and the constructed nature of class identities among factory workers and soldiers. But beyond Donald J. Raleigh's pathbreaking study of Saratov, we still know little about provincial cities in 1917, especially the small, nonindustrial cities that constituted the majority of Russia's urban centers.[1] Focusing on the city of Smolensk, this chapter provides a detailed description of one tile in the mosaic of provincial urban politics, as a step toward understanding the whole.

Smolensk, an ancient city on the upper reaches of the Dnepr River, served as the center of a grain-poor agricultural region on Russia's border with its western provinces. A border town of historic military-strategic importance, Smolensk also served as a crossroads between Moscow and the west. On the eve of World War I, the city's small population (75,000 residents in 1914) included "colonies" of merchants, tradesmen, and artisans from the western provinces (Poles, Lithuanians, and Latvians), and a community of nearly 7,000 Jews. Trade, not industry, formed the basis of the city economy. Half the population worked for wages, but only a small fraction was employed in factories. During the war, an influx of refugees swelled Smolensk's population to just over 85,000. The city became a staging base for Russia's western front, and its garrison grew to nearly 25,000 soldiers by 1917.

My particular concern is the political conjunction of social geography, living conditions, labor conflict, and the moderate socialists' discursive

160

strategies in representing fundamental problems of the urban experience in Smolensk. For most of 1917, the city was a Socialist Revolutionary (SR) and Menshevik stronghold. SRs ran the local press and, together with the Mensheviks, controlled the soviet of workers' and soldiers' deputies from March until late October. SRs and Mensheviks dominated the city's trade unions, workers' clubs, student groups, and most voluntary organizations (such as the Society of People's Universities, which organized adult education classes). Yet all of this changed rapidly in late summer. The moderate socialists had risen to power by politicizing problems of daily life and framing them within a "politics of class" that resonated with a majority of the city's population. Their failure to solve problems that they had politicized and "classed," their defense of state over class interests, and their employment of a "rhetoric of crisis" undermined their popular support and led to the fall of Smolensk's moderate socialists.

Revolutionary politics in Smolensk: an overview

Between March and early August 1917, the SRs and Mensheviks steadily consolidated control over local politics.[2] On 3 March moderate socialists pushed their way onto the city's newly formed Provisional Executive Committee (PEC), and in April they "democratized" city institutions, which in practice meant that socialists joined the administration. From June an SR served as provincial commissar of the Provisional Government, and in July the SR and Menshevik-led "socialist bloc" took over the city council or duma in a stunning electoral victory, winning 20,830 votes compared to 5,820 for the Constitutional Democrats (Kadets) and 1,235 for the Bolsheviks.[3]

Smolensk's SR and Menshevik leaders were well-known "locals" – they had spent their adult lives in the city, participated in its legal voluntary organizations as well as underground party activities, and worked at local self-government agencies. SR leader Boris Podvitskii, for instance, grew up in Smolensk and served as a zemstvo (elective district council) agriculture instructor; Menshevik Michael Davidovich, a statistician in the city administration, had organized the city's largest cooperative. This local experience shaped their approach to politics in two ways: it promoted interparty cooperation, and it reinforced ideological tendencies (especially among the Mensheviks) to view the state as a critical tool to building a new life. Smolensk's moderate socialist leaders were as familiar to local workers and employees as to professionals.[4] Both parties successfully recruited members in the spring of 1917, and by July the Menshevik organization had nearly 600 civilian members and the SRs nearly 2,000 (in addition to 1,000 members in the garrison).

Smolensk's Kadet leaders, with whom the moderate socialists wrestled for power in the spring of 1917, also had local roots, although these did not extend far beneath the strata of the local elite. Kadet leader M. A. Kvaskov, for instance, was a respected doctor; liberal A. M. Tukhachevskii was an important zemstvo activist. Liberal leaders (most of them doctors or lawyers) were well known to the city's professionals and propertied elite, but had little currency with its lower classes. At its peak in April, the Kadet organization had fewer than 300 members.

Smolensk's Bolsheviks were outsiders compared to the liberals and moderate socialists. A garrison Bolshevik circle created by Ekaterinoslav party agitator V. A. Smolianinov brought together about a dozen soldiers at the First Rear Automobile Workshop. In 1916, this circle joined a handful of SRs in forming a United Military Organization, which played an incidental role in Smolensk's February Revolution. Although the garrison Bolsheviks had some minor success in garnering support from soldiers in the spring of 1917, they had almost no contact with civilian workers.

A smaller, local Bolshevik circle formed during the war as well. Composed of secondary-school students, it badgered the older, defensist socialist leadership. S. L. Samover, V. Z. Sobolev, and a few other young Bolsheviks had some contacts with local workers through their activities at the All-City Medical Fund. But the young radicals' circle was still floundering in mid-April 1917, when an emissary from the party's Moscow Oblast Bureau fused it to the soldiers' circle and created a formal Bolshevik organization. Even then, party work remained sporadic and poorly coordinated, a criticism driven home repeatedly by the party machine in Petrograd and Moscow. The local Bolshevik organization had no newspaper, printed few leaflets, and organized only a handful of meetings. Beside soldiers in a few garrison units, the party's greatest support came from Lithuanian refugees at the Viliia Metalworking Plant (evacuated from Vilnius to Smolensk during the German advance in 1915), and from a small core of wood and leather workers. In late July, it had fewer than 200 members and held only 27 seats in the soviet (compared to 83 for the Mensheviks and 110 for the SRs).[5]

Then, in late August, the trajectory of local politics began shifting dramatically. The longer the moderate socialists controlled the city government, the more their influence seemed to decline. In the weeks after the Kornilov Affair, the SRs and Mensheviks found themselves eclipsed in the soviet by left socialists. In mid-October, the local Bolsheviks still controlled only 80 of 220 places in the soviet, but they could now outvote the moderates as part of an informal left-socialist bloc that included Left SRs and nonparty deputies. On 21 October, the soviet's SR and Menshevik leadership declared that they had lost support of the soviet majority, resigned their posts, and passed control to Bolsheviks and Left SRs.[6]

At this point, the majority of the city's workers actively supported neither the radical nor the moderate socialists. Most workers and soldiers remained neutral on 30–31 October, as the Fortieth Orenburg Cossack Regiment fought a bloody but indecisive battle against the soviet's left faction. No clear winner emerged from the skirmish, and a four-month interregnum began during which the soviet displaced Provisional Government and duma institutions piecemeal.[7] November's Constituent Assembly elections illustrated the depth of the moderate socialists' decline and of their former supporters' political disengagement. The SRs and Mensheviks combined won only 4,475 civilian votes, while the Bolsheviks took 4,041 votes (in addition to winning 7,098 of 10,131 votes in the garrison). The Kadets, who represented themselves as the most coherent opponents of Bolshevik "anarchy," captured a plurality with 6,976 civilian votes. Perhaps most significantly, more than 10,000 civilians who had voted in July now stayed away from the polls.[8] A similar phenomenon occurred among the city's Jews, most of whom had been ardent supporters of the moderate socialists in July. In November elections to the council of the local Jewish communal organization (*obshchina*), only 2,228 of 4,600 eligible voters cast ballots; of these, less than 40 percent voted for socialist candidates. The center had dropped out of local politics.[9]

How can we explain the course of revolutionary politics in Smolensk? In *Smolensk Under Soviet Rule*, Merle Fainsod described November's election results as "an impressive testimonial to the ability of the Bolshevik minority to identify itself with mass grievances, to mobilize them, and to use them as a catapult to power."[10] But there is precious little evidence of effective Bolshevik political organization, propaganda, or mobilization in the city of Smolensk. (Roberta T. Manning's essay in this volume makes a similar point for the province's rural Sychevka District.) [The reference is to the volume from which this essay is taken: Donald J. Raleigh, ed., *Provincial Landscapes: Local Dimensions of Soviet Power, 1917–1953* (Pittsburgh, 2001): 36–58 – ed.] One might argue that Bolshevik rule emanated from the barrels of soldiers' guns – after all, their strongest support came from the local garrison, and their ability to hold power depended upon soldiers' support and willingness to use violence. But that does not explain the moderate socialists' rise and fall, particularly among the city's civilian population.

Understanding Menshevik and SR leaders' discursive strategies is critical to untangling local politics in Smolensk. The city's moderate socialists, who defined themselves as the voice of the Democracy (the parties to the left of the Kadets), rose to power by politicizing issues of daily life and, most critically, articulating a politics of class that resonated with a majority of the city's population. This was possible because social geography, the conditions of daily life, the rush of popular organization after the February Revolution, and unfolding labor conflicts all helped forge a broad working-class identity. The politics of class associated class

163

identity with political party identification; in effect, the Democracy became conflated with class identity.[11] In framing themselves as the defenders of workers' class interests, the moderate socialists depicted poor living conditions as stemming primarily from bourgeois greed and mismanagement, defining their liberal opponents as a "bourgeois" party.

The politics of class propelled the moderate socialists into power, but from July they, not the Kadets, bore responsibility for declining living conditions. Resolved to regulate workers' activism in defense of state interests, the moderate socialists sought to balance class and state interests; this, however, proved no easier than preventing urban decline during wartime. City residents held the moderate socialists in the duma accountable for the breakdown of city life, while workers rejected the moderates' calls to compromise with management. Their disillusion with the moderate socialists knocked the center out of local politics, as reflected in November's elections to the Constituent Assembly and the Jewish communal council. As the moderate socialists' support dwindled, SR and Menshevik leaders depicted the city as caught in a maelstrom of crises. They rhetorically linked these crises, and the Bolshevik "ascendancy," to "anarchic tendencies" of the "dark masses." Like the Bolsheviks who subsequently seized power, the moderate socialists understood workers' changing political dispositions not as rational responses to conditions but as evidence that inadequate consciousness (*bessoznatel'nost'*) had left them vulnerable to manipulation.

Sources of working-class identity

How can we explain the Smolensk moderate socialists' political dominance in the spring and summer of 1917? The socialists (Bolsheviks included) represented themselves primarily as workers' or toilers' parties, but prewar Smolensk lacked any significant industry. Of its 75,000 residents in 1914, only 7,500 were employed in manufacturing, and only 1,500 of these in factories. Around 12,000 residents worked in the retail and wholesale trades, and another 12,000 as domestic servants, doormen, cabbies, or unskilled day laborers. Most wage earners were unmarried young men from peasant families.[12] This was certainly not the idealized working class with which socialist ideologues hoped to build a revolution. Still, during 1917, the disparate elements of Smolensk's laboring population identified themselves as members of the working class and, for a time at least, associated working-class identity with support for the moderate socialist parties.

The formidable historical literature on the sources of working-class identity in Russia investigates workplace social relations, the legal and social inequities faced by workers, the influence of the socialist parties, and workers' own efforts to define themselves.[13] Most factors discussed in this literature hold true for Smolensk before 1917: conditions and social relations in Smolensk's workshops resembled those in larger cities; since 1900, local socialist agitation had framed social relations for workers in class terms; and skilled workers in several trades (e.g., printers and tailors) had actively asserted their identity as workers. In 1917, though, workers' identity came to extend well beyond these skilled groups, thanks to the city's social geography, the flurry of public self-organization, and the political nature of the ascription and appropriation of public identity.[14]

Despite Smolensk's small size and relative lack of industry, its social geography sharpened distinctions between the lower and upper classes.[15] Most wage earners lived in the sprawling Third District, along the muddy gully streets of the Rachevka and Svirskaia Sloboda neighborhoods south of the river and on the swampy flats of the Iamskaia Sloboda and Petropavlovskaia Street neighborhoods in Zadneprove to the north. The district's poorly built wooden houses were desperately overcrowded and lacked electricity, clean water, and city sewerage. Its workshops spewed filth into the air, filth pooled in its streets, and city officials complained that its butcher and grocery shops and stalls lacked the most basic sanitation. Thieves congregated around its taverns and brothels and at the city bazaar.[16] Since the early 1890s, the duma had debated extending city water and sewer lines to the Third District, but it never did.

Conditions in the Third District worsened during World War I, as wartime shortages drove up prices and ate up workers' wages, while at the same time closing several workshops and creating greater unemployment. Thousands of Jewish, Lithuanian, Latvian, and Polish war refugees pushed into the district's poorest neighborhoods, aggravating already serious problems of overcrowding, food supply, and sanitation. By 1917, the city's civilian population had risen to 85,526.[17] While about 100 Lithuanians worked at the Viliia plant, which had retooled to produce army field kitchens, most refugees joined the ranks of the city's unemployed.

Smolensk's large wartime garrison of nearly 25,000 soldiers also strained resources in the Third District. At the onset of the war, Stavka (Supreme Headquarters of the Russian Army at the Front) designated Smolensk a staging base for the western front. Then, in 1915, the Minsk Military District Staff fell back to Smolensk during the Great Retreat. As a consequence, the garrison included several specialized technical and medical units as well as infantry and artillery reserves. Its two largest barracks complexes, in Svirskaia Sloboda and on Pokrovskaia Hill in Zadneprove, compounded neighborhood water and sanitation problems, while milling soldiers (especially those facing transfer to the front) introduced a volatile element in taverns and tea houses and at the bazaar. Requisition of apartments for the district command staff aggravated the housing shortage.[18]

Life in Third District neighborhoods contrasted starkly with that in the First and Second Districts, located on the plateau that formed the ancient city center. Smolensk's social and economic elite lived in the center – around 4,000 nobles and nearly 2,000 members of the families of merchants. It was also home to some 1,500 zemstvo and duma employees and their families, and as many doctors, lawyers, teachers, and clergy. A canopy of trees shaded its paved and lighted streets, broad sidewalks ran through parks and gardens, and splendid churches stood on every hill. The center boasted expensive shops and cafes, elite schools, a library, a concert hall, and several theaters.[19] At the end of 1916, the First and Second Districts each had more food-ration distribution points than did the entire, larger Third District; women waiting for bread in Rachevka frequently complained that residents of the center did not have to stand in long lines.[20] While the center's residents claimed that it was cramped and overcrowded, *Smolenskii vestnik* frequently carried advertisements for five- and six-room apartments near Blone Park, at the city's heart. On the fringes of the city center, though, employees, warehouse workers, and petty clerks lived in worn-down tenements.

The shared experiences of life in the Third District and on the fringes of the city center reinforced a broad sense of "us vs. them" that transcended particularistic identities based upon skill, trade, legal estate (*soslovie*), and ethnicity.[21] Workers at the Gergard Bobbin Factory (which had converted to war production) and sales clerks at upscale confectioneries lived on the same filthy streets and queued up at the same neighborhood stores. Jewish tailors and pharmacists' assistants in the Iamskaia Sloboda drank water from the same sulfur-tainted wells. And for artisans, sales clerks, and employees, the walk or tram ride to work in the city center was a journey into a different world, a juxtaposition of social spaces that made their own common condition even more palpable. Not surprisingly, controlling the city center had great symbolic importance in 1905 and 1917, and workers made Blone Park the terminus of all major demonstrations. Before 1917, the city's most politically organized workers had articulated the distinction between the "us" of the Third District and the "them" of the center in terms of class. In 1917, declarations of working-class identity became ubiquitous among residents of the Third District and the fringes of the city center.

In 1917, the complex web of identities among Smolensk's laboring population crystallized into a broad working-class identity. This was in part a spontaneous political phenomenon, spurred on by the flurry of organizational activities with which city residents greeted the February Revolution.[22] In joining trade unions and organizations, and in sending deputies to the Smolensk Soviet, thousands of men and women ascribed to themselves identity as members of the working class. Hundreds of workers and artisans unionized, declared themselves "comrade workers," laid out programs for asserting their rights as workers, and sent deputies to the soviet.[23] So did pharmacists, credit union employees, and court employees, members of professional groups that historians seldom describe as workers, but who nevertheless repeatedly chose to publicly identify themselves as such in 1917.[24]

Labor conflicts in the spring of 1917 both broadened and refined working-class identity. In April, in the midst of an inflationary spike, Smolensk's workers and employees demanded higher wages and impo- sition of an eight-hour workday (which the soviet had called for on 15 April). While some employers acceded to these demands, many small businessmen refused (including garment workshop and slaughterhouse owners), triggering a cluster of strikes. Striking tailors, butchers, and other tradesmen defined themselves as workers locked in conflict against capitalists. Work-control disputes accentuated such distinctions. While the Viliia Factory Committee, for example, insisted on workers' right to oversee hiring and determine work rules, plant director Iosif Esaitis claimed that only management had the right to decide such matters. On 16 April, the Society of Pharmacy Employees declared a strike against pharmacy owners, who had agreed to raise pay but refused to yield control over the workplace as a fundamental right. Striking pharmacists talked of defending "workers' interests" against the "capitalists," even though the "workers" involved were clerks and the "capitalists" small shopowners.[25]

During leisure time, too, working-class identity became woven into the fabric of public life. The revolution brought a frenzy of activities that helped construct working-class identity. The men and women who collected "red gifts" for soldiers at the front, sang in workers' choirs, attended workers' lectures and events at movie theaters, or participated in dozens of similar activities, explicitly subscribed to a worker identity. The same was true of the hundreds of people who joined the Lithuanian Workers' Club, the Jewish Workers' Club, the Socialist Club, and a half- dozen similar organizations that included not only workers, but also employees, students, and professionals who publicly appropriated a working-class identity.[26]

In practice, ascription and appropriation of working-class identity often became blurred with political party identification. While the moderate socialists' rhetoric simultaneously appealed to "citizens," members of "the Democracy," and "workers," underlying all of these designations was the political ascription of class identities. This is perhaps clearest in the case of Smolensk's Jews, who comprised 10 percent of the city's population. In the course of political competition, Jewish socialist parties ascribed different class identities to their supporters than they did to their opponents. Poalei-Zion, for instance, went to great lengths to define their supporters as workers and those of the nonsocialist Zionists as bourgeois and petty bourgeois. During the duma campaign, Jewish socialist leaders repeatedly defined nonsocialist Jewish groups as bourgeois, although in fact the nonsocialist organizations included many workers and the socialist parties included many nonworkers. Jewish socialists generally refrained from defining other socialists as petty bourgeois, but each party claimed to be the most authentic representative of the Jewish working class. This practice of political ascription of class identities characterized socialist politics in general, among non-Jews as well as Jews. And "politically inflected" class identity was not limited to party agitators' discourse – professionals and employees often associated their own support for the Democracy with appropriation of a worker identity.

Everyday life and the politics of class

As class discourse came to define public identities, everyday life became highly politicized. In competing for support, the parties, and especially the moderate socialists, strategically politicized such issues as food supply, public health, and crime.[27] Moderate socialist political rhetoric recognized that the revolution must overcome the legacies of autocracy and that rebuilding city life during wartime would be difficult. But it attributed urban problems primarily to the misrule and negligence of the city's "bourgeois" duma and defined the Kadets as the party of bourgeois interests. Only democratic (moderate socialist) control over the state apparatus, the SRs and Mensheviks argued, could bring a better life. The Kadets also politicized living conditions, but liberal political discourse rejected the class frame and held that citizens could improve city life only by rising above class distinctions and electing experienced (Kadet) leaders. Of these two positions, the moderate socialists' politics of class best resonated with city residents' broadened working-class identity, particularly given the apparent decline in living conditions.[28]

The revolution was no panacea for the problems of Russia's cities and did little to lessen the war's impact on living conditions in Smolensk.[29] Prices at the bazaar dropped in early March, but by April the cost of eggs, oil, meat, fish, and bread all surpassed their previous wartime highs. Despite rationing of kerosene, flour, bread, sugar, and sunflower oil, all remained in short supply. Consumers blamed shortages on merchants' greed (a charge leveled by competing merchants as well). As prices rose and supplies dwindled, Provincial Commissar A. M. Tukhachevskii appealed for patience. Despite his charge that citizens "not bring disorder into their city's life and tarnish the free people's hard-won achievements," fights broke out with regularity at Third District stores.[30] In May, the city received only three of 30 expected wagons of grain. Although the city administration warned of looming shortages, bread and other necessities remained available. It did, however, ban the sale of ice cream and pastries for lack of sugar. In June, it introduced a new ration system under which amounts and prices were adjusted weekly. Prices remained stable during June and early July, but the size of rations shrunk. Lines grew longer, especially in the Third District, and the duma repeatedly urged citizens to remain "patient and orderly."[31]

Besides waiting in long lines, residents of the poor neighborhoods still contended with terrible sanitary conditions. Emboldened by the revolution, they now freely demanded that the city take action. In the face of burgeoning complaints, the PEC appointed a new sanitation commission in mid-March. But while the commission spent the spring debating budgetary matters and reaffirming existing regulations for sausage shops and other food enterprises, conditions worsened.[32] The spread of epidemic diseases (especially scarlet fever) accelerated in March. Then, in April, the Dnepr River flooded its banks and filthy water inundated homes in the Iamskaia Sloboda, Petropavlovskaia Street, Svirskaia Sloboda, and Rachevka neighborhoods for an entire month. On 7 May, an anonymous letter to *Smolenskii vestnik* warned of a potential cholera epidemic in the Third District and decried the city's failure to address sanitation problems. Cases of smallpox, peritonitis, and the compound of intestinal ailments that Russian doctors referred to as bloody diarrhea (*krovavyi ponos*) were now alarmingly common. To the dismay of the city administration, public health appeared to be breaking down.[33]

The revolution also seemed to usher in a crime wave. The number of crimes reported to the militia in March 1917 doubled that of March 1916 (212 vs. 108). The trend continued through the spring: in April and May reported crime nearly tripled over 1916 levels (278 vs. 87, and 228 vs. 88). The rise in crime can be attributed in part to the release of dozens of criminals when crowds stormed the local prisons on 3 March, and in part to the temporary weakening of police activities engendered by the revolution. Several criminal gangs, some of which included soldiers who had deserted their units, operated with impunity in March and April, organizing a series of burglaries and armed robberies. The greatest number of reported crimes, however, had nothing to do with professional criminals; they were "survival crimes" committed by poor residents at the height of the spring's inflation. The overwhelming majority of crimes committed in spring involved nonviolent theft of either basic household goods and clothing or property valued at less than 300 rubles.[34] Crime began subsiding in late May, the very point at which crime became an issue in local politics.

In the spring and early summer, the moderate socialists attacked the Kadets for failing to improve living conditions and made these criticisms an explicit element of the politics of class. The SRs and Mensheviks accused the city provisions committee's Kadet majority of failing to assure an equitable supply of affordable goods and blamed the liberals for deteriorating sanitary conditions in poor districts. On 4 June, Dr. M. A. Abezgaus – a Bundist soviet deputy who had been appointed to the sanitation commission – charged that the city devoted too little money and personnel to public health. Abezgaus named specific streets in poor neighborhoods where garbage, human excrement, and polluted water posed severe hazards, and he warned that the wealthy could no longer ignore the problem because water sources in their neighborhoods had also been tainted.[35] The moderate socialists' emphasis on class inequities helped turn the problems of city life into effective weapons of political contestation.

It was the liberals and not the moderate socialists who first used the threat of crime as a political issue. Law enforcement had been one of the first aspects of city government "democratized" in spring, with the creation of a new city militia. Statistics on arrests suggest that the new militia fought crime effectively and succeeded in smashing the city's largest criminal gangs in April, but, in May, the liberals began insisting that the militia's ineptness had fomented a plague of lawlessness. Kadets explicitly cited the rise in robberies and "hooliganism" – acts ranging from crude remarks to women on the street to vandalism – as proof that order was breaking down and democratization had gone too far. Smolensk, they maintained, needed firm, experienced leadership. The moderate socialists soon seized on the issue as well and argued that the militia's failings proved that the city needed a new, socialist leadership. In their effort to turn public unease into political capital, both the liberals and the moderate socialists described crime as a looming crisis, even though reported crime actually had begun to decline.[36]

The moderate socialists made the problems of urban life a central feature of the summer duma electoral campaign, when Smolensk's Menshevik and SR organizations, like those in many other cities, formed an electoral bloc. In the weeks leading to July's duma elections, the socialist bloc's campaign focused almost entirely on crime, public health, food shortages, and similar issues. The bloc framed its detailed platform as a simultaneous appeal to "citizens" and to working-class identity. As the representatives of the Democracy, it alone could end shortages and build a "creative peaceful life" through programmatic reform. If elected, the socialist bloc would restructure the tax system, decentralize and democratize public services, expand the water and electrical grids and tram service, improve sanitation and health care, and reduce crime by reorganizing the militia. Although addressed to all citizens, the bloc's platform stressed that each reform and improvement in services would benefit the worker-residents of the city's poor districts, and it explicitly promised to run city government "in the interests and for the needs of the toiling classes, the interests and needs of the proletariat."[37] As the campaign intensified, the bloc drove home a simple message: the Kadets, a bourgeois party, had mishandled city affairs and would continue using local government for their own class interests. The only way to improve living conditions was to strip power from the bourgeoisie. So, socialist bloc literature concluded, "If you want a good duma, vote for the socialists."[38]

The socialist bloc's duma victory represented the resonance of the politics of class. A preelectoral meeting of Third District voters, for instance, resolved to vote for the bloc and against the "owners." The poor, they charged, live in filth and dirt, have no clean water and no lights, while the rich have paved streets and parks. The duma election would end such injustice.[39] The scale of the moderate socialists' victory (20,830 of 28,851 votes cast) reinforces the point that many of Smolensk's clerks and employees had appropriated the broadly defined worker identity that they associated with support for the socialist bloc. Many of the city's professionals also identified themselves with the Democracy and concluded that the socialists would do a better job running city affairs than had the liberals. *Smolenskii vestnik* editor Solomon Gurevich later concluded that citizens had voted for the socialist bloc expecting that it would improve city life.[40]

But moderate socialist control over city government could not end the war, alter structural factors driving inflation and unemployment, stop the spread of illness, or prevent people from committing crimes. Nor could the moderate socialists deflect the political consequences of these problems.

The breakdown of moderate socialist hegemony

The moderate socialists dominated city institutions through October 1917, but their political hegemony broke down already during the late summer and early fall. To a certain extent, national issues influenced local politics: citizens heatedly debated continuation of the war, the delay of land reform, elections to the Constituent Assembly, the causes of the Kornilov Affair, and the proper form of state power, and these debates helped shape their dispositions toward the parties.[41] Local conditions, however, played an even more critical role in undermining the moderate socialists. Three particularly important local factors subverted civilian support for the moderate socialists: the continuing decline in living conditions, the statism of SR and Menshevik leaders (best exemplified by their position on labor disputes), and moderate socialists' employment of crisis rhetoric.

Contrary to expectations, the moderate socialists could not improve the supply crisis. After the July duma elections, SRs and Mensheviks formed a majority in the city provisions committee; however, citizens reading regular transcripts of committee sessions in *Smolenskii vestnik* would have seriously doubted the moderate socialists' effectiveness in power. Much of the committee's time was spent in partisan debate, and the moderate socialists continually complained of Kadet stonewalling, which they seemed unable to curb. Moreover, the city depended upon fragile regional distribution networks that were simply beyond the moderate socialists' control. In July, Smolensk received just half its anticipated grain deliveries. Heavy rains then ruined local rye fields, the province's only significant grain crop. Food supplies waned. Prices for rationed bread remained stable, but rations were halved from one to one-half pound per day. At the bazaar, prices for staples like sunflower oil and potatoes fluctuated wildly. Sugar prices soared and the city ran out of tea and coffee. The supply situation deteriorated further as fall approached. Grain deliveries in August, September, and October all fell far short of the city's minimum needs.[42] Consumers did not feel the effects immediately; prices for rationed bread increased only slightly in August and September, as did the cost of commodities at the bazaar. In October, though, the consequences of shortages became painfully clear. Bread and flour prices doubled, as did that of potatoes, and the cost of clothing soared. Workers across the city raised new demands for higher pay, but even in the few cases where they succeeded, wages did not keep pace with inflation.

As rapid inflation seriously eroded popular faith in the moderate socialists' ability to govern, tensions rose in connection with warnings of impending starvation. Rumors spread that garrison soldiers – pushed to the verge of mutiny by shortages – were planning a food riot. On 29 September, these rumors gave way to panic in Iamskaia Sloboda, when Jews feared that soldiers ordered to search warehouses for hoarded goods would launch a pogrom. Residents of the city's poor neighborhoods swamped the soviet with accusations against alleged speculators and complaints that city officials were not punishing speculation adequately. In response, soviet and duma leaders formed a Commission for the Struggle with Speculation on 11 October. Moderate socialist leaders pleaded with citizens to remain orderly and abide by the law, but recognized their own diminished influence. As commission chairman V. Ia. Burgonov (an SR) admitted on 14 October, they were helpless to affect "the masses' psychological mistrust of traders."[43]

Just as the moderate socialists could do little to control inflation, the best efforts of activists like Dr. Abezgaus had little impact on public health. The volume of complaints to the city about poor sanitary conditions began rising after June. Abezgaus himself charged that the (democratized) militia did not treat sanitation violations seriously. Moreover, public turf wars erupted between bureaucratic departments responsible for sanitation and elected neighborhood sanitation trustees.

Despite their experience in the local bureaucracy, the SR and Menshevik leadership seemed overwhelmed by these disputes and appeared impotent in the face of growing health problems. The incidence of bloody diarrhea doubled in August, and typhus and typhoid fever spread in September and October. Renters in the poorer neighborhoods began blaming the moderate socialist-run duma for the growing piles of garbage in the streets. In an angry 7 September letter to the duma, residents of Nikolaevskaia Street (on the fringe of the First District) charged that they had complained for weeks about the filth and excrement in their street and that the city had done nothing.[44]

The moderate socialist-led local government also seemed impotent against crime, even though reported crime fell during the summer. The moderate socialist leadership took no notice of the drop in crime, and the press and party activists seemed obsessed instead with the danger of mob justice (*samosud*). Three times in late June and July, crowds of men and women, soldiers and civilians, lynched suspected thieves at the train station.[45] The moderate socialists and the Kadets both argued that mob justice threatened the revolution by undermining the rule of law,[46] but street crime again grabbed their attention in the weeks after the Kornilov rebellion. Reported crime increased along with prices in September and October. The majority of crimes were still small-scale thefts (116 of 179 crimes in September, and 147 of 218 in October) that should be interpreted as survival crimes. Dramatic, violent crimes had become more common, however, and were described in florid detail by *Smolenskii vestnik*, so that the threat of crime haunted residents of all the city's neighborhoods.[47]

The rise in crime, the breakdown of public health, and the fall's inflationary spike all undermined the moderate socialists' political support, not only among the workers, but also among professionals who had looked to them to improve city life. Menshevik S. E. Galperin later recalled that the local population had lost faith in the moderate socialists' "ability to handle the administrative and economic life of the city."[48] At the same time, deteriorating urban conditions contributed to a new cycle of strikes that further eroded support for the moderate socialists among Smolensk's workers.

Unlike the spring strikes, which were led by unions closely tied to the moderate socialist parties, labor unrest that fall centered on unions in which the Bolsheviks and Anarchists were influential.[49] Moreover, strikes by the left socialist-led unions now succeeded while those of moderate socialist-led unions failed. The woodworkers' union (which included several Bolsheviks) sparked a cycle of labor conflict when it struck for higher wages against the Litvin Lumber Mill on 6 August. The strike, which the soviet did not authorize, ended when Litvin promised a 50 percent wage increase on 9 August. On 12 August, the Anarchist-led leatherworkers struck for higher wages against three leather-making plants. Again the soviet did not endorse the action, yet one by one, plant owners agreed to the union's terms. On 16 August, one of the city's best-organized moderate-socialist unions, Needle Shop, declared a strike against garment workshops that had refused to raise wages. The strike failed, and after a week the union's Bundist-Menshevik leadership ordered its members back to work.

Labor unrest intensified in the weeks after the Kornilov rebellion. On 7 September, the Bolshevik-led metalworkers' union struck for higher wages and increased control over management decisions. More than 400 metalworkers went out, shutting down the Viliia and Gergard plants and the Reshitnikov String Factory for an entire month. The metalworkers' strike began a cascade of labor actions. In September and October, nearly 1,000 members of the union of cooks and waiters, the bakers' union, pharmacy employees, and a half-dozen other unions ignored the moderate socialists' calls for conciliation and went out on strike. Again, while the metalworkers' union prevailed in its strike, those by the pharmacy employees and other moderate socialist-led unions failed.

The left socialist unions' success owed less to the attributes of their leaders than to the fact that they struck against plants engaged in defense production, where both the owners and the state had a special interest in maintaining production. Still, the failure of strikes by moderate socialist-led unions carried a political message for Smolensk's workers – the moderate socialists were no longer effective leaders in labor conflicts. Moreover, the moderate socialist leaders had not publicly supported workers' strike actions. Instead, the moderate socialists told workers that they should not strike and that they should continue seeking compromise, even as inflation ate up their salaries, their employers stubbornly resisted raising wages, and the Kornilov rebellion seemed to demonstrate a right-wing conspiracy to crush "their" revolution. On 3 September, Smolensk's labor commissar, Menshevik S. P. Shur, told all "conscious workers" to "return to your benches and machines. ... At the present grave moment [the aftermath of the Kornilov Affair], I consider strikes impermissible, and I appeal to you, comrades, to decide all conflicts through arbitration."[50] *Smolenskii vestnik* would not endorse strikes and gave workers' demands only cursory coverage. The reason was rooted in ideology. In power, Menshevik and SR leaders became – as Ziva Galili has put it – statists, in that they believed state interests had to take precedence over class interests, at least for the time being.[51] Their statism manifested itself in a number of issues, ranging from democratization of rural government to labor conflict.[52] Party leaders feared that labor unrest would disrupt the war effort, accelerate the country's economic collapse, and undermine the stability of the state. They therefore urged workers to seek compromise rather than strike.

The public stance taken by Labor Commissar S. P. Shur epitomized moderate socialist statism. In April, in his capacity as a leader of the soviet, Shur had warned that workers must recognize the "all-state significance" of their actions. He resigned from the soviet upon appointment as labor commissar on 12 July, as he believed that the commissar must put state interests before class interests. In a letter to all "comrade workers," Shur explained that as an activist he had represented the proletariat, but as commissar "I will represent the interests of the provisional revolutionary government."[53] Commissar Shur continued urging that the "class-conscious, politically educated proletariat" seek mediation with employers rather than strike. As already noted, in the days after the Kornilov Affair he insisted that workers not strike, and throughout the fall he called on workers to put the state's interests before their own.

Shur's public statism contrasted sharply with his private interpretation of labor conflict. Shur went to great lengths to present himself as a neutral arbitrator during talks between the union and management, which dragged on from 26 August through 8 October.[54] Before and during the month-long strike, neither the union's Bolshevik negotiating team nor the owners' representative (Esaitis) would compromise. Both claimed to be defending the revolution and accused their antagonist of undermining order; both expected Shur to intervene in their favor. On 3 October, Shur angrily told union and management representatives that "in addition to the interests of both sides, there is here a third interest – that of the state." His job was to protect it.[55] But in his private correspondence to the Moscow region labor commissar, Shur struck a very different tone, blaming the strike on the owners and describing union demands as "important" and "directed toward improving the workers' condition." He begged the Moscow commissar to send a delegation to pressure the owners into accepting arbitration – Moscow could do this while appearing impartial, whereas Shur could not without jeopardizing the neutrality of his state office. He put the issue plainly:

> What is at stake here is the authority of a workers' organization – the Trade Union of Metallists. . . . It is impossible to refuse the workers this demand without striking a serious blow against our workers' organizations, their authority, and their strength.[56]

The apparent contradiction between the moderate socialists' public position of statism and their claim to represent workers' interests (which had been central to the politics of class) proved too great for workers and employees who in July had supported the SRs and Mensheviks. In the context of failed strikes and further-declining living conditions, calls for conciliation seemed irrational. In early September, workers and employees began recalling their moderate socialist soviet deputies, as did garrison soldiers.[57] The moderates lost influence and the Bolsheviks increased their strength in the soviet (but never achieved a plurality). From early October, Bolshevik and Left SR resolutions consistently won soviet majorities, and on 21 October the soviet's Menshevik and SR leaders admitted that they had lost authority among workers and soldiers and resigned. Shur stepped down as labor commissar two weeks later, citing "the shift in the mood of Smolensk's working masses."[58]

The way that moderate socialists rhetorically framed the breakdown of urban conditions was also a factor eroding their political hegemony. From late July, SR and Menshevik leaders began employing crisis rhetoric to explain declining living conditions. The provisions situation, for example, became a "provisions crisis," and all discussions of food supply were laced with warnings of impending hunger. From August through October, local officials and the press constantly warned that the city was on the verge of starvation. By emphasizing that such issues constituted crises, the moderate socialists ironically spurred on perceptions that they could not govern effectively and accentuated the political damage. This discursive strategy points to a continuity between moderate socialist and Bolshevik political rhetoric: like the Bolsheviks during the Civil War, the moderate socialists blamed their own political decline on the inadequate class consciousness of the "masses."

Crime had been the first urban problem that the moderate socialists, following the example of the Kadets, described in crisis terms. At the very beginning of the duma campaign, preelection rhetoric focused on the failings of the local militia. Blaming the militia for crime remained an element of crisis rhetoric through the fall, but with a twist – moderate socialists increasingly criticized militia members' "low level of consciousness." In late July, a new target emerged as the focus of moderate socialists' discussions of crime: undisciplined elements in the garrison.

The marauding soldier, robbing civilians and terrorizing the countryside, was a stock figure in the provincial press in late summer and fall 1917. The editor of *Smolenskii vestnik* in particular used cases of mob justice to exemplify the threat that undisciplined soldiers posed to revolutionary order. In its reports on lynching in July and August, *Smolenskii vestnik* attributed anarchic violence to soldiers and undifferentiated members of the "crowd" that milled about the railroad station and the bazaar, and highlighted the ostensible distinction between "politically unconscious" (*bessoznatel'nyi*) rural and semi-rural elements and the "disciplined" working class.[59] The moral was twofold: dark (politically unconscious) masses posed a threat to order, and the politically enlightened elements must maintain their discipline. Press reports from July through October blamed "criminals in soldiers' uniforms" not only for lynching, but also for thefts and other crimes. It is clear that discipline did break down in the garrison in late August, and militia records suggest that the number of soldiers arrested rose that fall, but the press seriously inflated soldiers' participation in criminal acts.[60]

The pitch of moderate socialists' crisis rhetoric regarding crime rose in the fall, as Smolensk's SR Provincial Commissar, S. D. Efimov, repeatedly warned that the city was sinking into a state of criminal anarchy.[61] *Smolenskii vestnik*'s coverage of crime became graphic and shrill, and helped drive popular perceptions of a crisis. Although the militia reported that there were fewer crimes in fall than in spring, the duma's moderate socialist majority claimed that "fear . . . is the mood of the day" and that Smolensk was becoming "another Kronstadt." By early October, SR and Menshevik leaders were convinced that the "crime crisis" required emergency measures. The duma and soviet formed an Executive Commission to Defend Order to battle crime, but few moderate socialists expressed faith in its abilities; a series of hyperbolic articles in *Smolenskii vestnik* warned that the crime crisis would not abate.[62] On 18 October, the soviet desperately pleaded with citizens to shun anarchic violence. Even Commissar Efimov conceded that "local authorities are powerless to fight lawlessness."[63]

The moderate socialists' crisis rhetoric escalated as their influence waned, since the rhetoric of crisis gave the moderates a way to comprehend both deteriorating urban conditions and their own political decline. After the Kornilov Affair, moderate socialist crisis rhetoric began linking crime and mob justice to rising Bolshevik influence and presented this as evidence that the masses had been overwhelmed by anarchistic tendencies. References to the "working class" virtually disappeared from the moderate socialists' discourse and were replaced by generalizations about the "masses." Linking low levels of consciousness to both crime and Bolshevism emerged as a dominant theme in local moderate socialist rhetoric in the days after the Bolshevik seizure of power in Petrograd. On 4 November, SR leader Petr Bukhshtab explained his decision to quit the soviet's executive committee by saying that he would not work with "lynchers" and "thugs." On 5 November, Gurevich described the Bolshevik uprising in Petrograd as a "bloody crime" and accused the local Bolsheviks of "preying upon the instincts of the dark elements and the unconscious masses."[64] Crime and the new left-socialist majority, then, could be bundled together and explained through the same phenomenon: the masses' inadequate consciousness. In local SR and Menshevik rhetoric, it was not the moderate socialists, whose campaign promises could not be fulfilled and whose public positions undermined workers' support, who had failed; the masses had failed.

Conclusion

Smolensk's moderate socialists presented themselves as both the voice of the Democracy and the representatives of the toiling or working

177

classes, but in the practice of politics the concept of the Democracy became conflated with a broad working-class identity. The moderate socialists rose to power because the politics of class resonated with a majority of the city's residents. The politics of class involved attributing class characteristics to problems of everyday life and ascribing bourgeois class identity to the liberals. The politics of class proved powerful because Smolensk's social geography, the realities of daily life, grassroots political activism, and labor conflict encouraged many people whom the moderate socialists (and later historians) considered peripheral to the working class to define themselves as workers. From spring until fall 1917, Smolensk's "workers" saw the moderate socialists as the best representatives of their class interests. But the politics of class could work against the moderate socialists, too. After July, the moderates' failure to fix problems of daily life that they themselves had politicized and "classed" undermined their claim to represent workers' interests. At the same time, the moderate socialists' attempts to defend state interests required that they mute workers' class-based demands at the very point when class conflict seemed most acute, and this further eroded their position among workers. Although the Bolsheviks, Left SRs, and Anarchists won the active support of only a minority of self-defined workers, the collapse of the moderate socialists had given the left bloc a plurality in the soviet. The moderate socialists, who seem to have had little more faith in the rationality of the common people (the *narod*) than did the Bolsheviks, interpreted the turn in local politics as evidence that the masses simply lacked adequate consciousness and were being manipulated.

While the course of politics in Smolensk might at first seem little more than a recapitulation of patterns familiar from Petrograd and Moscow (and Saratov, for that matter), it is in fact quite instructive. Social histories of Russia's largest cities in 1917 have concentrated on industrial workers and hence place class conflict in the factories at the epicenter of grassroots politics.[65] While many historians have noted that everyday life shaped workers' political dispositions, few have examined urban living conditions and their politicization.[66] The case of Smolensk reveals the politicization of daily life as a critical element of the politics of class in a small city without a large constituency of industrial workers. It suggests that we must look more closely at the many factors besides industrial labor conflict that shaped local politics in provincial centers. In particular, we need to look more closely at political contestation and the ways in which parties and groups framed and conducted politics during the Revolution of 1917.

The rhetoric of politics employed by Smolensk's moderate socialists also highlights important continuities linking Russia's socialist parties. The politics of class as practiced by all socialist parties depended upon the ascription of different class characteristics to supporters and adversaries. The Bolsheviks were not alone in ascribing bourgeois or petty-bourgeois class identities to their political opponents, nor was their propensity to bemoan the masses' low level of consciousness unique among the socialist parties.[67] At the same time, the fall of Smolensk's moderate socialists points to an important difference between the Bolshevik and SR-Menshevik practice of politics. When the politics of class undercut the moderates' popular support because they could not defend what they themselves had defined as the workers' interests, they stepped down from power. The Bolsheviks would prove no better at stemming the tide of crime, hunger, or sickness than had been the SRs and Mensheviks. But when they lost workers' support, the Bolsheviks proved far more willing than the moderate socialists to replace democratic politics with rule by force.

NOTES

Reprint of essay in Donald J. Raleigh, ed., *Provincial Landscapes: Local Dimensions of Soviet Power, 1917–1953* (Pittsburgh: University of Pittsburgh Press, 2001), pp. 14–35.

1 For overviews of the literature on 1917, see Ronald G. Suny, "Toward a Social History of the October Revolution," *American Historical Review* 88, no. 1 (1983): 31–52, and idem, "Revision and Retreat in the Historiography of 1917: Social History and Its Critics," *Russian Review* 53, no. 1 (1994): 165–82; Steve Smith, "Writing the History of the Russian Revolution After the Fall of Communism," *Europe-Asia Studies* 46, no. 4 (1994): 563–78; and Edward Acton, Vladimir Iu. Cherniaev, and William G. Rosenberg, eds., *Critical Companion to the Russian Revolution, 1914–1921* (Bloomington, 1997). The best monograph on a provincial city in 1917 is by Donald J. Raleigh, *Revolution on the Volga: 1917 in Saratov* (Ithaca and London, 1986).

2 Although the Menshevik and SR organizations in Smolensk included members of both parties' respective left (internationalist), centrist, and right wings, the centrists dominated their leadership. On interparty divisions among Mensheviks, see for instance Vladimir Brovkin, *The Mensheviks After October: Socialist Opposition and the Rise of the Bolshevik Dictatorship* (Ithaca, 1987). On divisions among the SRs, see Michael Melancon's contributions to Acton *et al.*, *Critical Companion*.

3 Socialist blocs won majorities in duma elections in Moscow and several other cities. See William G. Rosenberg, "The Russian Municipal Duma Elections of 1917: A Preliminary Computation of Returns," *Soviet Studies* 21, no. 2 (1969): 131–63. On local politics in the spring of 1917, see my "Discourses of Public Identity and Liberalism in the February Revolution: Smolensk, 1917," *Russian Review* 55, no. 4 (1996): 615–37, and "Local Government and State Authority in the Provinces: Smolensk, February–June 1917," *Slavic Review* 55, no. 4 (1996): 863–81.

4 Several local SR and Menshevik leaders also headed up the local Jewish socialist parties to which they were affiliated (the Jewish Socialist Workers' Party and the Bund, respectively) and were well known among the city's

MICHAEL C. HICKEY

Jewish workers. See my "Revolution on the Jewish Street: Smolensk, 1917," *Journal of Social History* 31, no. 4 (1998): 823–50.

5 The most detailed materials on the Bolsheviks in Smolensk are memoirs collected by Istpart (Commission on the History of the October Revolution). See Tsentr dokumentatsii noveishei istorii Smolenskoi oblasti (hereafter cited as TsDNISO), f. 7, op. 1, dd. 55–131; and Partiinyi arkhiv Smolenskogo obkoma KPSS, *Ustanovlenie i uprochenie Sovetskoi vlasti v Smolenskoi gubernii: Sbornik dokumentov* (Smolensk, 1957), 42–43, 70–71, 77–78. See also Partiinyi arkhiv Smolenskogo obkoma KPSS, *Bol'sheviki Smolenshchiny do oktiabria 1917 g.: Sbornik dokumentov* (Smolensk, 1961), 225; Institut marksizma-leninizma pri TSK VKP, *Perepiska sekretariata Ts. K. RSDRP(b) s mestnymi partiinymi organizatsiiami*, vol. 1, *Mart–oktiabr' 1917* (Moscow, 1957), 488; and Partiinyi arkhiv Smolenskogo obkoma KPSS, *Ocherki istorii Smolenskoi organizatsii KPSS*, 2nd edn. (Smolensk, 1985), 1: 42–67.

6 For a Menshevik appraisal of the impact of the Kornilov Affair on local politics and of the Bolsheviks' growing strength in September and October, see TsDNISO, f. 7, op.1, d. 127, l. 94.

7 On this interim period, see my 1993 Northern Illinois University dissertation, "Revolutionary Smolensk: The Establishment of Soviet Power in Smolensk Province, 1917–1918," 631–752.

8 Among garrison soldiers, the Bolsheviks won 7,098 votes, the Kadets 1,120, and Mensheviks and SRs combined only 1,913. Half of the garrison soldiers abstained from voting (*Smolenskii vestnik* [hereafter *SV*], 15 November 1917, 3; and Gosudarstvennyi arkhiv Smolenskoi oblasti [hereafter cited as GASO], f. 7, op. 3, d. 3).

9 The February Revolution shifted Russia's political spectrum to the left, so that the moderate socialists constituted the center in relation to the Kadets on the right and the Bolsheviks and Anarchists on the left (Rex A. Wade, *The Russian Revolution* [Cambridge, 2000], ch. 3). On the *obshchina* elections, see *SV*, 28 November 1917, 2.

10 Merle Fainsod, *Smolensk Under Soviet Rule* (Cambridge, Mass., 1958; reprint, Boston, 1989), 30.

11 Orlando Figes and Boris Kolonitskii similarly argue that class discourse transformed the meanings of the term "Democracy" so that "the common people's understanding of 'democracy' was intimately linked with their social expectations and self-identity ... they also thought of democracy in class terms" (Figes and Kolonitskii, *Interpreting the Russian Revolution: The Language and Symbols of 1917* [New Haven, 1999], 122).

12 A. I. Kazakov, *Naselenie Smolenshchiny: Proshloe i nastoiashchee* (Smolensk, 1996), 31, 50, 58. The labor force remained mostly young, male, and single in 1917: of the 192 members of the bakers' union, for instance, 136 were male, 121 were younger than 25, and 117 were single (GASO, f. 1998, op. 1, d. 12).

13 For representative examples of this large and complex literature, see Victoria E. Bonnell, *Roots of Rebellion: Workers' Politics and Organizations in St. Petersburg and Moscow, 1900–1914* (Berkeley, 1983), and essays by Reginald E. Zelnik, Mark D. Steinberg, Heather Hogan, and Steve Smith in *Making Workers Soviet: Power, Class, and Identity*, ed. Lewis H. Siegelbaum and Ronald Grigor Suny (Ithaca, 1994).

14 See, for instance, Boris Kolonitskii, "Antibourgeois Propaganda and Anti-'Burzhui' Consciousness in 1917," *Russian Review* 53, no. 2 (1994): 183–96.

15 For comparison, see the discussions of urban social geography in James Bater, *St. Petersburg: Industrialization and Change* (Montreal, 1976); Joseph Bradley, *Muzhik and Muscovite: Urbanization in Late Imperial Russia* (Berkeley, 1985);

Daniel Brower, *The Russian City Between Tradition and Modernity, 1850–1900* (Berkeley, 1990); and Raleigh, *Revolution on the Volga*, ch. 1.

16 *Zhurnaly Smolenskoi gorodskoi dumy za 1913 gody* (Smolensk, 1914), 95, 147, 189; D. N. Zhbankov, "Nekotorye vyvody o sanitarnom sostoianii fabrik i zavodov Smolenskoi gubernii i dannye izmerenii rabochikh," *Vrach* 17, no. 13 (1896): 368; Sanitarnoe otdelenie Smolenskoi gubernskoi zemskoi upravy, *Svedeniia o zaraznykh bol'nykh i deiatel'nosti meditsinskoi organizatsii v Smolenskoi gubernii* 1913, no. 11: 492–505; and GASO, f. 65, op. 2, d. 1793.

17 Some 12,000 Polish, 3,000 Jewish, 2,500 Lithuanian, and hundreds of Latvian war refugees were evacuated to Smolensk Province in 1915–16. Most of the Jewish and Lithuanian refugees ended up in Smolensk city (GASO, f. 1, op. 8, dd. 738a, 763, 906, 914, 935; *Vestnik statistiki*, nos. 1–4 [1921]: 210; *Evreiskaia zhizn'*, 7 February 1916, 34, and 15 May 1916, 59; Mikhail V. Isakovskii, *Na El'ninskoi zemle, avtobiograficheskie stranitsy* [Moscow, 1973], 302–5, 317–20; and *Vestnik Krasnogo Kresta*, no. 8 [October 1916]: 2714–15, and no. 10 [December 1916]: 3376, 3384, 3388–89, 3399–406, 3421). For comparison, see Donald J. Raleigh, "The Impact of World War I on Saratov and Its Revolutionary Movement," in *Politics and Society in Provincial Russia: Saratov, 1590–1917*, ed. Rex A. Wade and Scott J. Seregny (Columbus, 1989), 255–61; and Peter Gatrell, *A Whole Empire Walking: Refugees in Russia During World War I* (Bloomington, 1999).

18 GASO f. 65, op. 2, dd. 1805, 1811–13.

19 N. N. Chebyshev, *Blizkaia dal': Vospominaniia* (Paris, 1933), 9–11.

20 See, for instance, *SV*, 29 January 1917, 3; and 24 February 1917, 3.

21 On the broad "worker" or "toiler" identity that permeated other forms of identity in 1917, see Figes and Kolonitskii, *Interpreting the Russian Revolution*, ch. 4.

22 The four paragraphs that follow summarize evidence and conclusions presented in detail in Hickey, "Discourses of Public Identity" and "Revolution on the Jewish Street."

23 Records exist for only a few local unions. In the fall of 1917, the metal-workers' union had 472 members; the woodworkers, 400; the bakers, 200; the meatworkers, 300; the cooks and waiters, 261; the commercial employees, 300; and the postal telegraph employees, 300 (GASO, f. 1994, op. 1, d. 1, ll. 9–10 ob., 221; and f. 1988, op. 1, d. 12; and TsDNISO, f. 1, op. 1, d. 384; and f. 7, op. 1, d. 132, 1. 32).

24 Rhetorical distinctions between "employees" and "workers" were far less pronounced in Smolensk than in larger cities, perhaps because the industrial work force was so small. Compare records of the metalworkers' union and the Viliia plant committee (GASO, f. 1994, op. 1, d. 1; and f. 146, op. 1, d. 21) to discussions in David Mandel, *The Petrograd Workers and the Fall of the Old Regime* (New York, 1983) and idem, *The Petrograd Workers and the Soviet Seizure of Power* (New York, 1984); S. A. Smith, *Red Petrograd: Revolution in the Factories, 1917–1918* (Cambridge, 1983); Diane P. Koenker, *Moscow Workers and the 1917 Revolution* (Princeton, 1981); Diane P. Koenker and William G. Rosenberg, *Strikes and Revolution in Russia, 1917* (Princeton, 1989); and William B. Husband, *Revolution in the Factory: The Birth of the Soviet Textile Factory, 1917–1920* (New York, 1990).

25 TsDNISO, f. 7, op. 1, d. 132; GASO, f. 146, op. 1, d. 21, ll. 238–53; and *SV*, 17–25 April 1917.

26 There are few precise figures on the number of workers' club members in 1917, but by 1 April one of the smaller clubs, the Jewish Workers' Club, had 260 members.

27 William G. Rosenberg, *Liberals in the Russian Revolution: The Constitutional Democratic Party, 1917–1921* (Princeton, 1974), 158–59.

28 This discussion concerns living conditions for the civilian population, but living conditions were also important to garrison politics. See, for instance, Howard White, "1917 in the Rear Garrisons," in Linda Edmondson and Peter Waldron, eds., *Economy and Society in Russia and the Soviet Union, 1860–1930: Essays for Olga Crisp* (London, 1992), 162.

29 I. A. Baklanova, *Rabochie Petrograda v periode mirnogo razvitiia revoliutsii, mart–iiun' 1917* (Leningrad, 1978), 38–53; Z. V. Stepanov, "Ekonomicheskoe polozhenie rabochikh," in A. L. Fraiman, ed., *Istoriia rabochikh Leningrada* (Leningrad, 1972), 2: 40–41; and M. N. Gernet, *Izbrannye proizvedeniia* (Moscow, 1974), 423–24.

30 Data on prices are from *Smolenskii vestnik* and materials in GASO, f. 1, op. 8, d. 921; f. 12, op. 2, d. 20; and f. 65, op. 2, d. 1770. For Tukhachevskii's statement and charges against merchants, see *SV*, 29 March 1917, 2; and 16 April 1917, 3.

31 On the city's provisions administration in spring, see GASO f. 65, op. 2, d. 1770. On debates over democratization of provisions and assessments of the supply situation, see *SV*, 14 May 1917, 2; 27 May 1917, 2; and 1 June 1917, 3.

32 On the sanitation commission, see *SV*, 16 March 1917, 2; and GASO, f. 65, op. 2, d. 1802, ll. 1–18.

33 GASO f. 65, op. 2, d. 1801, l. 1.

34 Ibid., f. 578, op. 3, d. 22, ll. 5–39 ob.; and f. 578, op. 1, d. 4; and my "Moderate Socialists and the Politics of Crime in Revolutionary Smolensk," *Canadian-American Slavic Studies* 35, nos. 2–3 (2001): 198–218.

35 *SV*, 4 June 1917, 3. Property owners mobilized around the issue of sanitation: the Union of Homeowners formed in June listed it as a primary concern (*SV*, 16 June 1917, 2; and GASO, f. 65, op. 2, d. 1801, ll. 3–16 ob.).

36 *SV*, 26 April 1917, 3; 13 May 1917, 3; 19 May 1917, 2; and 11 June 1917, 3; and *Smolenskie Gubernskie Vedomosti* (hereafter cited as *SGV*), 1 June 1917, 1.

37 *SV*, 16 June 1917, 2; and 14 July 1917, 2.

38 *SV*, 22 June 1917, 2; 25 June 1917, 3; 27 June 1917, 3; and 8 July 1917, 3.

39 *SV*, 27 June 1917, 3.

40 *SV*, 3 August 1917, 2.

41 On local reverberations of national issues, particularly the Kornilov rebellion, see Hickey, "Revolutionary Smolensk," chs. 4, 7, 8, and 9.

42 In September, the province received less than one-third of scheduled grain deliveries (181 wagons). *SV*, 4 August 1917, 3; GASO, f. 12, op. 2, d. 20, ll. 144 ob., 147–47 ob.

43 *SV*, 14 October 1917, 3; TsDNISO, f. 7, op. 1, d. 132, l. 35; and GASO, f. 12, op. 2, d. 20, ll. 157–57 ob. From 10 September, the Smolensk garrison received half-rations (M. Dalian, *Smolensk v revoliutsii 1917 g.* [Smolensk, 1927], 31). And, on 17 October, the militia barely averted a riot at the store of a merchant "speculating" in galoshes.

44 GASO, f. 65, op. 3, d. 1801, l. 79, passim.

45 In each case, someone in the crowd identified the suspect as an "outsider" – either a *burzhui* (a derisive term for the bourgeoisie) or a "known criminal."

46 *SV*, 19 July 1917, 3; and 20 July 1917, 3. Differences between local Menshevik, SR, and Kadet understandings of legality are discussed in Hickey, "Local Government" and "Moderate Socialists."

47 GASO, f. 578, op. 3, d. 22, ll. 9, 21–23; f. 578, op. 3, d. 16, ll. 131–33, 191–92, 199, 247; and f. 884, op. 1, d. 143, 1. 86. Compare the florid account of an armed robbery in *SV* (14 October 1917, 3; and 15 October 1917, 3) to the militia's version in GASO (f. 578, op. 1, d. 7, ll. 57–64 ob.).

48 TsDNISO f. 7, op. 1, d. 127, 1. 94.

49 The following two paragraphs are based upon Akademiia Nauka SSSR, *Revoliutsionnoe dvizhenie v Rossii v auguste 1917: Razgrom kornilovskogo miatezha* (Moscow, 1959), 250–51; GASO, f. 1994, op. 1, d. 1, ll. 11, 231; National Archives Microfilm Publication T-87, Records of the Smolensk Oblast of the All-Union Communist Party of the Soviet Union, 1917–1941, reel 2, file WKP 1, 87, 99, 105, 108; various reports in *SV* from late August through September 1917; TsDNISO, f. 7, op. 2, d. 132, passim; and *Ustanovlenie i uprochenie Sovetskoi vlasti*, 95–96, 109.

50 *SV*, 3 September 1917, 3. On strike activity in the provinces in general, see Koenker and Rosenberg, *Strikes and Revolution*.

51 See Ziva Galili and Albert P. Nenarokov, "The Mensheviks in 1917: From Democrats to Statists," in Acton *et al.*, *Critical Companion to the Russian Revolution*, 267–80; and William G. Rosenberg, "Social Mediation and State Construction(s) in Revolutionary Russia," *Social History* 19, no. 2 (1994): 169–88.

52 On the moderate socialists' efforts to limit what they saw as disruptive democratization in the countryside, see my "Urban *Zemliachestva* and Rural Revolution: Petrograd and the Smolensk Countryside in 1917," *Soviet and Post-Soviet Review* 23, no. 2 (1996): 151–54; and Roberta T. Manning's essay in this volume. [Reference is to the volume from which this essay is taken: Donald J. Raleigh, ed., *Provincial Landscapes: Local Dimensions of Soviet Power, 1917–1953* (Pittsburgh, 2001): 36–58 – ed.]

53 *SV*, 6 April 1917, 3; 16 July 1917, 3; and 27 July 1917, 3; and GASO, f. 799, op. 1, d. 1, 1. 200.

54 GASO f. 1994, op. 1, d. 1, ll. 233–35, 25–218.

55 Ibid., ll. 41–42.

56 Ibid., ll. 33–34.

57 S. E. Galperin recalled that after the Kornilov rebellion the soviet became populated by "new people" whom the Menshevik and SR leaders did not know (TsDNISO, f. 7, op. 1, d. 132, 1. 37).

58 *Protokoly Tsentral'nogo komiteta RSDRP (b), avgust 1917–fevral' 1918* (Moscow, 1958), 40; *Ustanovlenie i uprochenie Sovetskoi vlasti*, 94, 99–105; and *Bol'sheviki Smolenshchiny*, 234–40. For resignation speeches by Menshevik leader S. E. Galperin and SR leader P. I. Bukhshtab, see *SV*, 25 October 1917, 2; for Shur's resignation, see *SV*, 9 November 1917, 3.

59 See editorials in *SV*, 19 July 1917, 2; 20 July 1917, 2; and 21 July 1917, 2.

60 Hickey, "Moderate Socialists."

61 See, for instance, SGV, 10 August 1917, 1; *SV*, 6 September 1917, 2, and 7 September 1917, 3; and Efimov's August–October correspondence with the city militia commander in GASO, f. 578, op. 1, dd. 5, 7, 8 and esp. f. 799, op. 4, d. 3,1. 203.

62 See Solomon Gurevich's page 2 editorials in *SV*, 10–15 and 18 October 1917.

63 GASO, f. 578, op. 3, d. 16, 1. 205; and *SV*, 26 October 1917, 3, and 21 October 1917, 3.

64 *SV*, 5 November 1917, 2; and 7 November 1917, 2.

65 See Koenker, *Moscow Workers*; and Smith, *Red Petrograd*.

66 The notable exception is the work of Tsuyoshi Hasegawa. See his "Crime, Police, and Mob Justice in Petrograd During the Russian Revolution of 1917,"

in Charles E. Timberlake, ed., *Religious and Secular Forces in Late Imperial Russia: Essays in Honor of Donald W. Treadgold* (Seattle, 1992), 241–71 [Chapter 3 above]; and idem, "Crime and Police in Revolutionary Petrograd, March 1917–March 1918: Social History of the Russian Revolution Revisited," *Acta Slavica Iaponica* 13 (1995): 1–41.

67 Peter Holquist calls attention to the repertoire of political practices that the Bolsheviks shared with other parties, both inside and outside of Russia, in his 1995 Columbia University dissertation, "A Russian Vendee: The Practice of Politics in the Don Countryside" [since published as *Making War, Forging Revolution: Russia's Continuum of Crisis, 1914–1921* (Cambridge, MA and London: Harvard University Press, 2002) – ed.].

Part IV

RETHINKING THE BOLSHEVIK SEIZURE OF POWER

9

LENIN, TROTSKII AND THE ARTS OF INSURRECTION

The Congress of Soviets of the Northern Region, 11–13 October 1917

James D. White

This essay reflects several important issues in the writing of the history of the Russian Revolution. It illustrates the continued importance of political history (despite what we have said about new approaches such as social history and language) and of the study of the Bolshevik Party including, but not only, Lenin. It also demonstrates that within a political approach, the old focus on Lenin as the unquestioned leader of a unified party and organizer and director of a coup d'etat misses the point of what happened. Alexander Rabinowitch had much earlier demolished the myth of a tightly unified Bolshevik Party, but the nature of Lenin's leadership role in the October Revolution was not really questioned. Similarly, although Robert V. Daniels asked important questions about the nature of the October Revolution as early as 1967, historians generally failed to follow through with new research on the October Revolution itself. Surprisingly, given its importance, the October Revolution has remained one of the least examined and most poorly understood aspects of 1917.

White undertakes to examine how the October Revolution came about by focusing on the Congress of Soviets of the Northern Region and, through it, the complex way that Bolsheviks and other radicals prepared for a transfer of power to the soviets, the Second All-Russia Congress of Soviets in particular. In looking so closely at what Lenin was actually calling for and in laying that so carefully alongside the Congress of Soviets of the Northern Front and surrounding events, he moves the focus away from Lenin and the myth of a well-planned coup executed under his direction, to the much more complex question of what Bolshevik leaders – Trotsky in particular – were actually doing. He makes clear that Bolshevik preparation for taking power was done very differently from what Lenin was proposing. Indeed, he inverts the traditional picture, making it clear that it was Trotsky's approach to having power taken by the Second Congress of Soviets that prevailed. This approach bypassed

Lenin's calls for an armed insurrection and especially his wild ideas about a military attack on Petrograd as the way to seize power. White's article also reminds us of the importance of the military situation in the events and mood leading to the October Revolution. How the revolution took place is the theme of the next essay in this collection also, and although quite different from White's in nature, the two together present the newer approach to the history of the October Revolution.

Readers might note that White often talks about the All-Russia Congress of Soviets as being set for October 20 – this was the original scheduled date, but it was postponed at the last minute until the 25th, the date by which it is remembered historically. The discussion in the article refers to the same congress, whichever date is used. Also, White uses the 1917 Russian place names for some important cities: Helsingfors for Helsinki and Reval for Tallinn.

* * *

By rights the Congress of Soviets of the Northern Region (CSNR) ought to be one of the best-known episodes in the history of the October Revolution. It took place in Petrograd between 11 and 13 October 1917, and thereby began on the day after the Bolsheviks adopted their famous resolution to take power. In fact the Bolshevik resolution of 10 October specifically mentions the Congress of Soviets of the Northern Region in the context of the armed uprising which the Bolsheviks proposed to organize.[1] In view of all that has been written about the Bolsheviks in the October Revolution it is, on the face of it, surprising that the Congress should be so little known.

The main reason why the CSNR tends to be ignored by historians is that apparently it did not lead to anything. Although the Central Committee resolution of 10 October mentioned it as a potential platform for launching an armed insurrection, this obviously did not happen. Therefore, as far as historians are concerned, the CSNR cannot be considered as one of the events which led up to the accession to power by the Bolsheviks; it was at best a false start. It is in this light that the CSNR is presented by those few historians who have mentioned the subject at all.

Both Robert Daniels and Alexander Rabinowitch in their detailed histories of the October Revolution treat the CSNR as an institution which was intended to launch an armed insurrection, but failed to do so. Daniels, for example, states that Lenin had hoped to use the CSNR as a "vehicle for insurrection", but concedes that: "In the end, the meeting of Northern Soviets did nothing of substance in this direction; it dispersed on 13 October with a feebly routine appeal that the national Congress of Soviets not be disrupted."[2]

Alexander Rabinowitch also presents the CSNR as a gathering which was intended to initiate action against the government. As it did not in fact do so, he feels obliged to suggest factors which might explain "the failure of the Northern Region Congress to trigger an uprising".[3] But if the CSNR failed in this function, did it achieve anything at all? Here Rabinowitch is in accord with Daniels in thinking that this was not of much substance. He considers that: "As it turned out, the Northern Region Congress was for the most part a thundering, highly visible expression of ultraradical sentiment".[4]

In this essay I should like to suggest that the CSNR did achieve a great deal of substance towards bringing about the October Revolution and that it is a key event which led directly to the Bolsheviks' conquest of power.

The political background

The political background in which the CSNR was held was formed by the collapse of the Kornilov affair at the end of August 1917 and the subsequent growth in Bolshevik influence in the soviets in the Baltic region. Bolshevik influence was also strong in those organizations which had been specially set up to counter the military threat from Kornilov's forces. In Kronstadt this organization was the Military-Technical Commission, which included representatives from the Kronstadt soviet and the naval base.[5] In Helsingfors a similar organization was established, the Revolutionary Committee, with representatives from local soviets and from Tsentrobalt (Executive Committee of the Baltic Fleet), which extended its jurisdiction over the entire territory of Finland. Even after the immediate danger of the Kornilov affair had passed, the organizations to combat it continued in existence, even though Kerenskii demanded their dissolution.[6] At the Third Regional Congress of Soviets of the Army, Navy and Workers of Finland, meeting from 9 to 14 September in Helsingfors, the Revolutionary Committee was replaced by a new Executive Committee under the chairmanship of the Bolshevik Ivars Smilga.[7] On 20 September the Regional Committee could claim that it had control over the whole of Finland, and that "not one order of the Coalition Government [. . .] is carried out without the consent of the Regional Finnish Committee".[8] The Helsingfors soviet also fell to the Bolsheviks in September, the Bolshevik Aleksandr Sheinman being elected its chairman on 20 September. In Helsingfors, moreover, the entire Socialist-Revolutionary organization went over to the Left Socialist-Revolutionaries and began to co-operate with the Bolsheviks. Both parties demanded the convocation of the Second All-Russian Congress of Soviets.[9]

A joint session of the Reval soviet, the Executive Committee of the Soviets of the Estonian Region and representatives of soldiers' and sailors' organizations meeting on 27 September gave overwhelming support to the Bolsheviks and demanded the transfer of all power to the soviets. The chairman of the meeting, the Bolshevik Ivan Rabchinskii, sailed to Petrograd the following day to report the event to the party's Central Committee. On the way he stopped off at Helsingfors to speak at the First Conference of Bolshevik organizations in Finland, and to confer with Smilga and Vladimir Antonov-Ovseenko.[10]

On 27 September Lenin, then in hiding in Vyborg, wrote a conspiratorial letter to Smilga, the Chairman of the Regional Committee of the Army, Navy and Workers of Finland, asking for the latter's co-operation in enlisting the troops in Finland to march on Petrograd and overthrow the Provisional Government. In Lenin's words:

> It seems to me we can have *completely* at our disposal only the troops in Finland and the Baltic fleet and only they can play a serious military role. I think you must make the most of your high position, shift all the petty routine work to assistants and secretaries and not waste time on "resolutions"; *give all your attention* to the *military preparation* of the troops in Finland plus the fleet for the impending overthrow of Kerenskii.[11]

Lenin was insistent that the time for passing resolutions was over; it was now a matter of military preparations, especially since there was a danger that the Provisional Government would find a military pretext to remove the troops from Finland. He was also adamant that the Bolsheviks should not wait until the Second Congress of Soviets met on 20 October and take power then. This was Trotskii's preferred course of action.[12] Lenin thought it foolish to postpone action for so long and to rely on the Bolsheviks having a majority in the Congress. From this time onwards Lenin was to put forward consistently the idea of mounting an offensive on Petrograd with troops from Finland. It is easy to overlook the fact that this was Lenin's conception of how power should be seized because one tends to assume that what Lenin was advocating in the weeks before the October Revolution was more or less what actually happened, and also because Lenin's use of the term "armed insurrection" leads one to envisage action which took place entirely within Petrograd. But Lenin's subsequent letters all make it abundantly clear that Lenin's plan for an insurrection involved a fairly large-scale military advance on Petrograd.

Lenin's letter reached Smilga during the Second Congress of the Baltic Fleet, chaired by Pavel Dybenko, which met from 25 September to 5 October in Helsingfors. One of the main Bolshevik speakers was the Finland Regional Committee member Vladimir Antonov-Ovseenko, to whom Smilga showed Lenin's letter. Despite the fact that in his letter Lenin stressed that the insurrection should precede the Second Congress of Soviets, Smilga, Antonov-Ovseenko and Rabchinskii made military preparations which were not offensive, but defensive in character, ones designed to protect the Second Congress of Soviets and to ensure that Kerenskii would not be able to send troops to Petrograd to dissolve it. They would do this by co-ordinating the activities of the Bolshevik-controlled Soviets in the approaches to Petrograd, and to this end they decided to convoke a CSNR. According to Antonov-Ovseenko, the idea was that the proposed Congress of Northern Soviets would "throw around revolutionary Petrograd an iron ring, which would defend the centre of the revolution, the capital, if the need arose". Antonov-Ovseenko got the idea approved by the First Conference of Bolshevik organizations in Finland, which was held between 28 and 30 September, by the Helsingfors soviet and by the Bolshevik Central Committee in Petrograd.[13] An organizational bureau was set up to take care of arrangements for the Congress, consisting of representatives from the Finnish regional committee, the Helsingfors soviet and Tsentrobalt. An invitation was sent out to twenty-eight soviets to the Congress scheduled to be held in Helsingfors on 8 October.[14]

Just at that time the political climate in the Baltic region changed dramatically in favour of the defensive tactics that Smilga and Antonov-Ovseenko had initiated. The German fleet made an attack on the Moon Sound in an operation intended to clear Russian defences in preparation for a renewed German offensive on the Northern Front. Against a numerically superior and better armed opponent the Russian Baltic Fleet put up a spirited defence, the sailors maintaining discipline and carrying out orders given by their officers, and often showing bravery under fire. They were encouraged in this by the Second Congress of the Baltic Fleet then in session. Although the Germans managed to achieve their objective and remove the Russian defences from the Estonian islands, the Baltic fleet was able to inflict serious casualties on the German navy and prevent further German advance.[15]

The Baltic sailors were elated by the battle and by the degree of success they had had in resisting the German attack. They were therefore understandably irritated when instead of praising them Kerenskii reminded them of an incident when five officers had been summarily executed on board the *Petropavlovsk* on 31 August, demanding that the crime be expiated and that the sailors do their duty. The sailors sent a strongly worded declaration in reply, saying that they did their duty not on the orders of some tin-pot Napoleon, but at the prompting of their revolutionary consciousness.[16]

The conviction that it was not Kerenskii, but the sailors, soldiers and workers who were the real defenders of the revolution and the country was reinforced when, on 4 October, it became known that following the Germans' capture of the Estonian islands Kerenskii and his ministerial colleagues had discussed the possibility of evacuating the government and the Pre-Parliament from Petrograd to Moscow.

These developments in the strategic and political situation caused the Bolshevik Central Committee to revise its arrangements for the CSNR. On 5 October on the advice of Sverdlov, the Bolshevik Central Committee resolved to postpone the opening of the CSNR until 10 October and to convene it in Petrograd. To make arrangements for holding the Congress in Petrograd the Baltic fleet sailor Aleksei Baranov was sent from the Finland regional committee to the capital, where he received the assistance of Leonid Karakhan.[17] In the capital the organizers of the Congress would also be able to count on the support of the Petrograd soviet, which had recently fallen under Bolshevik control and whose chairman was Trotskii.

On the eve of the Congress there was obviously a conflict of views among the Bolsheviks about what the role of the CSNR ought to be. Trotskii, who regarded the Congress as a means of ensuring that power would pass unhindered to the Second Congress of Soviets, did not argue his case publicly, but two of his sympathizers, Smilga and Karakhan, did. In an article in *Rabochii put'* on 8 October Smilga predicted that the forthcoming Congress of Soviets of the Northern Region would play an enormous part in the political life of the country. This was in connection with the campaign that was then being waged against the convocation of the Second Congress of Soviets. It was completely obvious, Smilga argued, that if people simply waited passively for 20 October when the Congress was scheduled to open, it would never happen. It was necessary to ensure that any second Kornilov affair would end in failure as the first one had done. Smilga, however, predicted that the Petrograd workers and soldiers, in concert with the revolutionary workers and garrisons of the Northern Region, would not allow the Congress on 20 October to be disrupted. In connection with events at the front the Provisional Government had shown itself, Smilga declared – in a phrase that was to be repeated by Trotskii three days later – incapable of either waging war or concluding a just peace. Things, Smilga concluded, were coming to a head, and at that moment the Northern Region could have an enormous significance.

Two days later *Rabochii put'* carried a report on the meeting of the Petrograd soviet on 9 October. There Karakhan had announced that the soviet executive committee had decided to participate in the CSNR because until then "the soviets of the Northern Region had not been united together. And now in connection with the threatening situation in which the country in general and the northern region in particular found itself, such a unification was extremely necessary". The Petrograd soviet would accordingly send a delegation of thirty people to the Congress, comprising fifteen Bolsheviks, ten Socialist Revolutionaries and five Mensheviks. The item concluded with the information that originally it was intended that the CSNR would discuss only the question of power, but the executive committee had decided to discuss the question of power in connection with the defence of the northern region.[18] This suggests that by 10 October Trotskii's policy on the CSNR had won in the executive committee at least.

On 8 October Lenin wrote two letters concerned with the CSNR, "Advice of an Onlooker" and "Letter to the Bolshevik Comrades Attending the CSNR". Both of these develop the ideas for an offensive on Petrograd that had been outlined in the letter to Smilga of 27 September. "Advice of an Onlooker" sets out the general principles of insurrection which Lenin has gathered from Marx's writings. As applied to Russia in October 1917, Lenin explains, this means:

> A simultaneous offensive on Petrograd, as sudden and rapid as possible, which must without fail be carried out from within and without the working-class quarters and from Finland, from Reval and from Kronstadt, an offensive of the entire navy.[19]

Lenin went on to emphasize that "to encircle and cut off Petrograd; to seize it by a combined attack of the sailors, the workers and the troops" was a task which required art and enormous audacity.[20] The "Letter to the Bolshevik Comrades Attending the CSNR" repeated Lenin's demand that the entire Baltic fleet and contingents of troops from Finland, Reval and Kronstadt should advance on Petrograd. Lenin made plain his impatience with the tactic of voting, of attracting Left Socialist-Revolutionaries and holding congresses of local soviets; he demanded immediate military action. He pointed out that Finland, the fleet and Reval were represented at the CSNR, and that these together could start an immediate movement on Petrograd.[21] In Lenin's view the CSNR could be used to launch the armed insurrection against the Provisional Government.

The Bolshevik Central Committee meeting of 10 October

On the eve of its opening the CSNR was postponed until 11 October so that the meeting of the Bolshevik Central Committee could take place. This was the meeting at which Lenin was present and the famous decision to seize power was taken. Before that meeting the polemical edge of Lenin's letters had been directed against the tactic of taking power at the Second Congress and onto preparing the ground for this at local congresses of soviets like the CSNR. But starting from the Central Committee meeting on 10 October until the Bolsheviks came to power on 25 October Lenin's energies were taken up with refuting the arguments of Zinov'ev and Kamenev who did not want an insurrection at all. This new polemic eclipsed the older one between Trotskii's and Lenin's approaches to methods of taking power.

Although the minutes of the meeting do not make it clear, Lenin argued in favour of an offensive from the Baltic area "to encircle and cut off Petrograd", seizing it by a combined attack of the sailors, the workers and the troops. This emerges from the letter Zinov'ev and Kamenev wrote after the meeting in response to Lenin's arguments. In it Zinov'ev and Kamenev, in indicating the strength of the armed forces at the disposal of the Provisional Government, pointed out the "large amount of artillery deployed in a fan around Petrograd".[22] This point would not be relevant unless Lenin had proposed the kind of advance on Petrograd he had described in the letters he had sent to the Bolshevik delegation to the CSNR on 8 October. That Lenin had argued in this way helps us understand the alarm Zinov'ev and Kamenev felt at the prospect, and why they felt so compelled to do everything in their power to make sure that Lenin's brand of armed uprising would not be launched.

Lenin had been encouraged by an offer from the Bolsheviks in Minsk to send forces to Petrograd.[23] He accordingly proposed that "the CSNR and the proposal from Minsk should be used to start decisive actions".[24] Upon the insistence of Trotskii, however, into the resolution that was adopted there was inserted the phrase "the withdrawal of troops from Petrograd". As he subsequently indicated: "This was the sole hint of that plan of insurrection which was subsequently dictated by the course of events in the capital."[25] The phrase served to justify the continuation of Trotskii's tactics based on defence of the capital and the role he had assigned in this to the CSNR. His insistence had the alleged weight of a Petrograd soviet decision behind it, for as Karakhan had stated in the issue of *Rabochii put'* published that day, the Petrograd soviet had resolved that the CSNR should discuss the question of power in connection with the defence of the Northern Region.

At half past ten on the morning of 11 October the Bolshevik delegation to the CSNR had its meeting. There is no systematic record of what took place on this occasion, but on the face of it all the ingredients were there for a difficult session. The delegates would have received Lenin's letters demanding that the Congress should signal the beginning of a military offensive on Petrograd. In fact Boris Breslav, the Bolshevik delegate from Kronstadt, writing in 1934, recalls that all the Bolsheviks at the Congress had the impression that the Central Committee might give the signal to start the insurrection at any minute.[26] Perhaps that is true, but the Bolshevik delegation also had serious cause to doubt that any such signal would come. For they had a copy of Zinov'ev and Kamenev's letter arguing that there should be no insurrection. Moreover, according to Breslav, Sokol'nikov made a report on the current situation on behalf

of the Party Central Committee. He would naturally have read the resolution that had been adopted during the previous night. The wording
of this resolution that Trotskii had insisted on had ensured that to carry
out the orders of the Central Committee there was no need for the
Congress to launch any immediate insurrection; the Bolshevik fraction
could adhere to the resolution and still go ahead with the Congress as
it had originally been conceived.[27] According to Antonov-Ovseenko the
speeches to be made at the Congress, the reports from the localities, draft
resolutions and the agenda were all finally approved. The proceedings
of the Congress certainly suggest that this was an event which had been
well prepared beforehand and in which very little was left to chance.

The first session

There were delegations to the Congress from Petrograd, Moscow,
Novgorod, Staraia Russa, Borovichi, Reval (Tallinn), Iur'ev (Tartu), Narva,
Arkhangel'sk, Wollmar, Kronstadt, Gatchina, Tsarskoe Selo, Chudov,
Sestoretsk, Schliesselburg, Vyborg, Helsingfors, Abo and Botok. There
were also representatives from the soviet of peasant deputies and from
the district Congress of the Baltic Fleet. Some organizations, however, had
not sent a delegation. These included soviets from Pskov, Petrozavodsk,
Tikhvinsk, Walk (Valk) and Wenden.[28] There were originally ninety-four
delegates in all, but four Menshevik-Defencists left the Congress on
the second day. The remaining ninety delegates comprised fifty-one
Bolsheviks, thirty-four Socialist Revolutionaries, four Maximalists and
one Menshevik-Internationalist.[29]

The first session of the CSNR opened in the Smolny Institute at five
o'clock in the afternoon on 11 October with an introductory speech by
Antonov-Ovseenko on behalf of the organizational commission. He
explained that the idea of calling a regional congress had originated in
Finland in the regional committee, that the Congress had first been scheduled to open on 8 October in Helsingfors, but in view of changes in the
strategic position and the political situation in the country it had been
decided to transfer it to Petrograd.

In stating the aims of the Congress, Antonov-Ovseenko repeated the
formula he had first enunciated in Helsingfors. This was to "unite in a
single powerful organization the Soviets of the Northern Region, bind this
organization more closely with the Petrograd soviet, creating around the
latter – in the surrounding hinterland of the focus of the revolution –
strong revolutionary support". He went on to state that such a union was
now essential to strengthen the Revolution and that the present Congress
was in its way the forerunner of the All-Russian Congress of Soviets.[30]

The chairman Nikolai Krylenko (Bolshevik) gave a brief survey of the
current political situation within the country. In the past seven months

of revolution, he said, nothing had changed to improve conditions for
ordinary people. The peasant movement had now become so extensive
that there was nothing the government could do to quell it. The economy
was in a parlous state which the Provisional Government had done
nothing to put to rights. On the chief question of the Revolution, that
of war and peace, while the soldiers at the front insistently demanded
that the fighting cease, the Provisional Government was planning a new
winter offensive. The soviet leadership, moreover, the Central Executive
Committee (CEC), continued to collude with the representatives of
the bourgeois circles in government. M. I. Skobelev, for instance, was
going to attend the Inter-Allied Conference in Paris on the Provisional
Government's behalf.[31] But, Krylenko concluded, public opinion had
become disillusioned with this kind of policy, and the present Congress
and the Second Congress of Soviets which was to follow would deliver
their verdict on that policy.

Krylenko's speech was followed by an emergency resolution proposed
by Antonov-Ovseenko on behalf of twenty-seven people still languishing
in Kresty prison who had been arrested during the July Days and who
were now on hunger-strike. The resolution was adopted unanimously.
This was the emotionally charged prelude to the first of the reports from
the localities which was given by Trotskii as the representative from the
Petrograd soviet.

Trotskii's speech was the highlight of the Congress, because its scope
went far beyond giving an account of the current situation in the
Petrograd soviet. The report from the soviet served merely as a pretext
for a carefully crafted piece of oratory. It was a speech in which Trotskii
set out to mobilize two contradictory sentiments prevalent at the time:
one was the patriotic feeling that had been generated by the naval battle
in Moon Sound; the other was the long-term war-weariness that
demanded a speedy termination to all hostilities.[32] Accordingly, in the
course of the same speech Trotskii would appeal both to those who had
tasted victory and to those whose greatest desire was peace.

Trotskii began his speech by referring to the recent elections in which
the Bolsheviks had now gained a majority on the Petrograd soviet. What
accounted for this success, he said, was that the public had finally become
disillusioned in the policies promoted by the previous soviet leadership,
which involved the continuation of the war; and to senseless offensives
on the front, like that of 18 June. Now, Trotskii stated, the Petrograd
soviet was in conflict with the Provisional Government and those parties
which supported it, in particular on the question of withdrawing some
of the garrison from Petrograd.

This brought Trotskii to the main theme of his speech: the defence
of Petrograd. He contrasted the actions of the Provisional Government
and its supporters, the Menshevik defencists, who were ready to abandon

Petrograd to the Germans, with those of the Baltic sailors, who had actually resisted a German attack. Trotskii repeatedly stressed the irony that the "defencists" did not deserve their designation, because they were not actually prepared to put up any defence of the capital city or of the country.

In this connection Trotskii deployed a piece of biblical knowledge to good effect when he stated that:

> The plan to desert and surrender Petrograd is dictated not only by the inability to organize the defence of the capital, but also by hatred for revolutionary Petrograd. Petrograd, as the Gospels say, is the "city that is set on an hill"; everyone can see it. Everyone knows what we think and what we do.[33]

Trotskii went on to say that the military staff had come up with the plan of withdrawing two-thirds of the Petrograd garrison from the capital. The Menshevik defencists in the Petrograd soviet had decided to go along with the military experts on this matter, though they themselves did not trust the army officers. However, according to Trotskii: "The Baltic fleet says otherwise. It has declared that it doesn't believe one word the Provisional Government, this veritable government of national betrayal, says. Nevertheless, the Baltic fleet will die heroically defending the revolution."[34] The Baltic fleet of course had already shown its heroism in defence of the country, and in doing so had acquired an authority which Trotskii was able to draw upon.

In an emotional passage Trotskii came to the main message of his speech: it was, he said:

> a matter of the fate of Petrograd, and we wish to decide this question with you, the representatives of the regional soviets. If anyone has the right at this moment to speak on behalf of the Petrograd proletariat and about the defence of its vital interests – it is the Petrograd soviet. At the first sign of danger which may threaten Petrograd the Provisional Government will flee the city. It is no secret for anyone that it is preparing to leave and to surrender Petrograd. The Provisional Government can flee from Petrograd, but the revolutionary people will not budge from Petrograd; they will defend it to the end. (Stormy applause.)
>
> After the surrender of Petrograd, where there is half of the industry working for defence, the defencists will be ready to surrender everything that is left. Let the defencists, together with the government which they support, flee whither they will. The Petrograd soviet will not leave and will defend Petrograd together with the Petrograd proletariat and its garrison to the very end. (Applause.)[35]

Trotskii concluded by saying that the time was close at hand when the soviets would have to take upon themselves the defence not only of Petrograd but also of the country as a whole. The best defence of the country would be the immediate proposal of peace to the peoples of the whole world over the heads of their imperialist governments. "Shall we", Trotskii asked, echoing Smilga's words in *Rabochii put'* on 8 October, "entrust the conduct of the war to those who know neither how to wage war nor how to conclude peace?" The answer was clear; there was no one but the soviets who could do this, and consequently it was necessary that the question of the country's fate should be decided by the All-Russian Congress of Soviets.[36]

The reproach that the Provisional Government could "neither wage war nor conclude peace" was a phrase which caught the paradoxical nature of Trotskii's appeal to his audience. For the implication was that he, Trotskii and the soviets, *were* capable of both waging war and concluding peace. The tactic Trotskii was adopting was to tap into the two powerful popular sentiments current at the time: one was the desire to bring the war to an end, and the other was the impulse to defend the country from German attack, which the Baltic fleet had recently done with such heroism.

The repeated references in Trotskii's speech to the Baltic fleet had prepared the ground for the contribution to the Congress by Dybenko, the chairman of Tsentrobalt. Dybenko lost no time in reminding his audience that even as he spoke Baltic sailors were dying heroically in battles against the numerically superior German fleet. He pointed out that despite the dedication of the sailors the Baltic fleet was hated by the Provisional Government because it was a hotbed of revolution. A great chasm, he said, had opened up between the Provisional Government and the Baltic fleet.

Dybenko then provided an explanation for why the Baltic sailors should have shown such close co-operation with their officers during the battle of Moon Sound. He recalled that just before the battle the commander of the Baltic fleet had appeared at the Second Congress of the Baltic fleet and asked whether military orders would be carried out. The answer was that they would, but only on condition that control over operational matters was in the hands of the sailors themselves. This had been agreed, and the Moon Sound operations had been carried out in this way. The arrangement, in Dybenko's view, had been extremely successful, because the losses on the German side had been much greater than those suffered by the Russians. The Baltic sailors had fought with honour, and, Dybenko emphasized, they fought not because they wanted to expiate their guilt before the Provisional Government, as Kerenskii seemed to imagine, but because they were defending the Revolution and all it stood for with all their might.[37]

Dybenko concluded by confirming what Trotskii had said in his speech concerning the disbelief of the Baltic fleet that the withdrawal of troops from Petrograd was necessary for strategic considerations. According to Dybenko the contention that it was necessary to withdraw the Petrograd garrison from the city in order to defend its approaches, and in particular to defend Reval, was simply not credible. Reval could be defended by the Baltic fleet. In Dybenko's opinion the Provisional Government was preparing to desert Petrograd, and this would be a strategic error of massive proportions, since it would deprive the Baltic fleet of support from the land. Then all the heroism of the sailors would be in vain.[38]

At the end of Dybenko's speech Trotskii read a greeting from the Congress to the sailors of the Baltic fleet who "are dying like heroes, paying with their lives for the crimes of the bourgeoisie of all countries". The Congress then rose and stood to attention to pay its respects to the sailors and soldiers who had been killed in battle.[39]

Dybenko's speech had introduced the theme of military orders being subject to confirmation by the sailors of the Baltic fleet. Subsequently in a series of reports from the localities the idea of the soviets or similar bodies exercising control over the military authorities was repeated. The first speaker to do this was Antonov-Ovseenko in his role as representative of the Finnish regional committee. This was a committee, he said:

> which arose after the Kornilov offensive. The committee monitors the activities of the government officials, takes care of counter-intelligence, and regulates life in the area. The committee has in all respects become the organ of revolutionary power. Not a single order of the Provisional Government is carried out in Finland unless it is signed by the commissar of the regional committee.[40]

The report by Sheinman for the Helsingfors soviet was much briefer than Antonov-Ovseenko's but was of a similar content. The record states that Sheinman "greets the Congress from a soviet which long ago took power into its own hands".[41]

The report by the Maximalist Kudinskii from the Kronstadt soviet was somewhat fuller, stating that:

> Kudinskii the representative of Kronstadt says that power has been in the hands of the soviet for some time. No instruction in Kronstadt is carried out if it is not approved by the Military-Technical Commission attached to the soviet.[42]

A similar report could have been made by the delegate from Reval, Rabchinskii, because following the German invasion of the Estonian islands the Reval soviet had set up a committee for the defence of the naval fortress and the surrounding area, a committee which concentrated in its hands all the military authority of the region.[43] The manner in which the orders of the military authorities in the localities mentioned were sanctioned by the local soviet, or special body acting on behalf of the soviet, seems to anticipate what was to happen in Petrograd on 21 October, when commissars of the Military Revolutionary Committee (MRC) went to the Commander of the Petrograd military district and demanded to countersign any order he might issue. In fact, on 22 October Antonov-Ovseenko was to give a report to the Petrograd soviet on the activities of the Petrograd MRC in terms similar to those [in which he had] spoken of the Finland regional committee:

> In all military units commissars have been appointed. ... No orders or instructions will be carried out without the sanction of the commissars.[44]

This kind of continuity raises the question of what the relationship was between the CSNR and the MRC. The logic of the reports from the localities was that some new body would be created, attached to the Petrograd soviet, which would exercise control over the military authorities in the capital, just as similar organizations monitored the military authorities in towns in the Baltic area. This would mean that power would *de facto* have passed to the soviet. No doubt up until 9 October the organizers of the CSNR had intended to propose the establishment of a body of this kind. On that day, however, the Mensheviks on the executive committee of the Petrograd soviet, in an effort to escape the charge of abandoning Petrograd to the Germans, had suggested co-operation between the soviet and the Petrograd military district involving the setting up of a "committee of revolutionary defence", which would concern itself with the question of the defence of Petrograd and its approaches, and would draw up a plan for the defence of Petrograd.[45]

Since it was conceived as a propaganda measure, the Bolsheviks were initially unenthusiastic about the proposal. But at the Soviet plenum meeting on 9 October Trotskii and Antonov-Ovseenko changed their tactics and seized upon the idea, drawing up a constitution for the new organization, to be called the Military Revolutionary Committee, which was more in line with the kind of body they were about to set up at the CSNR. The constitution for the MRC was approved by the executive committee of the Petrograd soviet on 12 October. When the CSNR met on 11 October the establishment of the MRC was well under way, directed by the same group of people who were organizing the CSNR. On 21 October the MRC did in fact send its commissars to demand to countersign orders issued by the Commander of the Petrograd military district, in the manner the CSNR had no doubt envisaged.

Because it existed already, the CSNR had no need to propose setting up the MRC. It could already proceed to a more advanced stage. The records of the CSNR contain two mentions of the MRC, and, typically, these are co-ordinated. On the first day of the Congress, in his report from the Reval soviet, Rabchinskii expressed the conviction that the time had now passed when power could be transferred peacefully and that it was necessary to organize oneself for the struggle ahead. "Therefore", he concluded, "we have to follow the example of the Petrograd soviet and set up military-revolutionary committees everywhere."[46]

At the session of the Congress on 12 October the Bolshevik delegate Lashevich, in speaking about the removal of units of the Petrograd garrison from the capital, mentioned that:

> In Petrograd at the present time there has been created a special soldiers' revolutionary committee embracing military units of all descriptions in whose hands will be concentrated *de facto* the ability to dispose of military force. The speaker advocated following this example in the localities.[47]

This proposal was duly approved by the Congress, and the corresponding arrangements for setting up the network of Military Revolutionary Committees were made towards the end of the Congress.

The second session

The second day of the Congress, 12 October, began with a speech of protest from Bogdanov on behalf of the Mensheviks. He referred to a resolution that had been adopted the day before by the Bureau of the CEC which pointed out that the Helsingfors soviet had no right to attend a congress of soviets of the Northern Region, because it itself was not part of the Northern Region, nor should there be representatives from Moscow, which also lay outside the Northern Region. The resolution also objected that the CEC had not been informed in advance of the Congress, and in the light of these considerations concluded that the gathering could not be considered as an official congress of soviets, but merely a private gathering.[48] Bogdanov also gave vent to his suspicion that invitations had been sent to local soviets selectively, so that the delegations came overwhelmingly from those which were dominated by the Bolsheviks.

As the spokesman for the Congress's Organizing Commission, Antonov-Ovseenko replied that the Finnish Regional Committee had convoked the Congress in conjunction with the Reval soviet (presumably he had Rabchinskii in mind), and that there had been no selectivity employed in the sending out of invitations. As this was hardly a crushing rebuttal of Bogdanov's case, Trotskii was required to deploy his oratorical skills to reinforce what Antonov-Ovseenko had said. Trotskii remarked with some sarcasm that he had the honour to be a member of the CEC – a very dubious honour – and that the Bolsheviks had not been involved in the decision taken by its Bureau that Bogdanov referred to, since they had been busy with other things. Trotskii added that it was untrue to say, as Bogdanov had, that the CEC had not been informed of the forth-coming Congress, because the executive committee of the Petrograd soviet, with the Mensheviks in attendance, had resolved unanimously to participate in the CSNR. When the question was put to the vote, the Menshevik motion was defeated, causing them to declare that they would take no further part in the proceedings, but would remain as observers.[49]

The main business of the Congress's second day was a discussion of the current situation. Trotskii was again the main speaker. His tone was more reflective than on the day before, and his speech was concerned with placing the present juncture within the context of the Revolution as it had developed so far. It was in its way an interpretation of the 1917 Revolution, and one which saw the Second Congress of Soviets as the point at which the proletariat would be restored to its rightful heritage of power. In Trotskii's view:

> In our country the proletariat has not shown sufficient will to seize power, although all the circumstances prompt it to do this.
> The bourgeoisie, on the other hand, is sufficiently prepared to do so. It seized power at the beginning of the Revolution and the proletariat did nothing to prevent it. The petty bourgeoisie came to power, basing itself on broad sections of the peasantry, because the peasantry was organized into the army before any awareness of its own interests had been formed. The peasants entrusted their interests to the petty-bourgeois elements, who even now speak on their behalf and utilise this to disrupt the All-Russian Congress of Soviets, which they find inconvenient.
> The cause of all the present crises is the fact that in the first days of the revolution the proletariat did not take power into its hands.[50]

Trotskii was also anxious to counter interpretations of 1917 which he did not agree with. Kerenskii had declared that the July Days had given rise to the Kornilov affair. In Trotskii's opinion this was quite wrong; the Kornilov affair had been brought about by Kerenskii's unsuccessful military offensive launched on 18 June. Trotskii was adamant that the July Days had not been a rebellion but a purely spontaneous move-ment.[51] Trotskii's intention here was probably to dispel an idea encouraged by Zinov'ev and Kamenev's letter, and which might well be current at the Congress: that the Bolsheviks might be leading their supporters into a repeat of the July Days, which would be followed by a new period of reaction. Trotskii's speech gave the reassurance that when the proletariat took power it would be part of a natural progression, a stage which the Revolution would necessarily undergo.[52]

Among the contributions to the discussion on the current situation, the one by Breslav, the Bolshevik delegate from the Kronstadt soviet, is especially significant because it provides a foil against which one can view Trotskii's speech on the day before. It is even in its way a response to Trotskii's speech. In Breslav's opinion the main question to be decided was that of power, because on this question all others depended. "In whose hands power resided would determine the land question, the question of war and peace, or, more correctly, war or peace." If the proletariat took power, Breslav predicted, then the imperialist war would be immediately brought to an end and land would be given to the peasants. The dimension of defending Petrograd against attack, so prominent in Trotskii's speech and serving as a preliminary to establishing the MRC, was entirely absent in Breslav's address to the Congress.[53]

Breslav's perspective was very different from Trotskii's. Later he recalled that what made the deepest impression upon him at the Congress were the speeches by soldiers representing military units at the front. He was aghast at the descriptions they gave of life in the trenches. Soldiers had no boots, no clothes, no ammunition; they sat in stinking dug-outs and literally rotted away.[54] For these men, peace could not come quickly enough, or, what in Breslav's reasoning amounted to the same thing: revolution could not come quickly enough. Identifying with these soldiers, Breslav would find it difficult to see the point of Trotskii's tactic of utilizing the defence of the capital to take power by stealth. Breslav recalls that he and other people at the grass-roots found it hard to imagine why the Bolshevik Central Committee did not simply issue the call to insurrection and have done with it.[55]

Breslav's current of opinion at the Congress, and the presence of the soldier delegates who sustained it, implies that care had been taken by the organizers to ensure that on the first day the tone of the Congress would be set by the Baltic sailors and the renewed will to resist the Germans which accompanied their success. Breslav's opinions on the urgency for an uprising to begin allows us to place in context his assertion that "all the Bolsheviks at the Congress had the impression that the Central Committee might give the signal to start the insurrection at any minute". This was something Breslav and his friends might hope would happen, but it was certainly not something that defined the character of the Congress.

At the end of its second day the Congress discussed the military-political situation. The report given by Antonov-Ovseenko returned to the theme of the removal of troops from Petrograd. Thereafter Lashevich and the SR Chelingorian proposed establishing military revolutionary committees throughout the Northern Region which would be analogous to the one being established in Petrograd. A resolution to this effect was duly passed.[56]

The final session and the follow-up to the Congress

The last day of the Congress was dominated by a discussion of the agrarian question, the main speech being made by Kolegaev for the SRs. He argued that arbitrary seizures of the land ought to be discouraged, and the land transferred to the peasant committees in an orderly way. Kolegaev believed that this was the means to ensure that the peasants would vote in the forthcoming elections to the Constituent Assembly. This positive reference to the Constituent Assembly was an unusual phenomenon at the Congress, where in general the Assembly had no place in the political perspectives of the participants. In fact, although the Constituent Assembly appeared on the Congress's agenda it was removed when the topic was about to be discussed, it being the opinion of the Organizing Bureau that the question had been sufficiently aired in foregoing resolutions.[57]

The resolutions in question arose from the discussion on the All-Russian Congress of Soviets, which did loom large in the political thinking of many participants in the CSNR, as this was envisaged as the body to which power would pass from the Provisional Government. But, as Lashevich, the main speaker on the topic, explained, the moderate socialists on the CEC were conducting a campaign aimed at stopping the convocation of the All-Russian Congress, arguing that the elections for this Congress would obstruct the elections to the Constituent Assembly. They even claimed that the soviets were now superfluous, as their function was soon to be taken over by the Constituent Assembly.[58] The CSNR resolved to send out an appeal to soldiers, sailors and workers to counter these arguments and ensure that arrangements for the All-Russian Congress went ahead.

The last piece of business to be transacted at the CSNR came under the heading of the organizational question. It was at this point that Antonov-Ovseenko translated into organizational form the argumentation and the resolutions of the previous two days. He proposed and had unanimously adopted the establishment of an executive committee of the Northern Region, which would ensure the convocation of the All-Russian Congress of Soviets and would be a focus for co-ordinating the activities of the local soviets of the region.[59] The Committee consisted of seventeen people, eleven Bolsheviks and six SRs. Quite a few members of the Executive Committee of the Northern Region became members of the Petrograd MRC. These included the Bolsheviks Antonov-Ovseenko,

Dybenko, Krylenko, P. V. Dashkevich, Rabchinskii, Raskol'nikov, P. Stuchka and the SR S. D. Kudinskii.[60] According to Antonov-Ovseenko, the Executive Committee of the Northern Region and the Petrograd MRC soon merged completely.[61]

The MRC in Petrograd was closely co-ordinated with the MRCs in other parts of the Northern Region, so that Petrograd and the approaches to Petrograd were covered by the same organization. In his memoirs Rabchinskii confirms that careful planning went into the network of MRCs designed by the CSNR. Rabchinskii recalls that: "In general here at the CSNR a unified plan of action was worked out, the procedure for maintaining communications etc. Every participant knew what he had to do and how to act."[62]

In the case of Estonia where Rabchinskii was based, it had been decided that Jan Anvelt had to take over the running of the Reval soviet while Viktor Kingissepp would take charge of the Executive Committee of the Estland soviet. Rabchinskii himself was charged with secretly organizing the transfer of power to the soviets, and crushing any resistance on the part of the SRs, Mensheviks or officers. According to Rabchinskii, the overall policy he was following was to ensure that not a single hostile soldier would be sent to Petrograd through the territory of Estland, and he was able to state with some pride that this had in fact been achieved.[63]

For the organizers of the CSNR there was the problem that not all the organizations in the Northern Region had sent delegates, and therefore there might be gaps in the defensive ring around Petrograd. This was no doubt why Antonov-Ovseenko travelled to Walk on 16 October to address a specially convoked conference of Latvian Social-Democrats. According to a participant at the conference, Antonov-Ovseenko reported that the Bolsheviks had decided to take power, that the Petrograd MRC had already begun to operate, that the workers, soldiers and sailors of Petrograd were getting ready to fight, that the Latvian Riflemen in the 12th Army should support Petrograd, and that their chief task was with arms in their hands to forestall any attempts of the counter-revolutionaries to send troops to Petrograd.[64] In essence, therefore, what Antonov-Ovseenko said to the Latvians was a summarized version of what they would have heard at the CSNR.

On the evening of 16 October the Bolshevik Central Committee held a meeting with representatives of the St Petersburg Committee, the Military Organization, the Petrograd soviet, trade unions, factory committees and other bodies to review progress on organizing an insurrection since the Central Committee meeting of 10 October. Lenin attended the meeting on 16 October, but Trotskii did not, being at that time occupied with getting the constitution of the MRC approved by the plenum of the Petrograd soviet.[65] What is striking about the CC meeting of the 16th is how little it seemed to know about the CSNR and its significance. Most speakers had the impression that since the 10th nothing had been done in the way of organizing an insurrection and that the resolution of the 10th had remained a dead letter. One of the participants even pointed out that the Bolsheviks did "not even have a centre yet" with which to prepare an armed insurrection.[66] A Military Revolutionary Centre was duly formed at the meeting of which Stalin was famously a member along with Sverdlov, Bubnov, Uritskii and Dzierzynski. But as the Centre joined the Petrograd MRC it was probably little more than the Bolshevik contingent representing party military organizations, provided for in the constitution of the MRC.[67]

A significant speech made at the meeting on 16 October was that by Krylenko, who of course knew all about the CSNR and what it had set in motion. The speech, however, had an elliptical nature and only hinted that preparations for taking power were already well under way. According to Krylenko the Bolshevik Military Organization was unanimous that "things were near enough to the boil", and thought it wrong to rescind the resolution that had been passed on 10 October. He said he disagreed with Lenin on the question of who would start the insurrection and how. He thought it unnecessary to enter too much into the technical details of the insurrection, but also considered it inadvisable to set a definite date for it. Nevertheless, he thought that the withdrawal of troops from Petrograd was a point of contention at which a fight could start. Krylenko concluded by saying that there was no point in worrying about who was to begin since a beginning had already been made.[68]

Significantly, in his *History of the Russian Revolution* Trotskii, after drawing attention to the fact that Krylenko had been involved in organizing the CSNR along with Antonov-Ovseenko and himself, reproduced Krylenko's speech at the meeting on the 16th. He appended to it the comment: "Krylenko was expounding and defending the policy laid down by the Military Revolutionary Committee and the Garrison Conference. It was along this road that the insurrection continued to develop."[69]

As we know, the body which did take power in October 1917 was the MRC or – perhaps it would be more exact to say – the MRC and the Executive Committee of the Soviets of the Northern Region. The transfer of power, moreover, came about on the day the Second Congress of Soviets met, much in the manner Trotskii had advocated. The great advantage of this means of taking power was made clear by Trotskii on the afternoon of 25 October, when he reported to the Petrograd soviet that so far there had been no bloodshed. He went on to say that he knew of no other example where a revolutionary movement involving such great masses of people had been carried through without bloodshed.[70] It is most unlikely that the same could have been said if Lenin's preferred method of taking power had been adopted. But the Lenin cult ensured that only rarely, and only fleetingly, did Trotskii ever allude to the differences which separated himself and Lenin on the method of taking power. But in 1924 Trotskii recalls that as Bolshevik control extended over Petrograd in October 1917 Lenin made the grudging admission that "Well, I suppose you can do it that way too; as long as power is taken."[71]

An examination of the CSNR, the circumstances in which it was held and the consequences to which it gave rise reveals some interesting and significant facets of the way the Bolsheviks came to power. The most striking of these is that the picture is incomplete and misleading if one looks at Petrograd alone. The geographical area which is involved is Petrograd and the approaches to Petrograd – the Northern Region. This is logical, because there was little use in taking power in the capital if troops could be brought in from the Northern Front – as they were in the July Days – and the revolution crushed.[72]

From the wider geographical perspective of the Northern Region as a whole, the character of the October Revolution is significantly different from that which emerges when the focus is on Petrograd alone. For if one considers developments in the capital in isolation there is much about the Bolshevik seizure of power that seems fortuitous and accidental. The full extent of the planning and organization which went into the October Revolution only emerges when one looks at the wider context which the CSNR reveals.

The CSNR is an essential stage in the evolution of the MRC. This was the background against which the MRC originated. It has its prototypes in organizations in the Baltic region set up in the wake of the Kornilov affair, and in its turn it was to serve as the model on which local MRCs in the Northern Region were to be based. The MRC was from its inception not just a Petrograd organization but the centre of a network covering the approaches to the capital.

The CSNR helps throw light on one of the most persistent mysteries of the October Revolution, such as what Trotskii was actually doing at the time. The materials relating to the CSNR make it plain that this was an episode in which Trotskii invested a great deal of time, effort and organizational talent. The road to power which lay through the CSNR was Trotskii's road, and as Trotskii indicated, it was the road which led to the desired destination. But it was also one which bypassed Lenin, and since Trotskii was always anxious to demonstrate his Leninist credentials, this is no doubt what led him to devote only scattered references to the CSNR in his *History of the Russian Revolution*.[73]

The CSNR is part of a coherent sequence of events whose dynamic runs from September 1917 right to the October Revolution. It was a major, if unacknowledged, landmark in the process which brought the

Bolsheviks to power. It was a process that was briefly in danger of being thrown off course. That was when Lenin demanded that the CSNR be used as the platform from which to launch an armed uprising. This danger, however, was successfully avoided, and the CSNR was allowed to continue organizing the transfer of power in its own way.

NOTES

Reprinted from *The Slavonic and East European Review*, 77: no. 1 (January, 1999), pp. 117–139.

1 The passage in question is:

> Considering, therefore, that an armed uprising is inevitable, and that the time for it is fully ripe, the Central Committee instructs all party organizations to be guided accordingly, and to discuss and decide all practical questions (the Congress of Soviets of the Northern Region, the withdrawal of troops from Petrograd, the action of our people in Moscow and Minsk, and so on) from this point of view.
>
> (*Protokoly tsentral'nogo komiteta RSDRP(b) Avgust 1917–fevral' 1918*, Moscow, 1958, p. 86; V. I. Lenin, *Polnoe sobranie sochinenii*, 55 vols, Moscow, 1958–65, XXXIV (hereafter *PSS*), p. 393)

2 R. V. Daniels, *Red October: The Bolshevik Revolution of 1917*, London, 1967, p. 84.

3 A. Rabinowitch, *The Bolsheviks Come to Power*, London, 1979, p. 211.

4 Ibid., p. 214.

5 S.S. Khesin, *Oktiabr'skaia revoliutsiia i flot*, Moscow, 1971 (hereafter *Oktiabr'skaia revoliutsiia*), p. 345; Norman Saul, *Sailors in Revolt: The Russian Baltic Fleet in 1917*, Lawrence KS, 1978 (hereafter *Sailors in Revolt*), p. 146.

6 V. Antonov-Ovseenko, *V revoliutsii*, Moscow, 1983 (hereafter *V revoliutsii*), p. 94.

7 *Sailors in Revolt*, p. 165.

8 *Zvezda*, 22 September 1917, quoted in G. F. Sivolapova, "S"ezd sovetov severnoi oblasti v 1917 g.", *Istoricheskie zapiski*, no. 105, 1980 (hereafter "S"ezd sovetov"), p. 49.

9 *Oktiabr'skaia revoliutsiia*, p. 91; *V revoliutsii*, p. 375.

10 *Znamenostsy revoliutsii*, Tallinn, 1964, p. 116; M. A. Petrov, "Rol' i mesto Estonii v leninskom plane podgotovki Oktiabr'skogo vooruzhennogo vosstaniia", *Lenin i Oktiabr'skoe vooruzhennoe vosstanie v Petrograde*, Moscow, 1964, pp. 374–75.

11 *PSS*, p. 265.

12 A. Lunacharskii, K. Radek, L. Trotskii, *Siluety: Politicheskie portrety*, Moscow, 1991 (hereafter *Siluety*), p. 68.

13 "S"ezd sovetov", p. 50; A. V. Rakitin, *V. A. Antonov-Ovseenko*, Leningrad, 1989, p. 114; E. Mawdsley, *The Russian Revolution and the Baltic Fleet*, London, 1978, p. 106.

14 *V revoliutsii*, p. 110.

15 Ibid., p. 107; *Sailors in Revolt*, pp. 158–60.

16 *V revoliutsii*, p. 108; *Oktiabr'skaia revoliutsiia*, pp. 538–39; *Sailors in Revolt*, pp. 148, 161.

17 *V revoliutsii*, p. 110.

18 *Rabochii put'*, no. 32, 23 (10) October 1917.

19 *PSS*, p. 383.
20 Ibid., p. 384.
21 Ibid., pp. 389–90.
22 *PSS*, p. 91.
23 I. I. Saladkov, "Trudiashchiesia Belorussii i pobeda Oktiabr'skogo vooruzhennogo vosstaniia v Petrograde", *Lenin i Oktiabr'skoe vooruzhennoe vosstanie v Petrograde*, pp. 348–53.
24 Ibid., pp. 84–85.
25 L. Trotskii, *The History of the Russian Revolution*, p. 1000.
26 B. A. Breslav, *Kanun Oktiabria 1917 goda: s"ezd sovetov Severnoi oblasti 11–13 oktiabria 1917 goda*, Moscow, 1934 (hereafter *Kanun*), p. 22. Breslav was a Bolshevik delegate from Kronstadt and one of the two secretaries at the CSNR.
27 *V revoliutsii*, p. 114.
28 *Rabochii put'*, no. 32, 23 (10) October, 1917; *Rabochii put'*, no. 35, 26 (13) October, 1917; *Kanun*, p. 28; "S"ezd sovetov", p. 54.
29 *Kanun*, p. 17; "S"ezd sovetov", p. 55.
30 *Kanun*, p. 28.
31 R. P. Browder and A. F. Kerensky (eds), *The Russian Provisional Government 1917*, 3 vols, Stanford, CA, 1961, II, pp. 1127–50.
32 The fullest version of this speech is given in *Kanun*, pp. 32–35, though the speaker is only identified as "the representative of the Petrograd Soviet". A summary of this version appears in A. Breslav, "15 let tomu nazad", *Katorga i ssylka*, no. 11/12, 1932, pp. 54–55. A shorter variant of Trotskii's speech appears in *Rabochii put'*, no. 35, 26 (13) October 1917. The *Rabochii put'* version was reproduced in L. Trotskii, *Sochineniia*, Moscow, 1925–26, vol. 3, part 2, pp. 5–6. It appears in French translation in S. Oldenbourg, *Le coup d'état bolcheviste*, Paris, 1929 (hereafter *Le coup d'état*), pp. 41–42, and in English translation in S. Lovell (ed.), *Leon Trotsky Speaks*, New York, 1972, pp. 59–60.
33 The quotation is from Matthew 5.14.
34 *Kanun*, p. 33.
35 Ibid., p. 34.
36 Ibid., p. 35.
37 Ibid., pp. 35–37.
38 Ibid., p. 38.
39 Ibid., pp. 38–39; *Rabochii put'*, no. 35, 26 (13) October 1917; Trotskii, *Sochineniia*, vol. 3, part 1, pp. 7–8.
40 *Rabochii put'*, no. 35, 26 (13) October 1917.
41 *Kanun*, p. 42; *Rabochii put'*, no. 35, 26 (13) October 1917.
42 Ibid.
43 J. Saat and K. Siilvask, *Velikaia oktiabr'skaia sotsialisticheskaia revoliutsiia v Estonii*, Tallinn, 1977, p. 230.
44 *Rabochii put'*, no. 45, 7 (25) October 1917.
45 *V revoliutsii*, pp. 119–20.
46 *Kanun*, p. 45.
47 Ibid., p. 62; *Rabochii put'*, no. 36, 27 (14) October, 1917.
48 "S"ezd sovetov", pp. 57–58.
49 *Kanun*, p. 50; *Rabochii put'*, no. 35, 26 (13) October 1917.
50 *Kanun*, p. 52; *Rabochii put'*, no. 38, 30 (17) October 1917; Trotskii, *Sochineniia*, vol. 3, part 1, p. 8.
51 *Kanun*, p. 53; *Rabochii put'*, no. 38, 30 (17) October 1917; Trotskii, *Sochineniia*, vol. 3, part 1, p. 9.

JAMES D. WHITE

52 *Kanun*, p. 54; *Rabochii put'*, no. 38, 30 (17) October 1917; Trotskii, *Sochineniia*, vol. 3, part 1, p. 10.
53 *Kanun*, p. 56.
54 Ibid., p. 73.
55 Ibid., pp. 72–73.
56 Ibid., pp. 63–74.
57 Ibid., p. 71; *Rabochii put'*, no. 37, 28 (15) October 1917.
58 *Kanun*, pp. 67–68.
59 Ibid., p. 69.
60 *Rabochii put'*, no. 37, 28 (15) October; *Kanun*, p. 71; 'S"ezd sovetov', p. 65.
61 Antonov-Ovseenko, "Baltflot v dni Kerenshchiny i Krasnogo Oktiabria", *Proletarskaia revoliutsiia*, 1922, no. 10 (hereafter "Baltflot v dni Kerenshchiny"), p. 123.
62 I. V. Rabchinskii, "Oktiabr'skie dni v Estonii", *Pobeda velikoi Oktiabr'skoi sotsialisticheskoi revoliutsii*, Moscow, 1958, p. 414.
63 I. Rabchinskii, "Oktiabr'skie dni v Estonii", *Klassivoitlus*, vols. 67–68, 1925, p. 7.
64 R. Kisis, "Ot iiulia k oktiabr'iu", *Pobeda velikoi Oktiabr'skoi sotsialisticheskoi revoliutsii*, p. 468.
65 *Le coup d'état*, p. 64.
66 *PSS*, p. 100.
67 *Petrogradskii voenno-revoliutsionnyi komitet: dokumenty i materialy*, vol. I, Moscow, 1966, p. 40. There is an indication in the Central Committee minutes that Stalin was not unaware of the Military Revolutionary Centre's place in Trotskii's overall strategy for taking power. For Stalin's contribution to the discussion includes the remark that: "The Petrograd Soviet has already embarked on an insurrectionary course by refusing to allow the troops to be removed" (*PSS*, p. 100). As a member of the Military Revolutionary Centre Stalin was acting in a minor capacity to further the progress of Trotskii's method of bringing the Bolsheviks to power. This would explain why in later years Stalin would claim to have played a major part in the October Revolution by virtue of his membership of the Military Revolutionary Centre, but be unable to elaborate on what the significance of that body had been. To have done so would have revealed Trotskii as one of the main architects of the Bolshevik Revolution.
68 *PSS*, p. 98.
69 Trotskii, *Sochineniia*, p. 1009.
70 *Rabochii put'*, no. 46, 8 November (26 October) 1917.
71 *Siluety*, p. 70.
72 This is stated explicitly in "Baltflot v dni Kerenshchiny", p. 118.
73 These are on pp. 933–35, 988–89, 998–1000, 1007, 1009, 1045, 1197–98. I am indebted for this exhaustive list of references to Dr Ian Thatcher.

210

10

"ALL POWER TO THE SOVIETS"

The Bolsheviks take power

Rex A. Wade

This selection looks at the October Revolution in the broader political and social-economic context that created the rising demand for "all power to the soviets" and made a new revolution increasingly probable by October. In this respect it might be contrasted to White's detailed examination of the events surrounding a specific event, the Congress of Soviets of the Northern Front, although the conclusions of the two essays match. The book from which this essay is drawn argues that a political realignment followed the February Revolution that resulted in the emergence of multi-party political blocs; this selection starts by discussing the Bolsheviks within a larger radical left that agreed on many fundamental issues, including the need to replace the Provisional Government by a new government, probably one based on the soviets. It also blends social-economic history into the political story, showing how important that was to the situation leading up to the October Revolution (an earlier part of the book gave an extensive overview of popular aspirations and organization). It relates that to the immediate pre-October Revolution events in Petrograd, especially the "Day of the Petrograd Soviet" (October 22) and other aspects of a general mobilization behind the idea of power being taken by the forthcoming Second All-Russia Congress of Soviets. Looking more closely at what happened during October 22–24, it emphatically revises the traditional story of a Lenin-conceived and Lenin-directed conspiratorial seizure of power on the eve of the Congress of Soviets. It also carries the story forward to the events of October 24–25, the "October Revolution itself," and the initial steps in consolidation of power, steps that would set the Bolshevik government on the path to dictatorship and a very different regime from what most participants in the October Revolution expected.

* * *

211

The rise of the Bolsheviks and the radical left

The Bolsheviks started in the spring of 1917 as the least influential of the three major socialist parties, but grew rapidly in size and importance. By fall they had surpassed the Mensheviks and were challenging the SRs in popular support; in Petrograd and many urban centers they had surpassed both parties. The reasons are complex. One was the Bolsheviks' success in positioning themselves as the opposition to both the government and Soviet leadership, attacking their failure to deal decisively with the land issue and blaming them for the deteriorating economy, for mishandling the nationalities question and for a host of other problems. The Bolsheviks hammered the Revolutionary Defensists for failing to end the war and for their commitment to coalition government (which was increasingly unpopular with workers and soldiers). They accused them of counterrevolutionary sympathies and even, ironically as it proved, of plotting to prevent the Constituent Assembly from meeting. As the Provisional Government and Revolutionary Defensist leaders failed to solve the problems of Russia and to meet the aspirations of society, the radical left prospered. The Bolsheviks in particular became the political alternative for the disappointed and disenchanted, for those looking for new leadership.[1]

The Bolsheviks' appeal was not merely negative, however. They also drew support for the policies they advocated. They promised quick action on the problems facing Russia: immediate peace, rapid and complete land distribution, workers' supervision in industry and various other social-economic changes. They were able to champion the demands of specific groups, such as the *soldatki* [soldiers' wives] for stipends and the "over 40s" for discharge from the army, in a way that the parties responsible for government or even Soviet actions could not. Moreover, they provided clear and believable, if often simplistic or even erroneous, explanations for the complex problems and uncertainties of the times. Their explanation that the problems of society grew out of hostile actions of "capitalists," "bourgeoisie" and other privileged elements was more easily grasped than was the working of complex and often impersonal forces. That some known or unknown "they" threatened the revolution was a popular belief in the unsettled world of 1917; few asserted it more forcefully or more effectively than the Bolsheviks. The lesson to be drawn, of course, was that therefore the problems of society could not be solved as long as the capitalists and bourgeoisie held any share of power.

Excluding the upper- and middle-class elements from power and the demand for radical change were both neatly summed up in the call for "All Power to the Soviets," which both the Bolsheviks and growing numbers of the population embraced but which the Revolutionary Defensist leaders stubbornly rejected. The Bolsheviks capitalized on the growing correspondence of their views with those of the workers and soldiers by waging an energetic propaganda campaign in the press and by orators, in which they drove home their criticism of the government and Revolutionary Defensism and highlighted their own prescription for radical change. Their politics of sweeping change, of a revolutionary restructuring of society, aligned them with popular aspirations as the population turned toward more radical solutions to the mounting problems of Russia.

The party's success also grew in part out of its organization. The Bolshevik Party in 1917 was a unique combination of centralization and decentralization. A small Central Committee served as its top decision-making body. Below it were city and provincial committees, of which the most important was that in Petrograd, the Petersburg Committee. Further down were the district committees in large cities and the smaller regional organizations countrywide. At the bottom, at the grass-roots level, stood the party committees in factories and army units. The Bolsheviks also had a special Military Organization to work among the soldiers. Not being distracted by the problems of central and local governance that affected other parties, the Bolsheviks were able to devote more energy and personnel to party organizational work and to gaining new supporters among the mass organizations and committees. Moreover, the party leadership was more cohesive than the other major parties. The others suffered from numerous deep splits, most significantly the Defensist versus Internationalist division. The Bolsheviks did not have that division, Lenin having crafted the party along strictly Internationalist lines and any Defensist-oriented members having left the party already.

Not that the party was without internal divisions. Despite Lenin's traditional emphasis on leadership and discipline, the lower party organizations had considerable freedom to adapt to the demands of their worker or soldier constituencies and to changing circumstances. They sometimes challenged or ignored the policies of the top leaders. Although Lenin temporarily abandoned the slogan of "All Power to the Soviets" following the July Days, for example, most of the party, especially at the lower levels, never ceased to support it. The lower-level party organizations tended to be more radical and more activist than the upper-level organizations. This reflected the fact that the Bolshevik Party, as the party of radical extremism, attracted the most radical and impatient individuals from the factories and garrisons. The top party leadership, on the other hand, was concerned with broad strategic issues and was of necessity somewhat more cautious than the rank and file. The leadership sometimes found it difficult to keep their more impatient members in step with overall party policy and strategy, as the July Days had shown. There were important disagreements throughout 1917 among the party leaders as well, especially over taking power in October, but the Bolsheviks were still the best organized and most cohesive, and had the most clearly authoritative central leadership of any of the revolutionary parties. . . .

The Bolsheviks, however, were not the only political group advocating sweeping changes and reaping the benefits of popular dissatisfaction with government and Soviet policy. Others shared their criticism of the government and Soviet leaders, offered similar analyses of why things were wrong and held out visions of a better future. The rise of the Bolsheviks was in fact part of a broader phenomenon of the growth of the radical left. Radical victories in soviets and workers' and soldiers' organizations in late summer and early fall usually rested on a left-bloc coalition of Bolsheviks, Left SRs, Menshevik-Internationalists and other smaller groups such as the anarchists, among whom Bolsheviks were usually but not always the predominant group. What unified this left bloc was opposition to the Revolutionary Defensist leadership of the Soviet and a call for different policies. They opposed continuation of coalition government and stressed class hostility instead of cooperation. They opposed continuing the war and demanded immediate peace. They insisted on quicker action on social and economic reforms and called for some form of Soviet power or all-socialist government. Many so-called Bolshevik resolutions were in fact joint left-bloc resolutions, and this left bloc provided the majority in many local soviets and other organizations often described as "Bolshevik" by later accounts and even by some contemporaries.

The Left SRs were the most important group, next to the Bolsheviks, in the radical left bloc. The left tendency within the SR Party emerged as a potent force on the radical left in the summer and early fall. It took clearer form as it became increasingly vocal in its opposition to the Revolutionary Defensists – and thus the right and center wings of the SR party – on the above issues. Their opposition to the offensive and the reimposition of the military death penalty swung the vote of many garrison soldiers to them within the SR Party. Left SR spokesmen such as Spiridonova, Kamkov and Natanson bitterly attacked the government, Kerensky (still officially an SR), Chernov and the SR leadership for continuing support for the war, for continuing coalition with the Kadets and for failing to deal decisively with the land question and other social issues. By fall the Left SRs became the major force in the Soldiers' Section of the Petrograd Soviet and in some other soviets as well. This plus some support in the workers' sections made them increasingly influential in the soviets generally. Their influence also grew inside the party. The leftists won 40 percent of the vote at the SR Party council of August 6–10, before the Kornilov Affair. On September 10, after Kornilov, the leftists won control of the Petrograd SR Party organization. This gave them control of its newspaper and thus of an important vehicle for putting forward their views. On September 14 they issued a manifesto in the paper demanding a general armistice, an end to coalition, workers' supervision, land to the peasants and the convocation of a new congress of soviets. The leftists were also gaining influence in the party across the country. They already controlled party organizations at the northern naval bases (Kronstadt, Helsinki, Reval), in widely spread cities such as Kharkov, Kazan and Ufa, and in many army committees. Their strength continued to grow and by fall the majority of SR Party organizations were for Soviet power, despite the official position of the central party leaders.[2] . . .

The left-wing Mensheviks were the third significant part of the left bloc. They emerged in late spring as a loosely knit group critical of the policies of Revolutionary Defensism, to which the Menshevik Party was committed under the leadership of Tsereteli and Dan. The left Mensheviks found leadership with the return in early May of prominent exiles, most importantly Iulii Martov, a founder of Menshevism. They adopted the name Menshevik-Internationalists to distinguish themselves from the Revolutionary Defensist leadership under Tsereteli, but did not leave the parent party. Like the Left SRs, they hoped to gain control of the entire party. In fact they did gain strength within the party in the late summer and fall, garnering over a third of the vote at the Menshevik Party congress in August, holding a loose majority in the Petrograd city organization and becoming the dominant faction within the party in some provincial cities (Kharkov, Tula and elsewhere). Popular support for Mensheviks of any variety was fading rapidly, however, as shown in disastrous electoral results of late summer and early fall. . . . Some of the Menshevik-Internationalist leaders abandoned the party; a large group led by Iurii Larin joined the Bolsheviks in August.

The anarchists rounded out the radical left bloc. Their absence from "high politics" of the government and Soviet masks the fact that all through 1917 they were important at the lower levels of politics, and especially in the factories of Petrograd. They focused their energies at the factory level and pinned their political ambitions to the factory committees in particular. This paid dividends. By late summer and fall elections at a large factory, as Paul Avrich has noted, "might have elected a dozen Bolsheviks, two anarchists, and perhaps a few Mensheviks and SRs."[3] The anarchists were a constant source of antigovernment, anti-Revolutionary Defensist, anti-factory management rhetoric, and they articulated worker discontents while helping to reorient them toward more radical politics. . . .

By August the radical left's criticism of the failure of the moderates, its advocacy of radical reform, and its calls for Soviet power began to translate into institutional power. Factories and army units continually reelected deputies to soviets, something the Bolsheviks and Left SRs pressed for in the name of accountability and democracy. As a result a combination of Bolsheviks, Left SRs and Menshevik-Internationalists took control of one after another of the Petrograd city district soviets in the summer, dominated the Petrograd trade unions and the factory committees, and gained control of some provincial city soviets and soldiers' committees. The process accelerated in September after the Kornilov Affair gave the left a gigantic boost. Especially important was the capture of the main bastion of revolutionary authority, the Petrograd Soviet. On August 31 a Bolshevik-sponsored resolution passed in the Petrograd Soviet for the first time. In response the Revolutionary Defensists put their leadership to a vote of confidence on September 9 and lost. On September 25 the Soviet elected a new radical left leadership. Leon Trotsky, who had joined the Bolshevik Party in July and swiftly became one of its most prominent leaders, became chairman of the Soviet, replacing Chkheidze. The new presidium had four Bolsheviks, two SRs and one Menshevik. Simultaneously the Bolsheviks took over the Moscow Soviet of Workers' Deputies, thereby giving them leadership of the two most important soviets. Victories in other cities accompanied this as the radical left bloc – and sometimes the Bolsheviks alone – won reelection campaigns in factories and barracks and took over control of soviet after soviet.

General elections to city and district government councils also revealed the shifting political loyalties. The Bolsheviks received a third of the votes in elections for the Petrograd city council on August 20, despite the absence of Lenin and some other top party leaders who were in hiding. In Moscow, Bolsheviks gained an absolute majority in voting for city district councils in September, a dramatic rise from June when they had obtained only 11.7 percent of the vote for the city council (the SRs won 58 percent in June but only 14 percent in September). These Bolshevik successes, it should be noted, came within the context of a dramatic falling off of voting in general. . . .[4]

Through these reelections of deputies and officers the Bolsheviks and other leftists were *elected* to leadership of the Petrograd and other soviets, and also of trade unions, factory committees, army committees and some public offices. They could reasonably claim *at this time* to speak on behalf of "Soviet democracy," the worker and soldier masses of the urban soviets and their demand for Soviet power. This control of the Petrograd Soviet and some other soviets allowed the October Revolution to take place; without it that revolution is difficult to imagine. Under Bolshevik leadership the Petrograd Soviet, the most influential institution in Russia, now became the main vehicle of the drive for Soviet power, supported by other soviets and popular organizations. Indeed, as it turned out, the October Revolution would begin as a defense of the Petrograd Soviet and the idea of Soviet power.

Soviet power, however, was an ambiguous slogan, meaning different things to different people, especially when it came to forming a government. For most it meant the Soviet in some way taking power and replacing the current "coalition" government (one including nonsocialists) with a new all-socialist multiparty government. The Menshevik-Internationalists and some others argued for a "homogenous democratic government," i.e., one that would include besides the soviets the representatives of other worker, peasant and even lower middle-class organizations such as cooperatives, democratically elected city councils, peasant organizations, etc. Many saw this as an alternative both to the old coalition government formula and to the Bolsheviks' narrower and more radical "Soviet power." It appealed to many socialists – including some Bolsheviks – who wanted to abandon governmental coalition with the liberals but who feared that a narrowly soviet-based radical government meant reckless policies, anarchy and civil war. Even some of the Revolutionary Defensists were moving toward this idea, while others still supported coalition. What was clear was the demand for a leftward, socialist reorganization of the government.

The crisis of coalition government

The Bolshevik and radical left rise in the soviets paralleled an ongoing government crisis that made government restructuring a pressing issue in the political life of fall 1917. The second coalition cabinet founded with such difficulty in July collapsed during the Kornilov Affair, and the parties and leaders that had championed coalition could not immediately agree on its reorganization. Therefore on September 1 the Provisional Government ministers turned the running of the government over to a Council of Five [headed by Kerensky]. . . .

Forming a new government, however, again proved difficult. . . . To help resolve this a "Democratic Conference," a gathering of representatives of socialist parties, soviets, trade unions, cooperatives and elected popular institutions such as city councils (which were mostly socialist-controlled) met on September 14–19. At this conference the Left SRs pushed hard for formation of a multiparty all-socialist government. After prolonged and acrimonious debate the conference passed muddled motions: first for the principle of coalition, then an amendment against including members of the Kadet Party, and then rejecting the whole resolution. The failure of the Democratic Conference to reach agreement allowed Tsereteli and the partisans of coalition, from their old base in the Central Executive Committee of the first All-Russia Congress of Soviets (June), to support Kerensky in forming a new Provisional Government, the "Third Coalition," on September 25. Headed by Kerensky and including Kadets, Mensheviks, SRs and other moderate socialists and liberals, it was even weaker than its predecessors, devoid of authority or significant support from any quarter. While formally a continuation of coalition, no one had much hope for it and all talk was of what would replace it.

The Democratic Conference revealed the extent to which the formerly unified ranks of the Revolutionary Defensists were in disarray. They no longer had an operable peace policy. Many of them had lost faith in coalition government, but clung to it because they feared the alternatives. The newspapers chronicled the steady erosion of their popular support, heralding an unbroken string of defeats by the radical left in factory and army committees, soviets, trade unions and other mass organizations. ... By the end of September the Revolutionary Defensist leadership had lost both its moral and main institutional authority (the Petrograd Soviet), although it still held on in the Central Executive Committee elected at the June Congress of Soviets. At the same time in the provinces many Menshevik and SR city committees were moving toward some kind of all-socialist-based political alternative to coalition and to the Provisional Government, toward local "Soviet power," despite the opposition of the Menshevik and SR leaders in Petrograd.

There is an appropriate symmetry to the coincidence that the "Third Coalition" government, headed by Kerensky and even weaker than its predecessors, was finally formed on September 25, the same day Trotsky became chairman of the Petrograd Soviet. The Bolshevik control of the Petrograd Soviet meant that the new government was faced with determined opposition there rather than the cooperation (even if sometimes strained) between the government and the Soviet that had been at the heart of the February System from March through August. It was the first cabinet of the Provisional Government that was formally denied the support of the Petrograd Soviet. Discussion of the government's pending demise and of how it might be replaced – by a broad socialist coalition or a radical Soviet government – or whether it might survive until the Constituent Assembly, began immediately. Moreover, the discussion went far beyond party leadership circles. It was the subject of intense debate in newspapers, in cafes, in barracks and factories, at public meetings and private clubs, on street corners and anywhere else people gathered. The question of some kind of Soviet power had existed since March, was argued ever more often and seriously as 1917 progressed and now became the chief topic of public discussion. What had changed was that, while previously the Petrograd Soviet leaders cooperated with the Provisional Government, the new leftist Petrograd Soviet leaders refused to do so and instead intended to replace it. Thus the government's weakness, combined with the new Bolshevik leadership of the Petrograd Soviet, gave urgency to the new question being posed in the streets and in the newspapers: "What will the Bolsheviks do?"

The popular mood – hopes and fears of the fall

The discussion of Bolshevik plans and the calls for Soviet power took place within the context of the deepening social and economic crisis and the growing popular demand for change. By late summer the revolution clearly had thus far failed to meet the aspirations of the people of the former Russian Empire. Indeed, unsolved political, social and economic problems created a mood of anxiety and tensions that fed directly into the growing clamor for a radical change of government. By fall Russians realized that they were suffering through almost continuous political instability punctuated by sharp crises marked by street demonstrations and loss of life. Newspapers and street orators traded recriminations over responsibility for the collapse of the summer military offensive and for the growing social and economic disorders. Strident demands by industrialists and workers, generals and soldiers, nationalities and others filled the air. Charges and countercharges among political parties resounded from oratorical platforms and filled the newspaper editorials. A sense of general crisis pervaded life, a feeling that things could not go on as they were. The latter was similar to the feeling that had preceded the February Revolution, that life could not long continue unchanged.

The war continued to loom as a fundamental problem. It put enormous stresses on the economy, which could not be corrected as long as war continued. The desire for peace became overwhelming by fall, among both soldiers and civilians. In addition, the unruly garrisons became ever more a problem for the government and for city administrations everywhere. Finally, the war fed into a major confrontation between the government and the Petrograd garrison which helped shape the October Revolution. The spark for the confrontation came from government responses to German military advances in September that threatened both land and sea approaches to Petrograd. On October 6 the government announced plans to send much – perhaps half – of the garrison to defend the sagging approaches to Petrograd. The garrison troops reacted to this news by vehement denunciations of the government, declarations of refusal to move to the front, pledges of support for the Petrograd Soviet and calls for Soviet power. Radical political agitators quickly tied the effort to move the garrison soldiers not only to a new "Kornilovite" counterrevolution, but to a possible subversion of the forthcoming Congress of Soviets. The controversy gave the Bolsheviks and radicals a golden opportunity to extend their influence in the garrison and further undermine government authority. The German military threat to Petrograd also worsened the government's relations with the workers as the government began planning for evacuation of key industries should that become necessary. As word of this spread the radical left denounced the government for preparing to abandon Petrograd, even charging that it was a counterrevolutionary scheme to choke off radical revolution.

Growing political radicalism fed also on the worsening economic situation. An important factor in the mood of fall 1917 was the sharp increase in prices coupled with growing scarcity of food and other supplies. The situation in Petrograd was both especially bad and especially critical, given its political importance and volatility. Bread had been rationed since spring, but in mid-October incoming bread supplies fell dramatically below daily demands. Although most attention focused on bread – the staple of lower-class diets – delivery of other foodstuffs also lagged dangerously behind previous consumption levels. By October only about one-tenth of the prewar milk supply was arriving in Petrograd, although the city had grown significantly. A conference on October 15 painted a bleak picture of a city with only three to four days of food reserves and little prospect for improvement.[5] Once again long lines snaked out from food shops . . . [and] prices rose rapidly, increasing about fourfold from July to October. The specter of starvation was real, especially for the lower classes, who were least able to take advantage of the flourishing black market with its high prices.

The problem existed in other cities as well. A survey of the food situation by the Ministry of Food Supply on October 12 registered for Novgorod the bleak entry: "starvation is appearing."[6] N. Dolinsky, a food supply official, wrote in the fall issue of the journal of the Ministry of Food Supply that "tragedy has become our everyday reality." A review of newspapers from around the country, he said, revealed that "ordinary labels such as *crisis, catastrophe* and so on . . . pale before the frightful hue of reality."[7] In Baku in September food shortages combined with labor conflict to stimulate demonstrations and riots. At the Baku Soviet one speaker stated that "Daily at the [food] supply center excited crowds gather, led by a few constantly active agitators, provoking the crowds to violence."[8] Indeed, the food lines emerged as important venues for political discussions and radicalization, including even debates over whether life was better under the old regime. "Every discussion in a public place in Russia now concerns food," wrote Morgan Phillips Price on October 8 at the conclusion of a long trip along the Volga River. "It is the essence of politics."[9] Moreover, the food crisis fed the general perception of the Provisional Government as having failed and of the need for radical change.

The industrial economy also continued to deteriorate, and that in turn helped drive other discontents. Whatever economic gains workers had made in the spring had long since been wiped out by skyrocketing prices, management resistance to new salary increases and wage losses due to factory closings and shortened hours. Production fell, the result of material and fuel shortages, falling productivity, and industrial strife. Strikes became even more bitter and politically polarizing. . . . The collapsing railroads moved less and less food and materials, compounding all other problems. In a desperate effort to improve fuel production, the government in October decided to dispatch a special military commissar with dictatorial powers to the coal-producing Donets Basin.[10] In Petrograd, management and government officials in October warned of forthcoming factory shutdowns, affecting perhaps half the city's factories, because of fuel and materials shortages. On October 9 the director of the Putilov factory, Petrograd's and the country's largest factory, reported that it had run completely out of coal and that as a result thirteen shops were completely closed and six would operate at partial capacity.[11] At the factory committee meeting the next day an anxious worker asked whether the fact that the factory was receiving one-third less fuel than it needed to operate meant that one-third of the workers would be laid off. The committee discussed various schemes for partial work and pay.[12]

. . . The crisis in the factories inevitably led the workers to the question of the use of state power to defend their interests. Worker conflicts with management and concern over wages, jobs and protection of their organizations led inexorably to a belief that those required a political solution. The issue before the workers by mid-October was not *whether* a socialist government, but *when* and *how*; whether to support a transfer of power at the forthcoming Second Congress of Soviets or wait until the Constituent Assembly. Either would provide a socialist government, with the radicals urging the former course and more moderate socialists the latter. In the mood of crisis that existed the former seemed preferable to ever more workers; steps were needed *now*. This was what the call for Soviet power meant – a government that would use state power in their interests, to solve their problems. . . .

Other problems heightened the sense of a society falling apart and in need of drastic measures. The growth of crime and public disorders intensified in the fall. The newspapers were full of reports of robberies, assaults and other violence. . . . Petty as well as serious misbehavior in public places – drunkenness, random shooting of firearms, looting, violence at train stations (usually by soldiers), a new rudeness of speech and behavior, open flouting of the law, unruly garrison soldiers – reinforced the impression. Continued lynch-law shocked Russians. . . . Travel became unreliable and more dangerous because of breakdowns on the railroads and the appearance of thieves and riotous soldiers – often deserters – on trains. Hundreds of thousands of soldiers from the front and garrisons roamed the country in the fall, pillaging, disrupting trains and towns, spreading rumors and violence, and offering fresh evidence of a social and political breakdown. The stock market collapsed after the Kornilov Affair, impoverishing portions of the middle classes and creating financial chaos. The government found itself less and less able to collect taxes. Continuing agrarian unrest and violence agitated the city as well as the countryside – large parts of the urban population, and especially garrison soldiers, had close ties to the villages. From the borderlands came news of nationalist movements demanding autonomy or even independence. The litany of problems was well summed up in an article on September 20 in the Moscow newspaper of the most moderate wing of the Socialist Revolutionary Party:

> Against the background of merciless foreign war and defeats of the armies of the Republic, internally the country has entered upon a period of anarchy and, virtually, a period of civil war . . .
>
> An open revolt flares up in Tashkent, and the Government sends armies and bullets to suppress it.
>
> A mutiny in Orel. Armies are sent.
>
> In Rostov the town hall is dynamited.
>
> In Tambovsk province there are agrarian pogroms; experimental fields are destroyed, also pedigreed cattle, etc.
>
> In Novgorod–Volynsk district the zemstvo storehouses are looted.
>
> Grain reserve stores in Perm province are looted.
>
> Gangs of robbers appear on the roads in Pskov province.
>
> In the Caucasus there is a slaughter in a number of places.
>
> Along the Volga, near Kamyshin, soldiers loot trains.
>
> In Finland the army and the fleet have disassociated themselves completely from the Provisional Government.
>
> Russia is threatened by a railway employees' strike . . .
>
> Unbridled, merciless anarchy is growing. Any cause is used.
>
> Events of colossal importance take place throughout the country. The Russian state collapses.[13]

The growing fears and fading hopes of the population demanded action either by the old leadership or by a new one. This set the stage for the struggle for power in the fall and the debates over Bolshevik intentions.

The Bolshevik debate over power

What were the Bolsheviks planning to do? That was the question on everyone's lips by mid-October. They debated it in the press, on street corners and in street cars, in food lines, at factories and army barracks, in political circles, even in the government. What, especially, were they planning for the upcoming Second All-Russia Congress of Soviets, originally scheduled for October 20 but then postponed to the 25th?

Apprehensions about Bolshevik intentions came to the fore when the Bolsheviks walked out of the Provisional Council of the Republic, or "Preparliament," on October 7. The Preparliament, another effort to strengthen the shaky government by convening a gathering of leading political figures from all groups, opened with a flurry of patriotic speeches and calls for revolutionary unity and discipline. Then Trotsky demanded the floor. Denouncing the government and the Preparliament as counterrevolutionary tools, he appealed to the workers and soldiers to defend Petrograd and the revolution. "Only the people can save themselves and the country! We turn to the people! All power to the soviets! All land to the people! Long live an immediate, just, democratic peace! Long live the Constituent Assembly!"[14] The Bolshevik delegates then rose and walked out amid jeers and taunts from the rest of the assembly. Their action intensified the debate about their intentions. What were the Bolsheviks planning to do?

That very question tormented Lenin as well. He feared that they would do too little, too late. From his Finnish hiding place – an order for his arrest dating from the July Days still existed – Lenin worried over Bolshevik intentions. He had already turned away from any idea of cooperation with the Mensheviks and SRs in some kind of shared Soviet power. Lenin's hostility to the moderate socialists and his view of them as betrayers of Marxism and accomplices of the bourgeoisie and the capitalists made cooperation within the generally understood meanings of Soviet power unacceptable. Bypassing entirely the debates going on in Petrograd about what kind of broad socialist government to form, Lenin in mid-September shifted to a strident call for an immediate armed seizure of power by the Bolsheviks. For him Soviet power meant a new type of government dominated by the Bolsheviks. From Finland he wrote to the Bolshevik Central Committee that "The Bolsheviks, having obtained a majority in the Soviets of Workers' and Soldiers' Deputies in both capitals [Petrograd and Moscow], can and *must* take state power into their own hands ... The majority of the people are *on our side*."[15] Limited in his ability to impose his will on the party from Finland, he sent message after message insisting that the time was ripe for a seizure of power and that the party must organize and prepare for it. In a letter of September 27 he wrote, in his usual polemical style with extensive use of stressed words, that there was a tendency

among the leaders of our Party which favours *waiting* for the Congress of Soviets, and is *opposed* to taking power immediately, is *opposed* to an immediate insurrection. That tendency, or opinion, must be *overcome*.

Otherwise, the Bolsheviks will cover themselves with eternal *shame* and *destroy themselves* as a party.

> For to miss such a moment and to "wait" for the Congress of
> Soviets would be *utter idiocy,* or *sheer treachery.*[16]

Lenin realized that the fall of 1917 offered a unique opportunity for
a radical restructuring of political power and for a man such as himself.
He believed that not only was the situation in Russia ripe for revolution, but also that in Germany and elsewhere in Europe. Like other
Russian socialists in 1917, Lenin saw the Russian Revolution as a central
part of a broader, sweeping world revolution. He saw it as a fundamental turning point in both Russian and world history: "history will
not forgive us," he wrote, if this opportunity to take power was missed.[17]
Moreover, he realized that the Bolsheviks had to move quickly because
the Menshevik and SR Parties were turning toward their left wings and
moving toward the idea of an all-socialist government – the recent
Democratic Conference had nearly achieved that. If a new effort were
successful that would placate one of the most insistent popular demands
and eliminate one of the mainstays of Bolshevik agitation. Lenin realized that even the more moderate wing of his own party supported the
idea of a broad socialist government. He had to move before that
happened and the Bolsheviks found themselves merely a part, perhaps
even a minority part, of a broad socialist government. The seizure of
power by the Bolsheviks was now his obsession.

Lenin's call divided the party leadership. A minority supported Lenin's
call to arms, especially the second-level leaders in the Petersburg
Committee and some district committees, but even there many doubted
the feasibility of such an action. Another group, led by Grigorii Zinoviev
and Lev Kamenev, two of Lenin's oldest and closest associates and most
authoritative party leaders, urged caution. They argued that the party
was growing stronger day by day and that it would be foolish to risk
that in an ill-conceived adventure that the government might yet have
the strength to suppress. Moreover, they had a different vision of the
future revolutionary government, favoring a broad coalition of socialists in a democratic left government (a position Lenin had held earlier
but now abandoned). They opposed any risky ventures even by the
Congress of Soviets. Their status in the party and Kamenev's prominent
role as a party spokesman in Petrograd – in contrast to Lenin's absence
– reinforced the influence of this position.

In between Lenin's demand for a violent seizure of power by the
Bolsheviks and the caution of Zinoviev and Kamenev, a third position
emerged. Increasingly identified with Leon Trotsky and probably representing a majority of the party's leadership, this looked to the
forthcoming Second All-Russia Congress of Soviets as the place and time
for the transfer of power. The Bolsheviks and other parties supporting
Soviet power would likely have a majority at the congress, and the

congress could then declare the transfer of power to itself. The government, they believed, would be helpless to resist this. The Bolsheviks would be the largest and thus most important party within the new soviet-based government. They would be its leaders, yet able to pose as the embodiment of "soviet democracy" and not as a single-party government. Moreover, they argued, the mood of the workers was such that they would "come out" for Soviet power, but not for a Bolshevik Party action. The Soviet had to be the focus of a transfer of power, of a second revolution. They correctly believed that the worker and soldier masses of Petrograd generally assumed that Soviet power meant a government of the socialist parties making up the soviets.

Despite Lenin's demands, therefore, the party's political effort focused on the forthcoming Second All-Russia Congress of Soviets as the means for a transfer of power. The Bolshevik Central Committee on September 24 ordered party members to press for reelection of local soviets that were still controlled by moderates and encouraged the convocation of regional soviet congresses and other activity to build support for a transfer of power at the Congress of Soviets.[18] From September 27 onward the main Bolshevik newspaper carried across the front page the headline: "Prepare for the Congress of Soviets on October 20! Convene Regional Congresses Immediately." Nor were the Bolsheviks alone in this focus: the Left SR newspaper carried a similar slogan, as well as regularly cautioning against any kind of "coming out" before the congress.

Getting the congress held and getting it to take power were sources of anxiety for the Bolsheviks and other leftists. Although the power of the soviets as institutions and the growing popularity of the Bolsheviks in them seems so great and unstoppable in retrospect, that was not at all clear at the time. The moderate socialists had agreed to convene the congress only reluctantly. The Bolsheviks and Left SRs labored under a constant fear that some kind of counterrevolution might yet block the congress, crush the revolution and snatch away their gains. They regularly warned that "counterrevolutionaries" might attempt to prevent the Congress of Soviets and appealed to workers and soldiers to be ready to defend it. Indeed, central to the campaign for Soviet power was precisely the argument that only Soviet power guaranteed the convening of the Constituent Assembly. Without remembering these fears, as well as the more general mood in October of disaffection, apprehension, desperation and growing social-political conflict, it is easy to misinterpret the mobilization of forces on the eve of the Congress of Soviets and the October Revolution itself.

Lenin did not share the Petrograd party leaders' focus on the Congress of Soviets. Frustrated and fearing that an irretrievable opportunity was slipping by, Lenin took the chance of moving from Finland to Petrograd. On October 10 he met, for the first time since July, with the Central

Committee of the party. After an all-night debate the Central Committee seemingly gave in to Lenin's passionate demands for a seizure of power. It passed a resolution stating "the Central Committee recognizes that ... [there follows a long list of international and domestic developments] all this places armed uprising on the order of the day."[19] This resolution later became central to the myth of a carefully planned seizure of power carried out under Lenin's direction. It was, in fact, something different and rather more complex than that.

What did this resolution mean, or not mean? First, it is important to note that it did *not* set any timetable or plan for a seizure of power. Rather, it was a formal reversion of Bolshevik Party policy to the idea that an armed uprising was a revolutionary necessity, after the interlude since July in which they had held that a peaceful development of the revolution was possible. After cataloging the international and domestic political situation, it asserted that "therefore ... an armed uprising is inevitable and that the time for it fully ripe," and instructed

> all Party organizations to act accordingly and to discuss and resolve all practical questions (the Congress of Soviets of the Northern Region, the withdrawal of troops from Petrograd, the reaction of the people in Moscow and Minsk, etc.) from this point of view.[20]

The resolution thus represented a shift in formal policy, but did not commit the party to a seizure of power *before* the Congress of Soviets or at any other specific time. Nor did it start actual preparations for a seizure of power. It was a general statement of policy for a turbulent and seemingly favorable period in the revolution, not a plan for the immediate seizure of power. At the most it was a statement of intent to overthrow the Provisional Government and replace it with a Soviet-based government when the time was right and a suitable opportunity arose, whenever that might be. This was hardly a new idea by October.

The resolution of October 10 did, however, do two things: it set off a vigorous debate within the Bolshevik Party about the meaning of the resolution and their future course of action, and it revealed the divisions in the party. A few interpreted it in a narrow sense, in Lenin's meaning, as a decision to launch an armed seizure of power as soon as possible. "The sooner the better," argued I. Rakhia at a meeting of the Petersburg Committee on October 15. Most, however, interpreted it in a broad sense, of meaning that a seizure of power would be carried out at some time, in some way, probably via the Congress of Soviets or in reaction to some government provocation. At the same meeting Andrei Bubnov, while pressing for action with the argument that "the general situation is such that an armed uprising is inevitable," admitted that "it is impossible to set a date for the insurrection, which will come of its own accord if conditions are right for it." Mikhail Kalinin expressed the uncertainty of many: he praised the Central Committee resolution of October 10, but added that "when this uprising will be possible – perhaps in a year – is uncertain."[21]

The Bolsheviks also debated the degree of popular support for a seizure of power and their own preparedness. At the meeting of the Petersburg Committee on October 15 speaker after speaker reported doubts that the workers and soldiers would come out in support of an attempt to seize power, especially before the Congress of Soviets, although they would rally to the defense of the Soviet and the revolution. Some, however, argued that the mood was ripe and that striking quickly was important. Still, everyone had to admit that little or nothing had been done to organize the soldier and worker supporters who would presumably carry it out, and nothing done to prepare Bolshevik cadres in key centers such as Moscow or to insure control of railroads and communications. Indeed, they had organized no central planning or directing center. The Red Guards, though militant and increasingly pro-Bolshevik, did not have any citywide central organization and the Bolsheviks had only a poor sense of their strength, mood and organization. A key party meeting (with Lenin present) on the night of October 16 reaffirmed the resolution of October 10, but one speaker noted that "If the resolution [of October 10] is an order, then it has not been fulfilled and we have done nothing about it."[22] This was six days after the October 10 resolution and fewer than four days before the congress was supposed to open – it was still scheduled for the 20th. Kamenev, who was strongly opposed to a seizure of power, argued that during the week since the resolution of October 10 "nothing was done . . . We have no apparatus for an uprising."[23]

The Bolsheviks were also debating the question of power in other settings, ones where Left SRs and other radicals participated. The Congress of Soviets of the Northern Region (CSNR) meeting on October 11–13 was especially important.[24] Its organizers, mostly Bolsheviks, saw it as a vehicle for organizing the Baltic–Finnish–Petrograd region troops, sailors and soviets behind the push for Soviet power and to insure the meeting of the forthcoming Second All-Russia Congress of Soviets. Although the question of an immediate seizure of power was raised, the CSNR leaders, Trotsky in particular, steered it toward preparations for the All-Russia Congress of Soviets and the assumption of power there. Lenin, however, in his writings specified the CSNR as a possible vehicle for seizing power. Lenin at this time was talking about an armed attack on Petrograd using troops from the Baltic fleet and northern region as the means of seizing power. The mingling of that idea with the resolution of October 10 and its reaffirmation on October 16 led Kamenev to declare that he so disagreed that he was willing to resign from the party's

Central Committee. Joined by Zinoviev, the two prominent Bolshevik leaders even took their case outside party circles, publishing their arguments against a seizure of power. This further stimulated public debate about Bolshevik intentions, as did Lenin's bitter attack on his old colleagues. As the Congress of Soviets neared the Bolshevik leadership was in disarray over how to proceed. In part by default and in part because that seemed to reflect the opinion of most party leaders, attention increasingly focused on the Congress of Soviets as the time, place and vehicle for the seizure of power, for making the new revolution called for in the Bolshevik resolution of October 10 as well as in hundreds of local workers' and soldiers' resolutions.

The debate about taking power was not limited to the Bolsheviks, who were not the only members of the leftist coalition that had been gaining power in city soviets in the fall and which would form the majority at the Congress of Soviets. The Left SRs and Menshevik-Internationalists totally opposed any action before the Congress of Soviets. Indeed, the influential Left SRs were focused on forming an exclusively socialist, but genuinely multiparty, government based on a broad spectrum of socialist parties. They had argued for such a government at the Democratic Conference and at the Preparliament, without success, and now turned to the Congress of Soviets as the vehicle for creating it. They approached late October trying simultaneously to prod their SR Party colleagues into agreeing to such a government while restraining what they feared to be Bolshevik adventurism. Left SRs were convinced that any solution to the crisis of power and to the social and economic problems and the war required an all-socialist government based on soviets. Many Menshevik-Internationalists had similar views. The Bolshevik leaders in Petrograd could not ignore the Left SRs' opinions, given their popular support in the garrison and factories. At the same time the Left SRs looked to the more cautious Bolsheviks such as Kamenev and Zinoviev and the Moscow leaders as evidence that such a course of action was possible in collaboration with the Bolsheviks. Even Trotsky's position was compatible with their approach.[25]

On the eve: the mobilization of forces

In the retrospective light of these debates and of the events of the next week that led to the October Revolution, the decision of the moderate socialist leaders on October 18 to postpone the opening of the Congress of Soviets from the 20th to the 25th looms fatefully momentous (it was postponed on the grounds that an insufficient number of deputies had arrived in Petrograd). This was wonderfully fortunate for the Bolsheviks, who were unprepared for and could not have attempted any seizure of power before the 20th even if they had so wished. The five extra days changed everything. They gave time for the further buildup of tensions, for a major struggle for control of the garrison, and for mobilization efforts by the Red Guards. Most of all they gave time for Kerensky's fateful decision to strike at the leftists on the 24th, which precipitated the armed seizure of power before the congress met. Without those events the October Revolution as we know it could not have occurred.

The mobilization of supporters during this period was especially important. A declaration of the transfer of power at the Congress of Soviets, however much expected, would after all be an insurrectionary action. The Bolsheviks and Left SRs could assume that Kerensky's government would try to resist. Therefore, they worked to insure that the Congress of Soviets could successfully take power upon itself and launched a series of measures designed to weaken the government and deprive it of its remaining legitimacy. They undertook to mobilize their own supporters, including a belated effort to create a Petrograd-wide Red Guard organization. They moved to take away the government's remaining authority over the garrison of Petrograd, thus destroying any ability of the government to use it against the seizure of power by the Congress of Soviets. They repeatedly called on workers and soldiers to be ready to defend the revolution and the Congress of Soviets. Seen in this light, as preparation to defend a transfer of power at the Congress of Soviets, the actions by the Bolshevik and Left SR leaders, the government, other political figures and local activists in October have a logic that they lack if one holds to the old myth of careful planning for a Bolshevik seizure of power *before* the congress.

It was as part of the efforts by the Bolsheviks and Left SRs to guarantee that they could successfully declare Soviet power at the congress that the Military Revolutionary Committee (MRC) and its attempt to neutralize government authority in the Petrograd garrison take on meaning. The idea of the MRC originated in the proposal by a Menshevik member of the Petrograd Soviet on October 9 to form a special committee to work on the problems of the restive mood of the garrison and the defense of Petrograd (a German attack was feared). Trotsky, as chairman of the Soviet, took up the idea and extended it, calling for a "revolutionary defense committee" to familiarize itself with all issues of defense of the capital and to supervise the arming of the workers. The purpose was to defend the city not only against any German threat, but against a "Kornilovite counterrevolution." It took form slowly and held its first meeting only on October 20 (i.e., not before the Congress of Soviets was originally scheduled to open). It selected a five-man leadership executive consisting of three Bolsheviks and two Left SRs, with one of the latter, Pavel Lazimir, as its chairman (he was also the chairman of the Soldiers' Section of the Petrograd Soviet). About the same time the Bolshevik leadership began to realize the MRC's potential as a vehicle for dominating essential armed power in the capital through its authority over the soldiers, and thus the role the MRC could play in enforcing a transfer of power at the Congress of Soviets.

Control of the garrison now became a key point in the developing struggle between the government and the left. Resolutions passed at an MRC-sponsored garrison conference on October 21 promised full support to the MRC and the Petrograd Soviet and called for the Congress of Soviets to take power and to provide peace, land and bread for the people. With this reaffirmation of the garrison's primary loyalty to the Soviet in hand, the MRC pressured the government. On the night of October 21 an MRC delegation called on General G.P. Polkovnikov, commander of the Petrograd Military District, and told him that "henceforth orders not signed by us are invalid."[26] Polkovnikov rejected their ultimatum. In response the MRC sent to all garrison units a declaration the next day that denounced Polkovnikov's refusal to recognize the MRC as proof that military headquarters was "a tool of counterrevolutionary forces." Therefore, it declared, protection of the revolution rested with the soldiers under the direction of the MRC. "No orders to the garrison not signed by the Military Revolutionary Committee are valid ... The revolution is in danger."[27] At the same time the MRC began to send its own commissars to replace the old, Revolutionary Defensist and pro-government ones in key military units, completing the process of transfer from moderate to radical socialist influence. By asserting this authority over the garrison the MRC not only challenged the essence of government authority – command control over the troops – but took a major step toward assuring the success of a proclamation of Soviet power at the Congress of Soviets. If the government could not call on the garrison, it would be helpless to defend itself.

Meanwhile Petrograd was the scene of numerous mass rallies, rumors and self-mobilizations. October 22 had earlier been proclaimed the "Day of the Petrograd Soviet," a day for meetings and demonstrations to raise funds and to consolidate support for the Soviet. Given the tension in the air, it now took on special significance. At mass rallies around the city the Bolsheviks and Left SRs worked to garner popular support for transfer of power to the Soviet. The aroused crowds roared their support. "All around me," wrote Sukhanov of a meeting where Trotsky spoke of the benefits of Soviet power, "was a mood bordering on ecstasy."[28] ... Rumors that "counterrevolutionaries" would do something that day led some Red Guard units to mobilize themselves and lent an air of nervous expectation. Some of these Red Guards decided to remain on alert until the Congress of Soviets met. The Vyborg district Red Guard staff ordered all units to hold themselves in full fighting readiness. A worker at the Vulkan Factory, F. A. Ugarov, wrote that "after the 'Day of the Soviet' the mood of the workers intensified. ... The bolts of rifles clicked. In the yard of the factory they fitted the trucks with sheet armor and mounted machine guns."[29] By the end of the 22nd everyone was expecting *some* kind of a revolutionary move, whether a classic armed rebellion (fueled by images of the French Revolution, peasant rebellions, and the July Days), an act by the Congress of Soviets, or even a counterrevolutionary putsch – something! A nervous tension rippled through the city.

Petrograd Soviet leaders, emboldened by support shown on the 22nd and having largely completed replacing old military unit commissars with new men – mostly Bolsheviks and Left SRs – escalated their challenge to the government on the 23rd. The MRC announced to the population that to defend the revolution it had sent commissars to military units and important points in the city, and only orders confirmed by them were to be obeyed. That evening the MRC won the allegiance of the garrison of the Peter and Paul Fortress after an all-day meeting where competing orators, including Trotsky, struggled for their allegiance. The fortress occupied the center of the city and its guns loomed over the Provisional Government offices in the Winter Palace across the river. On the evening of the 23rd the Petrograd Soviet meeting commended the efforts of the MRC, stating that their continuation would insure the meeting and work of the Congress of Soviets. Indeed, everything done thus far fitted within the framework of measures necessary to insure a successful transfer of power at the Congress of Soviets, or a successful defeat of the ever-feared counterrevolution if the latter did strike. . . .

Kerensky, the government members, and military commanders in Petrograd finally became alarmed at the trend of events: the massive show of support for Soviet power on the 22nd, the activities of the MRC, the behavior of the garrison and the Red Guards, and the looming Congress of Soviets. They made inquiries about the dispatch of troops from the nearby Northern Front, but these only raised doubts about whether such troops would support the government. Kerensky and the government were confronted with either waiting passively for the Congress of Soviets to declare their replacement or taking some sort of preemptive action. Finally, during the night of October 23–24, the government decided to act. Kerensky proposed arresting the MRC. The government instead agreed to initiate legal proceedings against some MRC members and Bolsheviks, and to close two Bolshevik newspapers in the city. For balance, two conservative papers would be closed also. They ordered military officials to assemble a reliable force at the Winter Palace. These proposed actions were so minor and inadequate that the government obviously did not comprehend either the popularity of the idea of Soviet power or the very real discontents felt by the populace. They clearly had not understood the fiery rhetoric of the past few days about defending against a counterrevolution. They completely failed to anticipate the firestorm of opposition that their actions would set off.

Such minor repressive measures by the government could hardly stop the rising tide of demand for Soviet power, but they could provide the very "counterrevolutionary" action for which the left had been watching. Kerensky unexpectedly handed Lenin his seizure of power *before* the Congress of Soviets.

The October Revolution: the armed confrontation

As most of Petrograd slept in the pre-dawn hours of October 24, a small detachment of military cadets and militiamen sent by the Provisional Government raided the press where two Bolshevik newspapers were published. They destroyed freshly printed copies of that day's paper, damaged the print beds, sealed the entrances and posted a guard. The alarmed press workers ran with the stunning news to the Smolny Institute, headquarters of the Petrograd Soviet, the Military Revolutionary Committee (MRC) and the Bolshevik Party. Unbeknownst to anyone, including the Bolshevik leaders, the October Revolution had begun. It began not in response to the demands of Lenin or a Bolshevik plan, but in response to the government's ill-conceived decision to launch a minor punitive action against the Bolsheviks.

Officials at Smolny quickly branded the press closure a counterrevolutionary move and summoned the leaders of the MRC, Petrograd Soviet and the Bolshevik and Left SR Parties. These (not including Lenin, who remained in hiding) assembled at Smolny to find that, in addition to the account of the printers, reports were coming in from various places around the city of suspicious troop movements. The MRC appealed for support:

> Counterrevolutionary conspirators went on the offensive during the night. A treasonous blow against the Petrograd Soviet of Workers' and Soldiers' Deputies is being planned. ... The campaign of the counterrevolutionary conspirators is directed against the Congress of Soviets on the eve of its opening, against the Constituent Assembly, against the people.

It then sent "Directive No. 1" to regimental commissars and committees: "You are ordered to bring your regiment to fighting readiness."[30]

The question was what to do next. Some of those present supported starting an armed insurrection immediately. Most, however, including Trotsky, focused instead on defensive measures designed to guarantee that the Congress of Soviets – which it was now clear would have a majority in favor of transfer of power – opened as scheduled the next day. Indeed, the Bolshevik Central Committee meeting which was hastily assembled concerned itself more with various aspects of the general political crisis than with the Provisional Government's actions that morning and their response to it; they did *not* discuss overthrowing the government before the congress met. That afternoon Stalin told a meeting of Bolshevik delegates assembled for the congress that there were two viewpoints within the MRC, "that we organize an uprising at once, and . . . that we first consolidate our forces," and that the Central Committee sided with the latter view. Trotsky's speech to the meeting reinforced Stalin's and stressed that the MRC's ordering of troops to reopen the closed Bolshevik newspapers was a defensive action.[31]

Through the morning and afternoon of the 24th the two opposing sides, each basically acting defensively, each accusing the other of betraying the revolution and each posing as its defender, tried to rally political and military support as the confrontation gradually gained momentum. Their efforts found very different responses. During the morning Kerensky and Petrograd military authorities tried without success to find reliable armed support. Government efforts to exercise authority in the Petrograd garrison were futile. The soldiers showed little enthusiasm for being used by either side, and the minority who did supported the Soviet. The garrison soldiers, when confronted with contradictory orders, usually either followed those coming from the Soviet and MRC commissars or did nothing; either way they were of no use to the government. Orders to send troops from outside the city either were countermanded by army committees or else the troops themselves refused to move after Soviet representatives told them they were being used for counterrevolution. By early afternoon the government managed to assemble only a small force of military cadets, officers, Cossacks and a detachment from one of the women's battalions to protect the Winter Palace and key government and communications buildings.

In contrast the Soviet found swift and vigorous support. Although most of the army garrison stayed in their barracks, some radicalized army units responded to the perceived threat of counterrevolution and came out in response to MRC appeals. Moreover, the actions of the government on the 24th galvanized the already agitated industrial workers and propelled their armed detachments, the Red Guard, into the confused struggle for control of the city. Virtually all Red Guards went into action, either on their own or in conjunction with groups of soldiers. Moreover, their *attitude* was especially important. Among the Red Guards there were no wavering units as there were among the soldiers, no forces that a worried Soviet leadership need fear might support the government. The problem for the MRC was that it exercised little direct control over the Red Guards, and even lacked a clear notion of their size and utility. Nonetheless, the Red Guards and those troops who came out gave the pro-Soviet forces preponderant armed strength in the capital.

The government and political opposition to Soviet power, meanwhile, was crumbling. Kerensky himself spent much of the afternoon of the 24th at the Preparliament trying to build political support. Indeed, virtually the entire political leadership of the country, except the Bolsheviks and Left SRs, spent the afternoon and evening there in fruitless debate. Although Kerensky won applause for denunciations of the Bolsheviks, after an evening of debate the Preparliament passed a resolution that effectively repudiated the Kerensky government – this in a body where most of the radical left representatives were absent. At the same time the moderate socialist leaders could not find any course of action other than issuing another tired resolution calling for restraint and warning of counterrevolution, such as the appeal on the night of October 24–25 that "An armed clash on the streets of Petrograd would untie the hands of the lurking bands of hooligans and pogromists ... [and] inevitably lead to the triumph of counterrevolutionary elements which have already mobilized their forces for crushing the revolution."[32] They still did not understand the deep popular roots of the demand for Soviet power, still seeing it only in terms of the danger of opening the country to counter-revolution. They still believed more in the phantom of a counterrevolution that had "mobilized" its forces than in the real popular movement.

While the politicians debated, while Kerensky sought support that would never come and while the Soviet and MRC leaders moved slowly to control key points that would be necessary to defend against a non-existent counterrevolution, groups of armed workers and soldiers began an uncoordinated but decisive struggle for control of the city. Most actions on the 24th were defensive and reactive. Red Guards and pro-Soviet soldiers mobilized to control the bridges over the river after the government endeavored to raise them to inhibit movement. Occupation of railroad stations followed rumors that the government was calling in troops from outside the city. This was mostly a process of push and shove, bluff and counterbluff, the government trying to use "reliable" units to maintain control, while pro-Soviet soldiers and Red Guards strove to take over buildings, bridges and key positions. Haphazardly and little by little, a transfer of armed power in the city took place through a series of nonshooting confrontations between armed groups in which the more determined side prevailed, and determination rested with the supporters of Soviet power. There was remarkably little actual shooting; no one was eager to die for the Provisional Government. By nightfall on the 24th the pro-Soviet forces controlled most of the city.[33]

Despite these successes, the Soviet and MRC leaders were still thinking about warding off a blow from the government and about the transfer of power at the congress. On the evening of the 24th Trotsky told the Petrograd Soviet that "All Power to the Soviets" would be implemented at the Congress of Soviets, and "whether this leads to an uprising or not depends not only and not so much on the Soviets as on those who hold state power in their hands contrary to the unanimous will of the people." He then warned that, "if the sham power [Provisional Government] makes a long-shot attempt to revive its own corpse, then the mass of the people, organized and armed, will give it a decisive rebuff."[34] Colorful imagery aside, this was a more realistic assessment of the situation than was coming from the other side.

Around midnight the gathering revolution shifted from defensive to offensive action. This was connected to two events: (1) a growing real-ization that the government was much weaker than thought and that the city was coming under the physical control of soldiers and Red Guards rallying to the defense of the Soviet, and (2) the arrival of Lenin at Soviet headquarters. Although he had been ordered by the Bolshevik Central Committee to stay in hiding, near midnight an agitated Lenin, aware that something major was happening in the city, left his hiding place to go to Smolny. Wearing a wig, a cap and a bandage on his face, he set off accompanied by a lone bodyguard. On the way they were intercepted by a patrol of military cadets but, mistaken for a pair of drunks and not recognized, allowed to pass. Then when they arrived at Smolny the Red Guard at the door initially refused them entry for lack of proper credentials. Only with difficulty did Lenin manage to enter what was becoming the headquarters of a revolution.[35]

The conjuncture of the dawning realization of the success of pro-Soviet forces and Lenin's arrival dramatically changed the situation. Lenin had not been part of the cautious defensive reaction of the 24th, and he was the one leader who had consistently urged an armed seizure of power *before* the Congress of Soviets met. Under his pressure and the reality of their growing strength the Bolshevik Soviet leaders shifted from a defensive posture to the offensive at about 2:00 a.m. on the morning of the 25th.[36] . . .

About the same time the MRC began to work out an elaborate plan for dispersing the Preparliament, arresting the Provisional Government and taking control of remaining key installations. They dropped the notion of waiting for the Congress of Soviets and commenced a drive to seize and declare the transfer of power immediately – before the congress – as Lenin demanded. By the time a cold gray windy day dawned on the 25th, pro-Soviet forces had extended their control to almost all of the city except the Winter Palace. There the members of the Provisional Government still sat behind a small, increasingly dispir-ited band of defenders, surrounded by a large but disorganized force of Red Guards and insurgent soldiers. The besiegers, however, feared that the government might have determined supporters who would inflict heavy casualties on any attackers and so were reluctant to attack. In fact, neither besiegers nor defenders were eager to risk bloodshed.

By mid-morning on the 25th the situation had progressed to the point at which, at about the same time, the Bolsheviks proclaimed the transfer of power while Kerensky fled the city in search of supporters. Kerensky had tried to find reliable troops in Petrograd and, being unsuccessful, decided to leave the city to seek troops at the front. He had trouble finding a way out of the city – the train stations were occupied by insurgents and the government could not find an automobile of its own – and not until about 11:00 a.m. did he speed past the besieging forces loosely surrounding the Winter Palace. While Kerensky searched for a car, Lenin at the Smolny Institute wrote the announcement of the overthrow of the government, which was immediately printed and spread throughout the city. On his way out of the city, in a borrowed car, Kerensky might have passed the first distribution of the proclamation announcing his overthrow. It read:

> To the Citizens of Russia!
> The Provisional Government has been overthrown. State power has passed into the hands of the organ of the Petrograd Soviet of Workers' and Soldiers' Deputies, the Military Revolutionary Committee, which stands at the head of the Petrograd proletariat and garrison.
>   The cause for which the people have struggled – the immediate offer of a democratic peace, the abolition of landlord ownership of land, workers' control over industry, the creation of a Soviet government – this has been assured.
>   Long live the revolution of workers, soldiers and peasants!
> The Military Revolutionary Committee
of the Petrograd Soviet
of Workers' and Soldiers' Deputies.
> 25 October 1917, 10:00 in the morning.[37]

That afternoon Trotsky opened a meeting of the Petrograd Soviet, where he announced the overthrow of the government and steps taken to secure power in the city. Lenin then emerged, his first public appearance since the July Days, to thunderous applause. The excited deputies and others who had crowded into the hall affirmed the transfer of power.

Trotsky's and Lenin's claims, while substantially true, ignored the inconvenient fact that, excepting Kerensky, the Provisional Government still sat in the Winter Palace behind a small defending force. It was a curiously unmilitary faceoff. On the afternoon of the 25th the radical journalist John Reed and three other Americans were able to bluff their way past the besiegers and simply walked into the palace unmolested by defenders. They wandered around the palace talking to various persons before walking back out past besieging Red Guards and soldiers and off to dinner.[38] All through the day and evening new arrivals of Red Guards and soldiers reinforced the besiegers, some of whom left, while some of the palace's military defenders changed their minds and marched away unhindered. During the afternoon a light, wet snow began to fall. Finally, during the late evening besiegers began filtering into the palace in small numbers, rather than actually "storming" it (paintings and motion pictures of a great charge on the palace were later fictional romanticizations). Toward midnight on the 25th those filtering in became a steady stream. As one defender described the process, "as long as the groups of Red Guards were small, we disarmed them. . . . However, more and more Red Guards appeared, and also sailors and soldiers of the Pavlovsky Regiment. The disarming began to be reversed."[39]

At about 2:00 a.m. on the 26th some of the attackers finally found the way to the room where the government ministers sat. At the sound of approaching insurgents the ministers ordered the cadets guarding the door not to resist, in order to save lives, and seated themselves around a table and waited. The door was suddenly flung open and, in the words of one government minister, "a little man flew into the room, like a chip tossed by a wave, under the pressure of the mob which poured in and spread at once, like water, filling all corners of the room." This was Vladimir Antonov-Ovseenko, one of the Bolshevik leaders of the MRC, who shouted, "In the name of the Military Revolutionary Committee, I declare you under arrest."[40] By the time of the arrest, however dramatic, the city was completely in the hands of pro-Soviet forces and the Congress of Soviets already in session. . . .

By the evening of the 25th it appeared that Lenin had obtained his goal of a transfer of power by a violent act of seizure before the Congress of Soviets. It is worth noting, however, that the transfer of power was in the name of the Petrograd Soviet and affirmed by it. It was not a revolution in the name of the Bolshevik Party, and the multiparty Congress of Soviets was still to be the ultimate legitimizing institution. Transforming a seizure of power in the name of Soviet power into a Bolshevik regime would depend on yet another unforeseeable stroke of luck, this one at the Congress of Soviets, comparable to Kerensky's blunder on the 24th.

The Congress of Soviets

As the armed struggle for control of Petrograd drew toward a close on the evening of October 25, the emphasis shifted to the political struggle at the Second All-Russia Congress of Soviets. Events unfolding there that night shaped the nature of the new government in ways no one, not even Lenin, could have foreseen at the time. They gave the Bolsheviks full control of the congress and the new government, contrary to all expectations, and transformed the debate about just what "Soviet power" meant now that it was a reality. They profoundly influenced the outcome of the revolution and the Soviet regime that followed for the next several decades.

The Second All-Russia Congress of Soviets opened at 10:40 p.m., October 25. The opening was delayed by the skirmishing in the city, the Bolsheviks being especially anxious to take the Winter Palace and capture the Provisional Government before it opened. The excited, milling crowd of delegates could no longer be put off, however, and finally the meeting opened amidst the sounds of weapons firing and with the palace still under siege. The Bolsheviks were the largest party, with about 300 of the approximately 650–70 seats (figures for the number of delegates and their party distribution are not precise). To obtain a majority they needed the support of other advocates of Soviet power, especially the about 80–85 Left SRs, who had not yet officially broken with the parent SR Party. Nonetheless, these numbers guaranteed that the new leadership would be from the radical left and predominantly Bolshevik. Most participants assumed that the congress would create a new government composed of a coalition of socialist leaders – Soviet power. The main question was its exact composition and how radical it would be. That depended to a large degree on the Left SRs and the Menshevik–Internationalists, who held the balance of power between the Bolsheviks and their moderate Menshevik and SR opponents.

Hardly had the congress begun when the sound of cannon was heard in the distance: the artillery on the Peter and Paul Fortress firing across the Neva River at the Winter Palace (which actually did little physical damage). An excited Martov, speaking for the Menshevik-Internationalists, proposed that, to avoid bloodshed, negotiations begin at once for a united democratic government of all socialist parties. This was endorsed by Anatolii Lunacharsky for the Bolsheviks and Sergei Mstislavsky for the Left SRs, and adopted overwhelmingly. This plan immediately went astray, however. A series of speakers from the SR, Menshevik, Bund and smaller parties rose to condemn the "conspiracy ... by the Bolshevik Party," which, they charged, preempted the work of the congress and "signals the beginning of civil war and the break-up of the Constituent Assembly and threatens to destroy the Revolution." Calling on congress delegates to join in a decision by Petrograd City Council deputies to march to the Winter Palace to support the Provisional Government and to prevent bloodshed, most Mensheviks and SRs then walked out. Martov, still searching for a compromise between the socialist moderates and radicals, then introduced an eloquent appeal to avoid civil war by forming a government "acceptable to the whole revolutionary democracy" (i.e., to the moderate Mensheviks and SRs as well as the Bolsheviks and radical left) and proposed that the congress suspend its work until this could be attended to.[41]

The Congress of Soviets, however, was now in no mood for negotiations. The speeches and departure of the moderate socialists not only left the Bolsheviks with an absolute majority, but also hardened feelings among those remaining, strengthening the militants and undermining those moderate Bolsheviks who were inclined toward concessions. Trotsky contemptuously rejected compromise: "you are miserable bankrupts, your role is played out; go where you ought to be: into the dustbin of history."[42] After passing a resolution (introduced by Trotsky) declaring that the "withdrawal of the Menshevik and Social Revolutionary delegates from the Congress is an impotent and criminal attempt to disrupt" its work,[43] the truncated congress continued to meet through the night, debating resolutions and receiving a string of encouraging reports. News of the taking of the Winter Palace and arrest of the government ministers buoyed spirits even further. Then came a series of reports of support from key military units. A kind of euphoria, not unlike that of February 27, set in as the long-discussed declaration of Soviet power seemed to be succeeding almost effortlessly. Finally, approaching 5:00 a.m. on October 26, Lunacharsky stood to read a proclamation of the assumption of power by the Congress of Soviets which Lenin – who still had not appeared at the congress – had just written. The proclamation not only announced that the Provisional Government was overthrown and that the Congress of Soviets had taken power, but also laid out a basic program which would appeal to most people of the Russian state:

> The Soviet Government will propose an immediate democratic peace to all the nations and an immediate armistice on all fronts. It will secure the transfer of the land of the landed proprietors, the crown and the monasteries to the peasant committees without compensation; it will protect the rights of the soldiers by introducing complete democracy in the army; it will establish workers' control over production; it will ensure the convocation of the Constituent Assembly at the time appointed; it will see to it that bread is supplied to the cities and prime necessities to the villages; it will guarantee all the nations inhabiting Russia the genuine right to self-determination.
>
> The Congress decrees: all power in the localities shall pass to the Soviets of Workers', Soldiers' and Peasants' Deputies.

After only brief discussion the congress adopted the proclamation with only two votes in opposition and a few abstentions.[44]

At about dawn on October 26 the exhilarated but exhausted congress delegates and Bolshevik leaders – some of whom had hardly slept for two nights – adjourned to try to sleep a little, to assess the events of the day and to plan for the second session that evening. At about the same time citizens of the capital awoke to quiet streets with little sense that any momentous event had occurred; seemingly yet another round of political turmoil, complete with armed groups in the streets, had been passed through. Proclamations, mostly in the name of the MRC, were posted, and although perhaps unsettling they gave little indication of the great events transpiring. . . .

The new government was, unexpectedly, made up entirely of Bolsheviks. This had not been envisioned in the many debates about a Soviet government, all of which had assumed some kind of multiparty socialist government. The walkout of the moderates changed that. The Left SRs insisted that they would join the government only as part of a broad socialist coalition, but with the moderates gone such a government was impossible. Therefore, an all-Bolshevik government was formed initially. Lenin became chairman of Sovnarkom and thus head of the government, with Trotsky as people's commissar for foreign affairs. The new government structure was completed when the Congress of Soviets chose a new Central Executive Committee (CEC). The Bolsheviks initially took sixty-two seats, the Left SRs twenty-nine and ten were divided among the Menshevik-Internationalists and minor leftist groups. The socialist parties that had withdrawn were unrepresented. The congress stated that the CEC exercised full authority in its name between congresses, including both general supervision of the government and the right to replace its members. However, the exact relationship of the CEC to the Sovnarkom, both approved by the congress, soon became a source of conflict between the Left SRs (who were in the CEC but not the Sovnarkom) and the Bolsheviks. Although the CEC with its non-Bolshevik minority did not seriously impede Lenin in his exercise of power, its multiparty structure maintained the image of a government based on a multiparty socialist coalition, a concept which enjoyed immense popularity as part of the slogan of Soviet power.

NOTES

This is an abridged and slightly modified selection from Rex A. Wade, *The Russian Revolution, 1917* (Cambridge: Cambridge University Press, 2000), pp. 206–244.

1 The Bolsheviks have been the subject of an immense literature. For studies of the party leading up to and during the October Revolution, see especially the two books by Alexander Rabinowitch, *Prelude to Revolution*, Bloomington, 1968 and *The Bolsheviks Come to Power*, New York, 1976, and Robert V. Daniels, *Red October*, New York, 1967. On Lenin especially see Robert Service, *Lenin*, 3 vols., London, 1985–94, and Neil Harding, *Lenin's Political Thought*, 2 vols.,

New York, 1977, 1981. Adam Ulam, *The Bolsheviks*, New York, 1965, provides another look at Lenin and the party.

2 Michael Melancon, *The Socialist Revolutionaries and the Russian Anti-War Movement, 1914–1917*, Columbus, OH, 1990, p. 282.

3 Paul Avrich, *The Russian Anarchists*, Princeton, 1967, pp. 145–46.

4 Diane Koenker, *Moscow Workers and the 1917 Revolution*, Princeton, 1981, pp. 202–10; Oliver H. Radkey, *The Agrarian Foes of Bolshevism: Promise and Default of the Russian Socialist Revolutionaries, February to October 1917*, New York, 1958, pp. 363, 443.

5 *Ekonomicheskoe polozhenie Rossii nakanune Velikoi Oktiabr'skoi sotsialisticheskoi revoliutsii*, Moscow, 1957, vol. II, pp. 351–52.

6 Ibid., p. 319. The deteriorating supply situation and its ramifications are a major thread running through the history of 1917. See especially Roger Pethybridge's fine summary in *The Spread of the Revolution: Essays on 1917*, London, 1972, esp. 1–56 and 83–110, and the books by Lars T. Lih, *Bread and Authority in Russia, 1914–1921*, Berkeley, 1990, and Mary McAuley, *Bread and Justice: State and Society in Petrograd, 1917–1922*, Oxford, 1991. Robert Paul Browder and Alexander Kerensky, eds., *The Russian Provisional Government, 1917: Documents*, Stanford, 1961, vol. II, pp. 615–708, offers documents on the economic situation.

7 Quoted in Lih, *Bread and Authority*, p. 111.

8 Ronald Grigor Suny, *The Baku Commune, 1917–1918: Class and Nationality in the Russian Revolution*, Princeton, 1972, p. 115.

9 Morgan Phillips Price, *Dispatches from the Revolution: Russia 1915–1918*, Durham, NC, 1998, p. 75.

10 Alfred J. Rieber, *Merchants and Entrepreneurs in Imperial Russia*, Chapel Hill, NC, 1982, p. 412.

11 *Ekonomicheskoe polozhenie Rossii nakanune Velikoi Oktiabr'skoi sotsialisticheskoi revoliutsii*, vol. II, pp. 163–64.

12 *Fabrichno-zavodskie komitety Petrograda v 1917 godu. Protokoly*, Moscow, 1979, pp. 490–92.

13 *Volia naroda*, September 20, as given in Browder and Kerensky, *Russian Provisional Government*, vol. III, pp. 1641–642, slightly modified.

14 Quoted in Rabinowitch, *Bolsheviks*, p. 201.

15 V. I. Lenin, *Collected Works*, Moscow, 1960–70, vol. XXVI, p. 19. Emphasis Lenin's.

16 Ibid., p. 82. Emphasis Lenin's.

17 Ibid., p. 21.

18 Robert H. McNeal, ed., *Resolutions and Decisions of the Communist Party of the Soviet Union*, Toronto, 1974, vol. I (ed. Ralph C. Elwood), pp. 284–86.

19 Ibid., pp. 288–89.

20 Ibid.

21 The debates at the Petersburg Committee are in *Pervyi legal'nyi Peterburgskii komitet bol'shevikov v 1917 godu: Sbornik materialov i protokolov zasedanii Peterburgskogo komiteta RSDRP(b) i ego Ispolnitel'noi komissii za 1917 g.*, Moscow-Leningrad, 1927, p. 316.

22 Quoted in Daniels, *Red October*, p. 94.

23 Quoted ibid.

24 On the congress see especially James White, "Lenin, Trotskii and the Arts of Insurrection: The Congress of Soviets of the Northern Region, 11–13 October 1917," *Slavonic and East European Review* 77, no. 1 (January 1999), 117–39 [Chapter 9 above].

25 On the Left SRs on the eve of the October Revolution, see Michael Melancon, "The Left Socialist Revolutionaries and the Bolshevik Uprising," in Vladimir Brovkin, ed., *The Bolsheviks in Russian Society*, New Haven: Yale University Press, 1997, esp. pp. 67–69.

26 Quoted in Rabinowitch, *Bolsheviks*, p. 241.

27 *Petrogradskii voenno-revoliutsionnyi komitet: Dokumenty i materialy*, Moscow, 1996, vol. I, p. 63.

28 N. N. Sukhanov, *The Russian Revolution 1917: A Personal Record*, London, 1955, vol. II, p. 584.

29 S.I. Tsukerman, "Petrogradskii raionnyi sovet rabochikh i soldatskikh deputatov v 1917 godu," *Krasnaia letopis'* no. 3 (1932), 64. See Rex A. Wade, *Red Guards and Workers' Militias in the Russian Revolution*, Stanford, 1984, pp. 192–94 for the Red Guard mobilization on the eve.

30 *Petrogradskii voenno-revoliutsionnyi komitet*, vol. I, pp. 84, 86.

31 Rabinowitch, *Bolsheviks*, pp. 252–54.

32 In Browder and Kerensky, *Russian Provisional Government*, vol. III, p. 1785.

33 For descriptions of the struggle in the streets see Wade, *Red Guards and Workers' Militias*, pp. 196–207 and Rabinowitch, *Bolsheviks*, pp. 249–300, *passim*.

34 Quoted in Robert V. Daniels, ed., *The Russian Revolution*, Englewood Cliffs, NJ: Prentice-Hall, 1972, pp. 131–32.

35 This episode is especially well described in Daniels, *Red October*, pp. 158–61.

36 Rabinowitch, *Bolsheviks*, pp. 268–69.

37 *Petrogradskii voenno-revoliutsionnyi komitet*, vol. I, p. 106.

38 John Reed, *Ten Days That Shook the World*, London, 1967 [1919], pp. 114–18.

39 Quoted in *Oktiabr'skoe vooruzhennoe vosstanie: semnadtsatyi god v Petrograde*, Leningrad, 1967, vol. II, p. 366.

40 Quoted in Rabinowitch, *Bolsheviks*, p. 300. In addition to the account of the siege and arrest of the government in Rabinowitch, Daniels, *Red October*, pp. 187–96, also gives a good account of the taking of the palace and the arrest of the government ministers.

41 Rex A. Wade, *Documents of Soviet History*, vol. I, *The Triumph of Bolshevism*, Gulf Breeze, FL: Academic International Press, 1991, pp. 2–5.

42 Sukhanov, *The Russian Revolution*, vol. II, p. 640.

43 Wade, *Documents of Soviet History*, vol. I, pp. 3–4.

44 Ibid., pp. 4–5.

11

THE ALL-RUSSIAN CONSTITUENT ASSEMBLY AND THE DEMOCRATIC ALTERNATIVE

Two views of the problem

Lev Grigor'evich Protasov

The long-awaited Constituent Assembly finally met on January 5, 1918, and after one meeting was forcibly dissolved the next day by the Bolsheviks. For a long time historians ignored the Constituent Assembly, for any of several reasons: because of its brief life and failure; because they felt that a democratic outcome of the revolution was no longer possible already by late summer or early fall and that it was either "Kornilov or Lenin"; and because of a certain tendency to focus on Lenin and October and ignore the weeks that followed, jumping instead directly forward to the civil war. More recently, however, some historians in the West and in Russia have assigned it greater significance, arguing that both the Assembly and the events leading up to its meeting and dispersal are important topics for investigation, and that its dispersal marks the effective border between the revolution and the civil war that followed. Since the collapse of the Soviet Union, scholars in Russia, previously prevented by the Soviet regime from attaching much significance to the Constituent Assembly, have turned to it with interest. Some have advanced arguments for its pivotal role in Russian history – Protasov's opening sentence even extends that to world history. Post-Soviet scholars in Russia have also been fascinated by the question of "alternatives," focusing especially on how the horrors of the Stalin years or even the whole Communist experiment might have been avoided had history taken a different path at one point or another during the revolutionary era. The Constituent Assembly is one such point. Protasov directs our attention to the importance of the idea of the Constituent Assembly as a factor in politics throughout 1917, to its significance for any chance for a democratic outcome of the revolution, and raises important questions about its relationship to the long-term political culture of Russia. An important

243

LEV GRIGOR'EVICH PROTASOV

theme of the article is how the Constituent Assembly fits into the Russian political tradition and its implications for current Russian political development, a broader theme that runs through many historical investigations today. For all these reasons, an article reexamining the importance of the Constituent Assembly in the history of the revolution, and which also reflects on its relation to issues facing Russia today, is perhaps an appropriate selection to end this volume.

* * *

The All-Russian Constituent Assembly was one of those world events that embody global tendencies in the development of human civilization and represent milestones in its history.

The epic of the All-Russian Constituent Assembly was the longest in its prehistory, the shortest if we speak of its one-day existence, and the most dramatic in terms of the magnitude of the hopes and disappointments associated with it. But its uniqueness rests in more than these. As a historical phenomenon it troubles scholars' minds with its long-standing and unresolved puzzle: how would the history of Russia have developed if the Constituent Assembly had had a different fate? For every lively mind, as Marc Bloch has shrewdly remarked, failures possess no less charm than successes.[1] It is appropriate to add that even the analysis of a historical alternative, if it is founded in the firm soil of specific facts, is technologically important and essential as a tool for a scholarly understanding of the past.

The Bolsheviks abolished the Constituent Assembly after its very first day of work. Its future would seem to have been doubtful even given a more indulgent attitude toward it on the part of the authorities. It might not have been able to cope with its tasks due to insurmountable internal differences of opinion and have deserved to be called just one more talk-fest [*govoril'nia*], or it might have become the victim of some other turn of events. The only certainty is that this all-Russian legislative assembly did not, in and of itself, provide guarantees for a democratic path of development; its fate is proof of that. But the forcible elimination of this irreproachably legitimate, supreme political, national institution, along with the subsequent tragedy of the Civil War, force us to see in the Constituent Assembly the unrealized democratic alternative to the Bolshevik regime.

Remarkably enough, the idea of alternatives is a constant theme in the historiography of the problem. In recent years, the old ideologized dilemma – bourgeois or proletarian democracy? – has been virtually supplanted by the general scholarly dilemma, democracy or dictatorship? Even the Marxist historical view of the October Revolution has evolved from an outright defense of the dispersal of the Constituent

Assembly, in the spirit of sacrosanct Leninist assessments, to pragmatic and completely plausible constructions in which this event is perceived as the sad but inevitable result of existing political circumstances. At least necessity is no longer passed off as a virtue.

However, a full scholarly analysis [*onauchivanie*] of the problem, which would overcome its politicization and the resultant inescapable mythologization, still lies before us; it requires a systematic investigation including the connections between the Constituent Assembly and the evolution of Russian statehood, society, national mentality, and so forth. To study its life and fate strictly through the prism of the political passions of 1917 and the conjuncture of events, itself not devoid of a touch of historical randomness, ultimately means returning to the fatal acknowledgment of the necessity of this precise variant of events. Not only because actual history is in general more convincing than hypothetical history but because the actions of the Bolshevik leadership in regard to the Constituent Assembly were in fact both logical and consistent, because they were appropriate to the political and ethical principles of the party.

The root of the question, however, is not how and why the constituent authority, which reflected the will of the people, came to be dispersed; rather, the question is why, despite all its legitimacy, it proved defenseless and helpless in the face of blatant usurpation in a democratic country. At that moment, after all, the Bolsheviks were not so powerful that they did not need to reckon with broad public opinion, with its firm and resolute position (the uncertainty of the Bolshevik leaders regarding the consequences of the step they had taken is revealed by Lenin's attack of nervous stress on the night the Constituent Assembly was dispersed, as described by N.I. Bukharin).[2]

Let us begin with the fact that we need a careful interpretation of the historically formed content of the very idea of the Constituent Assembly and its place in the structure of Russia's social consciousness, for without this, the whole problem would lack foundation. By 1917, the idea had a past more than a century old in Russia, but it constituted a basis for contemplation rather than for national ambitions. Carried by the winds of the French Revolution of the late eighteenth century into the eastern outskirts of Europe, into a country of autocracy and serfdom, the idea inevitably changed form, becoming a symbiosis of European political culture and Russian historical traditions. The idea of a Constituent Assembly was formed on the historical example of countries where the prerequisites had been created for a civil society and where the Leviathan state was not so omnipotent. In Russia, with its different types of feudalism and capitalism, given the political immobility of its society and its hypertrophic monarchy which maintained itself not only by coercive force but also by an ideology of its providential origins, as well as

245

by its practice of all-embracing state paternalism, throughout the nineteenth century there was no soil to nurture the concept of popular sovereignty.

From this it follows that the idea of the Constituent Assembly in Russia took on a meaning broader and larger than in the West – not only a political meaning but a social-philosophical one. From the second half of the nineteenth century, when the country's economic modernization intensified the need for appropriate state and social structures, and increasingly close ties with the West cast Russia's archaic character in even greater relief, this idea was given a new impetus and became a kind of symbol of the country's radical renovation, the elimination of its historical backwardness, and the solution to all its pressing social problems. Such an enlarged interpretation gave it a rather abstract, semilegendary character, which was fostered, too, by the complete absence of political rights and liberties in Russia until the early twentieth century. Not surprisingly, it also drew strength from such obviously vestigial sources as the communal-egalitarian organization of the village and historical reminiscences associated with *veche* [town-meeting] customs and Assemblies of the Land in Russia's past.

At the same time, the Constituent Assembly long remained an elitist idea because of the profound gap between the levels and, possibly, the type of political culture of the relatively thin educated stratum of society and the lower orders. The idea became part of the mentality of the Russian liberal-radical intelligentsia, its "bluebird," a generalized reflection of certain of its qualities such as its "nonbourgeois" character, its hostility to autocratic-bureaucratic and police tyranny (the Minister of Internal Affairs V.K. Plehve indeed defined the behavior of the intelligentsia as one of constantly discrediting the authorities),[3] and its traditional love of the people, which also included its guilt complex before the people. Moreover, various historical models, from the Convention (at the time of the Great French Revolution), which opened the way to power for the Jacobins, to the Constituent Assembly of 1848, which established the moderate regime of the French Second Republic, shaped popular views.

It is significant that the autocracy itself inadvertently served to disseminate the idea: by carrying out reforms it stimulated constitutional sentiments, and by persecuting the Constituent Assembly movement it enhanced the movement's romantic aura of self-sacrifice and martyrdom. In one 1917 newspaper we read "the history of the struggle for the Constituent Assembly was the Calvary of devoted heroism."[4] Remarkably, this struggle was also associated with those figures of the liberation movement who did not, in fact, advocate such an idea in their transformative schemata (for example, N.I. Novikov and A.N. Radishchev), and even with those who rejected it (like P.I. Pestel').[5]

In Russian social consciousness, the convocation of a Constituent Assembly was linked primarily to the introduction of a constitutional system; this is why historians' attempts to divide the methods of accomplishing it rigidly into revolutionary and reformist methods are incorrect, especially considering the changing evolution of the Russian state principle. Even Lenin early on, in the 1890s, allowed for the political liberation of Russia via a convocation of an Assembly of the Land by the tsarist government.[6] This assumption does not seem altogether unrealistic when we recall that the acceptance of the so-called draft constitution of M.T. Loris-Melikov was actually thwarted by the revolutionaries who assassinated Emperor Alexander II on 1 March 1881, not by reactionaries in the higher bureaucracy.

The first Russian Revolution [Revolution of 1905] brought widespread comprehension of, and hence popularity for, the idea of a Constituent Assembly. This was facilitated by the objective coincidence of two simultaneous processes: on the one hand, the increasing vertical social mobility of the population and the marginalization of society, a process that provided fertile soil for the growth of antigovernment sentiments; and on the other hand, the intensive party-political shaping of society – its "partyization." It is instructive that almost all of the parties incorporated in their programs both positive and utterly negative attitudes toward the slogan of convening a Constituent Assembly. The Union of 17 October, for example, while acknowledging the solidity of the principle of constitutional monarchy for Russia, nonetheless rejected the idea of a sovereign Constituent Assembly, as this would represent a complete break with the past, inevitably leading to severe revolutionary upheavals all over the country.[7] The rightist-monarchist All-Russian Patriotic Party declared that one of its first tasks would be to "oppose the convening of a Constituent Assembly and any other revolutionary acts that support civil strife."[8]

Given the crisis of authority which had progressively developed and the accumulation of an enormous potential for mass social unrest, convening a Constituent Assembly became a task of practical politics, provoking a sharp interparty struggle over the question both of the ways to create constitutional authority and of its tasks. The generally accepted criteria for radicalism, in our opinion, are in need of correctives, because the prospects for Russia's social progress depended not solely on how far it advanced along the path of revolution but also, and to no less a degree, on what type of civilized development it pursued. Westernization and models of Western democracy and reformist methods attracted not only liberals but also those Social Democrats who realized the need for a developed, law-governed society as the basis for future socialism. In terms of mentality, the Mensheviks were closer to the Kadets than to the Bolsheviks who were their fellow-thinkers in the faith. The Bolsheviks, in turn, resembled the SRs [Socialist Revolutionaries] and other *pochven-niki* [members of the "back-to-the-soil" movement] in their tendency to utilize Russia's historical uniqueness – in particular its exceptional, distinctly non-Western political culture, which was for the most part uncontrolled and destructive (the Westernizer-Marxist phraseology of Bolshevism does not change the essence of their position). In this way, unexpected political dispositions of forces and blocs came into being.

The idea of a Constituent Assembly triumphed in 1917, after the monarchy was toppled. Official Soviet literature refuses to call it a unifying idea, referring to the narrow party context in which different political forces interpreted it. However, on the night of 2 March, according to the terms of the well-known agreement on the establishment of authority in the country concluded, after lengthy and bitter disputes, between delegates of the Executive Committee of the Petrograd Soviet and members of the Temporary Committee of the State Duma, the exact legal status of the Constituent Assembly was worked out. It incorporated three principles: that elections would be by universal, free ballot ("the will of the people"); that the resolution of the main issues of state life, including determination of the form of government, would be the exclusive prerogative of the Constituent Assembly ("no prede-termination"); and that the Constituent Assembly itself, and it alone, would determine the range and limits of its tasks ("be master of the Russian land").

These conditions, hastily recorded by Soviet delegate Iu. M. Steklov "on a scrap of poor writing paper,"[9] in essence determined Russia's politi-cal *modus vivendi*, particularly between the two established institutional systems. On the same day, 2 March, *Izvestiia Petrogradskogo Soveta* stated, not without a certain condescension, that the Provisional Government did not have the right to institute any permanent form of government, and that its only purpose was to guard the people against the machi-nations of the counterrevolution and to help them to bring the Revolution to completion with the convening of the Constituent Assembly.

It is difficult to overstate the political significance of this decision. It secured the post-February regime in the country and established a balance of forces for a while, by uniting revolutionary and reformist tendencies. It partially curbed, although it did not end, party ambitions. This formula was accepted even by the monarchists, who sustained hopes of "rectifying" society and restoring the monarchy by way of the Constituent Assembly, which in this way acquired the support even of V.V. Shul'gin. The prestige of the Constituent Assembly as national arbiter grew to an unusual degree, especially among the middle strata, who more than anything craved peaceful resolutions to all social conflicts. This segment of society in particular voiced noble and naive appeals to end all political struggle in the country until the Assembly could be convened, so as to avoid violence to the will of the people, in the spirit of the Declaration of the Soviet of Deputies of the Working Intelligentsia, as announced at the State Conference in Moscow in August 1917.[10]

The farther things went, however, the more the reverse side of the transitional formula "no predetermination," which became fatal to the country, was exposed. The vacuum of legitimate authority grew larger, because both the Provisional Government and the Soviet parties themselves, which had placed the "bridle of no predetermination on it," wound up as its hostages. They were unable to wield the authority that had been conferred upon them for the purpose of reforming society, even to the extent that they were prepared to do so, without risking accusations, chiefly from the left, of infringing the rights of the Constituent Assembly. Meanwhile, this formula bound the left-extremist forces only to the extent that they recognized its right to apply definitive sanctions to their direct actions.

After the February Revolution, old analogies to the role played by the Constituent Assembly during the French or American revolutions became irrelevant, because the autocratic colossus fell apart, in a matter of days, under the blows of the rebellious people.[11] Its principal and traditional task had been accomplished – a democratic republic of maximum political legitimacy had been virtually established in Russia. But the elimination of the autocracy as a factor which had served to consolidate the opposition now served to split society, laying bare and exacerbating its glaring social contradictions. "Never before, anywhere, had it happened that a country had had to deal simultaneously with such a multitude of complicated and pressing problems – political, economic, social, and national," complained historian M.V. Vishniak, member and secretary of the Constituent Assembly. "These difficulties were made unbelievably more complex by the circumstances of the world war."[12]

After the February Revolution, the idea of the Constituent Assembly fell prey to the same kind of peculiar split that lies in wait for any lofty idea when it is shifted from the world of theories to the world of practice: an object of worship became the object of political passions, which openly took on the character of confrontation in the autumn of 1917. This clash with reality suddenly revealed the fragility of the idea of a Constituent Assembly, and its fatal dependency on society's level of political culture.

The problem was aggravated because the Revolution made a gigantic surge into the political life of the masses, formerly apathetic and even disdainful of politics. The masses brought their sufferings, their intentions, their social aggressiveness, and their inclination to use strong-arm methods to resolve conflicts, an inclination which had become unusually entrenched thanks to their recognition of their own striking role in liquidating the monarchy. Even more important, in Russia the lower orders were able in a short time to create their own representative bodies, which had claims, if not to power, then at least to their own share of the fruits of revolution. This, then, served as the sociopolitical "bouillon" for the most ambitious political forces, among which the Bolsheviks, headed by Lenin, stood out sharply by virtue of their willpower, their purposeful commitment, and their readiness to resort even to the most extreme measures in the name of these goals. It is appropriate to point out, incidentally, that the radicalized masses did not so much follow the revolutionary parties as push them on in their desire to realize all their expectations at once.

Under these circumstances, the burden of reforms which had histori- cally been held back fell upon the shoulders of the Constituent Assembly; every day of delay catastrophically multiplied this burden and undercut the chances of stopping the country's slide into universal crisis and civil war.

Nevertheless, throughout 1917 the Constituent Assembly embodied democratic prospects of development. Viewing the Revolution as an internally contradictory but logically ordered current of events running through the winding channel of alternative situations, we can say that the Constituent Assembly remained the steadiest constant in the vortex of events. Convening it was declared the primary task of all four compo- sitions of the Provisional Government – in the declarations of 3 March, 6 May, 8 July, and 26 September, respectively. General L.G. Kornilov justi- fied his putsch by citing "the necessity of leading the people to a Constituent Assembly in which the people themselves would decide their fate and choose the system for their new state life."[13] The Second All-Russian Congress of Soviets of Workers' and Soldiers' Deputies, after forming the Council of People's Commissars headed by Lenin, also stipu- lated its term of tenure – "from now until the Constituent Assembly is convened."[14] Finally, the "White movement," judging by its many official and unofficial documents, by no means rejected the idea of "no predetermination" and the convening of a Constituent Assembly.[15]

One might object that everyone had his own "constituent assembly" in mind, that each of the influential political forces was, so to speak, prescribing its own plan of social restructuring for the future supreme body. Lenin, for example, insistently emphasized that the Constituent Assembly would depend on who convened it,[16] and he frankly suspected Kerensky's government of intending to falsify the people's representa- tion. But regardless of motive, this had nothing to do with the Assembly itself. In addition, the possibilities for juggling the elections and the composition of the deputies were obviously exaggerated. The Constituent Assembly's democratism was guaranteed by the electoral law itself. It is no exaggeration to say that it was the most progressive electoral system of its time and later became the model for many countries. The ballot was universal, equal, direct, and secret. Even the fact that military deserters and members of the imperial Romanov family were deprived of the right to vote was not, given the circumstances of war and revolution, perceived as being in conflict with democracy.

Indeed we cannot deny the plausibility of the paradoxical opinion that the chief defect of the electoral law was its perfection.[17] The drafting of the law itself, and especially its implementation in a country which was not prepared for it either legally or technically, with almost 90 million voters, most of whom were illiterate and scattered over an enormous territory covering approximately half of Eurasia, represented an immense difficulty and required a great deal of time – and time was passing irretrievably. The time factor played a truly crucial role, perhaps the principal role, in the failure of the Constituent Assembly. But the customary explanations for the delay, namely that it was due to the bad faith of the Kadet jurists or the softness of the leaders of Soviet democracy, now seem too shallow; they fail to take into account the logic of the Russian Revolution, with its multitude of conflict zones, rivalry among power structures, mass character of participants, and so forth. Any limitation of electoral democracy to save time was interpreted in a purely counterrevolutionary sense, as an infringement upon the will of the people. As a result, the electoral law became both the zenith and the swan song of political democracy for Russia's entire history.

The Constituent Assembly's democratism was also manifested in the fact that the months-long preelection campaign under the changing kaleidoscope of political circumstances created an "aura" of legality for parties which found themselves at a disadvantage. After the events of July, Lenin protested against the persecution of the Bolsheviks, and appealed to the future Constituent Assembly.[18] The Kadets found themselves in similar circumstances after the collapse of the Kornilov campaign [kornilovshchina], as even moderate socialists did after the Bolsheviks seized power.

Recently, the focus of scholarly attention has been on the search for an alternative in the autumn of 1917, especially after it was determined that democratic options within bolshevism itself during the NEP [New Economic Policy instituted in 1921] were hopeless. The prospects of the various models of social development, including that of the Constituent Assembly, have been considered, although it is obvious that any of them would have been less frightful and destructive for Russia than the one that came into being as a result of the October coup.

Without exploring the entire spectrum of opinions in detail, we will put forth only a few thoughts regarding this question. The danger of a rightwing coup followed by a military-monarchical dictatorship, about which the Bolsheviks spoke so often in the autumn of 1917, now, from a historical perspective, seems to have been more of a bugaboo than an

251

actual threat. After the collapse of the Kornilov mutiny, the bourgeois counterrevolution was not in a position to take up arms and fight against united democracy. The leading anti-Bolshevik force, the Kadet Party, had retreated to the shadows and seemed to be demoralized. Nor is there any reason to think, as Lenin did, that the Provisional Government intended either to falsify the elections to the Constituent Assembly or to thwart them altogether; the former was not within its power, while the latter bordered on political suicide. Rather, the opposite was the case: the thoughts of Kerensky's cabinet in October were directed toward holding out until they could reach the safe haven of the Constituent Assembly. The All-Russian Commission on Elections categorically denied petitions from outlying areas to postpone the voting due to technical unpreparedness. "One might well assume that Kerensky's Provisional Government had a chance to lead the country to the Constituent Assembly, had it not been overthrown by October's armed uprising in Petrograd,"[19] V. Startsev wrote. While we agree with that opinion, we must add that that would have been the optimal variant of events.

The collapse of the Soviet form of statehood and government after seventy years of permanent crisis and vain attempts to make it viable impels us also to reexamine the problem of "The Soviets and the Constituent Assembly." As is well known, the democratic potential of the Soviets has not been disputed even by some Western historians (A. Rabinowitch, W. Rosenberg), who tend to assess democracy both as a system of representative institutions and from the standpoint of the masses' direct participation in resolving important social problems. Both of these are true: in 1917 the Soviets represented approximately one-third of the population,[20] but it was the lower orders that gravitated to them, seeing them as agencies of direct revolutionary action.

Relations between the Constituent Assembly and the Soviets constituted the essence of the differences of opinion among democratic forces on the question of power. The right-wing socialists, who until November 1917 had preserved the general leadership of the Soviet system, attempted to avert political rivalry between them and possible conflict on those grounds. On 12 October, the official *Izvestiia TsIK Sovetov* printed a lead article under the suggestive headline "The Crisis of Soviet Organization" [*Krizis sovetskoi organizatsii*]. The summary read:

> The Soviets were an excellent organization to struggle against the old regime, but they are absolutely incapable of taking on the creation of a new regime – they lack specialists, they lack the skills and abilities to run things, and, finally, they lack organization.

During that period, frequent warnings were heard to the effect that if the Soviets, led by the Bolsheviks, seized power in the country, it would

be the end of the Constituent Assembly, which would become unnecessary, because the Bolsheviks would be compelled to do the things for
which it had been convened. The essence of apprehensions like these
was not a fear that these things would come to pass – which seemed to
be only a matter of time – but the fear that they would be utilized by
extremist forces as a lever to usurp power. Iu. Martov, one of the most
left-leaning Mensheviks, who shared the idea of creating a uniformly
socialist government, nevertheless characterized the Soviets as a means
of "placing and entrenching a revolutionary minority in power."[21]

After 25 October, unquestionably the Constituent Assembly no longer
fitted in with the Bolsheviks' schemes of worldwide socialist revolution
and the building of a republic of Soviets. Moreover, it posed the threat
of drowning the social bulwark of bolshevism – the urban working class
and soldiers of the old army – in a sea of peasant votes.

To Lenin personally and the majority of his associates, the Constituent
Assembly was not a legal or moral imperative. As early as April 1917
he had expressed the conviction that life and the Revolution would
relegate it to the background.[22] At the same time, the Bolsheviks, reck-
oning with the possibility of different variants for the development
of the Revolution and gearing their tactics toward the main goal of
advancing the party to power, conducted a policy of flexible and circum-
spect improvisation with respect to the Constituent Assembly. Of no
small importance were the rich agitational possibilities of the slogan of
the Constituent Assembly, both to propagandize the Bolsheviks' garish
slogans and to discredit the Provisional Government and political rivals
for blocking its convocation. Typically, all the resolutions on authority
which the Bolshevik factions proposed to representative bodies such as
the Central Executive Committee, the Petrograd Soviet, and the Democratic Conference, included the demand that the Constituent Assembly
be convened immediately. L.D. Trotsky, in the name of the Bolshevik
faction, justified their conspicuous walkout from the Pre-Parliament, in
particular, by asserting that "the bourgeois classes directing the policies
of the Provisional Government have set themselves the goal of wrecking
the Constituent Assembly."[23]

One can hardly just call this hypocrisy; in politics there are always
elusive and variable factors which cannot be calculated in advance. It is
obvious that Lenin was impressed by the idea of a "combined type"
which would make the Soviets and the Constituent Assembly into
a whole. By the summer of 1917 he did not rule out the possibility that
the role of Constituent Assembly might be played by a Congress of
Soviets or a Council of Soviets,[24] or the possibility that the Constituent
Assembly, if it could be convened soon enough, would then turn power
over to the Soviets. In the autumn, however, the formula "the Constituent
Assembly plus the Soviets" had changed somewhat, to "the Soviets plus

the Constituent Assembly," but contrary to the mathematical axiom the order of the components radically changed the result.

It is not completely clear to what extent Lenin's plan for seizing power through an uprising was an attempt to forestall elections and the movement toward parliamentary democracy (certainly A.F. Kerensky thought so).[25] It is obvious, however, that taking up arms against a constituent body elected by all the people, without controlling the forces that promote power, would be political insanity.

In the post-October period, some Bolshevik statements created the impression of a sincere desire to find out the true will of the people ("We will submit all peace proposals to the Constituent Assembly for a decision")[26] and the Council of People's Commissars issued a decree guaranteeing elections on schedule, but all this belonged to a time when there were still hopes of obtaining a Bolshevik-Left SR majority in Parliament. Hardly had these hopes collapsed when esoteric discussions were launched concerning the superiority of proletarian democracy over bourgeois democracy and the preferable, extraparliamentary power of the proletariat, and an assertion was made that the fundamental problems of the Revolution generally could not be solved by the ballot.

It would seem that, having settled on a republic of Soviets ("Soviets are higher than any parliament and any constituent assembly"),[27] the Leninists subconsciously placed their hopes not on the presumed advantages that the Soviets had for uniting forces – since, with their class intuition, lack of professional administrators, and so forth, they relied on the initiative of the masses – but rather on the ease by which the ruling party, which possessed the secrets of social engineering, could manipulate them. In fact, the Bolsheviks did not for a minute intend to leave the Soviets to their own devices. For this reason, the emergence of a Party–Soviet "centaur" was absolutely predictable, and the Bolshevik leadership's sporadic attempts to prevent this are noteworthy for their complete lack of success. In all other attendant factors, the quasi-official nature of the Soviets as mass social-political organizations proved decisive. Both from the juridical-legal and from the general political point of view it seems quite doubtful that even multiparty Soviets whose authority was legitimized by the Constituent Assembly could have ensured the democratic development of society. To do this, the Soviet system would have to have been transformed into a traditional system of self-government – that is, it would have had to cease being what it was.

Therefore, even after the events of October, only the Constituent Assembly embodied democratic prospects for the development of statehood and society. Characteristically, the Bolsheviks, who derived their politics, their law, and their morality not from general principles of civilization but from the Revolution as they understood it, could not step over the Constituent Assembly or refrain from convening it; even Lenin failed to get his comrades-in-arms to change their minds on this.[28] And in the same way, not so much the Bolsheviks as Russian society – or, more accurately, its sociocultural condition – itself caused the death of this historical opportunity.

Scholarship has yet to make a correlative analysis of the idea of the Constituent Assembly in the structure of social consciousness in 1917, but some features are incontrovertible. The idea had not been poured uniformly on the various social "floors," so it depended directly on cultural and educational prerequisites. The cities, naturally, were in the forefront, while the countryside lagged noticeably behind. As stated in October [1917] at a session of the All-Russian Commission on Elections to the Constituent Assembly, "interest in the elections has not spread to the masses of the people but is confined to the upper strata."[29]

Again, the apperception of the Constituent Assembly was not uniform in terms of social stratum. For the middle strata, the "supertask" was to create a law-governed state while solving the crisis in the country by impeccably peaceful and reformist means. For the lower strata, especially their marginalized and lumpenized elements, the Constituent Assembly was attractive primarily as an opportunity to satisfy immediate social needs, generally interpreted as a simple leveling, a redistribution of the good things in life. (Moreover, the actual method of satisfying them was not particularly important; perhaps, in fact, coercive methods promised swifter and more substantial results, while considerations of legitimacy were less important.)

In this connection it is worthwhile to point out the ritual character of rally-style resolutions in support of the Constituent Assembly, which were always passed unanimously. Resolutions reflecting the current political moment generally ended with slogans such as "All Power to the Constituent Assembly!" and therefore sounded like incantations. They reflected the religious underpinnings of mass consciousness, a naive faith in the possibility of solving all problems at once (suggesting an analogy with that other popular slogan of 1917 – "Peace Without Annexations and Indemnities!" – both of which became mere fictions for most of their adherents). But this charisma of the Constituent Assembly in no way restrained the radical lower orders from taking things into their own hands to promote their interests – "God helps him who helps himself!"

Even before 1917 it was clear that the popularity of the Constituent Assembly was to a certain extent tied to the nature of the country's political circumstances; it waxed during periods of crisis and waned when things stabilized. In a society where power generally supplanted the law, its ideological roots were not deep, which indicated that at the critical moment the circle of those who championed the people's representation might turn out to be more narrow. Overall, the events of 1917 affirmed this tendency.

The core of the entire question, however, is the actual voting in the elections to the All-Russian Constituent Assembly, for this reflected most clearly the electorate's attitude toward the prospects of a parliamentary democratic government in Russia, and without that detailed statistical picture of the elections, any judgments regarding such prospects are as ephemeral as the smile of the Cheshire cat. It is also worthwhile to point out that the election statistics remain the Achilles' heel of the overall problem, and therefore, very likely, they merit special attention. In this connection, the present author has undertaken a series of specialized studies.

Despite the all-Russian election schedule stipulated by the law (12–14 November), in actuality the elections dragged on for more than three months. In Kamchatka the elections were held ahead of schedule, on 29 October, so that its sole deputy would have time to take the last steamship to the "Big Show." The final chord of the electoral symphony was sounded at the end of February 1918 – a month after the Constituent Assembly had been dispersed – in the Kuban, at a time when the Civil War was raging full force. For this reason, elections were held only in Ekaterinodar and in certain villages where the Kuban Territorial Council [Rada] still held power.

In practical terms, it has been established that out of eighty-one electoral districts (including the KVZhD [Chinese-Oriental Railroad] District and the district of the Russian Expeditionary Forces in France and in the Balkans, outside the borders of Russia), elections were held, in full or in part, in seventy-seven districts. They were definitely not held in the Syrdar'ia, Amudar'ia, and Transcaspian districts (which, by our estimates, included around 1.3 million voters);[30] the fate of the elections is unknown in the Russian Expeditionary Corps in France and on the Salonika Front, where voters numbered around 50,000 persons.[31]

Determining the total size of the electorate was especially difficult owing to the disarray in keeping the statistics under wartime conditions. Preliminary calculations (taken as the maximum) of the Statistical Conference headed by A.A. Kaufman and the estimates of individual experts enable us to calculate the maximum number of voters at 85 million (minus the population of the occupied territories).[32] In places where the elections were actually held, however, there were no more than 80 million voters.

Elections on such a scale had never before occurred in world history. Nor had history ever witnessed such organizational and technical difficulties, aggravated by the extremely unfavorable circumstances of two wars – the still-unfinished World War and the Civil War which had just broken out. All of this accounts for the deplorable state of the election statistics. In some districts, the elections were not carried through to completion (the Kuban–Black Sea, Terek–Dagestan, and possibly the

Steppe districts), while in other cases the returns were not tallied or else have not been preserved. For example, in the Orda District, located within the territory of the Bukei Horde in the Transvolga (with the center at Khanskaia stavka), the members of the district electoral commission were arrested by the local revolutionary committee just as they were tallying the votes.[33] The Council of People's Commissars' liquidation of the All-Russian Electoral Commission at the very height of the campaign led to the complete destruction of the electoral machinery, which obviously had serious consequences for future historians. Sad to say, our general familiarity with the state of archival and newspaper holdings leaves little hope that the national picture of the election results will ever be successfully reconstructed in full.

To get around or at least to diminish the gaps in the statistics, it would be useful to mobilize not only the tally results by districts but also empirically determined data in places where more complete results are lacking (the Bessarabian, Kamchatka, Kuban–Black Sea, Samarkand, Steppe, Terek–Dagestan, and Iakut districts). According to our observations, which are quite extensive but not exhaustive, more than 47 million persons participated in the voting, but still, about 2 million ballots were cast that are yet to be identified (L.M. Spirin's estimates, the most representative until now, covered less than 46 million voters).[34] The total returns of the voting in elections to the All-Russian Constituent Assembly are presented in Table 11.1.

One may note that the new figures correct only slightly the basic percentage indicators familiar to historians. It is easy to conjecture that a full voting picture will yield an increase in the proportion of national parties and tickets favored in outlying districts. We will not undertake an analysis of the electorate's party sympathies but will confine ourselves strictly to comments in keeping with the theme of the present essay. In this regard, the success of the SRs, who combined with the national SRs garnered more than half of the votes, was significant primarily because it demonstrated mass support for the centrist, conciliatory line rather than a triumph of party doctrine. In turn, the 23.2 percent of the votes which the Bolsheviks received reflected much more than an ordinary failure in the elections; in fact, it represented the population's vote of no confidence in the new regime. The defeat of the Mensheviks, as self-critically assessed by the party's leadership, emphasized the absence of conditions for realizing the orthodox Marxist ideas of socialist revolution. Such was the eccentric manifestation of the Mensheviks' correctness in this matter, which was so vital to the Marxists. The Kadet Party's relatively modest showing (4.6 percent of the votes) reflected not only its pro-Kornilov, bourgeois reputation in the masses' political consciousness but also the weakness of the liberal movement and the limited nature of its social base in Russia.

Table 11.1 Summary of voting for the All-Russian Constituent Assembly

| | All | | Separated by district | | | |
| | | | Rear | | Frontline | |
	Absolute	%	Absolute	%	Absolute	%
SRs	19,070,637	40.4	17,287,287	40.4	1,783,350	40.7
Bolsheviks	10,947,862	23.2	9,220,543	21.6	1,727,319	39.5
Mensheviks	1,380,649	2.9	1,240,309	2.9	140,340	3.2
NSes [People's Socialists]	374,518	0.8	363,521	0.8	10,997	0.3
Other socialists*	6,704,681	14.21	6,178,821	14.4	525,860	12.0
Kadets	2,172,187	4.6	2,098,588	4.9	73,599	1.7
Right-wing parties	279,227	0.6	279,227	0.6		
Landowners	191,109	0.4	191,109	0.4		
Commercial and industrial tickets	36,941	0.1	36,941	0.1		
Cooperative movement members	28,913	0.1	28,913	0.1		
Religious parties	301,514	0.6	301,514	0.7		
National parties	3,648,943	7.7	3,607,855	8.4	41,088	0.8
Cossacks	1,024,268	2.2	1,024,268	2.4		
Others	1,006,172	2.2	930,411	2.3	75,761	1.7
Total	47,167,621	100.0	42,789,307	100.0	4,378,314	100.0

*National parties of neo-Narodnik and SR profile, and also unified slates of socialist parties.

The right-wing parties and groups which had decided to participate openly in the elections suffered complete failure. In general, the small parties found themselves in the deep political shadows cast by the struggle of the giants. The Radical Democrats, for example, garnered a total of around 19,000 votes.

Because of the proportional electoral system, the composition of the corps of deputies corresponded overall to the results of the elections. Probably only the Kadets, who had avoided pre-election blocs, had any reason to complain that because of the distortions of the system they failed to obtain a dozen or so seats, having wrongly lost about 1.2 million votes.[35] Our observations encompass 765 deputies from seventy-three electoral districts (in the remaining eight, where the elections were not held or were not carried through to completion, another fifty-five deputies were to have been elected). Among them were 345 Russian and 47 Ukrainian SRs, 175 Bolsheviks, 17 Russian and 7 Ukrainian Mensheviks, 14 Kadets, and 2 People's Socialists. Affiliated with the socialist wing of the Constituent Assembly, as well, were 32 Ukrainian SRs and Social Democrats whom we have not been able to identify more accurately in terms of party affiliation, 13 Muslim Socialists and 10 Dashnaks [Dashnaktsutium, an Armenian revolutionary organization]. The remaining seats were distributed as follows: national parties and movements, 68; Cossacks, 16; Christians, 10; clergy, 1.

This, then, was the "Noah's Ark" of Russian statehood, which, like its biblical prototype, took aboard the entire species diversity of society in 1917.

These dry figures from statistical sources on the elections incorporate the subtle, sensitive, social-psychological mechanisms of the electoral behavior and reveal society's attitude toward the Constituent Assembly itself. What seems to us to be most significant in the vote is not its party coloration but rather the positive attitude of most of the population, as expressed by their participation in the elections, toward supreme constituent authority and its prospects. Among the complex tasks facing that authority starting in the autumn of 1917, the one that objectively came to the forefront was that of averting civil war, and to a certain extent the Constituent Assembly was the guarantee of civil peace.

This evidently constitutes one explanation for the electorate's high level of participation, which surprised many contemporaries. Counting invalid and annulled ballots, more than 50 million voters took part in the elections – that is, approximately 63 to 64 percent of the total. Considering society's political fatigue and conditions that were complex and in many places dangerous, this is a high figure.

What dismayed observers most was the broad abstention of the intelligentsia, in particular the urban intelligentsia. Having launched the slogan of the Constituent Assembly, at the crucial moment the intelligentsia took a passive position, thereby expressing their disenchantment with the prospects of popular rule in Russia. For the intelligentsia, the triumph of democracy had turned into a triumph of mob rule, and even sincere adherents of parliamentarianism turned away from it for a time, giving preference to a firm, authoritarian regime. The city-dweller who abstained from voting was revealing not only his apoliticism, he was also protesting against the starry-eyed inaction of the right-wing socialist leaders, against Bolshevik violence, and against plans to install a military-dictatorial regime in the country.

Judging by our estimates, in 220 cities of Russia having a total population of almost 7 million persons, about 4 million took part in elections to the Constituent Assembly – approximately 58 percent. But if we eliminate Petrograd and Moscow from this equation, because of their enormous and highly active electorate (about 70 percent), the percentage of those who voted drops to 52. This indicator fully reflects the average level of absenteeism in the provincial cities.

Equally surprising was the active voter participation in the countryside, which largely determined the basic national electoral parameters and saved the Constituent Assembly elections' reputation as a nationwide event. In a great many townships, villages, and hamlets the elections met with unfeigned enthusiasm, and 72 to 80 percent of the citizens took part. In the cities of Tambov Province, a typically peasant province, only 50.2 percent of the voters took part, whereas in the rural areas the figure was 74.5 percent. Participation in the elections ranged between 62 and 80 percent in agrarian Altai, Kazan, Kursk, Voronezh, Penza, Poltava, Chernigov, and other provinces.

Did this mean that the peasantry was really more highly politicized? By no means. The elections confirmed the traditionalist character of peasant consciousness. To the peasant, the political world, like the city world in general, was alien and incomprehensible; the peasants' electoral behavior, however, was dictated by practical considerations such as their attachment to the land, which determined their whole existence, and their fear that they would not be given land if they did not show up to vote. Another factor was the social-psychological makeup of the countryside: the communal custom of deciding things and acting "all in a heap," submissive obedience to directives from above, a mystical worship of anything incomprehensible and mysterious coupled with general apathy toward the question of political authority. People in the countryside dutifully went to vote for the Constituent Assembly, but once they received the landowners' land they became essentially indifferent to the Assembly's dissolution.

Although the expression of the peasants' will in the elections to the Constituent Assembly remained, in essence, unclaimed, it is unquestionably of scholarly interest. According to our figures, around 7 million persons voted in the cities. The author has statistical information regarding 6.2 million city dwellers. Extrapolating the basic results of the elections to the entire urban electorate (including settlements of the urban type), and subtracting from that total votes cast in the electoral districts of the hinterland, the remainder we get is a sufficiently reliable tally of the elections in rural areas (see Table 11.2).

The same factors, basically, operated in the peasants' and the soldiers' participation, but with a different slant. Because of the conditions of army life, soldiers became politicized with astonishing swiftness, but they represented a particular, marginalized political subculture. The soldier voted very actively, and primarily for the Bolsheviks. Statistics available to us show that among the 4,378 million soldiers of the front, votes cast were divided almost equally between the Bolsheviks and the SRs (39.5 and 40.7 percent, respectively). But among the 1,013 million servicemen in over 200 rear garrisons, the Bolsheviks got 55.8 percent of the votes, whereas the SRs got only 22.3 percent.

Unquestionably the slogan of peace was the magic crystal through which the soldiers looked upon all other social problems. Tempted by Lenin's promise of an immediate peace (essentially at any price) and the Bolshevik practice of social apportionment [delezh], the soldiers did not see any great need for higher legislative sanction. The Constituent Assembly could not give them what the new regime gave them. But this regime, too, proved to be in a certain sense a captive of the disintegrated army. The Bolsheviks became inadvertent hostages of the many-million-strong plebeian soldiery and had to adapt their policies to its wild impulses and actions, especially at the time of Brest. The bolshevization of the soldiers was not devoid of a certain peasant cunning: be a Bolshevik as long as it is profitable.

The urban workers also voted heavily, chiefly for the Bolsheviks. To be sure, it is hardly possible here to separate practical support for the party's policies from pursuit of the long-standing Social Democratic slogan. One suspects, in any case, that most workers did not go to the polls in the expectation that the Constituent Assembly would be dissolved. It was not long before the Bolsheviks came to realize the conditionality of that support and to become disillusioned with proletarian-messianic expectations. Among those who in January 1918 in Petrograd

Table 11.2 Election results in rural districts and in cities

Population	Bolsheviks	SRs	Mensheviks	Other socialists	Kadets	Others	Total
Urban	33.6	16.0	6.4	8.0	20.3	15.7	100.0
Rural	19.3	45.6	2.2	17.0	1.8	14.1	100.0

protested against the dismissal of the people's representatives were a great many workers.

It needs to be kept in mind, finally, that the Constituent Assembly was associated with the solution of a question of great urgency to Russia – the national question, the self-determination of Russia's peoples. Since the disintegration of the USSR, the national-state aspect seems the least risky of the historical parallels between 1917 and the present. Although the Bolsheviks formally proclaimed the right of nations to self-determination, their supranational revolutionary desires and their adherence to the unitary state made nationals of all political orientations extremely uneasy. Under such circumstances, elections in the non-Russian areas took on the character of a plebiscite regarding their future fate: a vote for non-Russian parties and slates rather than for empirewide ones became in effect a vote for one form or another of national self-determination. Overall, these garnered almost one-quarter of all the votes and up to 200 seats.[36]

Although the national idea, in the eyes of the voters who shared it and those they elected, was painted in various political and social hues, through this multicolored spectrum two key motifs showed clearly. First, the democratic idea of federalizing the country was dominant, and this was assigned to the forthcoming Constituent Assembly. Second, in the spectrum of the entire electorate's national-political sympathies an orientation toward socialist parties predominated (by a ratio of approximately 2:1).

On the night of 6 January 1918, the Constituent Assembly proclaimed Russia a democratic federative republic. But this act came hopelessly late. The Bolsheviks' accession to power had sharply intensified the separatist aspirations of the national leaders, who hastened to separate from the Soviet of Workers', Peasants', and Soldiers' Deputies to create their own states. The victory of bolshevism in the Civil War, over both the separatists and those who fought for a powerful, unified, indivisible Russia, created only an illusion that the national problem had been solved, as it cloaked the old imperial body with new ideological and political clothing. These days there is no doubt that a polyethnic community can be formed only within a democratic state.

The most delicate question to confront anyone researching the elections to the Constituent Assembly can be summarized as follows: were the elections really free enough to ensure the genuine expression of the voters' will? "They were far from exemplary, but neither, undoubtedly, were they farcical."[37] This is the conclusion reached by O. Radkey. Let us elaborate on this sensible conclusion. Russia was the freest country in 1917. The real level of political freedom, however, is determined not only by an aggregate of legal norms but also by the citizens' legal consciousness. Many of the violations of electoral democracy, chiefly on the part of the soldiers, can be accounted for by their understanding of it as "anything-goes." Even more important is that the elections themselves served as an object lesson in democracy for many millions of people who were illiterate in terms of politics and law.

On the whole, the elections to the Constituent Assembly revealed the weakness of the sociocultural prerequisites for shaping a political democracy of the Western type in Russia. For the majority, such abstract values as state, nation, and law and order, shaped and assimilated through society's lengthy cultural development, were quite remote. In general, revolutions are not the best time for such things, and the increasing bitterness of the interparty struggle in 1917, which dealt primarily in agitation populism, did not play a civilizing role. The extensive "partyization" of the population revealed in the elections[38] was deceptive, because most voters had a primitive concept even of "their own" parties.

The Bolsheviks were victorious in this struggle, but they also introduced their own disdain for democratic forms of government into the mass strata. And although the Bolsheviks had suffered an unconditional political defeat in the elections, garnering only 23 percent of the votes, it proved more important that most of the electorate was close to the Bolsheviks both in spirit and in methods of accomplishing their goals. To put it crudely, judging by the results of the voting, the people got not the regime they wanted but the regime they deserved.

The fate of the All-Russian Constituent Assembly showed the incompatibility of two methods of transforming society – the crude, coercive method, by means of an armed coup, and the democratic method, through the expression of the will of all the people. One of these must give way before the other.

In the history of the October Revolution, the dissolution of the Constituent Assembly has remained in the shadows, so to speak, of the main event – the uprising of 25 October in Petrograd. But in the history of Russian totalitarianism, the hierarchy of these events is different. In October the Bolsheviks seized power by overthrowing the unpopular Provisional Government, which they explicitly justified by citing the necessity of ensuring that a Constituent Assembly be convened as soon as possible. "Very likely, no one now would condemn the Bolsheviks for October 1917," one modern historian muses, "if they had carried out their promise to turn supreme power over to the All-Russian Constituent Assembly."[39]

On 6 January 1918, however, the Bolsheviks burned their bridges behind them, dissolving the absolutely legitimate – even from the point of view of "revolutionary law" – assembly of people's representatives, whom the socialists definitely dominated. It is essential, moreover, to take account of the compromised position of the opposition factions, which deliberately ignored the arrogant behavior of the Bolsheviks and the Left SRs and made pro-Soviet decisions concerning the democratic republic, the land, workers' control, and so forth. However, the door, which had been opened slightly for practical cooperation among the parties on a platform of Soviet rule, was demonstratively slammed shut without waiting for a final clarification of relations among the contending factions.[40]

After the Bolsheviks seized power, certain social circles maintained the hope that the Bolsheviks would soon discredit themselves and would be removed by the Constituent Assembly in a lawful manner. After 6 January, hopes for Russia's constitutional development vanished entirely.

In our opinion, the matter cannot be summarized simply by saying that the last chance to create a ruling coalition of socialist parties was lost, or that the Civil War, for which more than substantial cause had been given, was kindled. The liquidation of the Constituent Assembly and the whole complex of civil rights and liberties connected with it also contained in embryo the abolition of the democratic transformations for which the Revolution had been fought (direct rule by the people, productive democracy, land to the peasants, national self-determination, and so forth) and which were based on political and economic freedom. The inevitable consequences of this and similar steps included the party's monopolization of power, the indoctrination of society, the total statization of social life, and the equally irreversible self-isolation from the rest of the world. This act deprived the ruling power of its internal democratic potential, because it compromised those who favored compromise with the Constituent Assembly. The system that resulted came to be completely closed in character and proved incapable of self-regulation and self-renewal.

In conclusion, let us dwell on two prejudices that are rather typical of present-day historiography regarding the Constituent Assembly's potential as a factor in the democratic restructuring of Russia. The assertion has been made, not without a certain amount of historical cynicism, that the Constituent Assembly became, in essence, unnecessary, because all the goals of the Revolution had already been accomplished. This argument is surprisingly similar to the arrogant declarations of the Bolsheviks themselves, who used it to justify their actions against the Constituent Assembly. As a major objection to this, it is enough to point out that the problem of state authority founded on a civil consensus had by no means been resolved.

Another opinion which is becoming increasingly widespread is that Russia in the twentieth century was doomed to totalitarianism. It would be utopian to expect the All-Russian Constituent Assembly miraculously to solve all the burning social problems of its time; its chances for success were small, possibly infinitesimal. Every historical alternative in the "array of probabilities" has limits to its own feasibility; the one that triumphs is the one with the broadest limits. But because the democratic alternative in Russia was not realized with the Constituent Assembly by no means implies that it could not have been, that the country was traveling a path foreordained strictly by fate. Does not the very fact that the Constituent Assembly was democratically elected and convened, in and of itself, constitute a substantial argument against historical determinism? The recent collapse of the totalitarian regime in Russia, which, unlike other similar regimes, took place under pressure from purely internal factors, confirms that the sprouts of representative democracy were saved and survived.

In addition, human experience has shown that unrealized alternatives never disappear without a trace. This is even more true if they lead society toward progress. The revival of the idea of an All-Russian Constituent Assembly in present-day social consciousness is a vivid illustration of that.

NOTES

Reprinted from *Russian Studies in History* Vol. 33, no. 3 (Winter 1994–1995), 67–93. Original Russian text "Vserossiskoe Uchreditel'noe sobranie i demokraticheskaia al'ternativa. Dva vzgliada na problemu," *Otechestvennaia istoriia* (1993), no. 5, pp. 3–19.

1 See Mark Blok [Marc Bloch], *Apologiia istorii, ili remeslo istorika* (Moscow, 1986), p. 14.
2 See *Znamia*, 1989, no. 5, p. 78.
3 Quoted in G. Pomeranets, "Dolgaia doroga istorii," *Znamia*, 1991, no. 11, p. 187.
4 *Narodnaia svoboda* (Tiflis), 2 December 1917.
5 See *Priazovskii krai* (Rostov-on-Don), 29 December 1917.
6 See V.I. Lenin, *Polnoe sobranie sochineniia* [*PSS*], vol. 4, pp. 252, 370, 435.
7 See *Rossiiskie partii, soiuzy i ligi* (St. Petersburg, 1906), p. 33.
8 Ibid., p. 64.
9 Steklov displayed this document to delegates of the All-Russian Conference of Soviets on 30 March 1917 (see *Vserossiiskoe soveshchanie Sovetov rabochikh i soldatskikh deputatov: Stenografcheskii otchet* [Moscow–Leningrad, 1927], p. 108).
10 See *Gosudarstvennoe soveshchanie* (Moscow–Leningrad, 1930), p. 148.
11 See V.V. Zhuravlev and N.S. Simonov, "Prichiny i posledstviia razgona Uchreditel'nogo sobraniia," *Voprosy istorii*, 1991, no. 1, p. 3.
12 M.V. Vishniak, *Vserossiiskoe Uchreditel'noe sobranie* (Paris, 1932), p. 71.
13 V.D. Polikarpov, *Voennaia kontrrevoliutsiia v Rossii, 1905–1917* (Moscow, 1990), p. 185.
14 See *Dekrety sovetskoi vlasti*, vol. 1 (Moscow, 1957), p. 20.
15 See, for example, V.D. Polikarpov, *Ukaz. soch* [loc. cit., n. 13], pp. 372–73.
16 See Lenin, *PSS*, vol. 33, pp. 7, 9.
17 See Vishniak, *Vserossiiskoe*, p. 84.
18 See Lenin, *PSS*, vol. 34, pp. 7, 9.
19 V. Startsev, "Al'ternativa. Fantazii i real'nost'," *Kommunist*, 1990, no. 15, p. 36.

20 See S.V. Leonov, "Sovetskaia gosudarstvennost': zamysly i deistvitel'nost' (1917–1920)," *Voprosy istorii*, 1990, no. 12, p. 35.
21 Iu. O. Martov, *Mirovoi bol'shevizm* (Berlin, 1923), p. 39.
22 See V.I. Lenin, *PSS*, vol. 31, p. 110.
23 K. Riabinskii, *Revoliutsiia 1917 goda: khronika sobytii*, vol. 5 (Moscow, 1926), pp. 88–89.
24 See V.I. Lenin, *PSS*, vol. 31, p. 187; vol. 32, pp. 132–65.
25 See A.F. Kerenskii, "Rossiia na istoricheskom povorote," *Voprosy istorii*, 1991, nos. 7–8, p. 155.
26 See V.I. Lenin, *PSS*, vol. 35, p. 20.
27 Ibid., p. 140.
28 See L.D. Trotskii, *K istorii russkoi revoliutsii* (Moscow, 1990), p. 206.
29 E.A. Skripilev, *Vserossiiskoe Uchreditel'noe sobranie* (Moscow, 1982), p. 147.
30 See GARF (State Archive of the Russian Federation), f. 1810, op. 1, d. 472, l. 14, 19.
31 *Velikaia Oktiabr'skaia sotsialisticheskaia revoliutsiia: Entsiklopediia* (Moscow, 1987), p. 446.
32 See GARF, f. 1810, op. 1, d. 7, l. 127; d. 473, l. 1–2.
33 See ibid., d. 149a, l. 12, 13, 17.
34 See L.M. Spirin, *Klassy i partii v grazhdanskoi voine v Rossii (1917–1920 gg.)* (Moscow, 1968), pp. 416–19; L.M. Spirin, *Rossiia 1917 god: Iz istorii bor'by politicheskikh partii* (Moscow, 1987), pp. 273–328.
35 See N.V. Sviatitskii, "Itogi vyborov vo Vserossiiskoe Uchreditel'noe sobranie," *God russkoi revoliutsii, 1917–1918* (Moscow, 1918), p. 115.
36 This contradicts V.P. Buldakov's opinion that the positions of the national parties proved to be the weak ones in the elections to the Constituent Assembly. See V.P. Buldakov, "U istokov sovetskoi istorii: put' k Oktiabriu," *Voprosy istorii*, 1989, no. 10, p. 78.
37 Oliver H. Radkey, *The Elections to the Russian Constituent Assembly, January 1918* (New York, 1950), p. 50.
38 It is indicative that members of the cooperative movement, whose ranks numbered, according to various figures, between 10 and 24 million members, ran as independents and received only about 29,000 votes or less than 0.1 percent.
39 N.S. Simonov, "Demokraticheskaia al'ternativa totalitarnomu nepu," *Istoriia SSSR*, 1992, no. 1, pp. 55–56.
40 See V.V. Zhuravlev and N.S. Simonov, "Prichiny," pp. 6, 16.

FURTHER READING

Acton, Edward. *Rethinking the Russian Revolution*. London: Edward Arnold, 1990.
Clements, Barbara Evans. *Bolshevik Women*. Cambridge: Cambridge University Press, 1997.
Critical Companion to the Russian Revolution, 1914–1921, ed. Edward Acton, Vladimir Iu. Cherniaev, and William G. Rosenberg. Bloomington: Indiana University Press, 1997.
Daniels, Robert V. *Red October: The Bolshevik Revolution of 1917*. New York: Scribner's, 1967.
Ezergailis, Andrew. *The 1917 Revolution in Latvia*. New York: Columbia University Press, 1974.
Ferro, Marc. *The Russian Revolution of February 1917*. Englewood Cliffs, NY: Prentice-Hall, 1972.
Figes, Orlando. *Peasant Russia, Civil War: The Volga Countryside in Revolution. 1917–1921*. Oxford: Clarendon, 1989.
—— *A People's Tragedy: The Russian Revolution*. Harmondsworth and New York: Penguin, 1997.
Figes, Orlando and Boris Kolonitskii, *Interpreting the Russian Revolution: The Language and Symbols of 1917*. New Haven: Yale University Press, 1999.
Flenley, Paul, "Industrial Relations and the Economic Crisis of 1917," *Revolutionary Russia* 4, no. 2 (1991): 184–209.
Frankel, Edith Rogovin, Jonathan Frankel, and Baruch Knei-Paz, eds. *Revolution in Russia: Reassessments of 1917*. Cambridge: Cambridge University Press, 1992.
Friedgut, Theodore. *Iuzovka and Revolution*. 2 vols. Princeton: Princeton University Press, 1994.
Galili, Ziva. *The Menshevik Leaders in the Russian Revolution: Social Realities and Political Strategies*. Princeton: Princeton University Press, 1989.
Harding, Neil. *Lenin's Political Thought: Theory and Practice in the Democratic Revolution*. 2 vols. New York: St. Martin's Press, 1977, 1981.
—— *Leninism*. Durham: Duke University Press, 1996.
Hasegawa, Tsuyoshi. *The February Revolution: Petrograd 1917*. Seattle: University of Washington Press, 1981.
Hickey, Michael C. "Discourses of Public Identity and Liberalism in the February Revolution: Smolensk, Spring 1917." *The Russian Review* 55, no. 4 (1996): 615–637.
—— "Local Government and State Authority in the Provinces: Smolensk, February–June 1917." *Slavic Review* 55, no. 1 (1996): 863–881.
—— "Urban *Zemliachestva* and Rural Revolution: Petrograd and the Smolensk Countryside in 1917." *Soviet and Post-Soviet Review* 23, no. 2 (1996): 143–160.

—— "Revolution on the Jewish Street: Smolensk, 1917." *Journal of Social History* 31, no. 4 (Summer 1998): 823–850.

Holquist, Peter. *Making War, Forging Revolution: Russia's Continuum of Crisis, 1914–1921*. Cambridge, MA and London: Harvard University Press, 2002.

Kaiser, Daniel H., ed. *The Workers' Revolution in Russia, 1917. The View from Below*. Cambridge: Cambridge University Press, 1987.

Keep, John L.H. *The Russian Revolution: A Study in Mass Mobilisation*. London: Weidenfeld and Nicolson, 1976.

Khalid, Adeeb. *The Politics of Muslim Cultural Reform: Jadidism in Central Asia*. Berkeley: University of California Press, 1998.

Koenker, Diane P. *Moscow Workers and the 1917 Revolution*. Princeton: Princeton University Press, 1981.

Koenker, Diane P. and William G. Rosenberg. *Strikes and Revolution in Russia, 1917*. Princeton: Princeton University Press, 1989.

Kolonitskii, Boris. "Antibourgeois Propaganda and Anti-'Burzhui' Consciousness in 1917." *Russian Review* 54 (April 1994): 183–196.

Lieven, Dominic. *Nicholas II: Twilight of the Empire*. New York: St. Martin's Press, 1994.

Lyandres, Semion. *The Bolsheviks' "German Gold" Revisited. An Inquiry into the 1917 Accusations*. Pittsburgh: Center for Russian and East European Studies, University of Pittsburgh, 1995.

Manning, Roberta T. "Bolshevik Without the Party: Sychevka in 1917," in *Provincial Landscapes: Local Dimensions of Soviet Power, 1917–1953*, ed. Donald J. Raleigh. Pittsburgh: University of Pittsburgh Press, 2001.

Mawdsley, Evan. *The Russian Revolution and the Baltic Fleet: War and Politics, February 1917–April 1918*. London: Macmillan, 1978.

Melancon, Michael. *The Socialist Revolutionaries and the Russian Anti-War Movement, 1914–1917*. Columbus, OH: Ohio State University Press, 1990.

—— "The Syntax of Soviet Power: The Resolutions of Local Soviets and Other Institutions, March–October 1917." *Russian Review* 52, no. 4 (1993): 486–505.

Orlovsky, Daniel. "The Lower Middle Strata in Revolutionary Russia," in *Between Tsar and People: Educated Society and the Quest for Public Identity in Late Imperial Russia*, ed. Edith W. Clowes, Samuel D. Kassow and James West, 248–268. Princeton: Princeton University Press, 1991.

—— "Corporatism or Democracy: The Russian Provisional Government of 1917." *Soviet and Post-Soviet Review* 24 (1997): 15–26.

Pethybridge, Roger W. *The Spread of the Russian Revolution: Essays on 1917*. London: Macmillan, 1972.

Rabinowitch, Alexander. *Prelude to Revolution. The Petrograd Bolsheviks and the July 1917 Uprising*. Bloomington, IN: Indiana University Press, 1968.

—— *The Bolsheviks Come to Power: The Revolution of 1917 in Petrograd*. New York: W.W. Norton, 1976.

Radkey, Oliver H. *The Agrarian Foes of Bolshevism. Promise and Default of the Russian Socialist Revolutionaries, February to October 1917*. New York: Columbia University Press, 1958.

—— *The Sickle under the Hammer. The Russian Socialist Revolutionaries in the Early Months of Soviet Rule*. New York: Columbia University Press, 1963.

—— *Russia Goes to the Polls: The Election to the All-Russian Constituent Assembly, 1917*. Updated Edition. Ithaca and London: Cornell University Press, 1989.

Raleigh, Donald J. *Revolution on the Volga: 1917 in Saratov*. Ithaca: Cornell University Press, 1986.

Read, Christopher. *From Tsar to Soviets: The Russian People and their Revolution, 1917–21*. New York: Oxford University Press, 1996.

Rosenberg, William G. *Liberals in the Russian Revolution: The Constitutional Democratic Party, 1917–1921*. Princeton: Princeton University Press, 1974.

Saul, Norman E. *Sailors in Revolt: The Russian Baltic Fleet in 1917*. Lawrence, KS: Regents Press of Kansas, 1978.

Service, Robert. *Lenin: A Political Life*, 3 vols. London: Macmillan, 1985–1994.

—— ed. *Society and Politics in the Russian Revolution*. Basingstoke and London: Macmillan, 1992.

Smith, S.A. *Red Petrograd: Revolution in the Factories, 1917–1918*. Cambridge: Cambridge University Press, 1983.

Steinberg, Mark D. *Voices of Revolution, 1917*. New Haven and London: Yale University Press, 2001.

Stites, Richard. *Revolutionary Dreams: Utopian Vision and Experimental Life in the Russian Revolution*. New York: Oxford University Press, 1989.

Suny, Ronald Grigor. *The Baku Commune, 1917–1918: Class and Nationality in the Russian Revolution*. Princeton: Princeton University Press, 1972.

Swain, Geoff. *The Origins of the Russian Civil War*. London: Longman, 1996.

Wade, Rex A. *The Russian Search for Peace, February–October 1917*. Stanford: Stanford University Press, 1969.

—— *Red Guards and Workers' Militias in the Russian Revolution*. Stanford: Stanford University Press, 1984.

—— *The Russian Revolution: 1917*. Cambridge: Cambridge University Press, 2000.

White, James D. *Lenin: The Practice and Theory of Revolution*. London: Palgrave, 2001.

INDEX

Abezgaus, Dr. M. A. 170, 172
Abo 195
Aivaz factory 27
Aleksandrovich (SR worker) 146–8
Antonov-Ovseenko, Vladimir 189–91,
   195, 196, 199–206, 237
April Crisis 20, 21, 144, 151
April Theses 20, 21, 152
anarchists 24, 50, 173, 214, 215
Argunov, A. A. 145, 146, 156
Arkhangel'sk 108, 195
Armenia and Armenians 120, 122, 123,
   124, 133, 135, 259
Arsen'ev, N. A. 81
Avksentiev, N. D. 145, 146
Azerbaijan 122, 133

Belorussians 124, 134, 135
Berdiaev, Nikolai 77, 83
Bogdanov, B. O. 201, 202
Bolsheviks: Central Committee
   meetings of October 10 and 16,
   193–5, 205–6; and coalition
   government 20; Congress of Soviets
   190–208 passim; 222–40; Constituent
   Assembly 243–66 passim; and crime
   46, 66–7; and CSNR 187–208, 227;
   debate over power 135, 222–8; First
   Conference of Bolshevik
   Organizations in Finland 191;
   government 240; and history of the
   revolution 1–4, 6, 8, 13–15, 28, 264;
   July Days 22–3, 213; and language
   of democracy 75, 77, 81–4, 86, 94;
   MRC 228–30, 231, 232, 233–5;
   nationality question 126–36 passim;
   peasants 109, 112, 113–14; October
   Revolution 27–31, 205–8, 211–40
   passim; and Provisional Government

145, 156, 212, 217–18; radical left
   bloc 211, 214–16; in Smolensk
   162–83 passim; sources of support
   14, 21–31, 152, 155, 212–13, 216;
   strikes and 36–7, 43; and workers
   control 24–5
Breshko-Breshkovaskaia, E. K. 145
Breslav, Boris 194, 196, 203
Bubnov, Andrei 206, 226
Buchanan, Sir George 83
Bukharin, Nikolai 245
Bukovinians 127
Bunakov, V. 145
Burgonov, V. Ia. 172

Chamberlin, William Henry 2, 3
Chernigov 49, 128, 260
Chernov, Viktor (Victor) 145, 146, 148,
   151, 153, 156, 214
City Militia 47, 58–61, 67–8, 172
Congress of Soviets: First All-
   Russia(n) 23; Second All-Russia(n)
   29, 187–92, 195–206 passim, 211,
   215–19, 221–40, 250
Congress of Soviets of the Northern
   Region see CSNR
Constituent Assembly 8, 243–66;
   alternatives 243–4, 251–3, 264–5;
   Bolsheviks and 243–66 passim; and
   democracy 80–1, 92; elections 29,
   106, 108, 131, 163, 164, 256–62;
   electoral law 251, 152; historians
   and 243, 145–6, 264–5, 266n; idea of
   245–51, 255; moderate socialists and
   249; nationalities and 128, 129, 131;
   October Revolution and 212, 223,
   225, 232, 238, 239, 253–5; peasants
   and 93, 95, 106, 108, 109, 111, 128;
   Provisional Government 248–52;